If You Don't Weaken . . .

THE AUTOBIOGRAPHY OF OSCAR AMERINGER

Oscar Ameringer

If You Don't Weaken ~

THE AUTOBIOGRAPHY OF
OSCAR AMERINGER

WITH A FOREWORD BY
CARL SANDBURG

If You Don't Weaken ~

THE AUTOBIOGRAPHY OF
OSCAR AMERINGER

WITH A FOREWORD BY
CARL SANDBURG

GREENWOOD PRESS, PUBLISHERS
NEW YORK

46543

TO

MY MOTHER, AND DAUGHTER

SUSAN

WHO BRIGHTENED THE MORNING AND THE EVENING

OF MY LIFE

CONTENTS

ILLUSTRATIONS

ACKNOWLEDGMENTS AND SUNDRIES

EXCEPT that I inherited certain characteristics from an unknown number of unknown ancestors, was deeply influenced by persons most of whom were dead before I was born, and shaped by circumstances over which I had no control, I am a self-made man. But being all that, let me caution the reader at the very outset not to regard the following pages as my formal autobiography, for such autobiographies are only written by people who have great achievements to record, who have influenced the course of human events or flatter themselves that they have. As for myself, I never marched an army up the hill, down the hill or left it buried on the hill. I never wrote a law, and broke but few; was never honored with a public trust, nor damned for breaking one. And if occasionally I ran for some high office, my prospective constituents always saved me from being included among the rascals they threw out at the next election.

Least of all should this book be mistaken for the story of a poor immigrant boy who, by the exercise of hard work, thrift, and frugality, founded a house on Easy Street to live happily ever after on the hard work, thrift, and frugality of other poor immigrant boys—and native sons. Measured by the golden yardstick, and deducting liabilities from assets as good bookkeepers should, I am but little better off in earthly goods than when I landed at Castle Garden in the winter of 1886.

On the other hand, if, as some philosophers claim, the most important job is to live as long, happy, and useful a life as one may, I truthfully can call this life of mine a success. For in these three score and ten years—still going strong—mine has been the love of good women, the friendship of brave men, the approbation of fine souls, the precious gift of appreciating beauty in art and nature, the confidence and affection of the hundreds of thousands of humble men and women whose joy and sorrow I shared, whose hopes and aspirations I voiced.

I have seen my three sons grow into good husbands and fathers, all making a decent living by honest work except my youngest, who was cruelly mangled in the Argonne Forest. For this and for the loss of a career as a brilliant musician, he draws a pension of one hundred dollars a month. I see my five grandsons and one granddaughter following in the footsteps of their fathers, each healthy in body and mind, paying me the highest tribute a parent may receive by sharing granddad's notions, ideas, and ideals, while wisely side-stepping his mistakes. And then, the crowning happiness of all, the chubby hands of my baby daughter, patting the cheeks of a daddy past sixty. . . .

There have been, of course, days of heartache, worry and remorse. But what would harmony be without discord, light without shadow, good without evil? I have always been able, still am, to meet the blows of fate, if not always with a smile, at least with a grin. Hard aroused to anger, ready quickly to forget and forgive, I have only rarely suffered from the poison of hate. Never far ahead of the wolves, I had, with the few exceptions to be noted later, all the money I needed, which I dare say few multimillionaires will admit. And if, as frequently happened, one of my brain children found itself in hot water, somewhere some sympathetic soul would always come to its rescue.

On the whole, a quite successful life from the personal viewpoint. And yet not a personal achievement. For into the composition of this life have gone many lives, and all of them deserve acknowledgment. But how can one in the space of a few pages acknowledge the contributions of hundreds, even thousands of people in all walks of life, scattered over many lands, and most of them in the Rooseveltian category of forgotten men? I am, therefore, able to render acknowledgment to only a few of my co-authors.

Charles Ervin, wartime editor of the New York *Call*, who, in spite of his advanced age (Charlie is four years older than I) and his arduous duties as spiritual adviser and trouble shooter of the Amalgamated Clothing Workers and its foster child, the Textile Workers Union, has served as Washington correspondent of *The American Guardian*, to which he has contributed some twenty-five hundred words per week for the past ten years— gratis, including the cost of secretarial service, stationery and postage.

Carl Leathwood, for twenty years my coworker on the Oklahoma *Leader*, *The Illinois Miner*, and *The American Guardian*, to whom, in the position of managing editor, interpreter of my wretched handwriting, and occasional pinch hitter for my nom de plume, Adam Coaldigger, my journalistic reputation owes much.

My son, Siegfried, whose loyalty and devotion as circulation manager of four of my journalistic offspring has relieved me of the twin banes of my life—correspondence and detail work.

Among the outstanding angels and life-savers who, when one of these ventures was about to go down for the last time, always pulled it back to terra firma, thanks are especially due to Robert Marshall who, scorning the existence of the idle rich, devoted his own all too short life to enrich the lives of all; to George Marshall and his wife, Betty, fervently devoted to the same cause; to Ethel Clyde, daughter of a Scottish laird and shipmaster, but minus Scotland's most renowned characteristic, giving freely to every forward cause out of the riches of heart and purse; to the late Paul Pierce, Chicago manufacturer with highly developed social instincts and sympathy for the class from which he sprang; to Abraham Levin, retired capitalist of Los Angeles who, besides material financial contributions, secured thousands of readers to *The American Guardian* for the sheer love of serving mankind; to my old friend and stand-by, Jim McGill who, though a self-confessed exploiter of labor and hard-boiled agnostic, religiously lives up to the divine injunction: "It is more blessed to give than to receive."

My thanks are also due to S. D. (Steuben De Kalb) Wham, of Illinois, one of the founders of the Populist and Socialist Parties who, in spite of his eighty years and an oil-begotten fortune, has forgotten neither the ideal of his early manhood nor the revolutionary tradition of his forefathers; to Henry Heitholt, in the long-ago a fellow cabinet maker, later frontier farmer, now retired oil man, though not tired radical, who repeatedly has come to the rescue of one or the other of my publications; and to Gottlieb Suberly, gentleman, lover of soil and men, whose companionship, and experience as a successful "dirt" farmer, contributed greatly to saving my Utopian excursion in the realm of landless men and manless land.

Foremost among the organizations which aided in shaping and smoothing the course of this life are those of the coal miners of Illinois, Oklahoma, Kansas, and Arkansas; the American Fund for Social Service, also known as the Garland Fund; the Amalgamated Clothing Workers of America who in a particularly critical crisis came to my support with a loan of twenty thousand dollars and promptly forgot it; and the Finnish Co-operative Publishing Company of Fitchburg, Massachusetts, which in a more-than-usually dark hour brought dawn with its collectivist soul and treasury.

To Charney Vladeck, Carl Sandburg, Art Young, John Dewey and Oswald Garrison Villard, whose friendship and sympathy has often sustained me in the hours of discouragement, to the Minute Men of *The American Guardian* who, without hope of any other reward than having done their bit toward a better life, have built the circulation of the *Guardian,* to all of these my profoundest gratitude.

My heartfelt thanks also to my immediate helpers on this book: to Helen Turner, whose gift of second sight, and angelic patience, transformed my Horace Greeleyan handwriting into type; to my old friend and coworker on *The Illinois Miner,* Oklahoma *Leader* and *American Guardian,* McAlister Coleman, to whose merciless criticism, counsel, rearranging, rewriting and proofreading the literary virtues of this book are attributable.

And lastly to my wife, Freda Hogan Ameringer who, in spite of her revolutionary youth, preserved sufficient bourgeois virtues to keep the home fires burning while I burned up the sticks.

Making due allowance for the above contributions and deductions, the rest is i.

FOREWORD

WHEN the going is good with the humorist Oscar Ameringer he is equal to the best of Artemus Ward and Petroleum Vesuvius Nasby. He was still a youth in Ohio when *Puck* and other national journals of fun were publishing his efforts and paying for them. He came near drifting into place as a fun maker—and that only. Definitely he did move into a supreme position in the American labor movement as a man of laughter, wit, satire.

I have seen him in Milwaukee and Chicago, taking the platform in a crowded, smoke-filled hall, facing rows of somber and sober-faced workingmen, talking to them about their troubles, about woe and injustice and inequalities, drawing contrasts, soon bringing smiles to the faces and finally roars of laughter.

No other orator or platform man in American labor history has had this gift and used it so richly and refreshingly as Ameringer. In his life story he gives his readers from this wellspring of fun and fancy.

Yet he is more often a man on fire over the injustice between man and man, over the chaos and darkness of so many human fates where he cannot be a silent witness, where, like William Lloyd Garrison, he feels he has icebergs of self-satisfaction, indifference, complacency, smug indifference to overcome. In these moods he often sings with words and colors with phrases.

He tells us of how he was both a painter and a musician, how he made good money in both those fields of the seven arts, how he could have gone farther and made a name for himself: he narrowly escaped a respectable career approved by all polite citizens. He has been an artist nevertheless.

There is the art of Aesop in many of the fables set forth by Adam Coaldigger. There is the art of a Diogenes in the method by which he insists on being a Free Man. And having as an artist developed a rare personality and a wide range of freedom for himself, he wants it for others. So he becomes a crusader.

xvii

As a crusader, however, he is limited by the fact of being a philosopher and endowed with a sense of humor. Had this humor been lacking in Ameringer he might have become an American Gandhi, though possibly no Gandhi could get far in this country because of the national sense of humor.

It should be understood that it was outside pressure that sent Ameringer to the writing of this book. He has ego, but not the kind of introspective self-importance that enjoys talking about itself for the sweet personal sake of its own self. Friends saw him as a significant figure who had moved and breathed in the noise and sweeping tumult of historic streams of human events, seeing the rise and the ebb of tides and trends, keeping his hope when others were sunk in despair, never lacking a basic reverence for humanity. These friends told him that now in his seventies he must do a book that might speak for him when he departs from the scene. So he has given us true stories, episodes that stand up as good story-telling.

Some of us will go back occasionally to read again his New Orleans saga of the brewery workers, or the tale of the plugged quarter dollar. As an entertainer he has the skill and the quizzical humility of Will Rogers or Mark Twain.

Then again he is solemnly, even forlornly and desperately, the Free Man seeking his way, inquiring, shading his eyes toward the future and asking, "Watchman, what of the night?"

He does not ask that we agree with him on every page. He is satisfied if we join with him at times in laughter at the Human Comedy in which he was a participant—and he is humble enough to be content if, in the face of the Human Tragedy he tells of, there may be more of us persuaded to be merely more sober and decent, recognizing how difficult is perfect justice, recognizing that human affairs are "an approximation lacking gravity and precision."

CARL SANDBURG

Harbert, Michigan
March, 1940

Book One

THE SIGN OF MARS

1

BOOM! boom! boom! One hundred booms. The cannon were thundering a salute impressive enough to announce the birth of a prince of the blood, but I was not a prince, even though I was about to be born. My mother heard the guns as she was busy making hay on one of her twelve acres in the bottom lands of the Danube valley. When the birth pangs came over her, she barely managed to load the hay and bring it, the wagon, the cows, and me safely home to Achstetten before I put in my appearance. That was the fourth of August in the year 1870, and the salute of one hundred guns was being fired from the bastions of the fortress of Ulm, twelve miles away from our peasant village in the Swabian Overland. The occasion was the victory of the German forces in the battle of Spicchern Heights during the early days of the Franco-Prussian war.

In those days we lived, as I was born, under the sign of Mars. My earliest recollections are concerned with "wars and rumors of wars." A picture from an autumn day as far back as 1873 is still bright in my memory: I was mounted on a lofty strawstack, in company with a number of the other village children. We were full of excitement as we gazed southward toward the Danube. Between the apple and pear trees lining the road from Ulm to our village, and as far as our young eyes could see, came soldiers. Sabers and bayonets glittered in the sunlight slanting through the fruit trees. The blare of distant bugles reached our enraptured ears. First came the red-breasted Uhlans, mounted on light horses, their long lances carrying fluttering pennons and fixed to stirrups and arm straps. Then a regiment of sky-blue and yellow-breasted dragoons. Each cavalry regiment was preceded by a mounted band playing merry tunes. After the horsemen came wave on wave of foot soldiers, singing marching songs whenever their bands stopped playing or their fife-and-drum corps quit drumming and doodling. Behind the infantry were long trains of artillery, each gun drawn by six horses, a mounted driver for each team, three cannoneers sitting on the caisson and two more hanging in a sort of basket on either side of the cannon barrel. After the artillery came endless trains of wagons carrying provisions for the troops, and fodder for the horses.

The stream of soldiers continued to flow into Achstetten until every house and barn and every available space around it was filled with soldiers. At night we could see the glow of their camp fires for many miles in every direction. Our family's house and barn, built together under one roof, were filled with soldiers sleeping on hay, straw, and fresh shavings from father's cabinet shop in the rear of our combination parlor, dining, and sitting room. I am able to fix the date at '73 because one of the infantry-men quartered at our home showed me the operation of his Zindnadel gun, a model which I learned later was supplanted by the Mauser rifle in 1874.

Another reason I can establish the date of the occurrence is that one day a fine carriage stopped on the highway close to our home, at the place where the road went up a steep hill. Soldiers were hitching an additional team of horses to the carriage. On the driver's seat were two uniformed coachmen in short boots and shining tile hats; on the rear seat two more coachmen were sitting with folded arms. On the middle seat of the carriage were two men who I knew must be high officials. The bigger of the two had large, bulging eyes, a bristling mustache, and a bull-dog face. He wore a white uniform, silver breast and shoulder armor, boots coming well above his knees, and held a large straight sword between them. The whole was surmounted by a silver helmet reaching far down his neck, from the pinnacle of which a white horsehair plume descended almost to his bushy eyebrows. All in all, he looked like a hefty personification of Mars.

The companion of the warrior in white was a small, delicate man with a beardless, wizened face. Perhaps I would have ignored the little fellow entirely had he not extracted from his breast pocket a perfectly clean white handkerchief which he used to brush the dust from his highly polished shoes. Handkerchiefs were rare, indeed almost unknown articles in our circle. Their functions were generally performed by the back of the hand and the coat sleeve. It was this all but sacrilegious misuse of the hand-kerchief that attracted my attention to Field Marshal von Moltke, the victor of Sadowa and Sedan. Mars the Magnificent was Prince Otto von Bismarck, of blood-and-iron fame. The military demonstration in force which I had observed could not have been an ordinary maneuver, not if these two idols of Germany honored our section with their presence in 1873.

I take it for granted that even in those far-off days my people were primarily concerned with making both ends meet. Yet, at this distant range, it seems to me that war and soldiers formed the center of their conversation. Perhaps the reason was an ancient one: our locality had been repeatedly invaded since time immemorial.

Less than thirty minutes' walk from our village passed a Roman road. In my childhood, peasants were still quarrying rock, for corner and tombstones, out of that Roman highway. Over it had passed the legions of Caesar, Marcus Aurelius, Nero, and Diocletian on their raids for slaves to man the plantations of the noble Romans—and Teutonic blondes for their harems. Over that road had passed the stragglers of Varus's army, routed in the Teutoburger Wald shortly after the birth of Christ. Hannibal on his march over the Alps must have used the southern end of it, his elephants and swarthy warriors floundering in the snow of the Alpine passes. Barbarossa of Hohenstaufen, the Red Beard, whose castle was barely a day's walk from us, marched along it in his many invasions of Italy and his struggle for mastery over Rome.

Charles Magnus rode over that road on his way to the Eternal City to be crowned emperor of Rome by a successor of St. Peter. Huns, Tartars, and Mongolians from the steppes beyond the Urals, driven by drought and the lure of green pastures, had passed along it and all the roads for hundreds of miles north, south, east, and west of it. Mohammedans shouting "Allah il Allah" had penetrated as far as Lake Constance, only some sixty miles from our village. The imperial soldiers of Wallenstein, murdered in Eger Bohemia, and the mercenaries of Tilly the Catholic had swept over that territory, robbing, plundering, raping, burning friends and foes alike until its inhabitants were reduced by two-thirds and cannibalism had reappeared. The Protestant armies of Gustavus Adolphus, bound to convert all southern Germany and Austria to their one true faith, had turned it into a veritable hell. In my days, mothers still rocked their babies to sleep with a lullaby:

> "Pray, little one, pray;
> Tomorrow comes the Swede,
> Tomorrow comes Oxenstiern,
> He'll make you babies praying learn."

Oxenstiern was a corruption of Oxenstjerna, the prime minister of Gustavus Adolphus, who carried on the work of reform after Adolphus' death by means of murder, arson, famine, and pestilence.

The Thirty Years' War barely over, the Baltringen horde of rebellious peasants, named after the village of Baltringen, four miles from our home, roamed over that territory, illuminating the nights with burning castles and decorating the great oaks with the swinging bodies of blue-blooded oppressors. In the garret of our home in Achstetten there were still a scythe, horizontally affixed to a long stout staff, and a long two-edged broadsword, which one of my unknown ancestors may well have put to good use during the peasant wars.

The last time that foreign invasion had cursed our naturally peaceful countryside was only sixty-five years before I was born. After Napoleon's victory over the Austrians at Ulm, a battle had raged through and around our village. My grandmother on my mother's side was an eyewitness of it. The French artillery, I heard her say, had been stationed on the eminence of Oberholzhcim where the poet Wieland, translator of Shakespeare's "Midsummer Night's Dream," and the author of "Oberon," was born. The Austrian artillery was stationed on another rise at the west edge of our village. She used to describe how her family had huddled in our cellar with their most precious single possession, the family cow, and how that cow had docilely followed her father, my great-grandfather Johannes Miller, down the narrow cellar stairway just as if she had known what the shooting was all about. Grandmother also told us how the Cossacks on shaggy little horses, armed with long staffs bearing iron spikes at their business ends, had come to our village, sleeping on the ice of the little river flowing through it and stealing everything they could lay their hands on that was not nailed down. Grandmother always cackled gleefully when she told how, in order to protect her few coins from pilfering fingers, she resorted to a device only a seamstress would have conceived. She had stuck a needle cushion into her skirt pocket with the needle points sticking upward to meet intruding fingers. It was a great joke on the Cossacks, as grandmother saw it. I am inclined to think that even the Cossacks got the point or points, for Cossacks from the far-off Don have a sense of humor, as I was to learn in after years.

In all these recollections of "battles long ago," I never heard any glorification of war from our people. On the contrary, every eclipse of the sun or moon, or the appearance of a comet in the sky, was followed by prayers and pilgrimages petitioning the All-Highest to avert the indicated calamity, which they felt sure would be a martial one. Neither were our folksongs of warlike character, and those that did deal with war were anti- rather than pro-war in sentiment. I remember especially one of them which told the feeling of a horseman greeting sunrise on the day of battle. Freely translated, it began:

"Morning red, morning red,
Glowing for my early dead.
Today on prancing steed,
Today my heart will bleed,
Tomorrow in the cool, cool grave,
I and many a kamerad."

Its closing stanza read:

"Heart be still, heart be still,
For 'tis but God's own will."

Another rhyme reminiscent of turbulent days which we young-sters used to sing when we were catching *maykaefer*—June bugs —was:

"May bug flee,
May bug flee,
Thy father is in war,
Thy father is in Polen Land;
Poland is a firebrand;
May bug flee."

The pugnacious "Watch on the Rhine" was not popular with our people, either.

As a member of the so-called "Aryan" race (which I under-stand came out of India somewhere near the end of the second Ice Age), I must belong to one of the oldest families of Europe. But of the thousands of my celebrated predecessors in the house of Ameringer * I know only four: my father, my mother, my

* The accent is on the first syllable and the "g" is hard.

grandmother on my mother's side, whose name I never learned, and my maternal great-grandfather Johannes Miller.

Grandmother died when I was about four. I remember that she peddled small notions, needles, pins, thread, buttons, and ribbons, which she carried in an oblong box strapped to her back, and more particularly that on her return she usually scattered bread crumbs from a pocket in her skirt among our chickens. I suppose the latter procedure made such a deep impression on me because among the bread crumbs I often found a pfennig or two and I had learned that these could be exchanged for candy.

Of great-grandfather Johannes Miller I know only the little my mother told me. From that little I gather great-granddad must have been a man after my own heart. My regret is that he did not keep a diary, a failure duplicated in his turn by his great-grandson. The story of Johannes Miller begins with his wedding night, in 1776. According to mother's version the Count von Welde, lord of the county in which Achstetten is located, was returning from Ulm to attend the wedding. (Why the count should have undertaken the journey to be present at the wedding of one of his serfs I can only explain by the hypothesis that in those times the "right of the first night" still existed.) While driving down a steep hill the count's coachman heard a moan, and turning, he observed his noble passenger slumping to the floor of the carriage. Someone had stabbed the blue-blooded wedding guest through the heart.

For some reason suspicion fell on great-granddad Miller, and the next heard of him in the family chronicles, he was playing the oboe in George Washington's band on the occasion of the first or second July Fourth celebration. How great-grandfather had made his getaway, and that done, had managed to join Washington's band, then sojourning in New Jersey, I can only surmise. My theory is that he crossed the Danube, only a half-hour's walk from Achstetten, thereby transferring himself from Austria to Germany, or rather the territory of the prince of Württemberg.

The prince of Württemberg was obsessed by a desire to outdo Louis XIV of France. Pursuing this ideal, he had built a little Versailles in which he maintained a number of ladies of the Du Barry type. When King George III was in the market for cannon fodder with which to pacify his rambunctious subjects in America, the prince of Württemberg, as a result of his liberal projects, was flat broke. Worse still, Württemberg was a constitutional monarchy, and both the upper and lower House were determined not to vote another penny to their profligate prince. However, the prince of Hesse, finding himself in a similar predicament, had just refilled his princely treasury by selling some five thousand of his subjects to King George for cannon fodder. With this new source of revenue in sight, the prince of Württemberg followed suit. He emptied the jails and workhouses, gathered all vagrants and fugitives from justice, and sold them to his brother-anointed of England. The price, if I remember correctly, was about twenty dollars per soldier who died for the glory of prince and fatherland on the field of honor in far-off America, but only ten dollars per lucky devil who returned alive.

Whether great-grandfather Johannes Miller deserted to the Continentals, or was among the prisoners taken at the battle of Trenton, I never learned. Historians nowadays are given a certain speculative license and I use it to figure that it may have occurred to my great-grandfather that it might be better to join the un-British forces who by force and violence were bent on overthrowing the established government of the land. At any rate, I was informed by my mother that Johannes, some time after the retreat through New Jersey, unexpectedly turned up as a musician in Washington's band. So now I can lay claim to the proud distinction of being a Son of the American Revolution—both sides of it, in fact.

I do not know how or why great-grandfather returned to Germany. My own guess is that he was drawn back by the memory of the woman he had married on the day Count von Welde was stabbed to death in his own coach. And again—perhaps his return was motivated by a desire to cheat the prince of Württemberg out of ten bucks.

Besides being an anti-monarchist and musician, great-grandfather possessed the rare accomplishments of reading and writing. At any rate, mother told me that during the Napoleonic campaign in our district he had acted as spy for the Austrians. In his capacity as spy he wrote the number of French regiments he met on his finger nails, and obliterated the numbers he had written simply by moistening his nails with his tongue, and wiping them on his breeches.

Great-granddad Miller went to his reward at the ripe age of ninety-six. While fishing, late in November, he slipped from the bank, caught one foot in a root, and died of exhaustion. Mother once told me great-grandfather had acquired a taste for hard liquor in America; he never went fishing without a small flask of schnapps in his pocket. So it may have been drink that killed him. . . .

I never heard "Deutschland Über Alles" sung until after coming to America. I had known the tune as the adagio from Papa Haydn's "Emperor Quartet," which, to the words of a good old Methodist hymn, was sung in American churches all through the World War. We in Achstetten were not a military folk. There was a saying going around in my childhood days to the effect that

> "When the king to war goes
> The people take the blows"

a saying as true today as ever, irrespective of whether the kings are God-anointed or gold-plated. But this understanding came, of course, much later. For the present it was the soldiers' life for us boys. And what a glorious time we had during their maneuvers!

How could it have been otherwise? My first ten years fell in

the *Grosse Zeit,* Germany's great epoch. The country was marching double-time ahead. Unification of the thirty-six Germanic
states had abolished tariff boundaries, conflicting weights, measures, and postal regulations, and concentrated the operation of
railroads. Industry, commerce, banking and foreign trade were
striding forward in seven-league boots. The one billion dollars
indemnity levied on defeated France had been paid in gold. In
my youth ten- and twenty-franc gold pieces, stamped with the
fatuous countenance of Napoleon III, were still in circulation.
Money was plentiful, work was easy to get, wages and farm income were rising.

Germany's development, arrested by the Thirty Years' War
and centuries of dissension between scores of wrangling and often
warring dynasties, was making up for lost time. Meanwhile England and France had parceled out a large part of the world
among them. Russia had reached the Pacific. Across the Atlantic
the young giant, the United States, was becoming a world power.
But wait, wait! Soon German merchantmen would plow the seven
seas, protected by German warships. There were still a few
colonies lying about to be bid for with the mouths of cannon,
the language England and France had learned to speak so well.
Then onward to Germany's place in the sun—by ever-mounting
military and naval might!

For, mind you, the material prosperity of united Germany was
not due to political unification, nor to the application of science,
to industry, nor to the discovery of steam power by an English
tinker a century ago. It was all brought about by "blood and
iron"—assisted, of course, by God on High.

Not only were we Germans God's chosen people, but unques-
tionably had helped Him make the selection. "We Germans fear
no one but God," Bismarck had boasted. "Gott mit uns" was inscribed on the spiked helmet. "Gott and I," as it was modestly
put a decade and a half later by the future woodchopper of
Doorn. How could any power, or combination of powers, defeat
a partnership of Gott and us?

It seems, however, that even Gott and us require cannon fodder for shaping destiny. And so, whatever school, church, and home could do to forge us youngsters into future cannon fodder was done. Merry Yuletide brought us, along with the company of angels, shepherds, sheep, oxen, manger and Christ-kindel, gifts of bugles, drums, papier-mâché spiked helmets, tin swords, and lead soldiers.

On the front wall of our school hung a wooden replica of the Prince of Peace flanked by Joseph and Mary, and right below it a scene from the Franco-Prussian War depicting a sky-blue Bavarian infantryman beating the brains out of a kneeling French Zouave in blue jacket and red balloon trousers. In school we learned soldier songs and military evolutions, armed with iron rods representing rifles.

During maneuvers, or whenever soldiers were quartered in town, there were military high masses in church bestowing God's blessing on everything martial from kaiser, king, flag, uniform, down to rifle and bayonet. What wonder then that we boys played soldier more than any other game? There were always two armies—German and French. The German army was invariably composed of the best and strongest scrappers. The French army was always composed of the weaker, less pugnaciously inclined boys. And the cowardly French army was inevitably defeated, as predestined by the All-High in company with German might and heroism. The historic fact that only seven decades previously these cowardly French had romped all over our heroic Germans was conveniently forgotten.

I still remember two local sons of Wotan. The first was Haag, the organ grinder with the wooden leg. Haag bore the distinction of having been trampled upon twice, first by the French and second by the Russians. He was one of the few survivors from the thirty thousand Württembergers who participated in Napoleon's retreat from Moscow. As a good Austrian he had fought against the French, for which he had received a pewter medal

from the good Kaiser Franz. When Napoleon defeated his future
father-in-law, he annexed southern Swabia to the domain of his
troublesome ally, the prince of Württemberg, and bestowed the
title of king on him for good measure. In return for the honor
and the real estate, the king of Württemberg lent his army,
Haag included, to Napoleon for his invasion of Russia. Haag's
reward was one medal earned fighting against the Corsican, and
another earned fighting for him, thus making Haag plus two
medals and minus one leg.

Haag used to point proudly to the two medals on his faded
uniform, saying, *"Wir Helden* (we heroes) need no beggar's
license to ply our trade. These medals are our license."

The other remnant of the Napoleonic wars was Braig, a retired
forester. At the time of the French invasion he was only ten years
old, too young to fight for God, kaiser, and fatherland. French
troops had been quartered in his family's house. One day two
French cavalrymen tied him between their horses and took him
to another town, some twelve miles off. A few days later he returned with his feet bleeding, almost starved. He had trotted
the distance back bare-footed on frozen, icy ground. Yet it was
not the suffering he experienced on this journey which caused
him to foam at the mouth whenever Frenchmen were mentioned
in his presence. The Frenchmen had killed and eaten his pet
rabbit before Braig's eyes. For revenge the boy had peed in their
own well. "And I'll do it again," he would cry vehemently
seventy years later, "if another goddamn Frenchman ever dark-
ens the door again."

The supreme climax of soldier life and soldiering was the
annual fall maneuvers, after the crops had been harvested. At
that season there was no end to the soldiers. Soldiers on foot,
hoof, and wheel. Soldiers making love to peasant girls behind
brush and trees. Soldiers in every tavern and beer garden roaring
soldier songs. And did I love it! I was daffy about those maneuvers. I was so daffy about soldiers, and soldiering, and sham
battles, rifle salvos, cannon thundering, all over the otherwise

placid countryside that after having exhausted every ruse and lie
I could think of for getting excused from school I caught a
bumblebee with my writing hand and let nature do the rest. It
worked. The swelling which resulted baffled all the medical
knowledge of the two doctors of our town as well as that of a few
old lady faith healers. After a few days the swelling went down,
of course, but there were other bumblebees where the first had
come from, and by the time the bumblebee poison had lost much
of its potency, the maneuvers were over.

I think it was during that particular set of maneuvers when I
was completely captivated by Unser Fritz, the future Emperor
Frederick II, father of the last of the Hohenzollerns. I was
perched in the lower limbs of one of the apple trees lining the
road from Laupheim to Baltringen. It was a fine perch just a
few feet above the heads of passing cavalry men.

One of them—oh, heart, stand still!—reared up on his horse,
lifted a kindly bearded face up to me and, gently shaking the
limb on which I was perched, said with a merry twinkle of his
large blue eyes, "Shall I shake down that red-cheeked apple?"
It was Unser Fritz.

Oh, to die for a prince like that! To sit on a prancing horse,
cleaving the cowardly head of a Frenchman with my shining
sword. Driving a lance into the fear-quivering breast of another.
Finding the yellow heart of a third with the leaden messenger
of my trusted carbine. Or if not all of that lofty ideal, at least
tooting a horn, leading the host of righteous into battle for God,
king, and fatherland!

Such is the stuff out of which cannon fodder is made.

But catch 'em young, gentlemen of the crown, hymn, text, and
checkbook! Drill, instill the poison into minds still pliant, carefully hiding the bitterness by patriotic sugar coating, pious soothing syrup, and chauvinist lying. Catch 'em young, gentlemen,
so that the soldierly ardors of youth may follow them to the
very grave. And even then, it won't always work. . . .

2

WHEN I was about six years old my father persuaded mother to sell the little twelve-acre farm she had inherited from her first husband. Father, a highly skilled cabinet maker and one of the last guild masters, had never been happy in our peasant village, especially since he was much traveled and had worked for many years as a journeyman in the capital of fine furniture, Vienna. With the proceeds of the farm my father had purchased a home on the Lange Gasse in Laupheim, the county seat, where he set up his cabinet workshop. There I spent the most miserable years of a long life, my seven years of school.

As I look back on those years, it seems to me there is not one single happy incident I can remember. In later days I have heard people talking about the high quality of German pedagogy. They are not making sense to me. I hated that Laupheim school as much as I am capable of hating anything. There were only two really devout and deep-felt prayers that I squeezed out of my tortured breast in those seven years—the first that lightning might strike the teacher, the second that the schoolhouse might burn down. Teacher never was struck by lightning. He died of delirium tremens. The school actually burned down, but it happened too late to do me any good. . . . I received the glad tidings only last spring in Beverly Hills, California, where I had paid a visit to the late Carl Laemmle, the motion picture magnate,

16

THE AUTHOR AND HIS FATHER

who hailed from the same village, and whose age was about the same as mine.

All my teachers had missed their calling. They would have made first-class animal trainers. To say they should have been shot at sunrise would in my opinion have been a stupid understatement. They should have been shot at sunset the day before. My war with teachers and authority in general started during my first morning in school. I had received an urgent call of nature. Had I been at home or out in God's free air I should have known exactly what to do. But this was school. I was a bit bewildered by the strange surroundings. So, instead of giving the proper answer to the call of nature, I did what almost any youngster situated in my position would do. Whereupon my animal trainer, instead of telling me that there was a privy for little boys connected with the school, gave me my first *Tatze*, and for good measure held me up to the ridicule of the whole class.

From that day on until the bitter end, seven years later, these tatzen constituted the chief elements of my "education." Tatzen were administered with hazelnut switches on the finger tips of the culprit. One tatze for small offenses, two tatzen for greater offenses, up to six tatzen for more serious offenses. If six tatzen—and how they hurt!—failed to instill the proper respect for authority and learning, the sinner was slung over the knee of the pedagogue, who thereupon administered hazel switch blows until he grew tired. For the ultimate height of boyish offenses there was the *Kartzer* or school dungeon in which I spent many happy hours dreaming of the licking I would give my teacher as soon as I was big enough to handle him.

And yet, I was not a vicious youngster or a *Galgenstrick* (gallows rope), as my trainer loved to call me. I was slow to anger, could readily forgive, would generously divide with others what I had been given or had pilfered, and only lied in self-defense or when the truth might have hurt others. Nor was I a dull boy. Whatever I loved I learned faster than my school mates. But my love of learning was confined to drawing, music, and composition. Whatever else they taught in that cursed school belonged in the category of torture. Among my aversions were grammar and arithmetic. To this very day I do not know a single grammatical rule, either in the German or the English language, and yet in the course of time I have managed to become articulate in both languages as a result of reading good literature outside of school. By some queer turn of mind, when it came to mental arithmetic I surpassed most of my schoolmates, but as soon as a row of figures was placed before my nose they started crawling around like so many ants until I became hopelessly lost.

Looking back, these many years afterward, I can see clearly that nature had cut me out for an artist, musician, writer, or under exceptionally favorable circumstances, all three. For it was in these callings that I made my living for more than half a century and to them I returned always whenever the course of life had led me into other fields. My school training was not exceptionally favorable for developing these natural gifts. On the contrary, it was as unfavorable as ignorant teachers could make it.

Take drawing. Before I was ten years old I could draw anything that took my fancy—chairs, tables, animals, trees, flowers, people. One day during recess I had even drawn a caricature of our teacher on the blackboard, a likeness so good that when he returned from his recess stein of beer a bit too soon and spied the work of art, he licked eternal hell out of me.

If my teacher had possessed the slightest inkling of the purpose of education, on beholding his counterfeit on the blackboard he would have lovingly laid hands on the head of the young genius and said, "Well done, my boy! There is an artist concealed in you. Now, let's see what we can do to bring him out."

But no, free-hand drawing was not for my kind. I was the son of a cabinet maker. Future cabinet makers must learn only mechanical drawing, and so it was triangle, compass, and T-square which I soon learned to hate with every fiber of my soul.

Yes, they might have made a painter out of me. The stuff was in me. The things I then wanted above everything else, and only my mother would give me when she could squeeze the money from her household expenses, were water colors and colored crayons. Years later I found a sketch I had made of the houses climbing slowly toward the church and castle on the hill crowning the town. To my great surprise, even the perspective was almost correct, and I cannot remember that previous to that sketch anyone had even mentioned, much less introduced me to, the mysteries of perspective.

And as with drawing, so with music. Regarding the latter, however, I must give credit for whatever was perpetrated on me, not to my school teachers, but to the retired, half-pay army musicians into whose hands a cruel fate had delivered me. In the end, they served me better than I had anticipated in my wildest boyhood dreams.

At school I usually sang second, indicating that if not my voice, at least my ear was above the average. At home there were always a number of wind instruments lying around because father, besides being a highly skilled cabinet maker, was also a musician. If I remember rightly, he had either played in the orchestra of Johann Strauss, or if not, was at least acquainted with the methods of the waltz king. At any rate, he told me that the waltzes of Strauss were not Strauss's exclusive handiwork, but were a sort of co-operative product of Strauss and his orchestras. In presenting a new waltz to his players, Strauss would usually supply only the first violin part and figured bass. The rest the orchestra filled or faked in. Only after the composition had reached its final form was it written into score. I also heard father tell of playing the French horn with the rival of Strauss, the now forgotten waltz composer Lanner. The combination of craftsman and French horn player in one of the leading orchestras of Vienna may sound irreconcilable, but in the first half of the nineteenth century, music still was so poorly paid, even in the world's capital of good music, that orchestra performers generally could follow their true love only as a side line.

How it came about that I aspired to become an army bandsman and how the blowing I did and the blows I received in the process eventually blew me clear over the Atlantic Ocean I shall relate later. At all events, in the Seventies the German army still maintained an institution called music apprentices. Talented boys received their training from retired musicians at greatly reduced cost. My music lessons cost thirty pfennigs, or less than eight cents an hour. In return for this reduction the apprentice pledged himself to enter the army at the age of sixteen to serve twelve years, at the end of which time he was entitled to a civil position such as policeman, letter carrier, or street-car conductor. Thirty years later he could retire on a life pension of "not enough to live on, and too much to die on," as the saying had it.

I loved music and I had played a yellow boxwood F-flute when my fingers were still too short to cover all of its six holes and two keys. But the army-style music course was something else again. The curriculum included one wood, one brass, and one stringed instrument. My teachers were first-class disciplinarians; their view was that music was a trade to be learned from the ground up. The ground was a blank music page. Below the staff I was ordered to make the whole note of C. From C below the staff I gradually worked up to C above the staff, then down to the C below the C below the staff. I was warned where half tones were placed in both minor and major scales. In the course of these inhuman events I constructed every scale under the sun, moon, and stars, and some the sun, moon, and stars would be surprised to see, or hear.

Having written the scales, I played them in whole tones, half tones, quarter tones, eighth, sixteenth, and finally, in thirty-second tones. I played them pianissimo, fortissimo, crescendo, diminuendo, until I was playing them with tears in my eyes and murder in my heart. After scales came arpeggios, or broken chords, as we called them, and I played *them* in every conceivable and inconceivable key and phrasing.

Between scales and arpeggios came finger exercises, and on the clarinet, which I had innocently tackled, exercises with accent on the thumb and first two fingers of the left hand, which are cursed with more chores than the good Lord Himself ever imagined three fingers could perform. By the time I had become a fairly good clarinetist, passable trumpeter, and indifferent violinist, I hated music and everything and everybody remotely connected with it. But there was no way out. If I hit a wrong note, there was a box on the ear. If I failed to get my lesson, it meant a beating in the classroom and a beating at home until there was nothing left but to mourn and learn. Verily, if there was ever a mortal who had music physically pounded into him it was the young Oscar Ameringer. And still my tormentors could not kill all the inborn love of music in my soul. As good luck willed it, the financial agreement provided that our tormentors could employ us at dances, weddings, and other festive occasions requiring music. Our pay went to the instructors, of course, which was all right with me, for I would rather have played dances and marches gratis than play scales, arpeggios, and finger exercises for all the gold of Midas. I am sure it must have almost broken the hearts of our trainers to allow us to play merry and stirring tunes; however, the market for scales, arpeggios, and finger exercises was not good, and even half-pay army musicians cannot live solely by browbeating boys.

Come to think, now, I must recall that previous statement to the effect that my seven school years were all black, for I hugely enjoyed playing for dances. Moreover, I enjoyed tooting my little C clarinet or low-E-flat trumpet so hugely that I would rather keep on tooting than take time off to learn dancing, the art which everyone should acquire for the sake of grace and which I myself have missed.

I especially enjoyed playing for peasant weddings. Some of these actually lasted three days; *Polter Abend,* a sort of house-

warming before the wedding day proper, then the after-
wedding, largely devoted to sobering up. On the morning of the
wedding day itself, our band of from four to six pieces would
escort the bride, her bridesmaids, friends and relatives to the
village church. That done, we escorted the groom, his best man,
friends and relatives to church. In church we played Mendelssohn's Wedding March or Wagner's Bridal Chorus from *Lohengrin*. And please imagine Wagner's Bridal Chorus played by
clarinet, cornet, alto, and bass, and at best swelled by the addition
of tenor horn and second alto!

From church the happily spliced couple and united processions
marched to the tavern. Arrived there, everybody, except the
musicians who supplied the table music, sat down to the wedding
feast, and the amount of food those peasants could stow away!
There were Peter Brueghel paintings brought forward two
centuries!

At the weddings of richer peasants, that is, of Croesuses who
owned twenty acres and up, worked horses in place of cows, and
boasted the largest manure pile beneath their parlor windows, the
groom paid all the expenses: food, drinks, and music. At the weddings of poor peasants the guests, on congratulating the bride,
would leave a coin in her hand to help her set up housekeeping.
Everyone paid for whatever he consumed, while the musicians
paid themselves, taking up a collection after every third dance. In
either case, dancing was opened by a solo dance of first bridesmaid
and best man, followed by a solo dance of bride's father and
mother-in-law and vice versa. After that, all fell to dancing.

Somewhere between midnight and four A.M. of the wedding
day proper, fighting generally started at these peasant weddings.
This was especially the case when bride and groom hailed from
different villages and the former had brought a sizable dowry to
the opposition clan. At these pleasantries chairs and table legs
would frequently be converted into war clubs; beer mugs flew
through the festive atmosphere; knife blades occasionally slipped
between the ribs of more or less innocent bystanders. From all

this we musicians enjoyed immunity, thanks to the breast-high grating around the musicians' platform behind which we could always dodge when beer mugs came too fast and furious. Poor peasants usually managed to slip into the holy bonds of matrimony unaccompanied by assault, battery, and mayhem. Whether this was true because there was little or nothing to fight over, or because they possessed a larger measure of brotherly love, I leave for others to figure out.

I have already mentioned that besides my talent for drawing and music, I had a powerful urge for *fabulieren*, as Goethe called the art of story-telling. Moreover, by the time the age of school essay-writing came around I was by far the best-read boy not only of my class but probably of the whole burg. Somehow my peasant mother had come by a small library of German classics, containing part of the works of Goethe, Schiller, Hauf, Lessing, and, unfortunately for me, a history of the Reformation written by a Huguenot heretic named d'Aubigné, a book that wrought a veritable revolution in my head, resulting in no end of spiritual and bodily agony.

Shortly after digesting that history of the Reformation, we were called upon to write an essay on the *Glaubenstrennung*, or the split of the faith, as the Reformation was called in our Catholic circles. The reason for this distinction, I take it, was the fact that "Reformation" implied there might have been something in the Church of Rome requiring reformation.

By that time the province of Württemberg in which we lived had come under the spiked helmet of Protestant Prussia. It was therefore no longer healthy to call Lutherans heretics. The line between hell-bound and heaven-bound was the Danube River. Our religious convictions were determined by geography and history.

Up to 1805, upper Swabia, or the southern part of Württemberg, stretching from the Danube to the Lake of Constance, had belonged to Austria. When the Reformation broke out, in the sixteenth century, the emperor of Austria remained a faithful son of the Roman Church, and his loyal subjects judiciously followed suit. In all likelihood the people of the lowlands of old Württemberg would have remained Catholic, too. However, by the time part of northern Germany and most of the free cities had forsworn the old and embraced the new faith, the germinating democracy of old Württemberg had run off its own prince. The reason why the peasants and burghers of his realm had run him off was that the anointed was a drunkard, profligate, and all-around wastrel of the first order.

The jobless exile sought sympathy and succor at the court of Prince Johann of Saxony. Saxony was then the California of continental Europe. As in the adjoining Sudetenland of recently chloroformed Czechoslovakia, both gold and silver were mined in its hills and mountains. Since kingdoms and principalities were at that time the private estates of their rulers, Johann of Saxony, holding the longest purse string in the Holy Roman Empire, had become emperor maker, emperors being elected by the votes of the princes of the realm. In short, Prince Johann of Saxony was in his day a combination Warwick, Mark Hanna, and Pierpont Morgan. On top of that he had become the protector of Martin Luther.

This explains how it came about that, some time later, when Martin Luther went to Worms to defend his heresies before a conclave of Roman bishops, he got away with a whole skin, instead of being burned at the stake as had happened to poor Johann Huss at the conclave of Constance a century before. And so to Johann of Saxony went the ejected prince of Württemberg with his troubles.

He found a sympathetic listener. Johann had already become the leading light of the faith of Luther. At the same time he felt a bit lonesome and craved allies. The upshot of the powwow between the two was that Johann offered the prince of Württemberg his army and war chest with the understanding that, having licked his rebellious subjects, he would convert them to the new faith.

The exile did both, and in due time went to his reward *via* a combination of syphilis and delirium tremens.

Now much of this and other interesting information I had gleaned from the history of the Reformation by Huguenot d'Aubigné and perhaps some other book in mother's hope chest. So that when an essay on the Reformation came along I was swimming in duck soup. And I put it all down, the greed, immorality, and rapacity of the popes with sidelights on the greedy, immoral, and rapacious princes of the Church and princes of the blood, God-anointed though they might style themselves.

I told the story of Tetzel, who had come to Germany selling indulgences in the pious effort to raise the coin to finish the dome of St. Peter's, the fisherman follower of the humble carpenter. I told of Tetzel's box bearing the inscription,

". . . As soon as the coin in the coffer rings,
The soul of the sinner out of Purgatory springs. . . ."

I told the story of the cutthroat who had asked Tetzel if indulgences could be purchased covering prospective sins. Then, having received the assurance that matters like that were easily arranged with the heavenly judiciary, he paid the price and a few nights later robbed Tetzel of his box and contents. All this I put in that memorable essay on the split of faiths.

The effect of that historic masterpiece was electrifying, the literal sort of electrification one achieves in getting hold of a live wire. Where in the so-and-so had I learned those lies? Who in the so-and-so had stuffed me with all that blasphemy? Come across, 'fess up, or take the consequences. So ran my teachers' reactions.

Judging from the violent eruption I had created, I scented foul weather ahead. I would not give my mother away, come what might, and so I took the consequences—six tatzen on the finger tips, followed by others until the last hazel switch had gone the way of all flesh, followed by six hours' solitary confinement minus bread and water in the school dungeon.

But glory, hallelujah, I had not peached on my mother.

Next day my scholastic animal trainer ordered me out to the local thickets to replace the hazel switches worn out trying to beat a confession out of me. I refused point-blank. No more hazel switches available, I was treated to a series of blows on the cheeks by the huge hands of my teachers. All in vain. More docile and obliging schoolmates returned with the hazel switches requested. Another and for all I know more merciless beating followed. No use. No good. I was past thrashing. Past crying. Past feeling. Past everything but burning hate. They could have killed me before I would tell on mother.

A few days later, animal-trainer Schmidt, priest Hepp, and chaplain Hertzer formed a sort of holy inquisition endeavoring to extract that confession. To the honor of the last two named, they refrained from employing the third hazel-switch degree on me. I was prayed over, flattered, almost wept over. I was not altogether lost. Blasphemous, heretical as the essay was, it did show precocity and serious study. But would I not tell the source of my information?

Too late, too late. I had had the last atom of respect to both temporal and spiritual authority beaten out of my miserably bruised body and I didn't give a damn what might happen to me either here or in the hereafter.

There remained, however, a slight, almost hopeless chance of snatching my soul from the burning brand. The slight chance was a pilgrimage to the shrine of Mother Anna, mother of Mary. The shrine was located in the village of Schoenenberg, some three hours' walk from our home. The way I understood it, Mother Anna would intercede for me with Mary, her daughter, who would intercede for me with her Son, who would put in a good word for me with his Father. Thus in this roundabout way, leading through the heavenly Cabinet, I still might find salvation.

I was not impressed. I knew Mother Anna. She was a three-foot wooden statue, whittled out by some forgotten village sculptor. Centuries of wax-candle and incense smoke had given her the

complexion of a full-blooded Moor. Moreover, the ancient village sculptor had employed badly seasoned wood. As a result,
deep cracks had appeared on Mother Anna, extending from her
blackened wooden face to her blackened wooden feet. I couldn't
see how the collection of blackened wood and yawning cracks
could be of assistance in my case. What's more, I didn't care.

However, my restless, ever-willing feet did not object to the
long journey to Schoenenberg, rightly so called because the name
means "beautiful hill." From Beautiful Hill one could look
northward to the Danube winding its blue, leisurely way through
the green meadows of the valley; behind the Danube rose the
Jura mountains, or Swabian Alps. Westward you saw the somber
hills of the black forests, crowned by the almost mountainlike
hill on which stood the old chapel immortalized by Kreutzer in
the beautiful song, *"Droben stehet die Kapelle."* The same composer, born in my province, had also composed the well-known
song "Sunday Morning" which is still the favorite of German
singing societies. Southward one saw the glistening waters of Lake
Constance and beyond, the majestic snow-capped Alps of Switzerland. A beautiful country, inspiring poetry and song, explaining
perhaps why that little Swabian Overland had given Germany
one of its major poets, Friedrich Schiller; why some seven minor
poets sleep in a graveyard near Stuttgart, the capital of our province; and why such sweet singers as the aforementioned Kreutzer,
after whom Beethoven named his well-known sonata, and Silcher,
the composer of the music of the Lorelei, hailed from that little
neck of the woods, smaller than many Texas counties. So also it
came about that on my pilgrimage to Mother Anna on that Sunday morning the ever-healing balm of *Gott in der Natur* had lovingly healed the wounds of my soul, and body as well.

On my departure, mother had given me her rosary and one
mark in cash. I had invested ten pfennigs of the latter in a box of
cigarettes. There remained twenty-two and a half cents equivalent
in American money. At peace with the world once more, rosary

in my pocket and cigarette between my lips, I arrived in Schoenenberg just as its one church let out and its worshippers filed through the hospitable door of the Black Bock, Schoenenberg's principal tavern, handily located opposite the church. Not in a hurry to be saved, I joined the merry throng.

Spying an empty seat at a table, I ordered a seidel of beer, reducing my capital to the tune of ten pfennigs. At the table sat four young peasants a little older than myself, shaking dice out of a leather box. The object of their gambling was a very large pretzel, whose dimensions exceeded those of the pretzels you see sold in Reading and Allentown, Pa., by some five hundred per cent. The cost of the grand pretzel was forty pfennigs. Dividing forty pfennigs by four peasants makes ten pfennigs each. Presently one of the pretzel gamblers was cleaned out, leaving three. I joined the pretzel game.

Fate, if not faith, was with me. Perhaps it was only beginner's luck. Anyhow, by the time the noon meal was announced I had accumulated besides a small stack of pretzels a goodly stack of chicken feed. The chicken feed came in because when one had accumulated more pretzels than he knew what to do with he sold them back to his less fortunate compatriots. And so it came about that I earned my first meal—consisting of noodle soup, veal roast, potato salad, rye bread, and beer—by shaking dice while engaged on a pilgrimage to Mother Anna.

Of course I had been warned against the sinfulness of young boys drinking beer—alone. Drinking beer accompanied by our elders was all right. A still greater sin was smoking cigarettes. The last word in sin was shaking dice for money. However, when a fellow is thirteen, has money in his pocket, and has defied authority, divine, temporal and pedagogic, he's got to celebrate independence somehow, and that's the way I did it.

After my glorious independence-day dinner, other pretzel gamblers appeared. Having tasted blood, I joined them. Either the particular guardian angel who has stuck to me all through life directed my dice, or Satan had a hand in the game. I had been

told Satan went to no end of trouble and expense recruiting boys
for his domain. For the present, my luck only confirmed my conviction that all my trainers had told me about the dire consequences of sin was fiddle-faddle.

At the fall of dusk, I had hoarded ten pretzels. My pockets
bulged with small change and my tummy with lager. There must
have been as much as seventy-five cents' worth of coins, all copper—quarter-cent, half-cent, one-and-a-quarter-cent and two-and-
a-half-cent pieces. Had that pretzel game continued long enough
I might be living on the interest of my winnings to this very day.

However, it was getting dark. There was still three hours'
walk, mostly through pine forests, before me. It was time to go,
and so, stringing my ten pretzels on the walking stick I had cut
on the way, I bade Godspeed to my fellow pretzel gamblers and
started for home.

Getting home was another problem. I was loaded down with
pretzels, chicken feed, and lager. But villages are only a few miles
apart in that region, and every village harbors one or more places
where, as the saying went, the good Lord holds out the hand of
welcome.

It felt mighty good, entering those places, importantly order-
ing a seidel of lager, then importantly pulling a fortune out of
my pocket and tipping the plump waitress girl with a quarter or
half cent according to plumpness and looks.

Nearing our home I observed a light in the living room above
the workshop. Mother was waiting, perhaps praying for the return of the prodigal. But console yourself, mother. I have the surprise of your life for you. And holding up my string of giant pretzels in one hand and a fortune in loose change in the other, I
kicked the door open and triumphantly entered.

Mother was far from greedy, but it took money to supply the
wants of a youngster who was always pestering her for water colors, boxes of colored crayons, lead pencils, and sketching paper.
Well, here it was. Oodles and oodles of money. And so instead
of the welcome kiss, kissing being unknown in our circles anyhow,

mother gleefully started counting the fortune I gradually dis-
gorged from my pockets. At length, when the last quarter cent
was fished up, mother caught herself.

"But where, where, *bueble*, did you get all that money?"
("Bueble," let me say, is the diminutive of "boy" in the Swabian
dialect.)

I told her the truth, the whole truth, and nothing but the truth.

And when she had listened to my story in all its naked simplicity she exclaimed in dismay: "But, but . . . bueble, did you
see Mother Anna?"

I hadn't seen Mother Anna. I had completely forgotten
Mother Anna all the time I was shaking dice for pretzels. I hadn't
even thought of Mother Anna on that three-hour walk home in
the dark. And that was the truth, the whole truth, and nothing
but the truth, so help me.

The pilgrimage to Mother Anna was the last bright spot of my
school days. That fatal essay on the Reformation had cooked my
hash definitely and permanently. I had become the heretic and
pariah of the town. Even the few schoolmates who had put up
with me that far now shunned my company. Fortunately, there
was a fairly large Jewish group in our town. The ancestors of
some of those Jews had come into our country with the Roman
invaders in the early centuries of the Christian era. Nevertheless,
they were not to be regarded as Germans, but foreign interlopers
and heretics, and Christ-killers to boot. On top of all that, they
were better heeled than us Aryans, engendering a strong undercurrent of anti-Semitism in the hearts of the true believers.

Even before my final slip from grace I could not share in the
smoldering manifestations of anti-Semitism. On the contrary, I
had early learned to like the Jews. The Jewish boys I had come
in contact with seemed just a little brighter than our boys.
Mother, too, shared my sentiments. Had we not read together
Lessing's *Nathan the Wise*, she filling the role of commentator?
The Judenberg, or ghetto, where the less fortunately situated

Jews were located, was but a few blocks from our home. The Juden Gasse, later baptized Kappellen Strasse (Chapel Street), where the better- and best-heeled Jews were located, was only a little further away. Besides, misery loves company and so it came about that I spent a great part of my last school years in the company of Jewish boys.

Occasionally some of them took me to their homes. Compared to my own house, theirs were luxurious. Many of them already boasted pianos. There were always books lying on tables or stored in book cases, and I loved books. Also, compared to my own and neighboring homes, they were havens of peace. This was especially true by contrast with my own, for the marriage of my parents was not happy. Father being now almost, but not quite, a furniture manufacturer, felt he had married below his caste, although it was mother's money that had set him up in business. There were frequent quarrels. Father even anticipated Hitler by burning some of mother's books.

The mothers of my Jewish friends treated me most kindly. On the occasion of Passover, Jewish New Year, and other festivities, they would give me matzoth and other kosher tidbits. Their fathers were always sober and they, too, sneaked me an occasional five-, ten-, or twenty-pfennig piece. I also loved listening to the stories and Talmudic wisdom of the gray-bearded "Fathers," some of whom still wore the long kaftans and earlocks of their ancestors.

Perhaps these people had learned the story of my delinquency and, being in a way heretics and pariahs themselves, sympathized with my predicament. However that was, I learned to respect the Jews. That respect only deepened after I learned how much they had contributed to art, literature, and science in the long, cruel road they had traveled before and since their dispersion.

Besides my Jewish friends there were books to lighten my social outcasting. Books good, bad and indifferent, down to yellow-backed ten-pfennig blood-and-thunder tales and luridly illustrated Indian and Wild West stories, most of them located south of the shining big sea waters, east of wild and woolly Ohio. I read them all. *Pathfinder, Leather Stocking, The Last of the Mohicans,* the American adventure of Gerstäcker, author of *The River Pirates of the Mississippi,* and similar hair-raisers. Naturally, these volumes did not come from mother's book chest. Across the street from our house lived a Protestant merchant whose son, Paul, was about my own age. Besides being heretics, we both were voracious readers, but while thus far my literary predilection had largely run to classics and forbidden history, Paul's was blood and thunder. Cash registers with bells on them had not been invented yet, so there was always the primitive cash drawer of Paul's parents to draw on. Paul gave me the money. I bought the books, and Paul borrowed them from me. After reading them he returned them to their "rightful" owner who read them, if he hadn't read them before. In this way I acquired an overpowering urge to devote my life to avenging the bloody wrongs which palefaces had inflicted on my heroic red men. . . .

There was other literature. Mother belonged to a small reading circle largely composed of Protestants and Jews. The reading circle would subscribe to certain weekly and monthly periodicals. One of my chores was to collect the periodicals at the homes of the members. That operation was subject to numerous delays on my part, depending on the reading matter contained in the particular issues. On the whole it was good stuff, as witnessed by the total absence of holy pictures and miraculous adventures of dead saints. One of these periodicals was the *Gartenlaube,* which, on account of its anti-clericalism and liberalism, stood in very bad odor in our pious town. In fact, such liberal ideas as those sponsored by the *Gartenlaube* had the same odor in those days that bolshevism has now.

As I look back over those years I can't believe mother was the devout Catholic she seemed to be. Surely the reading of the German classics must have left its influence on her mind. Indeed, I heard her speak approvingly of Frederick von Hutten, Goetz von Beringen on the *Ironfist* (immortalized by Goethe), and of

Johann Huss and other heroes of the Reformation. She was also an admirer of Carl Schurz, Hecker, Siegel, and other '48 revolutionists, of whom I heard her speak long before I met their names in print. I suspect that her devoutness and regular attendance at masses and pilgrimages were largely a matter of protective coloring to shield her unhappy life from additional abuses. Poor mother! What a wealth of fine thought and feeling was concealed in her one-hundred-pound peasant body.

Besides mother, there was only one other person not yet convinced of my utter depravity, and that was the chaplain, Hertzer, who participated in the inquisition which sentenced me to the pilgrimage to Mother Anna. Realizing that beating the rebel would get nowhere, and very likely opposed to that method of reformation and conversion (he had a rather fine, sensitive young face), he tried books. Unfortunately, I was too far gone from grace for the kind of book he handed me. It was written by Alban Stoltz, a religious fanatic and hard-boiled Puritan belonging to the species of Calvin, Briar, and Cotton Mather. Everything that people enjoy in the world and costs a little money was sin, according to Alban Stoltz. Dancing, love making, playing cards, drinking, merrymaking of every kind and description was verboten and properly punished in eternal hell, as testified by the illustrations in Alban's book: there were poor souls, hands pitifully raised above surrounding flames. There were no end of horny-headed devils sticking red-hot pitchforks into bellies of damned sinners standing chin deep in boiling oil. I read *Zeit und Ewigkeit* by Alban Stoltz on top of Goose Hill, with the sleepy town in the peaceful valley beneath me, and there was no one between heaven and hell who could persuade me that the Maker of all this could so cruelly torture his children.

Returning the book to the young priest, I told him freely what I thought of it. However, instead of reaching for a hazelnut stick, as I had confidently expected, he only pitied me, which hurt deeper. I still hear his words ringing in my ears, words he spoke when on parting he laid his hand on my rebellious young head and said with an almost tearful choking voice, "*Armes Kind, armes Kind, is da kein Weg deine Seele zu retten?*"—"Poor child, poor child, is there no way of saving thy immortal soul?"

No, it won't do to condemn a whole religion, any more than to condemn a whole nation. But how could I, who had already read Goethe's *Faust,* who could recite by heart its magnificent dedication and all of the Easter Morning monologue and many other passages—how could I who had already read Schiller's *William Tell, Mary Stuart, Maid of Orleans,* swallow that stuff? Very likely I was still a long way from grasping the true import of the revolution these classics had wrought in me. But what I did not understand, I felt deeply, and what one feels deeply often surpasses understanding.

The German classics, Goethe, Schiller, Lessing, and later Heine, have remained my faithful companions, friends, and guides to this very day. And so has classical music. But how, the reader may want to ask, did the musical drillmasters, who pounded into me until they almost succeeded in pounding it out of me, introduce me to classical music? Well, they didn't. I got my first taste of good music from a Jewish girl. Her father was a doctor. Their house was not very far from ours, and every time, morning, noon, and night, I passed the place, I heard that Jewish girl pounding scales, arpeggios, and finger exercises on her piano till I often felt like throwing a rock through her window. Why couldn't she play a snappy march, waltz, polka, schottische, mazurka, or plain folk tune once in a while? Why always these confounded scales, arpeggios, and finger exercises which I hated like poison?

And then one morning I heard a sweet, simple melody, as sweet and simple as "The Lorelei" or "Silent Night." I lingered and listened and the more I listened the better I liked that piece. The theme which had first stopped my bare feet kept weaving back into it over and over again. Other melodies as lovely as the first one kept coming in, and all were so skillfully and naturally

interwoven that scales, arpeggios, and finger exercises were completely gone, their places taken by heavenly joy.

At the end of the piece I crawled through the picket fence,
raised myself up by the window sill, and said, "Fräulein Rosenthal, will you tell me the name of the piece you just finished?"

She answered, " 'The Variations in A Flat,' by Beethoven."

And that was my introduction to Ludwig van Beethoven, and
through him to the glorious realm of classical music. From distant
Oklahoma, over three thousand miles of land and sea, over sixty
intervening years, go my heartfelt thanks to Fräulein Rosenthal;
may a kind fate have closed her eyes before the assassins of our
Germany, the Germany of Goethe, Schiller, Lessing, and Heine;
Bach, Beethoven, and Wagner, clumped onto the stage of history.

3

SCHOOL at last gratefully behind me, I became an apprentice in father's cabinet shop. The machine age had already come in, but as far as our shop was concerned we were still in the handicraft era. Furniture was not made wholesale, but by order. Everything was done by hand and very much in the same manner and with the same tools as were used by the Egyptian joiners who dovetailed those wooden caskets for the glorification and preservation of Pharaoh and Co., which I was to see later. Wood was bought standing. Hands felled the trees. Hands loaded it on lumbering wagons and hauled it to the saw mill. More hands assisted by a slow-turning water wheel sawed it into boards and beams. Hands piled the sawed lumber in the lumber shed behind our home and shop. Hands, my own included, turned it over regularly, assuring straight and uniform seasoning.

The customer selected what he wanted from drawings made by hand. Price was set by the quality of wood and workmanship. Slighting workmanship for speed was a deadly sin. The customer's selection made, we transferred the drawing to wood, sawed out the wood by hand, dressed it, put it together, planed, shaved, sandpapered it until the last blemish had vanished, then polished it by hand and finally delivered it by wheelbarrow or pushcart, propelled by hand.

It was slow work. I remember it took us a week to make an ordinary dresser, and two weeks or better for a fine or extra-fine

one. Everything else was in proportion: a primitive way of making furniture, the same way many generations of cabinet makers
had employed between Pharaoh's and father's time. I noticed,
however, when I came to observe some of those Pharaoh's coffins,
that they were still beautifully intact. By the same token, I am
certain that most of the furniture made in father's shop is still
doing duty.

Father was a guild master. Indeed, he was more than that. He
was the master of the guild of joiners of the town. At the height
of his career, father employed four journeymen and two apprentices. Master, journeymen, and apprentices shared the same roof
and ate at the same table. The best went to the master. Second
best to journeymen. Apprentices took what was left, paid for their
tuition, and for good measure, washed dishes, ran errands,
watched babies and changed diapers.

When an apprentice had served his three years, he made his
"journeyman piece" in the shop of another master. If then, in
the opinion of a committee of masters, he had demonstrated the
proper qualifications, he was sent on the *Wanderschaft*, journey, to
perfect himself in his craft in other cities and lands. The wandering journeyman was not a hobo. He was entitled to all the rights
and privileges of a journeyman and future guild master. Entering
a workshop of his craft he would say, "God greet thee, masters
and journeymen of my guild." That done, and no work available,
he would receive a definite, stipulated journeyman's stipend from
his fellows, double the amount from the master, and so continue
his journey.

In the larger towns there were *Herbergen*, shelter homes,
houses in which guild journeymen found welcome overnight. In
the larger cities there were shelters for each separate guild. When
the journeyman returned and passed his mastership, he was
crowned master.

Father's shop was also the meeting place of the remaining guild
masters. In it I learned many things not found in books about the

troubles caused by the changing order. The age of handicraft was fading. Discussions were often heated and highly uncomplimentary to the new dispensation. There ought to be laws prohibiting machines, the guild masters would argue. There ought to be laws to forbid people who had not served their time as apprentices, and journeymen, and made their masterpieces, from plying their particular trades. "Free trade," by which they meant the privilege of plying trades without having acquired the lore and sanction of the respective guilds, must be done away with. One fellow, they pointed out, with no more experience in the art and mysteries of furniture-making than a new-born babe, had already established a furniture store in town. Another one, and a despised Jew at that, was operating a furniture factory by the grace of water power and free trade. And what's the world coming to anyhow, with unfair competition and chiselers all around? These good guild masters talked almost like General Hugh Johnson sixty years later, when the NRA was in flower, and to the same effect. The machine had come. Their breed was doomed. Work in the guild shops dwindled. The machine output was trash, of course. However, it was cheaper. People could see what they bought before they bought it. One after the other, guild masters gave up the ghost, were sucked into factories, or did home work serving the machine Moloch.

Father never became a machine hand, a term which connoted something considerably lower than a mangy hound suffering from flea bites and moral turpitude. Father died with his guild boots on. Just once I can remember he came near falling from grace. The local furniture factory had received a large order for the kind of box in which artists carry their tubes, brushes, and palettes. By then the Moloch had learned almost all the operations which go into the making of artist's boxes except the dovetailing of their four sides. We were masters at dovetailing. I heard father say, addressing an unseen machine, "Go ahead, damn you, but dovetailing is one thing you never will learn!"

I had not minded learning the furniture trade, although painting would have suited me better. There is something fascinatingly
creative about helping a dead piece of wood evolve into a thing of
beauty and service to man. But young as I was, I foresaw the end
of the golden age of handicraft. There was still the career of military bandsman, future policeman, letter carrier, street-car conductor and poor but deserving pensioner to fall back on. But in
the meantime something else had happened.

I was still enamored of soldiering, even though I despised my
military music trainers, who had cuffed, slapped and abused me
until I hated their very guts. I had heard them and other ex-
soldiers discuss, as if the words were sweet on their tongues, how
they had abused, insulted, and browbeaten underlings, or how
they themselves had been abused, mauled and browbeaten by
their superiors. I had seen a sergeant on a drill ground in Ulm
slap the cheek of a private, spit in his face, and for good measure
kick him in the crotch with heavy hobnailed boots. The king's uniform, it had finally dawned on me, was a fine thing to look upon
from the outside, but a mighty poor thing to be wrapped up in.

The climax that finally caused me to take the most decisive step
of my whole life was one of those accidents that so frequently
shape the destiny of us "self-made men." Our band was playing
in the beer garden of another town. A young country yokel, under
the influence of too many steins, had made what I thought a
harmless nuisance of himself, and a policeman, clad in the regulation spiked helmet and blue brass-buttoned uniform of his calling, ordered the exhilarated youth out of the beer garden. The
youngster was rather happy where he was; an argument started.
The peasant was dragged towards the exit, belabored on the way
with the flat part of the policeman's drawn saber. Without a moment's thought I jumped on the back of the law, wrapped my
arm around its neck, and tried my best to choke the life out of it.
The beatings I received in return, then and there and later at
home, still linger in my memory. . . .

There were other factors. I was already the town pariah. In the opinion of its burghers and burgheresses, all but mother, I was doomed and damned. There were only two courses for young hellions like me. Gallows and hell—or America. So to America I went, partly pushed, but mostly drawn, some eight months before my sixteenth birthday, at which time I was scheduled to enter the army and toot my horn for *Gott, Koenig* and *Vaterland*.

There were no tears shed at my departure, save mother's and mine.

Book Two

MY FIRST AMERICA

4

BOMBARDED by a thousand and one new impressions, I can remember but little of my first journey to America. There was the ill-smelling steerage with its seasick passengers; a cursory immigration examination in Castle Garden, New York a sea of houses, deafening elevated trains pulled by steam engines, rattling express wagons, horse-drawn trucks and street cars, peddlers shouting "ana banana," dirt, dust, and smoke.

Then the train and Oswego, a name known to me through one of Fenimore Cooper's Indian tales, but not an Indian in sight. A long ride on a spring wagon in Buffalo, transferring from one depot to another, but nary a buffalo. Clanking, bell-ringing trains in switchyards electrically illuminated. Great stretches of rolling hills. A deep pain in the heart called homesickness. Finally Cincinnati, where an older brother had preceded me, though not for the same reasons at all.

My reputation had gone before me and my brother shared none of my views. He was none too pleased to have the black sheep of the Ameringer fold wished on him, and moreover, he had his hands full with a growing family. The atmosphere of his house was too much like what I had left behind me in Germany, and we soon parted company.

Thinking back over the years I am sure the fault was rather mine than that of brother. I was an adolescent, though it would be decades before I learned that term and its implications; like

most youngsters of that age, I knew a great deal more then than
I know now. Neither did I realize at that time that the restraints
of my early youth had already made a full-bloomed rebel of me.
Nowadays we know more about the lasting effect of early impressions and how to counteract them, but at sixteen neither I nor
my surroundings had the slightest inkling of the forces that shape
the minds of men.

In the meantime, however, brother had helped me to secure
a job in a small furniture factory, and so back to wood shavings
and sawdust.

There was no resemblance between the work in that furniture
factory and father's shop. Here everything was done by machine.
Our only task was assembling, gluing together, and finishing, at
so much a chair or table, the two specialties of the factory. Speed
came first, quality of workmanship last. So long as the product
passed the inspection of the foreman, well and good. How soon it
would fall apart was the least of his and our worries.

The work was monotonous, the hours of drudgery ten a day,
my wages a dollar a day. Also, spring was coming on. Buds and
blue hills beckoned. And so, when agitators from the Knights
of Labor invaded our sweat shop, preaching the divine message
of less work for more pay, I became theirs from toe to forelock.
The general cause of labor did not enter my head—all I knew
was that what these organizers talked about was what I wanted.

In order to become a member of the Knights I was compelled
to add two to my almost sixteen years. But whatever I lacked in
age I more than made up in enthusiasm for the cause of less work
and more pay. The organization I had joined was a branch of the
Deutsche Holz Arbeiter Verein—German wood-workers' union
—affiliated with the Knights of Labor. The wood-workers' union
was an industrial, or vertical, union. It embraced all wood-workers
with the exception of basket weavers and wooden-shoe makers.
The membership was almost exclusively German and seasoned
with a good sprinkling of anarchists. Prior to the first of May,
1886, when the eight-hour-day strike was to be launched, there

had been groups of older or more militant members manufacturing bombs out of gas pipes. All of us expected violence, I suppose.

Too young to be admitted to the inner circle, I had converted a wood rasp into a dagger, in anticipation of the revolution just around the corner. The prelude to the revolution was the May Day parade in which I marched, bloody upheaval in heart and dagger beneath my coat tail. Only red flags were carried in that first May Day parade, and the only song we sang was the "Arbeiters Marseillaise," the battle cry of the rising proletariat. Even the May Day edition of the *Arbeiter Zeitung* was printed on red paper. Testifying further to the revolutionary intent of the occasion, a workers' battalion of four hundred Springfield rifles headed the procession. It was the *Lehr und Wehr Verein,* the educational and protective society of embattled toil.

Unfortunately for the pending revolution, the forces of law and order in the city made no attempt to interfere. Whether plutocracy had already abdicated or, considering that it takes two to make a fight, had taken the wiser course, I never discovered. And so we just marched and marched and sang and sang, until with burning feet and parched throats we distributed our forces among the saloons along the line of march where we celebrated the first victory of the eight-hour movement with beer, free lunch, and pinochle.

Next day the strike started. It was a jolly strike. Victory was dead certain, for did not almost everybody belong to the Knights of Labor? Butchers, bakers, and candlestick makers, doctors, preachers, grocerymen and boarding-house keepers. What could be easier? With everybody quitting work the surrender of plutocracy was a foregone conclusion. In addition, there was the union treasury. The first week "out" married men received six dollars in strike benefits, single men, three. The second week out was not so good. Married men received three dollars and single men nothing. And the third week out all were placed on a basis of American equality, everybody getting nothing. In the meantime, something happened which took much of the original starch out of strikers and sympathizers alike.

I was standing on the picket line when an express wagon drove up unloading bundles of papers. Soon newsboys were rending the air with the ominous cries: "Anarchist bomb throwers kill one hundred policemen in Haymarket in Chicago—Anarchist bomb-throwers kill one hundred policemen in Haymarket in Chicago—Anarchist—"

Things were getting serious. Many of us had called ourselves anarchists without, I am sure, being able to distinguish between arnica and anarchy.

The bad news from Chicago fell like an exceedingly cold blanket on us strikers. To our erstwhile friends and sympathizers the news was the clarion for speedy evaporation. Some of our weaker fellow Knights broke ranks. The army of the social revolution was visibly melting away. The police grew more numerous and ill-mannered. And so did the tempers of our diminishing irreconcilables.

I was standing opposite the main entrance of the furniture factory, warming half a brick under my coat tail, when one of the erring brothers came along. If he had been content with entering the building, I might still be a poor but deserving factory hand. However, before entering, he stuck out his tongue and made a long nose at me, whereupon I let fly my half brick.

Had the erring brother been an American versed in the art of baseball, he would have caught the brick and hurled it back at me, or would have sidestepped the missile. However, being a low Dutchman, he closed both eyes, stooped down and met the brick head on.

It was a lucky strike. I was proud of it and no doubt would have gloated over the body of the fallen foe had not two police-men appeared on the run, making it advisable for me to seek more congenial surroundings.

Owing to that and other overt acts, my name became emblazoned on the blacklists of Cincinnati's employers, so much so that when the strike was finally broken I experienced no trouble living up to the obligation I had assumed when joining the Knights of Labor to the effect that I would not return to work in that or any other furniture factory until our just demand, the eight-hour day plus a twenty-per-cent increase in wages, was granted.

5

FREE as a bird and an outcast once more, I was sitting on a bench in Washington Park in Cincinnati when the young man next to me started a conversation, addressing me first in English and, that failing, in German. The young man, it turned out, was a musician. So was I. He played the cornet. So did I. Moreover, he was the proud possessor of two cornets, while I had none. The upshot was that the young man invited me to his home to play cornet duets.

It was a pleasant home. We played about equally well. The mother of the young man was one of the very motherly German *Hausfrauen* who loved cooking, music, and boys. At the end of our rehearsal I was invited to remain for dinner. When I departed it was "Please come again and as often as you feel like it." I felt like coming soon and thereafter often, and no matter how often it was, it was always "Won't you stay for lunch, dinner, or supper?" as the case might be.

These rehearsals were mutually beneficial. My cornet playing was no better than that of my young friend. But I was a more experienced all-around musician and my appetite was decidedly superior to his, something his mother seemed to enjoy even more than my playing.

Back in practice, I secured a catch-as-catch-can job playing on a borrowed cornet in Bellstaedt's band. Old man Bellstaedt, the father of Herman Bellstaedt, one of the outstanding cornetists of

48

that day, operated a saloon. As a matter of fact, virtually all band and orchestra leaders of that time were saloon keepers. Both bands and orchestras were largely recruited from their customers, and the better the customer, the better his chance for engagement.

Owing to this custom our pay was usually spent for beer before it was earned. However, with beer went free lunch and a loafing place. The effect on the morale of us musicians was not too good. There was considerable truth in the saying, "Alle Musikanten sind Lumpen, aber nicht alle Lumpen sind Musikanten."—"All musicians are booze hounds, but not all booze hounds are musicians."

Our main jobs were playing for serenades, dances, picnics, and funerals, as all German mutual benefit and burial societies provided bands for the last rites of deceased members. The wages fluctuated between a dollar and a half for funerals and three dollars for all-night dances, including food and drink—with the accent on the drink.

The most I ever earned in those days was playing for an all-night carousal in one of the aristocratic bawdy houses on Longworth Street. Some big butter-and-egg men had arranged the affair in honor of their visiting customers. Everything was free. Everybody got gloriously soused including the ladies, their gentlemen callers, the 'cello, guitar, violin, and flute.

When I came to next morning, my fellow artists had already departed. The young lady in bed with me was still sleeping the sleep of the just, and well she might, for I realized only on awakening that I had not slept alone. Even then I grasped it only dimly, thanks to the pain in my head. Madam, however, was already up and doing, like the efficient business woman she was.

Spotting my forlorn self, she ordered me to take a hot bath and then come into the kitchen for breakfast. Hot bath taken, I went into the kitchen, where Madam served me a most excellent breakfast. Then, raising her skirt, she extracted a five-dollar bill from her private bank. It was more than I had hoped for, considering

sundries and incidentals. So I thanked her profusely, expressing
the sincere hope that whenever she was in need of a competent
flutist she would remember me.

"No," she replied, almost angrily, "I don't want to see you
again in this place. You're too young for this sort of thing." Then
extracting another fiver from her private bank she lightly kissed
my cheek, saying, "Now take this and get the hell out of here."
Queer critter, that Madam. Gives me ten dollars, a kiss, and tells
me to get the hell out of her place. . . .

Occasionally there were better paid and more respectable jobs.
For a while I played clarinet in Brand's Symphony Orchestra at
the Sunday Pops. Still later I played second cornet in a Hessian
military band holding forth in Hartman's Concert Hall over the
Rhine. The weekly wage at Hartman's was sixteen dollars plus
eight beer checks a day. I also played some months in Kohl and
Middleton's Dime Museum at the same pay, minus beer checks.

On the whole it was a hit-and-miss sort of life. Music was
neither a trade nor a profession. Outside of New York and
Chicago there were no permanent symphony orchestras; up-and-
coming males looked upon music as effeminate, something for
girls to catch and hold beaux with; large permanent bands, such
as Gilmore's, Sousa's, and Pryor's, were still to come, although
with one exception, strangely enough. Every state penitentiary
boasted a whopping big band. Either musicians were easily caught
in the meshes of the law, or when caught served longer terms
than ordinary lawbreakers, for those penitentiary bands were invariably the best in the state.

But with the growth of the musicians' union, penitentiary bands
declined in quantity, quality, and stability. I have no history, if
there be one, of the American Federation of Musicians at hand,
but if I recollect rightly, this is how it came into existence. Some
of us younger, and consequently more radical, musicians resented
the treatment extended by our saloon-keeper band and orchestra
masters. While there was no particular objection against beer,

free lunches and loafing places, even a musician wants to handle a few dimes now and then. As a result of this laudable ambition, some two dozen of us launched a short-lived co-operative saloon. One of the city's breweries supplied fixtures and credit for beer. Hopeful butchers, bakers and grocers gave credit for free lunch. The big idea behind the collectivist saloon was that since musicians and saloons are inseparable, the band and orchestra leader desirous of our services should come to our saloon. Moreover, we bought our beer at wholesale while they sold us theirs at retail and kept their own books to boot.

Our saloon-musicians' headquarters was a few doors north of Henck's Opera House on Vine Street, the heart of the Cincinnati amusement center. The society we had organized bore the significant name of *Aschenbroetel Verein*, or Cinderella Society, out of which grew Local Number One of the American Federation of Musicians. If my memory does not fail me, John Weber, for almost a half a century president of the Federation, was a member of our Cinderella Society. His father, a band leader, also operated a saloon on Elm Street opposite the Music Hall. But the youngster stuck with us and, if still living, still sticks, God bless him.

And so, whenever in the long years after I met a clean, nattily dressed young fellow with an instrument case in hand, wending his way to work, I would say to myself, "Young chap, you do not know the old fellow you passed. But the good clothes on your back and that self-respecting mien of yours might never have come your way had it not been for the collectivist beer I absorbed long ago in the moist atmosphere of the Cinderella Society."

6

WHILE I was playing at Hartman's Concert Hall, clothed in a Hessian uniform—stripes, brass buttons and all—a musical variety company played its acts at the same stand. Its name was "The Street Pavers of Paris," its director a small, heavy-set, and pock-marked Italian by the name of Pavanelli. Most of the troupe members were Italian and French, while the manager was a Russian count, Von Felixi. Felixi was a linguist. He had to be.

Besides the French and Italians of the Pavanelli group there was a cornetist and pianist, Guillemino Renner, alias Willy Newman, from New York, who spoke only East Side English, and finally, a brilliant young German, whose English was somewhat below par. Oscarre Americolini, as his name appeared on the show bill, eventually had accepted the lucrative offer of sixteen dollars a week plus fame, as tendered by Count von Felixi. A wayward member of the group surnamed Quinto had entered one of the numerous Venusbergs on Longworth Street, from which neither threat of hell-fire nor promise of salary raise could pry him loose. It was necessary to replace him. Thus Hessian military bandsman Oscar Ameringer became Oscarre Americolini of the Street Pavers of Paris, directed by Signor Pavanelli of Naples, Italy.

Dressed as I imagine no street pavers of Paris were ever dressed, our troupe entered the stage, lugging the implements

52

of our calling. Among the implements were natural and synthetic paving blocks. A certain number of these were laid on sand bags. The synthetic ones, each hiding bellows and organ pipes, were carefully scattered among the natural ones. Each artist Street Paver was armed with three finely tuned hammers. My hammers hammered E, F, and F sharp. The rest of the troupe hammered the rest of the scale as far as it went. Since there were no pedals on our hammers for sustaining tones, we played music which leaned in the direction of staccato, such as "Yankee Doodle," a selection from Offenbach's *Orpheus in the Under World*, and the "Anvil Chorus" from *Il Trovatore*.

The paving stones safely hammered in place, we vanished and reappeared with the sort of hand-power pile driver with which street pavers are supposed to tamp down paving stones. These tampers were of papier-mâché and concealed brass instruments; mine hid E-flat bass. Gently pounding the pile drivers on the synthetic paving stones hiding a bellows and organ pipes, we played "Home, Sweet Home" and "Nearer My God to Thee." That done, we lifted the pile drivers to our lips and triumphantly marched off tooting Verdi's "March" from *Aïda*. In the last act we appeared with brooms, shovels, rakes, and wheel barrows to clean up the job. These implements of honest toil hid trumpets on which we trumpeted the "Soldiers' Chorus" from *Fra Diavolo*. Then Curtain.

When our engagement at Hartman's ended we took to the road. Then our troubles began. Our first engagement was in Hatzfeld's Concert Hall on Second Street in Hamilton, Ohio. Hatzfeld was a member of the well-known Von Hatzfeld family of Prussia, and a true nobleman, as we were about to learn. Madam Pavanelli, on her departure from Cincinnati, had forgotten a pair of new shoes in her hotel. One morning her faithful spouse went back to Cincinnati for them, and when Signor Pavanelli returned that evening, Madam Pavanelli was gone. So was our linguist manager, Von Felixi. So was a little leather satchel in which director Pavanelli carried the treasury and contracts of the Street Pavers of Paris. Worse still was the circumstance that Madame Pavanelli, a genuine Parisian, was our solo cornetist and the only one of the Street Pavers who looked good in tights. Finally, with three important notes missing, our hammer chorus was definitely on the blink.

Edmund von Hatzfeld owned a small farm some miles from Hamilton, and to the farm went the Street Pavers of Paris, where we made ourselves useful picking strawberries, killing potato bugs and whitewashing outhouses. Otherwise our position was deplorable. Tights, solo cornet, three notes, money, contracts and interpreter vanished, we were worse than stranded. The language difficulty alone presented an almost insurmountable obstacle. However, music is an international language, and by much rehearsing and rearranging we managed to reconstruct our acts. After some weeks of this, a new manager appeared out of the void. His name was Von Sanne, a giant Hollander who, besides singing a fair tenor, also gave a humorous monologue and spoke enough French, English and German to unite linguistically the Street Pavers of Paris.

The first engagement the new broom swept up for us was a three-night stand in the Red Star Opera House of Miamisburg, Ohio. The financial arrangements provided that receipts were to be divided evenly between the owner of the opera house and the Street Pavers. But, alas, we had fallen on evil days. It was June. On the first night of our stand, the G.A.R. was having a camp fire on the outskirts of town—admission free. The second night, the new Methodist Church was giving a strawberry and ice-cream social, admission ten cents, including strawberries and ice cream. The third and last night, the representative of a fire-engine concern was giving a free demonstration of the value of his machine by setting an old factory building on fire, and that done, saving it.

It was a most successful demonstration. I saw it myself; in fact, all the Street Pavers of Paris saw it, because no one showed up at the ticket window, and we had left the Red Star Opera House in search of solace and free entertainment.

That same night we met in the room of our new manager. The question before the house was: Shall we boldly face the owner of the hotel next morning and confess we can't pay and will he be kind enough to let us depart in peace, or shall we go piecemeal during the night? Opinion differed. I myself argued strongly in favor of going piecemeal, on the ground that no matter which method we adopted the hotel man wouldn't get his money anyhow, and that the piecemeal method might save a lot of unpleasantness.

No decision reached, I privately decided to fold my tent like the Arabs and silently steal away. Unfortunately, I fell asleep while waiting for sufficient silence. This explains why I left only after breakfast in the morning, which was better, after all, because the breakfast of oatmeal, ham, eggs, hot cakes, pie, and two cups of coffee seemed more valuable to me just then than the few things in my satchel. My most valuable possession, my trusted flute, I had left at the Von Hatzfeld farm, many miles away, toward which I turned with light steps and a trusting heart. I made the Von Hatzfeld estate by nightfall with the faint echo of that heavy breakfast still haunting my memory.

A few hours later, the majority of the Street Pavers showed up with only Signor Pavanelli and Monsieur Guillemino Renner from the sidewalks of New York among the missing. From what I could make out, my colleagues had all departed piecemeal, but later had met at the railroad depot of Middletown, halfway between Miamisburg and the Von Hatzfeld haven. Apparently the French and Italian members of the group still had a few coins in the sock, as is the custom of Frenchmen and Italians in general. Weary of walking, they had decided on taking the train. Guillemino from New York, to whom both French and Italian were Greek, had blissfully entered the train unaware that his fellow Street Pavers had left him out of the deal.

On the moving train, and in want of both cash and ticket, he

patiently explained to the conductor that being a member of the
assembled Street Pavers of Paris, it was up to its director, Signor
Pavanelli, to pay the fare. Signor Pavanelli, unable to grasp a
word of the negotiations, but sensing it had something to do with
money, of which he was inordinately fond, refused to shell out.
The three-cornered argument grew hotter. When Guillemino
finally snatched a small handbag which Signor Pavanelli had
managed to smuggle out of the Miamisburg hotel and tendered
it to the conductor in lieu of ticket or cash, a tussle started between
Naples and East Side New York. Whereupon the conductor
pulled the bell rope and with the aid of the brakeman put the
two combatants out in the open. After cooling off in a haystack
under the stars, they pulled up at the Von Hatzfeld estate next
morning, good friends once more.

In the meantime our new manager had departed in the general
direction of Columbus, Ohio. Thence, a few weeks later, came a
letter from Manager von Sanne bearing the happy tidings that
he had secured a six-weeks' engagement at a concert garden.
Pleasant surprise was the news that a definite remuneration was
guaranteed. Even more surprising, the letter contained the tickets
for getting there. And so to Columbus traveled the Street Pavers
of Paris, accompanied by the blessings and full lunch baskets of
Count Edmund von Hatzfeld, indicating that there are even
Prussian Junkers with hearts in their bosoms.

Hessenhauers' Beer and Concert Garden on South High Street,
Columbus, was the first and last place where the Street Pavers
received their stipulated sixteen dollars a week and keep. As for
myself, I did even better. The state fair being on, I played bass
drum in the Columbus band in the afternoon, adding nine dollars
more cash to my sixteen dollars net. Under these circumstances
I might well have saved something for a rainy day. But why
save money for rainy days when all a fellow can do then is
mope around the house? Or, for that matter, save money for

old age when the only pleasure left in old age is remembering the sins of youth, most of which take cash?

From Columbus the Street Pavers of Paris went to Newark, Ohio, where we met our Waterloo. The arrangement had again provided a fifty-fifty division between opera house and artists, which would have been fair enough had there been anything left to divide. During our week's sojourn in Newark we patronized, at reduced show rates, a one-dollar-a-day hotel nestling up against one of the locks of the Ohio-Lake Erie Canal. When the Street Pavers of Paris dispersed piecemeal for the last time, I remained. It was not a good hotel. But when a fellow has no other place to go to at all, why sneak away from it, be it ever so humble?

The hotel keeper, Leon Schmidt, had only recently arrived from Germany and had just bought the hotel. He did not know a word of English and consequently was unable to discover how rotten my English was, so he employed me as night clerk at one dollar a week, keep, and all the three-for-a-nickel stogies I felt like smoking.

Whether it was our inability to answer the questions of our guests, or lack of capital and hotel experience in general, I am at a loss to say. Anyhow, the hotel fared poorly. I never received my promised dollar a week and when stogies ran out, smoking ceased, too. However, there were compensations. My employer sang a magnificent *helden* tenor. His wife was an exquisite pianist. I played flute. And as we were rarely disturbed by guests, a glorious time was had by everybody until hard-hearted creditors closed the door of the hotel and broke up our trio.

From night clerk I advanced to custodian of lunch counters in the saloon of the then well-known German-American poet, Nies. My pay was room, board, all I could drink and smoke plus four dollars a week. I kept that job only a few weeks. Friends and fellow musicians of Schmidt had helped acquire a saloon for him, and a few days later I accepted the position of bartender therein. From the financial standpoint the new position was a demotion. Three dollars a week Schmidt felt was the best he could offer.

Also, he had saved only one bed from his hotel, and as that was occupied by himself, wife, and little daughter, other sleeping arrangements would have to be found for me. When and how he hadn't figured out.

As it happened, the saloon did as poorly as had the hotel. My sleeping quarters were the little side room in which we kept sawdust for the saloon floor. My bedding was *helden* tenor Schmidt's big ulster. Toward the end, even food ran low, to say nothing about my three dollars.

But again there were compensations. The beer went so slowly that we had to drink most of it ourselves. We used to tap a pony keg of beer in the morning and devote the rest of the day to keeping it fresh. It was about all two able-bodied men could do in a day's work, but by nine P.M. we usually had completed the task, whereupon we rolled the empty keg out on the sidewalk, making all the clatter we possibly could, to inform the neighborhood that we were still in business.

One day when Schmidt had gone to Columbus to make some credit arrangements with our brewery, leaving the task of emptying our daily keg to me, I fell asleep behind the bar. I was aroused by loud knocking, to discover a hard-hearing man with a powerful voice, pounding on the bar and demanding if I was a musician? When I confessed to the charge, he asked further if it was true that I played the clarinet and read notes?

By answering yes to both questions, I brought him to state his mission. He was the proprietor of a honky-tonk down by the Baltimore & Ohio tracks. He had an orchestra of piano, violin and cornet, all first-class musicians, but none able to read notes. Now he had a song-and-dance act specialty and would I accept the job of playing the music of the act on the clarinet until his orchestra got the hang of it? I accepted, but with the reservation that I did not possess a clarinet.

"Never mind," he replied, "I know where we can get one. I used to have a clarinet player in my orchestra. He could read notes, too, but he lost two fingers in the cigar factory where he worked in the daytime. We'll go hunt him up."

Closing the saloon, we looked for and found the clarinetist with the lost fingers. He was more than willing to co-operate. He lent me his whole set of clarinetti, A, B flat and C.

The all-by-ear orchestra caught on quickly. Between acts we waited on the tables. The daily stipend was a dollar and a half, augmented by free beer and the loose change dropped by inebriated patrons. After supporting my fellow trio members I had nine dollars in cash left by the end of the second week. This I split with the family Schmidt, and then deprived it of its good provider by taking a south-bound freight.

7

I COULD have made the hundred-and-fifty-mile journey from Newark, Ohio, to Cincinnati in a few days by hike and freight. But why hurry? There is nothing at the end of the road save the grave and the faster one goes the sooner he gets there. Besides, I had a lady friend in Columbus and four-fifty in my pocket. When I left the lady two days later, the four-fifty was gone but the memory of the two days I still have. On the night of my departure, I met that incredible thing, a sympathetic railroad policeman.

I was waiting in the switchyard for a handy freight train when I heard a voice in the darkness: "Say, bo, what are you trying to do, break in a car and steal something?"

"Both," I replied. "Break in a car and steal a ride." My English was improving.

The man was Irish—I remember he told me his name: it was Kelly—and consequently possessed a sense of humor. One word led to another until I had related almost the whole of my American odyssey, including my late experience with the Street Pavers of Paris. Perhaps my broken English lent charm to the tale. Anyhow, he told me of a crossing further down the track where freight trains stopped and were therefore easy to catch, and on parting, believe it or not, that railroad bull pressed half a dollar into my outstretched hand. Blessed, heaven-sent humor, how often have you greased the palm of life for me!

Now fifty cents is not exactly a fortune to live on. But youth, a winning smile, and a pair of merry brown eyes are more valuable than idle riches, as I learned on that lazy, leisurely journey. I had always been careful not to let my clothes run down, as there is nothing that covers so many sins as a clean collar and a fresh shine, and I walked up one day to the open kitchen door of a farmhouse and asked the lady there for the loan of shoe blacking and brush. The lady of the house complied. And as I was busily brushing my shoes, she began to ply me with questions, as lonely farm wives will.

Where was I bound?

I was bound for Cincinnati.

Where did I come from?

I came from Newark, Ohio.

Why was I walking instead of riding on the train?

I had no money.

Where did my parents live?

In Germany.

Was I all alone in this country?

I was.

Had I eaten anything this morning?

I was about to answer yes, but I caught myself and, not wishing to lie, merely shook my head.

Would you mind if I cook you a little to eat?

I didn't mind.

The "little" the lady cooked for me consisted of ham, eggs and potatoes, supplemented by preserves, two cups of coffee, three glasses of milk and two wedges of pie. Why beg in my America? After that, whenever my stomach announced meal time, I muddied my shoes preliminary to borrowing boot blacking and brush at a farmhouse. And it worked every time.

I even earned twenty cents in cash one day, and would have earned more had the cheerful donors possessed it. A flint-hearted brakeman had chased me off a gravel train, and as I walked the ties a horse and buggy with two lady passengers drove up. A passenger train was tooting down the track. There was plenty of time for crossing, but the ladies became excited and nervously pulled on the lines, frightening the horse into backing buggy, the ladies, and itself toward a deep ditch on the side of the road. Foreseeing danger, I ran, grabbed the bridle of the horse and saved the situation for all concerned. When the train had passed, the ladies started the customary questions: "Where did I come from, where was I going, why did I walk, where were my parents?" Result—the two ladies ransacked their purses, which unfortunately contained only two dimes.

Railroad bull, fifty cents. Ladies, twenty; and not a single meal missed. Why beg or steal in my America?

The last day of this anything but Weary Willie's *Rheinfahrt* was the most glorious of all. It started when about sunrise I piled out of my couch of gas pipes in a box car and beheld the most beautiful autumn morning of my young life. Oaks, maples, birches and pines were staging a riot of brown, green, purple, violet, crimson and gold. Birds soared singing in the azure sky, squirrels were busy harvesting among the rustling autumn leaves on the ground. Through the brilliant foliage I saw the silvery surface of a sleepy stream. Stripping quickly I dived into the molten, cooling silver; then, cleansed in body and soul, I got out my flute and, naked as a young Pan, played an ode to Indian summer until the very birds fell to listening and the squirrels sat admiringly on their haunches, waving bushy tails in applause. Concert over, and breakfast announced, I filled up by brush-and-shoe-blacking method at a near-by farmhouse. Then I returned to my furry and feathery audience, with whom I tarried until the sun stood high in the sky and the birds had ceased their trilling and trumpeting. Reluctantly I turned my face toward distant Cincinnati.

Somewhat past dinner time, according to my stomach, I spotted a large white house on the edge of a small hamlet that looked as if it might have brushes and shoe blacking to burn. I entered the well-kept rear yard and stepped on the clean back porch, when a girl of about my own age rushed through the kitchen door, threw her arms around me and covered me with kisses; then, holding me at arm's length, she uttered a wild scream and flew back into the house.

Here was something altogether unexpected, and yet so enticing as to call for investigation. There was no one in the kitchen. Through another door I saw a long table, indicating that the place might be a country hotel or boarding house. Entering the room with the long table, I observed the remains of the recently removed noonday meal. My appetite demanding action, I sat down at the long table and helped myself to milk, bread and butter. If anyone surprised me, I had the brush-and-blacking tale ready; if that did not work, there were seventy cents in my pocket, and twenty-five of them would buy a square meal in those days.

Presently an old lady entered, stopped suddenly, dropped her hands limply to her sides and gave me a bewildered look. I greeted the old lady with my most friendly smile and cheeriest good-day. There was no reply. I disarmingly vouchsafed it was a beautiful day. Still no answer. The brush-and-blacking tale was apparently out of question. I was stumped. Finally the old lady turned around and left the room, shaking her head in a manner that might say anything from "Why, the gall of the brat!" to "Did you ever see anything like that?"

A few seconds later she returned with an old man who walked with a crutch and wore spectacles pushed up on his forehead. He lowered his glasses to the ridge of his bony nose and peered; raised them again to his forehead; repeated the process; scrutinized me with head cocked first on one side, then on the other, sized me up and sized me down, intermittently shaking and nodding his head. Now the girl who had so affectionately bidden me welcome only a few minutes before peeped between the old couple, apron corner to lips, all giggle and titter.

There was something decidedly queer about the trio. I had

read something about private insane asylums. Perhaps I had hit
on one. Finally the old man and the girl departed, the one head-
shaking, the other giggling. The old lady walked up to me and
with the same puzzled, strange look in her eyes asked, "What
might be your name, boy?"

I gave her my name.

Are you sure that's your name?

I was.

Where were you born?

I told her.

Where do your folks live?

I told her.

Are you all alone in this country?

I was.

Sure, boy, you ain't stuffing me?

I was not stuffing her. And then the old lady, with a deep
sigh, said, "If that isn't the beat'nest thing a body ever saw.
You're the spitting image of that grandson of mine. Two years
ago the little scamp run off with a pony-and-dog show and we
haven't seen hair nor hide of him since. The girl out there is his
twin sister. Their parents died when they were only knee high
and so we raised them. But, boy, you're sure you ain't lying?"

Eventually I set the old lady's mind at rest about lying, and
then she enquired, "Have you had your dinner?"

I had not.

Are you hungry?

Not so very hungry. I had eaten some of that good home-
baked bread, fresh butter, and drunk the remnants of the sweet
milk on the long table.

But wouldn't you rather I'd cook you a warm meal?

I agreed that a warm meal would be most welcome.

Pots, pans and dishes clattered in the kitchen, and in course
of time the nice warm meal was set before me—enough of a meal
to gladden the hearts of a bunkhouseful of famished lumberjacks. And while I was eating, the old man and old lady sat by

and questioned me, and related incidents in the life of their wayward grandson.

There still seemed to be a lingering doubt in their minds which the old man finally dismissed, saying, "No, mother, it ain't our Willy. Tricky as the young rascal is, he couldn't imitate that German brogue."

Filled to the bursting point, I suggested it was time to go, as I hoped to make Cincinnati that night.

But why not stay overnight, and after a good sleep start bright and early in the morning?

I wanted to go. Something inside me was driving me out of that house. I wanted to be alone. I could laugh at hard luck. This was something different. I felt weak through and through. They —and that girl—must not see me crying.

"Well, if you must go, let me fix up a little lunch for the way." The old lady smiled at me and returned to the kitchen.

The little lunch turned out to be two whole pies and some cake, a number of sandwiches, radishes, salt and pepper wrapped in paper, a little tin box of butter, a white-and-red-checkered napkin, all lovingly stowed away in a large paper bag. This was too much. I must show them I was not an impostor or panhandler. I reached in my pocket and tendered Willy's grandmother my entire fortune of seventy cents.

"No, no, boy. You'll need that little change. We're not going to take it. Someone somewhere was good to our Willy or he would have come back by now, and that's all the pay we want."

I was finished. I slumped over my folded arms and cried my heart out. Willy's grandmother had become my own mother.

After I had quietly said good-bye to the old couple in the room with the long table, I walked through a hall to the front porch, where the girl was waiting and all was sunshine again. I explained to the poor young thing in all the English I could muster how sorry I was she had made the fatal mistake of kissing a total stranger, and how in after years, happily married and with children of her own, she would shudderingly remember that awful slip of her girlhood. Then I returned her kiss to make it all equal.

The girl slapped me. But as it was the kind of slap that makes you feel good, I didn't mind.

Some few minutes later, when from a bend of the road I took a last look at the big white house, old lady, old man and granddaughter were waving aprons and crutch in farewell.

That same evening I hit Loveland, Ohio. One of the first things that greeted me was a sign bearing the portrait of a foaming schooner. I had walked quite a stretch after leaving the big white house. It was still very warm. Cincinnati was only some twenty miles away, and the seventy cents had begun to feel heavy in my pocket. By the second glass, the bartender started the accustomed string of questions. Where was I bound for? Where did I come from? How was I traveling? and so on. The story of the Street Pavers of Paris seemed to amuse him especially. He laughed often, heartily and loudly. Other guests became interested. New guests appeared when old guests departed.

The story of the Street Pavers of Paris gained by repetition. As often as my schooner was empty, mysterious hands refilled it. Toward nightfall a kind-hearted, gently inebriated brakeman offered to take me to Cincinnati on "the cushions." And an hour later, full of good cheer, beer, a paper bag full of eats and seventy cents still in my jeans, I closed the episode of the Street Pavers of Paris where it had begun.

A kindly, friendly, hospitable America—my America, of the last two decades of the nineteenth century—full of opportunity for a boy capable of telling a good story and bright enough not to stoop to manual labor.

8

THE most important and fruitful discovery I made in the winter of 1887-88 was the public library of Cincinnati, Ohio. I stumbled on the place by sheer accident. One day while I was studying the want-ad page displayed in the window of the Cincinnati *Enquirer* I noticed a number of people entering the building next door. Finding nothing exciting among the want ads, partly because I had made no real effort to read English fluently, and partly because the little I could make out seemed to offer nothing but hard work at low pay, I followed the crowd.

The place looked good. It was warm and comfortable. In one of the large rooms of the ground floor people were reading newspapers and other periodicals, some of them in German, and all this was free. So I made myself at home. However, I had never been much of a newspaper reader. Besides, people were always going in and out of that room, creating drafts and confusion. What I was really looking for was a quiet, comfortable loafing place in which a fellow could enjoy a little snooze now and then. And I discovered that the Cincinnati Public Library harbored the very place I hankered for. It was the history room up on the third floor, and there I settled down.

The few others who patronized it occasionally were bespectacled young men who tended strictly to their own business, never spoke, and usually walked on tiptoe. There was the regular librarian,

an elderly maiden lady who was always too busy crocheting to
disturb the tranquility of the room. My particular method of
reading history was to extract a large volume from the book-
shelves, lay it on the table, spread my elbow-cradled face between hands and if there were illustrations, look at the illustrations. If there were no illustrations, I would snooze over the
English text.

Why should anyone want to read history? I knew all the
history I wanted to know. History was bunk. On a certain day in
the year 318 B.C. some great warrior marched up the hill and
down again. On a certain day in the year 318 A.D. a certain king
had done something unpleasant to the army of another certain
king, and so for centuries innumerable. So why actually read
history?

One day when I passed too close to the elderly maiden lady,
she looked up from her crocheting and asked me innocently,
"Young man, are you fond of history?"

Indeed I was. I would rather read history than eat. History
had been my passion since I was knee high. And all this because
I scented danger to my pet loafing place.

"Well, then," continued the crocheting maiden lady, "if you
are so fond of history, would you mind if I selected a course of
reading for you? I have noticed your reading is rather indiscrimi-
nate. You rarely select the same book a second time."

I was caught. From now on, it was either read history or
keep out.

The first book she handed me was a life of Tom Jefferson. It
was written by a '48 revolutionist who, like so many of my compatriots and his contemporaries, had escaped to America, fought
with Schurz, Siegel and Hecker through the Civil War, become
a member of Congress, returned to Germany after unification,
and later had been a member of the German Reichstag. The name
of the author was Kapp. Reading just the other day Oswald
Garrison Villard's *Fighting Years*, I learned that this Kapp was
the father of the Kapp who led the miscarried Kapp putsch

against the social-democratic regime of harness-maker President Ebert. Another example of how far some sons of revolutionists, also daughters, will stray from the path of their revolutionary ancestors!

I should add that this life of Tom Jefferson was printed in German, thereby closing my last avenue of escape from reading it. I didn't snooze over that book. On the contrary, it kept me so wide awake that when "lights out" sounded that night I was still reading, and next morning was first on deck in the history room. This Tom Jefferson was a man after my own heart! His whole crowd belonged to my league. These fellows had no more respect for high priests, princes, kings, and hand-me-down authority than I had. They were rebels from the word go. They had chased the soldiers God had anointed. Told the whole bloody outfit where to get off, or know the reason why. Had dissolved the unholy partnership between church and state. Declared that one man was as good as the next one and maybe a darned sight better. Had reveled in force and violence, going as far as I had in throwing bricks at scabs, or loyalists as they called them, when not riding the Tory strikebreakers tarred and feathered out of town on a fencerail.

The life of Jefferson swallowed in two bolts, the good teacher handed me the *Life of George Washington* by Washington Irving—still in German. That book was not quite as exciting as Tom's life, but interesting enough to keep me wide awake between eight A.M. when the library opened, and nine P.M., when it closed.

Others followed. A life of Benjamin Franklin, still one of my heroes. Stories of Ethan Allen, Nathan Hale, Mad Anthony Wayne, Lighthorse Harry Lee, and dozens more. Before the bluebirds came again I was so thoroughly imbued with the glorious traditions of America's revolutionary period that I haven't got over it yet; so thoroughly imbued that I was an old-fashioned Jeffersonian-Jacksonian American long before I acquired my naturalization papers. I knew all about Washington, Jefferson,

John and Samuel Adams, Alexander Hamilton, Tom Paine, Ben Franklin, Concord, Lexington, Bunker Hill, Valley Forge and Yorktown. I could recite the name of every President from Washington to Cleveland, including the forgotten ones. And most glorious of all, I could read English!

What a marvelous teacher that spinster lady was! "You are young enough to learn to read English," she told me one day. "Unfortunately, there are no schools for your kind and you haven't got the money for private lessons, but if I give you an English book I think you can almost read, will you try?"

I would. The book was *The Vicar of Wakefield*, by Goldsmith. There were many words in it I could not make out; sometimes whole sentences and paragraphs were too obscure for me. But when I got to the end I knew fairly well what the story was about. I had even—and oh, what joy—caught a fine joke in the book. It was the one when the vicar told how he rid himself of unwelcome friends and relatives by simply lending them a sheep, a little money, or a pair of boots, whereupon they usually remained absent for a long while.

After *The Vicar of Wakefield*, I was handed a book of poems by Robert Burns. How could that wonderful teacher know that I loved poetry and that Scots are more closely related spiritually to Germans than the English?

The next book that captured me completely was a collection of American humor compiled by Mark Twain. There were selections from Artemus Ward, Josh Billings, Bill Nye, Hans Breitmann and Mark Twain's own immortal "Jumping Frog of Calaveras County." How fresh, keen and all-around "don't give a damn for nobody" was that American humor! And always how much more spontaneous and bubbling than the beer-soaked, smoke-laden, mother-in-law belabored humor of Germany! And so, without homework, prescribed lessons, punishment, rewards or examinations, this best of all teachers led me from book to book, until, almost unaware, I had acquired the language, history, and some of the literature of my new homeland—my own, now, for life.

9

THE winter of 1887 was a little harder on poor people than usual. However, I was only financially poor. My health was excellent; I slept like a rock and my appetite was disturbingly keen. I had solved the problem of sleeping quarters by accidentally discovering an unoccupied flat on the top floor of a three-story building. The floor was heated from below. Better still, a chimney passing through a large closet made the closet comfortably warm. Also there was an old broom and mop in that closet. By placing the mop under my head in lieu of a pillow and using the broom as a shock-absorber between my shoulder blades and floor, I usually managed to sleep quite nicely.

In the daytime I patronized the public library. The problem of eating was solved by the greatest and most beneficent of all American institutions—the free-lunch counter. By investing five cents in a schooner of beer and holding on to the evidence of purchase, one could eat one's fill of such delicacies as rye bread, cheese, hams, sausage, pickled and smoked herring, sardines, onions, radishes, and pumpernickel. It is true I did not always have the required nickel. But by patronizing only the larger saloons through the rush hours one could always commandeer a partially filled glass some absent-minded cash customer had left unguarded, and by doing so escape the suspicion of being a deadbeat.

Nevertheless, and notwithstanding these favorable factors, I did require a little money now and then for sundries, incidentals, and tobacco. This I secured in the following manner: Coal in that day and place came down the Ohio River in large barges. From there it was loaded on two-wheeled carts and hauled to its destination, where it was dumped unceremoniously on the street. Having trailed the coal to its temporary lodging, I then would inquire of the housewife whether she would like the coal carried into the cellar, or wheeled to the coal shed in the rear, as the case might be. If the answer was in the affirmative, I carried out the commission. The honorarium was usually a dime.

One day, however, I struck a bonanza. I had carried a ton of coal up one flight of stairs to a lawyer's rookery and deposited it in a piano box standing outside the lawyer's office. The remuneration was a quarter, a whole quarter, the fourth part of a dollar! I had not seen that much money in one pile for months and, as unearned fortunes usually do, it made its recipient reckless.

I decided to invest the quarter in a legitimate meal. That is, a meal honestly earned and paid for. A meal, moreover, that could be eaten in peace, assured that no saloon bouncer would catch me in the act of obtaining nourishment under false pretenses.

There was a bakery just around the corner. I entered it, purchased a ten-cent loaf of rye bread, stuck it under my arm and proudly deposited my fortune on the counter. The effect on the baker was alarming. He rolled his eyes toward the ceiling. His mustache bristled, and his jaw dropped. "Boy," he roared, "how can you have the gall to try to pass that quarter on an honest man? Look," he continued indignantly, "the brass is shining out of it. Feel," he exclaimed in rising anger, "it feels like soap. Listen," throwing the quarter on the counter, "it sounds like lead, and you have the nerve to try to pass that quarter on me."

"But," I stammered crestfallen, "it's a quarter, isn't it?"

"Sure, it's a quarter, a counterfeit quarter, and the worst

counterfeit quarter anyone ever tried to stick me with. And you, an innocent-looking boy trying to hornswoggle an honest baker with a phony coin like that. You'll land in the pen. There's where you'll land. Now, hand me back that loaf, and get the hell out of here!"

I protested my innocence. I didn't know it was a counterfeit quarter. I had earned it carrying a ton of coal up a flight of stairs to a piano box standing outside a lawyer's office. The lawyer, a gentleman of the legal profession, an officer of the court, if you please, had given me that quarter in payment for an arduous task honestly performed. Besides, it was the only money I had. My parents lived three thousands miles away on the other side of the ocean. I was out of work. I had no friends to borrow from and no relatives to live on.

Never before and at no time in later years did I feel quite so crushed, lonely, and forsaken as at that moment, and no doubt I looked it. The baker's face relaxed. His breathing became easier. His color faded from beet red to pink. I had touched the soft spot under his white apron, so that when I picked up that quarter and handed him the loaf of bread he said, almost kindly, "Never mind, boy, take it with you. Mebbe you are hungry, so get out and guten appetite. Mebbe some day you can pay me that dime or hand it to another landsman out of luck."

Sure, the baker was a German. All bakers were German in those days, and so were butchers. All of which may explain why presently I found myself in a butcher shop negotiating for a dime's worth of sausage. By that time, I confess, I had a suspicion that the quarter in my hand was not all that it should be. But man does not live on bread alone. Also, hope springs eternal in the human breast. Moreover, the growl in my stomach had become clamorous. Come what may, my heart was set on a complete fill-up of rye bread and wurst. Let him who as a boy never rifled his mother's larder, never stole apples out of a neighbor's orchard, nor lifted tropical fruit from an Italian's stand while the owner was looking the other way, throw the first stone at a hungry sixteen-year-old with two men's appetite.

For some reason the butcher became even more indignant than the baker when I tendered him the quarter for the dime's worth of sausage under my arm. Worse still, in rendering his opinion of a boy that tried to pass as punk a counterfeit as that one on an honest butcher, he waved an ugly butcher knife two inches before my nose. Didn't I have eyes to see the brass where the silver skin had rubbed off? Couldn't I feel that the quarter was as greasy as soap? Didn't I hear the dull thud of lead when it was dropped on the counter, and me a greenhorn too, and hardly long enough in the country to acquire tricks like that? And where did I expect to land if I continued on the road of crime?

Again I explained the great stretch of geography that separated me from home and mother; the dearth of friends and relatives; the weary months without regular work and meals; the two tons of coal I had lugged up a flight of stairs and deposited in a piano box; the officer of the court who had bestowed that quarter on me in return.

With explanation came mollification. The butcher stuck his knife in the cutting block beside him, and when I offered the package of sausage as a peace offering, he declined in almost the identical words of the good baker and I departed with blessing, sausage, and counterfeit quarter.

As I was standing in front of that butcher shop, a great light dawned on me. I had read of the land of boundless opportunity and sure enough, here it was. That very morning I had risen from my couch of broom and mop, a poor homeless boy. And now, not yet noon, my fortune had mounted to forty-five cents, inventoried as:

One loaf of bread	10¢
One string of sausage	10¢
Cash	25¢

And finally, a perfectly true story worth untold sums.

So long as that counterfeit quarter held out, my fortune was assured. As far as the story went, like all good stories, it improved with age and repetition. The one flight of stairs gradually grew into two and finally into three. The one ton of coal gained two more in the telling. Touching up the high lights and deepening the shadows and adding an artistic flourish here and there eventually increased the human interest and drawing power to the point where I could purchase almost anything within reason, that is, anything from a quarter down.

It would be an overstatement to say that I lived on the fat of the land during the weeks I possessed that blessed counterfeit quarter. I still retained my lodging in the closet of that otherwise untenanted apartment. I patronized the free-lunch counters less. I might have tendered my precious quarter for a glass of beer and thereby have established a legitimate claim for free lunch, but the risk was too great. Barkeepers in those days had a habit of absent-mindedly sweeping coins off the counter into the spill tank below. Worse, and moreover, barkeepers were not always as sober as they might have been. What if some half-shot barkeeper accepted that quarter at its face value and handed me two legitimate dimes in change? No, the risk was too great. I would not trust my fortune in the hand of an inebriate.

My visits to the public library also became fewer and shorter. I had discovered how to travel and keep warm in street cars. Those street cars were either cable or horse drawn. The platform where the motorman or driver stood was unenclosed. Glass would have obstructed the vision of those functionaries. Sheets of rain and driving snow apparently had no such evil effect, neither did the frost that encircled their eyes.

The inside of the car, carrying the pay load, was enclosed, however, and for further comfort contained a coal stove. By sitting close to the stove, one could dream, or see the world go by. When the conductor came around for the fare, I proffered my quarter. Fortunately that quarter was so impossible that the mere touch of it sent a warning signal to the brain center of the con-

ductor, and there followed the recitation of my oft-told tale. If
the conductor was the right kind of man he returned the quarter
and walked off with shrugging shoulders. If he happened to be
the wrong kind of man, he pulled the bell rope and I stepped off
the car and took the next one. To the credit of those old-time conductors be it said that the overwhelming majority of them carried a generous load of the milk of human kindness, for many of
them took me to the end of their line and forgot to see me on the
return trip.

At last came the tragedy, the end of my dream of a life of peace
and comfort financed only by one bad quarter. One fatal evening
at the rush hour in an overcrowded car, I handed my precious
quarter to a flustered conductor, who transferred it to a new-fangled and thrice-cursed contraption dangling over his front elevation, from which he abstracted two perfectly good dimes in
change. Two hours later, I was a pauper again.

10

SOME time in the spring of 1888, while walking on Elm Street, near Sixth, I observed a boy of about my own age slowly revolve on his heels and then keel over. His body was in violent convulsion, his mouth foaming, his head battering the sidewalk. I rushed up, placed one arm under his head and, with the hand of the other, held down his jerking limbs. Up to then I had never seen a person racked by an epileptic fit. When the boy had recovered and the usual crowd dispersed, I offered to take him to his home. It was only five blocks away and there I met Lucy, his mother.

Lucy was a woman around forty—and to me the most gentle, charming and cultured woman I had met outside of my own mother. She was the daughter of a high official of the Prussian Railroad. She had studied singing and painting in Düsseldorf, then Germany's second art center, surpassed by Munich alone. She had married another official of the Prussian Railroad who, caught at peculation, had escaped to the United States. Lucy had followed but, soon separated from her spouse, she was now supporting her four children by teaching drawing and painting.

Lucy, grateful for the little service I had rendered her unfortunate boy, invited me to return. I did, of course, and thereafter often. Before many visits had elapsed, I was installed in her house, living more happily than ever before. The unconventionality of the situation bothered neither of us. Lucy was good, and

good, all good, was her influence on me. She introduced me to
Heine. She also introduced me to the stage where I first met
Shakespeare in *The Taming of the Shrew* and subsequently in
*Romeo and Juliet, King Lear, Midsummer Night's Dream, The
Merchant of Venice,* all in German translation. Later on, my
English improving, I attended these and other Shakespearean
plays given in the original. I saw Booth and Barrett, then at the
summit of their art, in *Julius Caesar* and other plays. Odd as it
may seem, I still prefer my Shakespeare in German. The reason
for this, and also, perhaps, for the popularity of "Unser Shakespeare" in the Germany of yore, is that he was translated by
dramatists as great or nearly as great as himself—such as Goethe,
Schiller and Wieland. Moreover, shorn of Elizabethan English
and expressed in the folksy language of Germany's greatest poets,
he is much easier to understand.

Through Lucy I met Frau Gehring, one of the few living
members of the Weimar Players, who were organized by Goethe
and rescued the Bard of Avon from virtual oblivion, for by that
time he was rarely played even in England. Frau Gehring, then
close to ninety, would painfully climb the three flights of stairs to
my studio, drop down on a chair, and for hours recite from the
glorious rôles of her prime. She used to tell me I was her last
audience. Her children didn't give a tinker's damn for drama, her
grandchildren no longer spoke German, and unless an old woman
could wag her tongue, it would most certainly kill her. Therefore
I was the hero that saved her life.

But what about that studio?

Well, as I have explained, Lucy taught drawing and painting.
One day, while she was drawing a flower set on a piece of white
silk, I offered to take the job off her tired hands. Lucy consented
and, when the drawing was done, exclaimed, "Why, you have a
remarkable talent." I had known all along that I had a remarkable talent for drawing, but Lucy was the first to tell me so, and
better still, she strongly advised me to perfect myself.

Things in general were easing up for me. My board and room

at Lucy's was only three and a half dollars a week. The Centennial Exposition was on. Musical engagements were more plentiful and better paid, thanks to the efforts of the Cinderella Society. Also, in a strange and sudden outburst of business enterprise, I had leased for four dollars a week a space near the Exposition with the honorable intention of conducting a cold-drink stand for the benefit of fair visitors. Then someone still more ambitious offered me eight dollars a week for my lease. I surrendered the document, netting an unearned increment of four dollars a week, which I invested in drawing lessons. Later I took painting lessons from an artist specializing in the painting of landscapes and still life on screens for saloon windows. The screens served the dual purpose of keeping flies out and concealing the customers. From screen painter I advanced to pupil of a fairly capable portrait painter by the name of Weber, brother of the Cinderella Weber mentioned in an earlier chapter. Lastly, I took a short course at the Eden Art School.

In the meantime I was making a fairly comfortable living painting landscapes and flower pieces in wooden bread bowls at one dollar a bowl. Some of these I painted on commission from the aspiring wives of middle-class Germans. Others I peddled around in modest art and picture stores in the manner of Adolf Hitler, not yet born, *Gott sei dank*. I painted butterflies on ladies' white slippers and forget-me-nots on the fronts of ladies' wrappers in the style popular at the time. I drew enlarged photographs in crayon and, toward the end, painted portraits from life in oil, aquarelle, pastels, or whatever the customer wanted.

I have a strong suspicion that my contributions to Cincinnati's art life were somewhat trashy. But the stuff sold. I was able to raise the price. My reputation spread. So that one day I received a request to draw the demised daughter of a prosperous doctor and druggist in Washington Court House, Ohio. How my reputation had spread as far as the birthplace of Harry Daugherty, Attorney-General of Ohio gang fame, I have forgotten. Anyhow, with an affectionate au revoir to Lucy and her family, to Washington Court House I went and reconstructed the daughter from a number of amateur snapshots to the entire satisfaction of doctor, family, friends, relatives and neighbors.

Next, a well-to-do widow, who had seen and admired the reconstructed crayon drawing of the doctor's daughter, gave me the commission to paint her brother, a prominent hardware dealer of Circleville, Ohio, in oil. Agreed honorarium, seventy-five dollars for hand painting. I was getting on and up.

In Circleville I registered at the best hotel: rate, American plan, two dollars, no ups, and a bathroom on each floor. Then I set up a studio in a large room with fair north light above Van Hyde's saloon on Main Street. The portrait of the prominent hardware dealer perpetrated to the satisfaction of everyone concerned, I was ready to return to Cincinnati when something else happened.

"Don't run away from this place," cautioned my friend, the saloon keeper Van Hyde, whose good customer I had inevitably become. "You are just getting started. Circleville is the capital of the Pickaway Plains, the richest farming country of the whole United States. South of here, past Chillicothe, through Waverly, and clear down to Portsmouth on the Ohio you'll find the richest farms and farmers in the land. Many of them are Pennsylvania Dutchmen who settled in the Scioto bottoms in the early days. Best farmers ever, and all lousy with money. I got a history of Pickaway County down in my safe. It contains the biographies and steel engravings of all the old settlers. Go and enlarge these steel engravings. They are good ones, and I bet you sell every one of them."

They *were* good steel engravings. Somewhat idealized, perhaps, but I dare say great improvements on the photographs and daguerreotypes they were taken from.

Following the advice of my friend I made half a dozen life-sized crayon drawings of old settlers, hired a horse and buggy from the livery stable around the corner, and sold every one of them before sundown at twenty dollars apiece.

With that good start my reputation spread like wildfire. Soon I painted and drew portraits all over the Pickaway Plains. These people were the second generation of Pennsylvanians who had moved from Lancaster and Bucks Counties to Ohio. The pioneering work was over. Log cabins had given way to substantial frame and brick houses. The stream bottoms, cleared of plum thickets, produced marvelous crops on the almost virgin soil. Farms were operated by owners who lived and worked on them, and they were large farms, frequently comprising three hundred acres and better.

Elsewhere, there was still the open frontier. Surplus children had already moved on to Indiana, Illinois, Iowa, Kansas and Nebraska, avoiding the division of old homesteads. Moreover, these Pickaway farmers were—and for all I know, still are— farmers by the grace of God. To them soil was not dirt under their feet to be ruined, raped, and robbed. They were not dirt farmers, but *Landbauern,* soil builders. Farming was a noble calling, far above, that of merchant, lawyer, politician or money lender. Mortgaged farms and tenants were still rare. These people were a proud, self-respecting lot all around. Many of them wore tailor-made clothes, and regularly affixed a "Mister" when naming one another. At the same time, they were the living personification of democracy. The hired girl was neither maid nor servant, but "the young lady who makes her living with us"; farm hands were "our help."

At the home of Dan Hitler, a confirmed bachelor, and no relative of that other one, I'm sure, some five miles south of Circleville, Lizzie, the housekeeper, Marie, the young lady making her living with them, Hank and Hiram, "our" help, Dan, myself, and the regular week-end guests, used to sit around the fireplace in the big sitting room on winter evenings, our collective socks smoking in front of us, debating every problem under the sun on the basis of one-hundred-per-cent democracy and equality. Dan's eight-room brick house had running water in the kitchen and a bathroom on the second floor. The water was pumped by hand into a tank located in the garret, but it was running water, by grace of gravity, just the same. Every bedroom had its fireplace.

I still remember one cold morning when, coming down in bare feet as usual, I heard Dan say to the housekeeper, "Now, Lizzie, it's all right with me that you had a fire in Oscar's room last night. He's our guest. I want him to be comfortable. But I want you to understand once and for all that whenever it's too cold for Oscar to sleep without a fire, it's too cold for me, too. Get that."

Dan's farmhouse contained a well-read library, in which I became acquainted with Plutarch's *Lives,* Gibbon's *Decline and Fall of the Roman Empire,* Thackeray, Milton and Dickens, and renewed my friendship with d'Aubigné's *History of the Reformation.*

And was I popular! Especially with the young ladies. Can you imagine an easy-to-look-at twenty-year-old painter, musician, making money hand over fist, spending it like a fairy prince, and on top of all that, a rising author, too!

Author? Certainly. I have already mentioned the deep impression Mark Twain's compilation of American humor had made on me. Well, in between painting Pickaway Plain farmers and ancestors, playing flute obligatos for rising prima donnas, holding forth and holding hands at every social function of the best and very best families, I had started writing humorous stuff à la America. My English spelling was still bad, and has not improved much since. But there was always some nice young lady who knew how to hammer the typewriter, who could spell, and knew the places where dots, commas, and exclamation marks belonged.

So it happened in Circleville that one morning, looking through the show windows of Cook's bookstore, I saw a two-page illustrated spread in *Puck* captioned:

THE DUKE AND HIS DOG
A modern fable
by Oscar Ameringer

Oscar Ameringer's Portrait of Dan Hitler

BANDMASTER AT THE AGE OF THIRTY

The tale was a take-off on the sensational wedding of a Cincinnati heiress to the Duke of Manchester, whose claim to fame was the large Newfoundland that accompanied him on all occasions. Shortly thereafter I received a check for six dollars from *Puck*, accompanied by a request for more contributions. Painter, musician, writer, everything the animal trainers of my school days had done their level best to beat out of me! Not yet of age, I was already all three of them—almost.

Thus encouraged, I went on to write modern fables, nonsense rhymes, humorous poems and parodies in the style of Longfellow's "Song of Hiawatha" for *Puck* and *Judge*, then the two outstanding humorous publications, and also for *The Sunny South*, the Sunday supplement of the Atlanta *Constitution*.

Considering the state of my English in those days, coupled with the fact that I was actually paid for my efforts, it is quite possible that had I continued in this field I might well have become a minor American humorist. But something happened.

11

THE United Brethren were holding a revival at their church some five miles south and east of Circleville. I had heard of revivals. They sounded exciting. And so I hired my favorite red-wheeled buggy and an obliging old mare named Jenny, who could be driven with one hand and had a predilection for standing by the hour in dark places without being hitched. Off we started for Bethel Church, and arrived in good time—for Jenny, that is.

Since I was not in the market for salvation, I took a perch on a window seat. After some days of violent and exhausting general soul-saving, the congregation settled down and concentrated on saving the soul of Ike—the black sheep of the prosperous Muller family.

I knew Ike and liked him. One day, as I was busily enlarging father Muller in crayon, someone had entered my studio above Van Hyde's saloon, unobserved by me. The first intimation I had of company was when I heard a voice behind me say, "That's a goddamn good picture of dad. I'll take it." Turning around I beheld a small, barefooted man somewhere in the fifties, with a gray grizzly beard, gray curly hair on his partly bald dome, and grizzly gray eyebrows over a pair of mischievous, honest gray eyes. It was Ike.

"So you think this is a good likeness of your father?" I asked.

"Natural as life," replied Ike. "Here's your twenty. I'll take it home with me."

"Wait a minute," I replied. "In the first place, the portrait isn't quite finished yet. And in the second place, it was ordered by Dan Muller, who, I take it, is your brother."

"So he is," answered Ike. "But right here is one place where no brother of mine is gonna get ahead of me. So here's your twenty. The picture suits me as it is," and grabbing the picture, Ike marched out of the room.

Ike was a character, everybody agreed. What he would have been called had he been a poor man instead of merely the least well-heeled of his well-heeled tribe, I don't know. Ike walked barefoot winter and summer. Regularly every Saturday and occasionally during the week he would get more or less gently soused. A further testimony to the waywardness of Ike: while all his neighbors had posted signs bearing the legend: "No Hunting on This Farm," the sign on Ike's place read, "Hunt as long as you damn please, and when you hear the dinner bell, come up to the house."

Now the brothers and sisters of the United Brethren were ganging up to save Ike's barefoot soul. Everybody else present had already been saved.

The chief exhorter would utter groans and shriek windy prayers informing all present how badly Ike was needed in blessed Beulah Land. When the chief had run down or run out of wind and information, volunteers of both sexes hastened to the rescue with hymns and prayers. Sisters of the United Brethren would surround Ike, kneel in prayer before Ike, threaten brimstone and hell-fire to Ike; promise wings, palm-branch halos and harps to Ike. No use. Ike wouldn't testify. Ike wouldn't hit the sawdust trail. Ike wouldn't grace the mourners' bench.

This went on night after night, until at last Ike arose from his seat and drawled good-naturedly: "Well, neighbors, it looks like this shindy ain't gonna stop until I testify, so testify it is. But I want you to understand, testify is all you're gonna get out of me, and here goes:

"In the first place, I didn't come here to be saved. I came

because my women folks had pestered hell out of me to come.
In the second place, I don't like preachers nohow. Like all of
your dads, mine made me work like the devil as soon as I was
old enough to hold a plow handle and drive a horse. I, like you,
never got nary a cent of wages or dime of spending money. Year
in, year out, it was work, work and work again. At last, when I
was around thirteen, dad loosened up and gave me a colt. Some
of you remember that colt and how I loved it, curried it, combed
its mane and tail, and polished its hoofs like it was the most
precious thing in all the world, and so it was to me.

"Well, when I had the colt saddle-broke, one Saturday evening one of these circuit-riding preachers stopped at the house.
I didn't like circuit riders because ma and pa always made us kids
wait till they was through eating and by the time they was
through there was most always only the wings of the chicken
left.

"Well, this circuit rider stayed overnight and next morning he
asked dad could he have my colt for riding to Hallsville, where
he said some big church doings were going on.

"I didn't want that preacher to take my colt. But dad said
lending it to the preacher was serving the Lord, and you know
we daren't talk back to our dads. So that circuit rider rode away
to serve the Lord at them Hallsville doings and he musta kept
going for nobody ever seen anything more of him and my colt.
And I haven't liked preachers ever since.

"Some years later, the Civil War bust loose. Most everybody
around here was Abolitionists, talking always about how wrong
it was to enslave, beat, and sell God's children like they was
cattle. For myself, I always believed folks should be as good as
their words. So when Old Abe called for volunteers I skipped
out and joined the army, while the rest of you, or your dads,
got themselves substitutes and bounty jumpers in their places.

"Well, the three months for which Old Abe had called
stretched out to three years. War ain't a good place for learning
Sunday-school manners. With the rest of the boys I learned

drinking, gambling and whoring and might have gone clean to the devil if I hadn't caught a rebel bullet in my right heel that sent me home. For more than a year I couldn't wear a boot on my right foot. By the time it was good and healed I just kept on going barefooted.

"Some time in the seventies—I was already married—Prince Jones started a distillery down on the Scioto River. I'm sure you all remember Prince Jones, the richest man in the whole valley. Brother Dan sitting over there used to court Princess Ella Jones. Being such fine-haired folks, Dan used to go to their house in his greased boots with the parlor shoes under his arm. When he got to the Prince Jones gate, he'd put on the parlor shoes and leave the boots on the outside. One night somebody walked off with Dan's boots. He had to hike home in his parlor shoes and it almost killed him, they was that small. Didn't they, Dan?

"Well, everybody around here was hellbent for downing demon rum. Aunt Maria and Annabel over there even went to Circleville trying to pray the saloons out of business. But when Prince Jones started selling stock in his distillery every darn one of you bought it. You was against demon rum, but not against getting rich from his victims. I, too, bought some of that stock. I thought as part owner of a distillery I could get honest-to-goodness whiskey. I didn't have the cash. But Sam Peters of the First National Bank took my note for the five thousand I turned over to Prince Jones. Many of you had given notes for the same purpose. But when Prince Jones's distillery busted higher than a kite, most all of you found out your property belonged to your wives, or your dad hadn't properly signed it over to you, while last week, I, the black sheep of the whole settlement, paid old Sam Peters the last damned dollar I owed on that note.

"I know you've all been talking about me coming home drunk late at night. Well, I guess I was, but I never was so drunk that I couldn't see Frank up there, who does most of the shouting, steal corn from the piles on his own field, cheating the corn huskers whom he was to pay so much per bushel. And talking about Frank reminds me that tough as I am, all the girls that ever worked at our house got away clean, married, raised children by their husbands, while over at Frank's place I never knew of a girl that wasn't knocked up when she left, and if you folks are curious, I'll give you the names of every one of them!"

The folks weren't curious. As Ike's testimony progressed, more and more of the good brethren and sisters discovered they had more important business than saving Ike's soul. By the time he had reached the place where he would, at request, recount the names of the girls who had left Frank's place in delicate circumstances, only Ike and I were left. Even his women folk had deserted Ike. There was nothing else I could do but load the unrepentant into my red-wheeled buggy and get out the bottle of redeye I always carried for snake bites. We celebrated his single-handed victory over the United Brethren on the way home.

At the height of my Circleville fame I took out my naturalization papers. Van Cleave, editor of the *Democrat and Watchman,* with whom I frequently discussed the problems of the horse and buggy age in the thirst parlor beneath my studio, had become a judge. When I appeared before Justice Van Cleave, the judge was loaded for me. He had prepared a line of questions that might well have stumped an aspirant for the Supreme Court. I passed the examination with flying colors. Then, having passed, I asked the examiner to give me the names of the three Presidents who had preceded Buchanan. The examiner was stumped, whereupon examined and examiner adjourned to our pet corner in Van Hyde's saloon for celebrating the addition of one more citizen to the Land of the Free.

Strong, solid people, these Pennsylvania Dutch. Worthwhile people, too, were the Virginians who came from hills back of the Tidewater and settled the Virginia reserve east of the Pickaway Plains, land which was easier to clear than the plum-thicket bottoms of the Scioto river. What men and women the folk of those days were! One of them—grandfather Lutz—told me on

his hundred-and-third birthday how as a young man he had repeatedly made the long journey to New Orleans in "New Orleans
boxes" and returned on foot all the way through the Chickasaw
and Cherokee country. "New Orleans boxes" were barges on
which the early settlers loaded their corn meal, hams and bacon
and floated it all with the spring freshets down the Scioto, Ohio,
and Mississippi rivers, to the then nearest market, New Orleans.
Selling the cargo and barges they hoofed it home, always aiming
to make the fifty-odd-mile home stretch from Portsmouth to
Circleville in one day.

From grandfather Lutz, and from some of his descendants I
met later clear across the continent, I learned how the term
"hitch-hiker" originated. Two men, but with only one horse
between them, took a journey. The first man would mount the
horse and ride ahead. The second followed on foot. When the
first man had ridden his allotted distance, he would dismount
and hitch the horse on some tree or fence rail and proceed by
foot, whereupon the second man would mount the horse until he
caught up with the hiker.

It had been my firm intention to return eventually to Cincinnati and Lucy. However, one day I received a letter from my
mother telling me she was in very bad health and did not expect
to have many more years to live, and would I return to Germany
so she could see me once more? I determined to return to Europe
at once. But that required money. . . .

Some of my customers had paid me in cash, some in checks.
I spent whatever I wanted to spend, deposited the rest, wrote a
check now and then, but never kept track of my bank balance,
if any. In the forlorn hope of finding perhaps a hundred or a
hundred and fifty dollars in the bank, enough to pay my fare
back to Germany, I asked the cashier how my bank account stood.
And I received the staggering information that I had fifteen
hundred dollars in the bank.

"Fine," I said. "Let's have it."

"What do you want to do with it?" the cashier asked.

I said, "I am going to Europe."

"When do you want to go?" he asked me.

"The next train east leaves at three o'clock. I want to be on that train."

So he counted out the money.

Book Three

MUNICH, 1890 STYLE

12

WHEN I arrived home I found mother in first-class health, though nearing seventy. She had only been lonesome for her wayward youngest son, who was nearer to her heart than all her other children. But I was not angry at the ruse she had used to get me home once more. In fact, it was a remarkably pleasant feeling to return in triumph— the family's ugly duckling returning to the roost as a swan.

My deportment was anything but that of the prodigal son who came home after a session of husks and swine. I had over five thousand marks in my pocket; I sported a tailor-made broadcloth suit, brand-new tan overcoat, gold watch and chain and gold-rimmed glasses designed purely for show. I rolled the natives flatter than American pancakes. Here I was, the outcast, who everybody had predicted would end on the gallows, strutting about the burg like a millionaire, the envy of every father and mother—the idol of every girl—the crowning glory of mother.

On the evening of my arrival I met the teacher's pet, the shining example of my schooldays, Joseph Dilges. He was escorting a wagonload of manure hauled by a team of cows. Knock-kneed, splay-footed and already stoop-shouldered, the paragon of learning and virtue had flunked on his physical examinations for the army, where his docility and retentive mind might have been useful. His shabby lot made me doubly glad I had become an American.

Most of my schoolmates were either in the army, had strayed away, were working in some of the new factories, or had become cow chaperons, like Joe Dilges. Some of the girls were married. Many more had become servants in nearby Ulm. Others were helping their parents in fields and kitchen. While I, destined for the gallows rope, had been in America, had acquired a fortune, a strange language, an honorable profession, and no end of culture. And I rubbed the contrast in. I painted my father's and mother's portraits, had them framed in gilt, and exhibited in the window of the two-by-four bookstore where, in the days of my disgrace, I had bought the yellow-backed Indian-blood-thunder-and-gore stories with the money my friend Paul Gerhard swiped from his father's cash drawer. I painted Herr Gerhard and Frau Gerhard themselves, and let it be remembered that he was the richest merchant of that town. I painted the richest peasant for hundreds of miles around and his wife, and I painted them in their peasant costumes—low shoes, the man with his silver buckles, short pants, short jacket, with silver thalers for buttons, and the conventional three-cornered hat. The woman was in her manifold short skirts, velvet stays crisscrossed by silver chains, and the peaked bonnet of the Black Forest peasants. Those two were proud peasants, as proud and self-respecting as the farmers of the Pickaway Plains. Their estate must have comprised all of a quarter section—160 acres—by my American standards. They worked at least six horses, some oxen, and cows. There must have been a dozen hired men and maids on the place. All ate at the same table and shared the same roof. Their farmstead, I noticed, was laid out very much in the manner of that of the Pennsylvania Dutch farmers in the Scioto valley, but there were differences. These peasants were a great family in their way, but they were farming far more primitively than the Ohio families I had known. At the estate of Count von Welde, not far away, McCormick reapers and horse-driven threshing machines were already in operation, but on the estate of my peasant couple all work was still done by hand.

"Why install machines?" he parried when I asked why he

had not established more modern methods. "Our people must live all year 'round. It is better for them to spend their winters threshing than loafing." Perhaps he was right.

That peasant holding and the farms of my friends in the Pickaway Plains are still my idea of farm life, so much superior to some of the corporation farms and tenantry-cursed plantations I was to see later. These people were part and parcel of the soil on which they lived. The huge manure pile in front of their great barns was an earnest that the fertility of that soil would be preserved. Soil to them was not dirt, but something holy. The same thing is expressed in Schiller's "Song of the Bell":

> "To the holy womb of Mother Earth
> The sowman trusts his seed,
> Hoping for its resurrection
> As God decreed."

What a tragedy that so many American farmers have treated soil as the dirt under their feet! What a disaster that they did not look on farming as a great art, and the freest, most soul-satisfying mode of human living! Instead, they conceived it only as a means to make a profit, and so in the end made themselves the slaves of industry, capital, and speculators.

Wherever in my wanderings I found this type of peasant I saw good homes, schools, roads, prosperous towns, and a proud, free, self-respecting people. Perhaps there is a moral in that for us today. Democracy is rooted, somehow, in the soil.

During my two months' stay in Laupheim I even broke into the inner sanctuary of its masculine society, the Herrenzimmer, or smaller side room attached to every tavern where the officials, professionals, and clericals congregate. Not knowing how rich the American really was—and I had been free with money—I was received as an equal. The gentry graciously admitted I had been, if not a bad, at least a rather high-spirited boy—full of the devil, but at the same time, they had always known I would make good. Strange, how much a few American fifty-dollar bills exchanged at the local bank accomplished in altering their verdicts on my character!

But while consorting with the aristocracy of the town on the basis of equality, I let no opportunity pass without expressing my opinion regarding aristocracy, nobility and hand-me-down authority of every type. Finally I was warned by Chaplain Hertzer, the one man who, of all my tormenters, had had some faith in me, that perhaps it would be best for me to seek a freer, more tolerant environment. The rumor had got abroad that I was a democrat, which was true, an anarchist—there was something to that, too, remembering the wood-rasp dagger I had carried in that Cincinnati May Day parade—and finally, a socialist. Well, not yet—

Anyhow, I had shown them. Mother's life work was fulfilled. Even if we parted forever, she had reaped her harvest. I had still over four thousand marks in my possession. I was back in Germany. I wanted to become a painter, and so I departed for the painters' paradise of Germany: Munich.

13

THE name of Munich in these black years is a symbol of the despair and degradation which darken the European earth. But it was not always so. When I first set foot in Munich as a young art student some fifty years ago, it was one of the most charming, civilized and, ironically enough in the light of recent events, democratic cities in all Europe.

Munich's setting is a thing of beauty in itself. To the south tower the Tyrolean Alps with their crowns of purple-white snow. The green, foam-flecked, Alpine-born Isar River stretches two arms through the heart of the city. Along its banks marches the gracious English Garden until it disappears at either end in the stately pine forests of the Bavarian Overland. And to this natural beauty have been added architectural beauties which make the place a sheer delight to the sensitive eye.

These man-made adornments were largely contributed by a line of Bavarian kings who, in the opinion of the native Munichers, were "überschnapped," a term meaning badly cracked in the upper stories. Whatever may be said about these crowned eccentrics, they certainly were magnificent spenders. And more often than not their spending redounded to the greater glory of Munich.

One of them, King Ludwig I, was obsessed to make Munich a second Athens. Under a heady Periclean influence he built the old and new Pinakothek and the Glyptothek and filled them with

the sculpture and painting of both old and new masters. This
first Ludwig was the founder of the Royal Academy of Art.

Besides running to old masters, Ludwig had a compensatory
predilection for young and beautiful ladies. For one of them, the
Spanish dancer Lola Montez, he built one of the most charming
little villas I have ever seen. The location of the villa might have
been improved, perhaps, but as it was only a stone's throw from
the royal palace, it was a step saver.

Lola Montez, with her haunting Irish beauty, was the straw
which finally broke the royal camel's back, or rather exhausted
the patience of the Bavarian taxpayers. It was well enough for
His Majesty to found museums, art galleries and centers of
learning. Such things brought tourists and students to the city,
thereby helping to fill the pockets of the burghers. But building
a charming villa, costing goodness knows how many hundred
thousand marks, for a foreign dancer was too much. Bavaria was
then a constitutional monarchy, whose *landtag* or legislature
possessed the power to depose God-anointed persons for cause.
The cause was usually some royal dementia connected with what
Thorstein Veblen was later to entitle "conspicuous waste," and
Ludwig and Lola were so treated.

Maximilian, who followed Ludwig the First, appears to have
had little of his father's weakness for the fair sex, native or
foreign, but was just as strong for raiding the royal treasury to
beautify Munich. Among his contributions were Maximilian
Street, the Bavarian (now German) Museum, and the Maximil-
laneum, the ornamental structure of undefined architectural
provenance which crowns the end of Maximilian Street.

Maximilian's successor, Ludwig the Second, was also cracked.
He is known to history as "the mad king of Bavaria," although
why he alone is thus distinguished it is hard to explain. However,
he was so magnificently cracked that I have often wished some
of our economic royalists were similarly afflicted. Ludwig II
hated women and loved castles, of which, in the course of his
reign, he put up a surprising number. Many of them he built in

almost inaccessible places, to save them from souvenir hunters, I suppose. But they are still beautiful and in the course of time lured many millions of francs, liras, pounds, gulden, and dollars into the tills of Bavarian hotel and innkeepers.

Ludwig's other and more engaging affliction was Richard Wagner. Poor Richard had never learned to play any musical instrument sufficiently well to make an honest living. And as he could neither sing nor dance, he was naturally driven to composition. But at that time, the kind of music Wagner wrote was anything but popular; in fact, it was more than unpopular. It was downright revolutionary. Among other innovations, Wagner had conceived the weird notion that there should be some relationship between text, music, singer and orchestra. He called his musical bolshevism the music of the future, and so it was, then. And if there is a worse-paying job in this vale of tears than working for the future, history does not record it.

In all probability Wagner would eventually have succumbed to malnutrition had he not had the good fortune to run into crazy King Ludwig II of Bavaria. And so, whenever I hear the "Liebestod" from *Tristan and Isolde*, or "Ode to the Spring Night" in *Die Walküre*, or Wotan's "Farewell" from the same opera, or Siegfried and Brünnehilde's "Love Duet" in *Siegfried*, or Brünnehilde's heart-breaking cry before riding into Siegfried's funeral pyre, I think of the old, mad king, and hope that all is well with him in the hereafter. It is, I am sure, if the heavenly orchestra isn't all harps. It won't be heaven for Ludwig unless the Ultimate Orchestra contains a few hundred French and English horns, clarinets, bassoons, and trombones, plus trumpets and Siegfried horns for variety's sake, and tympani, cymbals, and gongs. Harps are all right, so long as they come in ones or twos, but an all-harp orchestra would be hell on a music lover of Ludwig's heroic stamp. . . .

Anyhow, it was this crazy Ludwig who took up Richard Wagner and supplied him with board, lodging, spending money, and protection—until the economy bloc of the Bavarian Legislature

declared the king insane and deposed him on a charge of extrava-
gance, boondoggling, and fiddle leaning.

Retired to the little Castle Berg on dreaming Starnberger Lake,
Ludwig shortly thereafter committed suicide by drowning. The
attendant assigned to him tried to save him, but lost his own life
when the king paused in the process of drowning himself long
enough to hold the loyal fellow under until he stopped struggling. After which, Ludwig walked out in deep water and finished
his interrupted job.

When Ludwig II was deposed, the legislature appointed his
uncle, Luitpold, as prince regent. The legitimate successor would
have been Ludwig's elder brother Otto, since Ludwig was child-
less, but Otto was hopelessly insane. On the other hand, in a
roundabout way, he was still, by the grace of God, king of Bavaria, hence there had to be a prince regent in his place.

Luitpold was neither skirt chaser, palace builder, art patron, nor
spendthrift. The reasons for his virtue were that he was well in
the sixties when he got the job, and the royal treasury was empty.
He also had solemnly promised the Bavarian legislature that in
the event of his selection he would make penny-pinching Article
One of his program.

Luitpold's only ambition was to go down in Bavarian history as
Luitpold the Good. In the pursuit of this laudable aim he courted
good will, wandering about Munich in civilian garb, buying can-
dies for street urchins and visiting the studios of forgotten artists,
while religiously abstaining from buying their works.

It was Luitpold's courting of popularity in this harmless way
that eventually brought us together. We met almost every morning in the English Garden, where he was taking his constitutional
on horseback, dressed in most unassuming civilian clothes. Of
course I knew who he was, but I had long since become an incor-
rigible antimonarchist, and so would offer his dignity nothing
more than a cold stare. This went on until one morning Prince-
Regent Luitpold bowed before the rising tide of democracy by

doffing his hat to me. After that we regularly exchanged the customary courtesy on the basis of prince first and me second.

What's more, the old gentleman seemed to enjoy this rebellious behavior on the part of a youngster. One day I was accompanying a delegation of home-town celebrities (who had come to Munich to order a bust of a demised burgomaster) on their way to the "Secession" which was the exhibition of young and therefore rebellious painters. We met Luitpold coming out of the show, dressed in Prince Albert and silk hat. When he spied me, he doffed his silk topper, according to our mutually adopted code.

"Bu-but," exclaimed my home-town celebrities, "isn't that Prince Luitpold?"

"Sure," I replied, with all the nonchalance of a twenty-one-year-old.

"Bu-but he knows you?" the celebrities inquired, with bated breath.

"I should say he does. Didn't you notice how he tipped his hat to me—first?"

Largely on the strength of my intimate connection with royalty, the commission to mold the counterfeit of the demised burgomaster of Laupheim went to a young sculptor friend of mine who needed the money badly—and was quite liberal with it when he got it. . . .

As a result of protracted experience with quixotic royalty, the common run of Munichers lost much of their respect for kings. The working masses had largely gone socialist by then, while the student population, hailing from every corner of the earth, naturally looked upon itself as inferior to no one and superior to everyone. The bulk of the burghers were an easy-going, beer-drinking, often- and prodigious-eating lot, who feared no one but God and restricted that to Sunday morning.

As verification of the democratic or, perhaps better, the "don't give a damn for anybody" character of Munichers in those times, I offer the following episodes in evidence:

First, somewhere around 1892, Emperor William the Second
—and last—honored Munich with his presence. With the tactless-
ness customary to the future woodcutter of Doorn, he entered in
the Golden Book of the city, in which the autographs of visiting
celebrities were inscribed, the words, "Whoever opposes me, I
shall crush with my might." Signed—"Wilhelm Rex."

In those days Bavarians still regarded themselves as Prussian
by compulsion only. They had fought Prussia in 1866 and had
only been united with it since 1871. "Big-snooted Prussian" is a
sympathetic translation of the customary term they applied to
their northern brethren, and now the biggest Prussian of the
whole tribe was threatening to crush good Bavarians if they refused to become yes men!

By nightfall of that day, every available wall space in Munich
was covered with the imperial threat. Next morning, when the
imperial train passed through Ludwig's Strasse on the way to the
maneuver ground, not a hat was lifted, not a single "hoch" disturbed the air, although the street was crowded to capacity. But
that afternoon, when Wilhelm Rex and his retinue returned,
every man on horseback was greeted with tumultuous applause
until William appeared. Then icy silence fell upon the dense
mass. Yes, Munich once knew how to deal with rulers who talked
too tough. . . .

Second, that same winter I attended the Artists' Masked Ball,
the outstanding social and artistic event of the season. With Wilhelm Rex in mind, I masqueraded as a sort of hit-or-miss Don
Quixote. My breast armor consisted of three pan lids. My shield
was one of those large square boards on which German house-
wives roll out noodles. On my right upper and lower arm were
two grating irons. I wore a felt slipper plus spur on the left foot,
a Wallenstein boot minus spur on the other. The whole was surmounted by a two-foot tin varnish can with peacock feathers waving from the cork. And in my hand a huge wooden sword, bearing
in blood-stained letters the legend: "Whoever opposes me, I shall
crush with my might." In any other German city of that time I

would have been arrested for lese majesty as a matter of course, but in Munich my take-off of the kaiser only made a choice contribution to the hilarity of the occasion.

Third, returning late at night from another festive occasion, with a group of haphazardly organized artist friends, I had my first contact with Munich police. It was a beautiful winter night, after a fresh snowfall. As we walked into the Königsplatz someone in our group made the observation that the square fronting the Glyptothek looked as inviting as a virgin canvas. Thereupon another conceived the brilliant idea of drawing the portrait of William of Hohenzollern on the snow. The motion was passed and we mounted one of the pedestals flanking the stair of the Gallery, from which a large urn had been removed.

One of us drew the spiked helmet; another the nose and upturned mustache, and so on down. However, by the time we reached the decorations on the breast of His Royal Majesty, our drawing material had run out. Fortunately, at that juncture, a bibulous member of the proletariat appeared on the scene, to whom we explained our predicament.

The man was willing, but declared between hiccoughs that being a machinist, portraiture was out of his line. Someone offered to guide his hand. The good Samaritan accepted. The portrait of His Majesty was almost complete when a policeman stepped around the corner of the Glyptothek. Things began to look more serious; however, after carefully scrutinizing the work of art he pronounced it a good job, considering the material we had to work with, but added the injunction, "Please don't let me catch you at this sort of doings in the daytime."

That may not be the politest of stories, but it illustrates the change between the Munich of my day and Hitler's. No doubt the snow is cleaner, now. . . .

In more concrete manner the spirit of old Munich's democracy was manifest in the management of the city's affairs. I doubt if democracy in any stage of its development has exceeded the performance of the German municipalities in the pre-war years. In Munich in my time the conception of public office as a public trust was so commonly held by officials high and low that any deviation was fatal. On such rare occasions as a municipal officer was caught grafting, it was taken for granted that he would commit suicide. If he did not, a loaded pistol was left in his cell as a hint.

Among the city fathers were the most distinguished men of science, the arts and professions of whom the town boasted. Before my time there was Baron Justus von Liebig, one of the greatest chemists of the nineteenth century. When I was there, one of Liebig's most brilliant students, Max von Pettenkofer, known for his metabolism researches, was serving on the city council. The mighty Diez, teacher of Frank Duveneck, the American painter who was to spread Munich's techniques throughout the studios of his native land, was a member of the council together with Franz von Lenbach, by all odds the top portrait painter of his time in all Germany.

Men like these served and served faithfully for the honor of it. Their only reward besides the consciousness of duty well done was the free lunch served after council meetings. This was a sumptuous affair washed down with vintage wines from the cellar of the council hall, the *Ratskeller*. It was well earned, for the affairs over which the council presided were of magnitude and complexity. Munich owned all its public utilities. Huge areas in and about the city were municipally owned and leased out by the city to tenants, whose rents financed most of the large-scale public improvements. Small wonder that there came to Munich American students of municipal government such as Richard T. Ely, Frederic Howe and Charles Zueblin to take back home stories of honest and efficient management that put to shame the inefficiency and corruption of our own cities. If Milwaukee today stands out as a notable exception to the run of American municipalities in the traditional integrity of its government, the credit for this is due to the Socialist immigrants who imported from Munich and other

German cities of the 'Nineties their standards of good government.

None of this is to indicate that my interests at the time of which I write were concentrated on municipal administration. Lenbach was a hero of mine, not because of his civic virtues, but rather because he could, with bold strokes, put on canvas the authentic lineaments of his sitters in a masterly manner that was the despair of us novices and quite often the cause of apoplectic fits on the part of said sitters. There used to be considerable high-brow chatter about the way in which John Singer Sargent "psychologized" his subjects, notably in his famous portrait of the elder John D. Rockefeller. Lenbach not only psychologized his high and mighty sitters, he rent them to shreds. His conventional portraits of Bismarck are best known, but then Lenbach admired Bismarck and in his mass production of the Iron Chancellor's features he mercifully omitted the bull-frog touch which I recall as Bismarck's most distinguishing characteristic. When it came to the Lenbach portrait of Emperor William I, the grandfather of the Doorn exile, Lenbach used the scalpel as well as the brush. He did a picture of a monarchial wreck, physical, mental and spiritual, which delighted the Socialists as much as it disgusted the Hohenzollerns, who refused to accept the painting. Not that Lenbach cared. He had put down his man as he had seen him, a wheezing, old stuffed shirt. Similarly he painted Queen Victoria as a petty-bourgeois bale of hay in a black sack over which vacuous blue eyes peered from a fat, baby face.

That Lenbach was capable of lavishing the most tender emotions upon an object of his love I was to discover when I watched him painting a portrait of his little daughter. The child stood slightly pigeon-toed, clad in a long blue gown, in her eyes a look of heavenly wonder. Somehow the hard-boiled Lenbach caught that look forever in his eternal tribute to innocence.

All that I have said about the high level of Munich's officialdom in no wise applies to the city's police. In my rôle as a Socialist organizer and self-appointed defender of the underdog in general I have met up with uniformed stupidity from Berlin to Jersey City, but never have I found the equal of the Munich police of the nineties. The dumb but fortunately good-natured leviathans were carefully selected from men who had served twelve years in the army and were discharged without a single black mark against them. Naturally such a process guaranteed a moronic docility that made the Munich police the butt of the beer-hall radicals.

Some three or four doors from the house in which I was living on Sismaringer Strasse in Haidhausen, a suburb of Munich, was a merchant-tailor shop in which, one night, a passing policeman observed two suspicious characters packing up rolls of clothing materials by the dim light of a lantern. Suspecting something out of the regular order, the policeman entered to investigate and soon elicited the information that the two visitors were burglars. Promptly he declared the pair under arrest.

However, before departing with the twain, handcuffed, one of the burglars announced he had left his cap up on the second floor, and could he secure it? As it was a cold winter night, the kind-hearted policeman gave permission, holding burglar Number Two for security. When, after some ten minutes, burglar Number One failed to reappear, the policeman arrived at the conclusion that there was something not altogether right in the delay. So he mounted the stairway in search of Number One, but not until he had received the solemn promise of Number Two not to stir from his place. Unable to discover anyone upstairs, the disappointed policeman returned to his charge below and naturally found him gone, too.

Now, any normal policeman the world over would have carefully kept the adventure to himself. But not this trusting soul of a Munich policeman. He dutifully reported the incident to his captain, not forgetting the woeful lack of veracity and all-around reliability of burglars. Whereupon the story of the disappointed policeman appeared in all the Munich papers. It was on this episode that Papa Geis, the most popular humorist of Munich's beer halls, evolved his tale of the stuttering policeman:

"As I w-w-was wa-wa-wa-walking down Da-da-da-dach-aur Strasse," the policeman reported to his captain, "who do you think I m-m-met but the ju-ju-ris-dididictionally ap-ap-apprehensi-si-sible heavy criminal. 'Cr-cr-crim-criminal,' I said, 'you are ar-ar-ar-arrested.'

"When we came to to the b-b-baker shop in Da-da-dach-aur S-s-strasse the c-c-c-criminal said, 'I am very hungry. I want to b-b-buy a bun.' I said, 'All right, you b-b-buy the bun and I w-w-wait at the d-d-d-d-door.'

"I wa-wa-aited f-f-f-f-five minutes. I w-w-w-waited ten m-m-minutes, and then w-w-went into the b-b-baker sh-shop, and asked the b-b-baker l-lady, 'Did you see the ju-juris-didictionally ap-ap-apprehensib-sible heavy c-c-criminal?' She said, 'He-he-he went out of the b-b-back door ten m-minutes ago.'

"Next day as I w-w-was wa-walking down D-d-d-dachaur S-s-strasse, who do you think I m-m-met again, but the self-s-s-same heavy c-c-criminal. Said I, 'C-c-criminal, n-now you go w-with me f-f-for sure.'

"When w-w-we came to the b-b-baker shop on D-d-dachaur S-s-strasse the c-c-criminal said, 'I am hungry. I w-w-want to b-b-buy a b-b-bun.'

" 'All right,' I s-s-s-said, 'you b-b-buy the b-b-bun, but this time I w-w-wait at the back door.'

"I w-w-waited f-f-five m-m-minutes. I w-w-waited ten m-m-minutes. The h-h-heavy c-c-criminal didn't c-c-come. Then I w-w-went into the b-b-baker shop and said to the b-b-baker lady, 'D-did you s-s-see the heavy c-c-criminal?' She said, 'Y-y-yes, he w-w-went out of the f-f-front d-d-door ten minutes ago.'

"Next day as I w-was w-w-walking down Da-da-dachaur S-s-strasse who do you think I m-m-met again . . . ? the self-s-s-same c-c-criminal. So I s-said to the c-c-criminal, 'N-n-now I've g-g-got you for g-g-good.'

"When w-w-we came to the b-b-baker shop on D-d-dachaur

S-s-strasse, the c-c-criminal said, 'I w-w-want to b-buy a b-b-b-bun.'

"'N-n-n-n-no!' I s-s-said, 'you are n-not g-g-gonna c-catch me again. This time I b-b-buy the b-b-bun and you w-w-wait on the outside.'"

Andreas was a friend and classmate of mine at the art school. He was born in Shanghai, China, the son of a rich Hamburg merchant with a branch office in that city. After the death of his father the family had returned to Hamburg, and now Andreas was studying art in Munich, for art's sake. That is, as a sort of finishing touch to his education. He was slated to be a highlight of Germany's diplomatic service in the Orient. With this aim he had, aside from an academic education, acquired a good working knowledge not only of German, French, English, and Italian, but Chinese and Japanese as well. He had studied these last two languages at the Oriental Institute in Naples, Italy. He was, in addition, an excellent violinist. And now he was studying art on top of all the rest. He was by far the most all-around educated mortal I've met before or since. Indeed he had so much learning in his head, by the time we met, that thinking on his own hook was definitely excluded.

One day a tailor had delivered to our studio a pair of trousers which Andreas had ordered. After trying the fit in back of a screen behind which models were dressing and undressing, Andreas hung the trousers on a nail and promptly forgot them, as usual. When I came to the studio next morning the male model of the evening before informed me that a friend of his had stolen the pants. It appeared that, after the students had departed, while the model was still dressing, this friend had come in to borrow a mark. Not having that much with him, our model offered to borrow it from the janitor—who happened to be the loan shark of the institution. Returning after successful negotiation, he discovered that his friend had vanished, and with him Andreas' new trousers. Having no desire to be himself accused of stealing, our model had peached on his friend, even to the point of telling his name, Johann Reisemeier.

Armed with the name, character, and working address of the culprit, I proceeded to the room of my friend, close by. It took some time to make clear to the over-educated mind of Andreas how, why, and whose pants had been stolen. Once convinced on these points, he wanted to know what was the customary procedure in such cases?

"Report the theft to the police," I suggested.

"Yes, yes, I suppose that's it," confessed the prospective plaintiff, "but will you go with me?"

"Sure," I replied. "You couldn't locate the police station. It's almost three blocks from here."

At the station we were ushered into the office of the captain on duty. The captain was a walking or rather a sitting advertisement for the high quality of Munich beer. He was barrel-shaped. His abdomen served in the double capacity of bay window and hand rest. His nose was carmine, shading into Prussian blue toward the lower end. His eyes were piglike, but blue and friendly. A short, cropped ring of red hair and beard surrounded the face in the manner of an aura.

After listening most sympathetically to my story of the purloined pants, the captain exclaimed in a combination of grunts, heaves, and Bavarian dialect, "Well, well, so Johann Reisemeier steals pants. Who would ever have thought that of the scamp, and most likely he has pawned them by now, as we soon shall find out. In the meantime, fetch me Johann Reisemeier, and I'll see what we see." At that, I mildly suggested to the captain that, since we were only art students, his own force was perhaps better qualified to apprehend Johann. To this the captain agreed with some misgivings, whereupon plaintiff and his chief witness departed.

Late that same afternoon there was a gentle knock at the studio door. It was our captain, cap in hand. Without the slightest attempt at military salute or heel-clicking, but with shining countenance, he informed us that he had seen pants-thief Reisemeier, who had confessed his guilt freely, but who assured the police that the pants were no longer in his possession. He had pawned them for the sum of four marks with the Widow Mueller, a pawnbroker on Cewuetzmiehl Strasse. To my inquiry as to whether Reisemeier was incarcerated he replied, "There is no need for anything as drastic as that, inasmuch as the police are in possession of his *personalien*," that is, his collection of birth, baptism, vaccination, and school certificates and passport, without which, sojourn in the German Empire was most difficult, if not impossible. He also assured us that in due time the criminal would be arrested, brought to trial and, if found guilty, suitably punished.

"But," I interjected, "have you recovered our pants?"

"No, not the pants," the captain replied with the utmost good nature. "As I told you, the pants were pawned with the Widow Mueller for four marks. The widow is a licensed broker and a most honorable woman. I'm sure you will have no difficulty in recovering your property by paying her the four marks she has advanced to Johann Reisemeier." We must have looked somewhat taken aback, for the captain added, "Of course, you could secure them again by civil action. But that would cost much more than four marks, and you young gentlemen certainly would not deprive a poor but honest widow of four marks. So I'm sure you will follow my suggestion." Giving us a roseate smile, the good officer departed.

"Well, what shall we do now?" my friend Andreas inquired. "Do now?" I replied, brimful of righteous indignation. "Report both case and captain to the chief of police! Do you think for a minute we're going to buy our own trousers back?"

The following morning we reported to the chief of police. His name was Von Stetten; I remember it because I was born in Achstetten, three miles from the town of plain Stetten. Chief von Stetten listened most politely to our complaint and informed us that, while the documents of the case had not yet arrived from the police station concerned, he was sure our story was true. He closed the interview by seconding the advice of our captain to recover our property by means of appeasement and purchase. A most estimable woman, that Widow Mueller, who, on no consideration, he knew, would lend money on stolen goods. Certainly we could rescue the pants by civil action, which, of course, would cost much more than four marks. Besides, he felt quite certain we were not the kind of young gentlemen to deprive an indigent and honorable widow of four marks.

"Well, what are we going to do now?" friend Andreas wanted to know after the door of Munich's police headquarters had closed behind us. "Next," I replied, having reached the state described as holy wrath, "we're going to call on Widow Mueller and get our pants."

The Widow Mueller was shocked at hearing our recital. Johann Reisemeier, whose watch and overcoat she had pawned many a time in her capacity as a licensed broker of the municipal pawnshop, had deceived us all by pawning stolen goods with her! Reisemeier was a scamp, a crook, a character assassin! But with all that the indignant lady would not dream of losing four hardearned marks by surrendering our pants. We finally compromised. We paid her four marks and got the trousers back.

Having lost the last vestige of faith I ever harbored for legal institutions and justice in general, I hunted up Johann Reisemeier. He confessed the truth and confessed it nakedly, inasmuch as I found him in the Roth sculpture class, posing in the altogether. But in reality, he explained, he had not *stolen* the trousers. He had only borrowed them. Seeing them hanging behind the screen where his friend and colleague was dressing, he felt quite sure he could pawn them for more than the single mark he was touching his friend for. He went on to vouchsafe his opinion of rich young men who tempt hard-working poor people by leaving brand new clothes hanging around in semipublic places. Finally, he was not a thief. His intention had been to redeem the pants from the Widow Mueller on next pay day and return them to the nail from which he had borrowed them.

In the end, we compromised again. Reisemeier promised me on his word to return the four marks his coming pay day. I promised on my word of honor not to press the case against him, provided he came across with the four marks promised. At any rate, why prosecute the poor devil? The Widow Mueller had her four marks, my friend Andreas had his trousers, and on the day promised, Reisemeier brought the four marks.

However, the case was still on the official police books, and the next problem was how to expunge it. My solution was based on five years' sojourn in the Land of the Free. Cited to appear in court against the defendant, one simply failed to appear, that was all. However, it developed that there was no relationship between American and Bavarian court customs. When I was cited to appear at nine A.M. on a certain day in May before the *Hohepolizei Gericht von München,* as chief witness in the matter of Andreas Stettinus versus Johann Reisemeier, Andreas and I would have been absent had not two policemen appeared at ten A.M. and marched us to the police court. There we found defendant Reisemeier sitting on the mourners' bench. Following introductions all around, Andreas testified to the ownership of the pants. I testified to the manner in which the pants had disappeared. The Widow Mueller testified she had lent Reisemeier four marks on the pants. Then I testified how I had paid her the four marks for the pants. Reisemeier testified when and how he had paid me the four marks and lastly Andreas testified that the pants he had on were the very ones that had disappeared.

The upshot was that nobody having lost anything, no theft had taken place, whereupon defendant Reisemeier drew one day in jail for misbehavior while plaintiff Andreas and chief prosecuting witness Oscar were sentenced to ten days in the *Bürgerstube* for contempt of court on the ground that we had not voluntarily appeared when the case was called.

The *Bürgerstube,* or citizens' room, was a sort of mild purgatory for respectable minor law-breakers. There were no bars on the windows, the door was never locked, and the jailers would carry beer for culprits, partake of their lunches, and, when time permitted, play pinochle with them. Another good feature was that you were allowed to serve time on the installment plan. And so by sleeping, eating and playing pinochle between seven P.M. and seven A.M. for twenty days in the *Bürgerstube,* the two of us attended our classes regularly and a good time was had by all.

14

THE leading industries of Munich were beer, art and education, and the chief of these was beer. Among the brews that made Munich famous were Spatenbrau, Pschorrbrau, Löwenbrau, Augustiner Brau and San Salvador Brau, all of which I studied diligently and frequently. I still believe that if the victorious Allies had accepted German war indemnities in Munich beer, this world would be a happier place in which to live. There was something so filling and soothing in Munich beer that I am certain its universal consumption would have served the cause of peace considerably better than the League of Nations.

The best beer that ever went down my grateful gullet was Kloster Andex Brau. The Monastery Andex was located some twelve miles south of Munich. Many a pilgrimage I made to that holy grail of beer, and made them on foot, too, which not only whetted the thirst, but also saved the money for quenching it.

When the Reformation abolished the North German monasteries in the name of the Lord and the new-born profit system, Bavaria remained in the fold of the Catholic Church, wherefore the Bavarian monasteries continued their communistic ways, including the brewing of beer designed solely for pleasurable consumption. But when in 1871 Bavaria came under the heavy heel of Protestant Prussia, the monasteries were deprived of most of their communist activities, including the brewing of beer. However, the reverence of Bavarians for good beer was so high that a special dispensation was granted the monks of Andex: they were allowed to brew, provided they religiously abstain from selling beer and thus deprive poor but deserving private breweries of divinely ordained dividends.

The thirsty pilgrim to Andex planted himself on the nearest smoke-blackened table, and one of those blessed roly-poly monks placed a stein of foaming lager before him. When the stein was empty another appeared, and so on. On leaving Klostergarten or Klosterstube, honorable and well-heeled pilgrims left a voluntary contribution for the monastery treasury, covering, or more than covering, the price of the beer within them. Busted but none-the-less honorable pilgrims departed with the beer in their midriffs and a pious "Vergelt's Gott" meaning "May God repay" on their lips. But in either case the parting "Behüt' dich Gott" of the father was just as friendly.

While Andex beer was not brewed for profit, I have a theory that there was another and perhaps deeper reason for its wondrous quality, and that is the two-hundred-foot-deep well from which the monks of Andex drew water in oaken buckets by hand-operated windlasses. Water acquired in so costly a manner was too precious to be spoiled by being treated with tiny quantities of hops and malt. The monks of Andex had to make the best of their water and they most certainly did. In this connection, I harbor a corollary theory that the poor quality of American beer is primarily due to the cheapness of water. By some tragic coincidence, all the principal beer cities of the United States are located on large bodies of water: Milwaukee on Lake Michigan, St. Louis and New Orleans on the Father of Waters, Philadelphia on the Schuylkill River, while New York is completely surrounded by water. I feel sure that if our great brewing corporations had as much trouble securing water as the good monks of Andex, they would refrain from desecrating it with corn meal, saccharine and licorice.

That grand old Andex beer held its foam for hours and one could float a dime on it. Nor did it rush down the throat as if afraid of missing the train. It met its destiny leisurely, winding several times around the heart, thereby engendering the kind of emotion that inspired Friedrich Schiller to pen the immortal words in his "Ode to Joy": "Be embraced, you millions, here's . . . my kiss to all the world." I never saw anyone drunk at Andex monastery. Neither did I ever overindulge at the place, although I confess that after the third stein I would occasionally take in the beautiful panorama seen from the Klostergarten— towering snow-capped Alps (twice as towering as normally) southward, sleeping Ammersee to the right, emerald Starnberger Lake to the left—and then exclaim, "Come on, fellows, how much do you want for the whole *schmier?* I'm paying cash."

It is astonishing, the amount of the milk of human kindness concealed in first-class beer.

15

THE foot of the Alps is only a few hours from Munich by hike. And to the Alps we went over week ends and during vacations, finances permitting. One of the longest of these walking tours took us over the Brenner Pass, down the valley of the Adige through Stertzing, Meran, Botzen and Lake Garda, to within sight of the Adriatic. That particular trip lasted forty days, cost me the princely sum of twenty-two American dollars, and was worth every cent of it. There were five of us: my friend Andreas; an art student by the name of Kubel from Dresden who, although an ardent socialist, had received a scholarship from the king of Saxony; a friend of Kubel's; a young school teacher also from Dresden; and myself. Besides being congenial walking companions, four of us made up a versatile quartet. Instrumentally, we performed on the violin, guitar, flute and mouth harp (a combination which composers have tended to neglect in their major opera); vocally, we professed to first tenor, second tenor, baritone and bass. The bass—myself—was not a strong singer, bass or otherwise. Bereft of keys and holes whereon to plant my fingers, I easily lost my musical bearings, but the others were good instrumentalists and vocalists as well.

Traveling extremely light in earthly goods, we relied largely on our artistic achievements to see us through. They did. For as the German saying goes, "Kunst bringt Gunst." Moreover, traveling for students was very cheap in those days. When one is young and has tramped fifteen or twenty miles a day, almost any rock will do for a bed. We carried our own commissary department, which consisted largely of rye bread and cheese or, sometimes, cheese and rye bread. Beer was around six cents the quart, wine was cheaper than that, and milk cheaper than either. For stormy weather there were Alpine huts and student taverns which granted a one-third reduction in price to any young hopes-of-the-future.

The Alpine or shelter huts were a peculiar institution. Located in less accessible localities, or where taverns wouldn't pay, they were in the care of the Alpine Society, a voluntary association of mountain climbers and lovers of nature in general. The bedding was hay. There was in each of them a small shelf of smoked, canned, pickled and curdled food. There was also a modest medicine chest and first-aid kit in case of accident. The price of the commodities was written on the packages; the cashier an iron box, into which the purchaser dropped the money, and every so often the stock of food, hay, and medicine was renewed. To my best belief and knowledge, those shelter huts were never robbed, and paid their own way. This was, of course, long before the world was made safe for democracy. Whether such automatic taverns would still pay I am in no position to know.

It was thanks to one of these shelter huts that I became acquainted with one of Germany's outstanding statesmen—Von— but never mind the name for the present. We had scaled the Tame Kaiser, a mountain range extending east from Kufstein on the Inn river. While preparing our noonday meal of rye bread and cheese, two mountaineers, one natural, the other synthetic, approached us. The natural mountaineer carried a heavy rucksack; the synthetic one an Alpine staff and monocle. After a somewhat half-hearted introduction on all sides, the natural mountaineer emptied his rucksack while the synthetic one with the Alpine staff and monocle looked benignly on. As the rucksack divulged its secrets, a veritable delicatessen store unfolded before our bulging eyes. Two roast chickens, sausages, cheeses, and preserves of all sorts were climaxed by six bottles of Rhine wine.

In spite of the monocle and Prussian dialect, the synthetic one was not bad at heart. He invited us to participate in the luscious feast at his feet. Need I say we fell to? When one has lived for days on a diet of cheese and rye bread, or vice versa, even Arkansas swine's bosom and corn pone would be welcome, and here was a feast to gladden the heart of a young god. I must have taken my first fatal step toward internationalism on this particular occasion. Up to then I had harbored a strong dislike for Prussians; now it appeared that even that grim species had a human side.

After the feast we parted with our good host. But that night we met again at the Pfandelhof, a well known tavern at the foot of the Tame Kaiser operated by a widow and her four daughters, strong, buxom females, and the mother so young that she could easily have passed as the older sister. I still regard those Tyrolean women as the crowning glory of their glorious sex. They were neither Teutonic nor Mediterranean, but a happy mixture of both. From the Romans who crossed through the Alpine passes for centuries they had inherited their dark eyes, hair, and slight olive complexion. From the Teutons came their tall, strong, graceful figures. Much outdoor life and the healthy exercise of mountain climbing had contributed rosy cheeks and full, kissable lips, while sharing the work of men made them a physical match to the best of that sex.

It happened to be Sunday night, so besides us wanderbirds and our monocled host of that noon, there were a good number of young Tyrolean bucks in the room, all dressed in their picturesque native costume. As a result of conflicting interests, our group hatched a sinister conspiracy. The big idea was to get the native roosters drunk and thus monopolize the country women for ourselves.

I would gladly have participated in this laudable endeavor, but alas, I had lost my watch in the hay of the shelter hut in which we had slept the night before. The watch was a medium-priced Swiss, but an excellent timekeeper, and above that, a veritable friend in need. Every time they gave *Tristan and Isolde* or *Siegfried* at the Royal Opera House, or some celebrated guest conductor directed one of my favorite Beethoven symphonies, the Third, or Fifth, or Seventh, or I had made an important date with some charming model who might require a modicum of expenditure, I was dead broke. At these frequent occasions, my faithful timepiece usually came to my rescue. The presiding elder of the Munich municipal pawnshop knew that faithful timepiece so well that whenever he spied me entering his door he started counting out the customary fifteen marks.

Now that rainy-day standby was lost. It was a choice between a two-hour climb in the dark back to the shelter hut in an attempt to recover my watch, or the opportunity to monopolize one member of the extremely attractive managerial staff of the Pfandelhof. Virtue triumphed and as a result I lost out both ways. I never found my watch, and on returning near midnight from the arduous climb I found my associates dead to the world, while the Tyrolean roosters were still dancing with our buxom hostesses. The only one of us outlanders still in a semivertical position was our host of that noon. Even he had reached the stage where he was weeping on the generous bosom of one of the Pfandelhof daughters.

Now it's one thing to get hilariously exhilarated in the company of genial souls and something else again to look with perfectly sober eyes on a bunch of drunks sprawled round a room in all possible and impossible positions. Utterly disgusted with the inebriety of an otherwise pretty decent set of friends, I retired to my room on the second floor of the tavern. However, the stamping, music and yodeling down below made sleep impossible, dog-tired as I was. I finally went out on the balcony and, drinking in the solemn beauty of the moonlight, meditated on the depravity of man, with special emphasis on the drunken outfit below.

After sitting there for some time, I overheard a mixture of love-making and argumentation going on under the balcony. Being no Peeping Tom, and not having any desire to wound my lacerated soul by further disgraceful conduct, I refrained from taking a bird's-eye view of the situation until I heard a noise that sounded like a hefty hand landing with considerable force on a fat cheek. Looking over the railing, I saw, sprawled on the dewy sod, the future Reich's chancellor and German Ambassador to Rome—Von Bülow.

Oh, well, we can't all be saints. Here's hoping that in the dark days to come the memory of that night in the Pfandelhof brightened his heart occasionally.

> "Oh, thou clear, blue heaven,
> How beautiful thou art.
> Would I could press thee
> To my joyous heart."

This was one of our favorite songs. We even sang it in the pouring rain on the eight-hour tramp from Epps on the River Inn to Meierhofen, the last village of the lower Ziller Thal, the home of most Tyrolean singers, yodelers, and zither players. Arriving at the student tavern, where we could get the customary reduction of thirty-three and a third per cent, we found it overcrowded. Perhaps we could find bed and board at the regular Gasthaus, the tavern keeper suggested. And there we went.

Yes, replied the keeper of the regular Gasthaus, he had room for all five of us.

True, but would he kindly grant us the customary reduction of thirty-three and a third per cent?

He would.

But considering there were five of us, would he be kind enough to shave that a little?

Well, considering it was a very rainy night following two very rainy days, and that he had the rooms, he would.

Entering the Gaststube, we found it three-quarters filled with disgruntled tourists of the better class. These people had started out to tour the Tyrol in the minimum possible time. Now for two solid days they had been rained in. Also, they were mostly north Germans, who take life much more seriously than south Germans. On top of that, we newcomers looked more like hobos than the future hope of German Kultur. We had frequently slept in our clothes, seedy enough at best, and we had solemnly promised each other to refrain from such luxuries as shaves and haircuts for the duration of the journey. Hence our welcome was somewhat cooler than a refrigerated icicle.

Scenting and resenting the implied snobbery, we took one end of a long table without going through the customary formality of introducing ourselves to our fellow guests at the other end. Then, to accentuate our protest, we declined to order the warm meal which we craved, extracted cheese and rye bread from our rucksacks, and ordered the cheapest *Landwein* of the house, cheaper even than beer.

Our modest repast finished, we pulled out fiddle, guitar, flute and mouth harp, drowning the halting conversation of the others. After a few marches and waltzes, the daughter of the tavern keeper volunteered the information that she played the zither, and on our cordial invitation, produced it. More marches and waltzes, and the zitheress revealed that her young brother played the harp. A few minutes later the young brother, barefooted and rubbing his sleepy eyes, appeared with an Italian harp. The orchestra was growing. Shortly it was sweetened still further by song. The rich harmony of "Oh, thou deep blue heaven" rang out into the chilly, rainy night. Music soothes even the Prussian breast. The ice melted. Someone sang second to somebody's first tenor. Somebody sang first bass to someone's second. Soon altos and sopranos joined in, and there was a full mixed chorus, with orchestral accompaniment. Wine bottles appeared and accumulated on every table, including that of the merry troubadors. After all, north or no north, these people were Germans, and so *Gemütlichkeit* rose to hilarity. . . .

Next morning when I threw the feather bed back a cloud of steam rose into the icy morning air from my fully clothed form. Apparently my undressing had stopped at removing only one hobnailed shoe.

We assembled at an early hour, considering the glorious preceding night, and ordered a sure-enough warm breakfast, fully intending to pay for it. But when we asked what we owed, the host replied, "All you young gentlemen owe me is a return visit at the same rate. In another hour that bunch of tourists would have gone off to bed sober. Thanks to your presence, I just helped the last two up to their rooms a few minutes ago. A very profitable night, I assure you, so *behüt' Gott und auf baldiges Wiedersehen.*" To the strains of "Oh, thou deep blue heaven" we marched forth into the now smiling, sunbathed landscape.

It was somewhere in the upper reaches of the high Ziller that we finally broke forces. Andreas and Kubel and the Dresden school teacher returned to Meierhofen to reach Stertzing by way of Innsbruck and the Brenner Pass. Zechlin and I took another pass to the same destination. Much of our journey was made in the clouds. And as clouds are composed of moisture, and it is cold in those high altitudes, eventually we were shivering all over. When we stumbled across two huts, one empty, the other holding Alpine hay, we stopped to dry out and warm up. We hung our soaking garments on an Alpine staff, affixed between the corners of the empty hut and, fetching hay from the other, soon had a merry fire blazing. The nature of the fuel required frequent trips in the altogether, and it was on one of these, the clouds having lifted in the meantime, that I saw a small village some thousand-odd feet almost directly below. Our intention had been to reach the village of St. Jacob a few hours distant, but evening was coming on, we had been delayed by the clouds, felt tired and hungry, and decided to risk the descent to our freshly discovered village. Had we been more experienced mountaineers we would have most respectfully declined the attempt. However, by careful clinging and much accidental sliding and the assistance of the Guardian Angel, we made it in one piece.

As we approached the first house in the little village, we asked the good housewife if we could secure a few litres of milk? Very sorry, but she had no milk. Then could we get a few bumpers of wine? Very sorry, but she had no wine, either. We assured her that we were not hobos, but respectable tourists, perfectly willing and able to pay, but that didn't help. The good housewife had committed herself.

I felt the woman wasn't telling the truth; there must be some other reason why people of her kind denied refreshment to weary wayfarers. And there was, as we presently discovered. The tiny village was too far from the main tourist paths to encourage commercial hospitality, yet it was near enough to be visited by an increasing number of tourists. So between not having learned to charge for refreshment and being unable to give it away free, the good woman had fibbed in self-defense. But she had no heart for fibbing, and besides, she must have lacked experience.

Just then the bells of St. Jacob rang out the Ave Maria and reminded me that the prayers I, on my teachers' knees, had had pounded into my young being with hazelnut switches were not lost motion, after all. Solemnly making the sign of the cross and reverently lifting my face to the crucifix in the corner over the table, I started rattling off the rosary. I say "rattling" with deliberation, for saying it slowly and, worse still, thinking about what I was saying, I certainly would have got stuck.

My companion was a Lutheran and consequently a total stranger to the rosary. However, being rather wide between the eyes, he kept one of them on the crucifix and the other on me, thereby getting by quite creditably. During the long recital one member of the family after another came trailing into the room—

father, grandfather, and five youngsters, ranging from five to fifteen. All joined in the prayer, with me still in the lead.

After the rosary there were exclamations: "Oh, you are Catholic, too!" "Why, I thought all Prussians were Lutherans." "And you are students. Perhaps studying for the priesthood?" And so on.

Really, it would have been a crime to have apprised these good souls of the sad state of our own. Meanwhile the father had disappeared somewhere, to return presently with a large jug of wine. Mother secured a large bowl of milk from some unknown source, and for good measure, placed a huge panful of oatmeal on the table. Soon the congregation was dipping oatmeal and milk out of the same pan and bowl, in brotherly fashion.

After the supper dishes had been cleared away the smaller youngsters were shooed to bed. With nightfall came the hour for story-telling. That is, having no desire to enter into any theological discussion in which friend Zechlin would most likely have stuck his neck out, I started reciting stories of the time when Napoleon and the king of Bavaria, the Corsican-Teutonic allies, were doing their best to deprive their brother ruler of Austria of his beloved Tyrol.

According to Heinrich Heine, the Tyroleans were fighting over the question as to which was preferable, an emperor in brown breeches living in Vienna, or an emperor in white trousers living in Paris. The Tyroleans voted unanimously to fight like Trojans for the emperor in brown breeches until he dropped his loyal Tyroleans like a superheated brick when his daughter became spliced to the emperor in white trousers. Since I had shortly before read Immermann's history of Tyrol, I had the story on the tip of my tongue: Andreas Hofer, betrayed and shot at Mantua by a French firing squad without the father-in-law of Napoleon lifting a finger to save him. . . . Speckbacker the redoubtable, and Geier Hansel, the twelve-year-old who rushed into the field of fire, picking up spent bullets since lead was scarce in Tyrol. . . . The girl who, under murderous strafing, had driven her loaded hay wagon into the pass near Stertzing, blocking the advance of the French. I knew them all, and all about them.

The audience was more than sympathetic. It was overwhelmed. How could I, a rank outsider, know so much more about the heroic struggles of their country than they? More astounding, I hadn't been there. And yet, grandfather assured them, it was all true. For had he not heard these stories over and over again from his own father and from many survivors who had lived through them and seen it all with their own eyes?

On our departure in the morning we offered the good housewife a few gulden as a small token of appreciation for the hospitality she had extended. She declined emphatically. She would not accept a penny from such fine, entertaining, Catholic gentlemen. Neither would Geier Hansel, as I had dubbed her twelve-year-old and berry-brown son, who could well have served as model for Lenbach's "Shepherd Boy." Geier Hansel accompanied us to the junction of the main road to St. Jacob; where, despairing of my power of persuasion, I finally laid two gulden on a rock with the advice either to take it or leave it to someone else.

Even then the boy would not take what must have meant a small fortune to him. It was only after we had walked a good distance that he slowly picked up the money and took his way home, troubled no doubt as to how to explain to his parents that he was returning with the two gulden in his brown fist.

At Stertzing, the southern terminal of the Brenner Pass, which now forms the boundary between Italy and Germany, our groups were reunited. Stertzing, we found, was a simon-pure medieval town. It had been built in one piece by the merchant prince Fugger of Augsburg for the protection of his salt and silver miners in the vicinity and the high road that carried his merchandise from the far Orient over the Brenner Pass and down the Bavarian lowlands to Augsburg. Boom-town Stertzing, built of six-foot walls surrounded by ten- or twelve-foot walls, entrance protected by bastions, watch towers, massive oaken nail-studded gates, is the same now as it was in the fifteenth century.

The tavern at which we stopped was operated by an elderly couple, both as broad as they were tall. Had they walked several times around each other every day they would, I am sure, have had all the physical exercise they needed. The food was plentiful and wholesome, the wine above mere drinkability, the beds clean and soft, and the price well inside the reach of our purses. Indeed, so well pleased were we with our host and his offering that we asked him why he didn't enlarge his tavern, thereby assuring greater revenue.

"Well," he replied, "there are numerous reasons. In the first place, there is no room to build a wing. In the second place, I'm not sure these old walls would support a third story. In the third place, there are only myself and my wife to be taken care of and we've got all the income we need. Why make more work for the sake of earning something we wouldn't know what to do with? And lastly, my father was born and died in the tavern. So was his father and the father of his father and the father of his father, and so on back for as long as anybody can remember. Many children have been born in this place, mated, died, and gone home to their reward. As far as I know, they all were good people, lived happily and died in the faith. So why should I break the chain?"

Nevertheless, we offered to draw plans for the expansion of his hostelry, just for the mere pleasure it would give us. The site we selected was the bowling alley adjoining the little beer, flower and kitchen garden in the rear of the tavern. The bowling alley was only about forty feet long and scarcely seven feet wide, but by allowing five feet by three per room we managed to crowd ten rooms in the space available. The guest stepped from a two-foot hallway through a two-foot door directly on the bed. Places for clothing, rucksack and other accoutrements were provided by a series of square-headed nails driven in the walls above the bed.

Square-headed nails were selected so as to harmonize with the square-headed nails on the shoes of mountain climbers.

As there was no way of reaching under the bed for whatever one might search for under a bed in those days, we provided for a small bay window extending from the two-foot hallway. In this bay a communal vessel was to be placed. The rooms being a foot or so short of holding the average guest, two holes were provided in each door through which he could extend his feet. One of the advantages of this arrangement was that in case the guest had left a call to be awakened at a certain time, tickling the soles of his feet would achieve the purpose without at the same time disturbing other guests by knocking at the door.

Whether our contented host ever executed this plan, I do not know, as we departed a few days later. But he got no end of fun out of it before we left. He had our blueprints and specifications framed and hung on the walls of the tavern, and explained the most intricate details of the layout to his other guests.

A queer sort of a human, that tavern keeper. By modern standards he lacked enterprise and the Chamber of Commerce spirit. But after all, what more may man achieve in this life than to eat, drink, mate, make merry, and sleep in the knowledge of having served his fellow tourists to the best of his ken?

Somewhere back in the fourteenth or fifteenth century, a collective-bargaining agreement was consummated not far from Stertzing. Its terms suggest that both the A. F. of L. and the C.I.O. are still a long way from catching up with the tactics employed by the guild of silver miners of that time and locality. Among other things, the agreement stipulated the six-hour day and five-day week. Saturday was set aside for shopping. Mines were to remain idle during all saints' days and holy weeks. When the absentee employer of the miners, a count of Tyrol, arrived at Stertzing for negotiation, he was met by a reception committee of five thousand miners, organized into companies of archers, crossbowmen, and spearmen who entertained him with their skill in

target shooting, fencing and military evolution. Whether these
militant maneuvers had anything to do with the liberal terms
of the agreement, history does not say.

In Stertzing, also, I met the first female barber. This was, of
course, long before emancipation had bestowed upon the physically weaker sex the glorious privilege of competing with the
stronger for jobs. As I have mentioned before, the five of us
had made a solemn promise neither to shave nor have our locks
shorn, and now one morning the whole outfit, myself excepted,
appeared clean-shaven, plus haircut. To my indignant protest
came the reply that there were highly mitigating circumstances.
The barber was a lady, who carried on her unladylike profession
in a small room in one of the town's watch towers. In spite of
my indignation, and driven no doubt by my inherent urge for
scientific inquiry, I proceeded to the scene of the outrage. It was
even as the boys had told me. There was the lady barber and a
rather good-looking, generously curved lady barber at that. Her
tonsorial equipment was a bit primitive. Her razor not overly
sharp. Her shears pulled more than they cut. However, employing her Mae West bosom as a headrest, one forgot petty details.

We returned to Munich over the Brenner Pass, lingering for
a day at Baerenbad. From its summit my patron saint, Goethe,
had several times cast longing eyes toward his beloved Italy, the
land *wo die Citronen blühen,* then, drawn by duty and love of
woman, reluctantly turned his face toward Weimar.

Goethe, dead many years before I saw the light of day! How
could you have dreamed of accompanying this Swabian peasant
boy along the complicated road of life, wisely counseling, gently
guiding, giving me a small measure of your boundless understanding, of sympathy for all manifestations of life, art, beauty
and science?

To my mind there has been but one American the peer of
Goethe: Benjamin Franklin. Both were scientists, statesmen, in-
ventors, discoverers, prophets, seers, lovers of all nature and of

men and women, and both were pagans. I have just been reading Carl Van Doren's great biography of Franklin, and wondering to what still greater heights that Boston Quaker boy might have risen had not his devotion to the cause of the American colonies absorbed the largest part of his long, useful, beautiful life. Fortunately the man in the Weimar tomb and the man under the flat stone in the Philadelphia Quaker graveyard are with us still. I often hear their voices above the wrangle and jangle of old and new world strife, hatred, fear, and shallow-pated politics. . . .

I parted from Tyrol and its warm-hearted people one unforgettable Sunday evening, with the full moon coming up over the corner of the Iselberg behind us, and the sun just set below the rolling hills of the Bavarian Overland before us, and still gilding its summits with rosy gold, while on the Inn river floated barges with cargoes of young people, singing, their voices carrying clearly over the waters.

16

DURING a previous visit to Ulm, I had managed to get tangled up in a love affair with the daughter of a well-to-do burgher. On Christmas eve, 1892, I was on a train bound from Munich to Ulm. As became my station, I traveled second class. It was a cold night. The second class compartments were small, stuffy, and held only four passengers, two facing forward, two backward. One of my fellow travelers was a Russian lady who spoke both German and English, as I discovered when I introduced myself.

I had eaten a good meal before departing from Munich, and was desperately itching for a smoke. But there was the small, stuffy compartment and the lady. How could I ask for permission to smoke? I didn't. It was the Russian lady who asked the privilege, and that being gladly granted by me, she fished a large package of jet-black Turkish tobacco out of an elbow-deep skirt pocket, followed by a large, silver, hand-operated cigarette-rolling contraption, a package of cigarette papers, and ultimately a box of matches. When she had rolled a dozen or so cigarettes, each the size of a hot dog, she lit one between her full and fully painted red lips, and that done, lifted the match to my waiting cigar.

Now ladies in those days neither smoked cigarettes, nor painted their lips. Cigarette smoking and lip painting were the exclusive prerogatives of ladies engaged in horizontal occupations, as Heine put it. This promised to be an interesting journey.

The lady turned out to be the champion female smoker of that day. She inhaled deeply and, having inhaled deeply, discharged two unbelievably dense columns of smoke through her nose back into her mouth and repeated the process. However, enough cigarette smoke escaped, no doubt through her ears or eyes, to make her invisible and me more than uneasy. I worried no more about the lady's occupation. In fact, I began to feel so desperately sick that I was compelled to ask her for permission to stick my head out of the window.

On my arrival in Ulm, my virtue unimpaired, I learned from the maid that my girl's parents, having intercepted a letter about my approaching visit, had taken the precaution of sending her to friends in Sigmaringen, capital of the province of Hohenzollern-Hechingen.

This was the spot whence the royal tribe of Hohenzollern started on its world-conquering career, which began, modestly enough, by a program of highway robbery. The site of the original Hohenzollern roost was well-selected for its purpose. Along the foot of the steep hill on which it was perched passed the road over which flowed the trade of a goodly part of continental Europe. From the falls of Schaffhausen, the river Rhine was navigable down to the North Sea at Antwerp. But at Schaffhausen the contents of the barges coming up the Rhine had to be transferred to horseback and wagon for delivery in Italy. By the same token the merchant caravans, carrying the silk, satin and spices of India over the Alpine passes to the Low Countries, went by the Hohenzollern place of business on their way to Schaffhausen for transfer to Rhine barges.

To the honor of the Hohenzollern family it must be said that its members were excellent business men, judiciously combining social-service with highway robbery. The Hohenzollern road was the best kept in all that country. The family tolerated no competition on the part of lower-grade highwaymen, nor did they ever demand more than the traffic would bear, for their commission. Consequently they never killed the merchant goose that laid the golden eggs.

The thrift, frugality, and enterprise of the family enabled one Papa Hohenzollern to send two of his younger sons to wild and woolly Prussia, where, accompanied by papa's blessing and loot, they purchased the Mark Brandenburg, in which Berlin is now located. By judiciously intermarrying with the East Elbian Junkers—who had settled the Baltic provinces (including their aboriginal slave population) after their return from the Crusades by conducting some hard-boiled real-estate deals and by doing considerable claim jumping—the Hohenzollerns finally acquired that place in the sun now symbolized by the woodpile in Doorn. In the process of acquisition, the northern Hohenzollern branch had found it advisable to change their Romanist religion for that of the up-and-coming Martin Luther, while the southern Hohenzollerns remained Catholic.

This is not a history of the Hohenzollern family. I inject this brief historical sketch merely to explain what followed my attempt to locate a certain Theresa in the residential city of Sigmaringen, capital of Hohenzollern-Hechingen.

Perhaps I had not read the papers, or reading them I had paid no attention to an event then exciting the capitals and chancelleries of Europe. Anyhow, stepping off the train at Sigmaringen (normal population five thousand, and all caterers to the court of Hohenzollern-Hechingen or serving in its five-hundred-headed armed forces) my astonished eyes beheld a triumphal arch and through it a gaily decorated, beflagged and bespruced street. When I jocularly thanked a passing burgher for the magnificent reception tendered me, I was indignantly informed that the decorations were not in my honor, but in that of the pending marriage of His Royal Highness, the Crown Prince of Rumania, and Her Serene Highness, the Princess Irene of Edinburgh, and that, moreover, the very next day the Allhighest Emperor William II would honor the city and occasion with his august presence.

I hadn't come to see the All Highest. All I wanted to see was lovely and loving Theresa, and I could not have selected a worse day for that purpose. The town was filthy with dukes, princes and kings attended by trainloads of blue-blooded chamberlains and chambermaids. These were big doings. Princess Irene of Edinburgh was a granddaughter of Queen Victoria. The Crown Prince, and groom, of Rumania was a scion of the Hohenzollern family of the Catholic branch, with the All Highest of the Protestant branch topping the whole *schmier*. Under these circumstances, there was little hope of locating Theresa. Indeed, all I accomplished that day was to locate a cot in the garret of the Golden Lion, one of the better taverns of Sigmaringen.

As I entered the large guest room of the Golden Lion that evening I found it filled with courtiers of both sexes. When at last I located an empty chair and, as is customary, introduced myself to my two neighbors, I was met first by four highly elevated eyebrows, and second by two broad, cold, gold-embroidered backs. I didn't give a hang for the snub, but I felt lonely and out of place. Fortunately, at another table, I observed what seemed to be some genuine human beings. There was considerable laughter at that table, and once in a while I caught a few English words.

I was not mistaken. The happy, democratic crowd at the table was composed of newspapermen from every metropolitan newspaper of Europe. The London *Times*, Paris *Temps*, *Figaro*, *Berliner Neueste Nachrichten*, *Pester Loyd*, were all represented by correspondents, and among them, a sketch artist, a representative of the London *Graphic*, who, on my approach, sociably made room for me on the half of the chair occupied by his other half. It was a good gang, as most newspaper crowds are. There was some difficulty finding one's way through the babel of tongues. However, at least I commanded two of them, and as it seems to be against the religion of English correspondents and Englishmen in general to acquire foreign languages, I presently became interpreter between the English and German representatives of the fourth estate.

Next morning, after a rather late night, and with no hope of finding Theresa, I pushed my way through the teeming multitude toward the town's single depot, where the All Highest was to arrive. I found the station roped off from the common or garden variety of citizens and taxpayers. But I was not one of them. I was an American citizen. Moreover, I had come to see Theresa, and consequently was dressed fit to kill. So I boldly pushed up the detaining rope and strutted toward the depot. There was none to stop me. Some of the soldiers and police on guard actually clicked their heels and saluted this prince in civilian garb. There really was no danger of being found out. No true law-abiding and royalty-worshipping German would have had the presumption to do such an unheard-of thing as passing a *verboten* barrier like that rope. Besides, I had worked that gag repeatedly. Whenever I passed over or around one of the *verboten* signs for which Germany is famous, and some officious official inquired who in hell I thought I was? or where in *Teufel* did I think I was going? I would inquire in my choicest English how best I could go to the place I apparently was going to? or would the officious official kindly explain what the writing on the *verboten* sign meant? or, pointing to my pipe, would merely strike an imaginary match on the seat of my pants, indicating, "Kindly give me a light." It always worked.

When I entered the *Wartesaal erste Klasse*, things looked a bit more serious. The place was littered with royalty. Besides some six or seven kings, I recognized my old friend, Prince Luitpold of Bavaria. The old boy might get it into his head to ask me how come? I also detected some English words in the overworked atmosphere. The least that could follow my exposure would be a few days' detention in the local hoosegow as a suspicious character, and I hadn't seen Theresa yet. But, like General Ulysses Grant, I believed that retreating through the door I had entered would bring bad luck. The only other door, opening to the train shed, was barred by a giant drum major filling all of the opening. Would the drum major move, if I gave him a gentle shove, and let me out? That was the question.

I had my doubts. But finally a chap of about my own age, dressed in the uniform of an Austrian Kaiser Jaeger, under the influence of mistaken identity waved his hand at me as if to say, "Just a minute, and I'll be seeing you." Well, I didn't want any prince asking me how my mother, the queen, was getting along, or had my old man, King So-and-so, got over the jag acquired at the big shoot on the estate of Prince Hohenlobe Hamburger von und zu Honseburg? So, with a peremptory gesture in the direction of my gold-braided drum major, I walked out on the platform.

My troubles had only started. There was no escape from that platform. The train shed was flanked by wrought-iron pickets and spiked helmets. Walking out on the ties was more than *verboten*. It was something that never did and never could happen in Germany.

To add to my worries, the Oriental rug on the platform, which in a few minutes would be honored by the spurred boots of the All Highest, was strewn with roses. I was not used to walking on roses. Somebody might not like it if I walked on roses designed for the feet of the All Highest. And then, just as things looked blacker than the interior of a black cat at midnight, in marched, flanked and escorted, my newspaper friends of the night before. They received me with smiles and handclasps and backslaps. A few minutes later, when I was safely in the bosom of the fourth estate, the All Highest stepped out of his imperial train.

I had seen the All Highest once before on horseback, and on horseback he gave the appearance of a good-sized man. Now the All Highest was on foot. And on foot he looked barely five feet six. His complexion was sallow, his eyes gray-black, his voice the snarl of the Prussian drill master. One of his hands was supported by his sword belt; with the other he shook hands with the royal brethren in the cases when he did not kiss them on their foreheads or one or both cheeks, all the while emitting a ceaseless rattle of "charmed," "delighted," "so happy," and other phrases from the vocabulary of convention.

The reception over and royalty departed, the sketch artist of the *Graphic* turned to me and inquired, casually, "Have you secured the press permit for the wedding?"

I replied, "Not yet."

He directed me to the Master of Ceremonies, Hofmeister von Arnim, at the castle.

Well, there is nothing like trying, as the good old American saying has it. To Hofmeister von Arnim I presented the card of an American living at so-and-so Rue Something, Paris, whom I had met some weeks previously. To this I had added "Representative of the Paris *Herald*."

Hofmeister von Arnim asked no further questions, but filled out the requested document, and to the wedding I went. There were three ceremonies, civil, Anglican and Greek Catholic. Princess Irene, by the grace of Henry VIII, was an Episcopalian. The Crown Prince of Rumania was the son of an ex-Catholic who had swapped his faith for the crown of Greek Catholic Rumania. If there are such things as the holy bonds of wedlock, that couple was in them.

For a preliminary, Princess Irene was rebaptised Marie—the Queen Marie of Rumania, who, before dying a year or so ago, described that very wedding in the *Saturday Evening Post*. It was all true. The old lady hadn't exaggerated. I was there and saw it all with my own eyes. After the rebaptising of Irene Anglican to Marie Greek Catholic came the civil wedding, in compliance with the German laws. The Anglican wedding was performed by a company of archbishops assisted by a battalion of low- and high-church functionaries. The Greek Catholic ceremony was performed by an orthodox Catholic archbishop or arch something, supported by a battalion of two-hundred-pound or better champion wrestlers. They had to be. No one out of the heavyweight wrestler class could have carried the tons of satin, silk, velvet, gold embroidery, rings and precious stones with which these followers of the humble carpenter were adorned. These were the boys who excommunicated Russia's first and only conspicuous Christian, Tolstoi, and went to their just reward shortly after Rasputin got his.

The three-ring wedding was a success except that when the All Highest distributed imperial smacks on the rose-strewn carpet of Sigmaringen, he passed me by. But a few days later I located Theresa. Who, at that age, wants to be kissed by a bristling mustache, anyhow?

17

AS I look back on my Munich days, I realize they were by no means the least fruitful of my educational experiences. They gave me a deeper appreciation of the special world in which dwell art and beauty. Things never looked or felt the same to me after that. Whether it was a stately building, a duck swimming on a shady pond, a tree lifting its branches to the sky, a passing cloud, a cud-chewing cow, a gamboling lamb, statuary, or a cotton-picking Negro, they were all endowed with fresh and additional charm. Seeing things rightly is an art in itself, just as listening to music, though more easily acquired than the art of seeing, is an art in itself. And though I was never an addict of what passes for popular music, it was perhaps in the same Munich beer hall where, as Henry Adams described it, the wall fell which had hitherto separated him from the unseen empire of sound, that I received my final initiation into the golden treasure house of the classics. That experience, I think, justifies the nearly five irresponsible years I spent in Athens on the Isar.

Another invaluable gain was the broadening of my understanding of people of other nationalities. All of us are drilled in the notion that the country into which the accident of birth has cast us is the greatest country on earth, and its people more or less superior to the rest of God's children. Munich in those days was full of all kinds of people hailing from many parts of the world.

Among my friends and acquaintances, besides Americans and Germans, were a Turk, two Chinamen, several Italians, Spaniards, Frenchmen, Englishmen, Scots, Scandinavians, a Russian nihilist, and, finally, an elderly Russian nobleman with a large estate near Odessa.

In his youth that nobleman had accompanied Prince Alexis on his tour around the world, which included a visit to the United States, where they had met President Grant and General Custer. Later he had been attached to the first Russian consulate in Tokio. From the stories he told me about the customs, manners and high culture of the Japan of those days, it must have been a delightful country. I take it for granted that my nobleman friend had little opportunity to study the bearers of water and hewers of wood who supported the charming life of the Japanese upper crust.

Now in his early sixties, the count was studying art, ostensibly. In strict privacy, he confided to me that life under Czarism had become unbearable to him, that the study of art, although he was a lover of it, served as the best possible explanation for his voluntary exile, and that he felt confident the crash of Czarism was not so very far off, in which event it would be well for his kind to be out of Russia. The first crash did come some ten years later; I doubt, however, if Count von Ruckteschell lived to know the final catastrophe twelve years after that, including the loss of his twelve-thousand-acre vineyard in the Crimea.

That there are so many different racial characteristics, personal traits, philosophies, notions, faiths, prejudices, and predilections in this human menagerie is always astonishing. Yet I soon learned that under the skin we are all alike, each a mixture of good, bad and indifferent. As a result of this lesson about the oneness of the human species, I could never in the years to come accept the notion that the checkerboard of life is composed of black and white squares, conveniently designated as devils and angels; even when the great madness of 1914-1918 swept many kindly, decent people into the whirlpool of nationalist hatred I never could think of Frenchmen, Germans, Italians, Russians, Englishmen, Americans as different species. When I read of this or that great victory in which so many hundred thousand hated enemies had bit the dust, I could not rejoice. Those dead men were the kind of youth I had been, no matter what their country.

There are no good people. There are no bad people. Take us by tribe, nation, or individual, we are human beings, and while that might be the worst that can be said about any animal, that's what we are—human beings, each fighting the battle of the Lord with the demon nature planted into our hearts, minds, and tissues. We are, as Goethe said of himself, as good and bad as nature.

In those Munich years most of us stood politically more or less to the left of center. That is, we were forward-looking. A rather amusing term, "forward-looking," because virtually all of the forward-lookers I have met since then have been so busy looking backward that they couldn't even see what was taking place under their very noses. Anarchists look back to Bakunin and Kropotkin. Socialists look back to Marx and Engels. Single-taxers look back to Henry George. Progressive Republicans look back to Abraham Lincoln, Progressive Democrats to Jefferson and Jackson. Progressive lawyers quote Blackstone while progressive parsons and rabbis vainly try to forget Moses and Genesis.

As for myself, I was even then a hard-boiled democrat with no more reverence for handed-down authority than the proverbial cat has for a queen. I was fairly well versed in history, especially American and modern European history. A Cincinnati cap maker had introduced me to Darwin, Haeckel and Huxley. Besides a liberal smattering of the German classics, I had read Kant's *Critique of Pure Reason,* which I cheerfully confess was over my head, but it did leave something behind. Always a strenuous reader, I had often pored over an interesting volume until gray morning crept through the window; even today I cannot go to sleep until I have read more or less, and usually more. Of economics, which I regard now as the rock bottom of social science, I knew nothing. However, my mind had been opened. The removal of the junk pounded into my young head by school and church had provided the blessed vacuum in which any new idea found welcome and lodging.

One of my closest friends, the royally endowed art student from Dresden, was a confirmed Social-democrat and bound to convert me to his faith. In the pursuit of this aim he dragged me to a number of Social-democratic gatherings; I remember especially one large mass meeting in the Münchener Kindelkeller. Wilhelm Liebknecht, the father of Karl Liebknecht, who was later murdered by the forerunners of Adolf Hitler, spoke to us. I can't remember a single sentence uttered by the speaker that day, but the deep seriousness of the man left an impression which all these many years have not wiped out. Whatever Liebknecht advocated, whatever he stood for, there could be no question but that it came from the very bottom of his heart and that, right or wrong, he believed it with every atom of his being. He was not an orator. He was one of those rare men who sway audiences not by oratory but by the very intensity of their faith and their firm belief in the inherent goodness and good sense of the mass. Gene Debs was another of that kind, so was Victor Berger and John P. Altgeld.

So, while I did not take the sawdust trail to the socialist converts' bench that day, I left with the profound feeling that these despised Reds were animated by something much higher than the itch for office, a feeling which afterward made me more receptive to similar ideas.

I knew even then that Wilhelm Liebknecht had been one of the five Social-democratic members of the North German Reichstag who had voted against the war budget of 1870. A year later he was one of the sponsors of the manifesto in which the Social-democratic Party warned against the dire consequences of the annexation of Alsace and Lorraine perpetrated at the first "peace" of Versailles. The reward for this manifestation of common sense and pure patriotism was some years of incarceration as political prisoners in a penal fortress. Of all the German statesmen of those days these five hounded, despised socialist "traitors" against Gott, Kaiser, and Fatherland were the only ones who foresaw the ruination of Germany in a world war—"not one of those localized wars," said the manifesto, "not the kind of war prattled about by our beer-hall Philistines, saber rattlers and jingo professors, but a world war between Germany and the united Latin and Slav nations." The manifesto, drafted by Karl Marx, then exiled in England, might have added England and America to the Slav and Latin nations which in 1918 defeated Bismarck's Germany. Otherwise, every consequence predicted in that prophetic manifesto came true to the last bloody dot.

Queer how the despised radicals are usually right in the end. Mankind seems to march forward only by marching left.

In one other respect Munich became an important turning point of my life. My not-too-earnest studies there completely wrecked my chance to become one of America's popular portrait painters.

I discovered that a new school of painting existed which bore no relationship whatever to the slick, pretty, almost enameled wax figures I had painted and mistaken for art. The things I had so carefully smoothed and polished had been very popular and well-paid, considering my age and experience, but they were not art. They were daubs. So, later, after my return to the States, commissions grew scarcer and scarcer until they ceased almost entirely. And yet, even dire want, or at least the fear of it, was not powerful enough to compel my return to the old technique. As Heine wrote, we're not the master of our ideas. They master us, and make us fight like gladiators for their existence.

However, I still had music in my quiver. And before my final return to America, I became a ship's doctor. It came about in a rather curious fashion.

Book Four

HOME TO AMERICA:
TEXAS INTERLUDE

18

THE job I actually landed with the North German Lloyd was that of 'tween-decks steward in the steerage. My principal task was to remove the visible evidences of seasickness, and in those days steerage stewards worked in pairs, four hours at a time. My partner in sanitation was a German count, Martin von Minden, who had fallen on evil days. Our equipment consisted of two large iron buckets—the first containing sand, the second either empty or containing sand and something else—plus one shovel, to spread the sand where it would do the most good, and one broom. The technique was simplicity itself: after spreading the sand from the first bucket, we swept it back onto the shovel with the broom, emptied the shovel into the second bucket, and at intervals, took the used sand away and threw it overboard.

By no stretch of the imagination could the whole enterprise be classed as an esthetic occupation. . . .

One day it was my turn to carry large iron bucket number two on deck and consign its contents to the briny deep. We were well out in the English Channel and the sea was choppy. A gray, melancholy drizzle shrouded the ship from stem to stern. That moment was one of the low points of my career; I had reached the particular point of *mal de mer* when the worst that can happen is welcome news and death loses whatever sting it possesses. I was feeling so wretched that I debated with myself whether it would be preferable to empty my bucket overside and go back to work, or hang on to the bucket and go overboard with it. At that critical moment, I heard a jeering exclamation behind me: "Some job for a rising artist!"

I had no idea anyone would know me on that boat, but I turned and there stood the natty, blue-garbed figure of the medical student who had occupied the room adjoining my own in a Munich tavern near the Karls Platz. Although we were not close friends, we had borrowed each other's books, periodicals, tobacco, and matches and kept each other company when we happened to be broke. Now it appeared that while I had descended the social ladder from would-be Leonardo to steerage steward, he had ascended from medical student to ship's doctor.

How had I fallen so low? he wanted to know.

I explained. I had gone broke once too often. There was no way a young, unknown artist who, moreover, wasn't an artist yet, could make a living in a great art center like Munich. I was on my way back to the States where art patrons were not so particular. Pawning a viola and watch, I had managed to get as far as the port of Bremen. Between Bremerhaven and the promised land there was an ocean too wide to swim, too deep to wade, and I could not walk on water, wherefore I was compelled to work my way across.

"Nothing wrong with that," replied the young medico, "but couldn't you find something better than 'tween-decks steward?"

"I tried," I told him. "I applied for the position of captain, and they turned me down. I applied successively for the position of first, second, third, and fourth navigation officers, and they turned me down. I applied for everything from chief cook to dish washer and chief engineer to stoker, and they turned me down. Eventually I landed in that epidemic of seasickness down below."

The medico meditated. "Do you know anything about medicine?" he inquired finally.

"Not a thing, thank God."

"Well, then, have you a decent suit of clothes?"

I had more than that. I possessed an almost new tailor-made broadcloth suit, a wide-brimmed, soft artist's hat, a smart tan overcoat, a pair of gold-rimmed glasses, and an assortment of flowing silk ties.

"Never mind the flowing ties," my acquaintance replied. "Go downstairs, shave, clean up, dress, then come to my office."

I did. When I came up for air, the doctor handed me a cap on which I read in golden letters the legend: *Assistenzarzt*—assistant doctor. He said, "See if it fits." The cap was a bit too large, but a wad of paper in the band would remedy that.

"And now that you have your doctor's hat," continued the doctor, "you take up your practice 'tween-decks."

Steerage passengers on the North German Lloyd in those days received free medical attendance including medicine, while first and second-class passengers were supposed to pay, and sometimes did pay, for that service. In cases where the first-class patient happened to be an unattached lady of uncertain age and loving disposition, and the doctor a good-looking male of easy adaptability, the remuneration—if not the practice—was frequently quite handsome. But nothing like that in the steerage, of course.

The prospect of returning to the 'tween-decks was not alluring. But at any rate, there would be no more large iron bucket number two connected with the work.

When we arrived at the field of operation my superior requested my former colleague, Count von Minden, to show him the sick list which the two of us had previously prepared. Certain facial contortions on the part of the count indicated that he recognized me in spite of my professional disguise and was itching for an explanation of the sudden transformation. However, intensely democratic as my instincts were, my new position of assistant doctor would not permit me to take cognizance of undignified mugging on the part of my ex-partner in large iron buckets numbers one and two. Moreover, I knew from having prepared that sick list what an astonishing number of patients awaited my ministration.

Lower bunk three was sick—seasick. I knew all the symptoms. I had experienced them in my own person. There were the watery eyes, the excessive flow of saliva from the exposed mucous membranes of the open mouth, the agitation of the muscles of the abdomen and chest, the sudden forward bending of shoulders and elongation of the neck in the effort to decrease the distance between the patient and the nearest receptacle. The diagnosis was clear in my mind. What I wanted to know was what the chief medico would do about it. My acquaintance addressed lower bunk three in the following words:

"Sick, my friend?"

Noises from the occupant of lower bunk three indicated something of that nature.

"Seasick?"

No reply.

"Vomiting any?"

The answer to that was only too obvious.

"Let me see your tongue."

The patient made a desperate attempt, alternately swallowing and projecting his tongue.

"Let me feel your pulse."

The patient made a heroic effort to extend one of his extremities.

My chief turned to me. "Doctor, give the patient the powder in the blue paper."

I made a note in a memorandum book: *Lower bunk No. 3, powder in blue paper.*

Lower bunk seven was sick. There was no question. He was seasick. The evidence was all about him. Nevertheless, the medical routine continued.

"Sick, my friend?"

A wild stare, blue lips, and a corpselike complexion indicated an affirmative reply.

"Seasick?"

"No, I'm just dying and don't care."

"Let's feel your pulse."

The case apparently was not hopeless. The man was still able to distinguish upper from lower extremities.

"Let's see your tongue."

The tongue was inspected.

Then to me, "Doctor, give the patient the powder in the blue paper." I made the entry: *Lower bunk No. 7, powder in blue paper.*

Lower and upper bunk thirteen were both sick. It was a case of interactivity complicated by sympathetic response. When one took sick, the other followed, and vice versa.

The prescription was powder in the blue paper.

By the time we had reached upper bunk forty-three I became curious. "What is the powder in the blue paper?" I inquired of my chief.

"Epsom salts."

"Oh," I ejaculated, "and is that the only medicine I am to practice with?"

"It's all you need," he informed me. "They are all seasick, and they will all recover in a few days with or without medicine. However, they are entitled to medical attention. Epsom salts hurts no one and, moreover, its therapeutic action is such that the patient knows something has been done for him and is usually contented with one application."

"Well, doctor," I said, "if that is the only treatment I have to offer, diagnosis has become a minor consideration. Why not let me practice on my own hook?" Like all ambitious neophytes I was eager to practice my new technique.

"Sure," replied the chief, "go ahead. If something important comes up, notify me and I'll see what I can do about it." With a single grin he left me to my own devices. I went ahead.

Upper bunk forty-six was sick. I went through the prescribed routine.

"Sick, my friend?"

"Seasick?"

"Vomiting any?"

"Let's see your tongue."

"Let's feel your pulse."

There really was no reason why I should have asked the last two questions. All tongues looked alike, and to the very end of my practice I never learned the exact spot on the wrist where the pulse was located. In spite of these shortcomings, I became a successful physician. In the twelve days of my practice I did not lose a single case, or have a dissatisfied patient leave the ship in search of another doctor. Had those thirteen hundred 'tween-decks passengers settled as a colony in the wide open spaces of the boundless West, I might still be their honored, revered, and respected doctor. This is not humorous bragging. Often I overheard such observations as: "I tell you, I was sicker than a dog, and that young doctor cured me with one dose!"

The business of medicine is largely a matter of confidence, plus a bed-side manner.

19

UPON my return to the United States the first job I landed was in Canton, Ohio. The celebrated front-porch campaign that hoisted William McKinley into the White House was in preparation. Part of the preparation for that, and every other political campaign before and since, was a band. The band on that occasion was the Grand Army Band, of which I first became second alto and later, first clarinet. And that is how I came to hear every speech, save one, which William McKinley made during that famous campaign, together with the oratorical offerings of innumerable minor prophets of prosperity such as G.O.P. governors, congressmen, senators, with a few future Supreme Court justices thrown in for good measure.

Well-financed delegations were pouring into Canton. Delegations of farmers from the sunburned prairies of the Middle West. Delegations of horny-handed sons of toil from the steel and tin mills of Pennsylvania. Delegations of Napoleons of finance and captains of industry. Delegations of lawyers and men of the cloth. Delegations of patriotic societies and hopeful postmasters. Delegations of Grand Army men and ex-Rebels from Old and West Virginia, Kentucky and Tennessee. Delegations from the rock-ribbed coast of Maine and the sun-kissed hills of California.

The *modus operandi* was always the same. Before the arrival of a delegation-swollen train, the band marched to the station, preceded by Joe Smith on a bicycle. Joe was private secretary to

Major and Governor McKinley. Later he became secretary to President McKinley. The band would line up in marching order in front of the depot. As the delegation tumbled out of the train, Joe Smith, tablet in hand, jotted down the name of its bellwether, along with local information for future reference.

After forming ranks, the delegation, headed by the band and Joe Smith's bicycle, started for the front porch on East Market Street. Depending on the regional character and type of delegation, we played appropriate marches . . . "Marching Through Georgia," "Dixie," "Onward, Christian Soldiers," or "The Girl I Left Behind Me."

Arrived at the front yard the delegates were ushered into a large circus tent on the grounds. If they hailed from wet territory they were regaled with two glasses of beer and one sandwich apiece. If the delegation hailed from dry territory, there were two sandwiches and one cup of coffee, followed by speeches of the minor prophets.

The ceremony in the circus tent was primarily designed to give Joe Smith time to compose the speech of the presidential candidate. Joe's speeches were always composed as a variation on three themes. Theme one dealt with how the Republican tariff had made Columbia the gem of the ocean, and contained a secondary theme touching upon the relationship of the McKinley tariff with the main theme.

Theme two was an adagio in minor, a sort of Wagnerian warning foretelling the dire consequence of fiat money. On delivering that one, the future President would extract a silver dollar from beneath his Prince Albert coat and solemnly recite: "My fellow citizens: The opposition will tell you that this silver dollar represents one hundred cents of American currency. Yet the same amount of silver contained in the dollar I hold in my hand will only purchase fifty-three cents' worth of merchandise in our sister republic across the Rio Grande," and so forth.

(I knew that dollar well. I had seen it before, or at least one exactly like it. A few years previous, while running for governor of the grand old state of Ohio, McKinley was speaking on the courthouse steps at Circleville, the capital of the Pickaway plains of Ohio. "The opposition," he said on that occasion, "will tell you that this silver dollar I am holding in my hand is worth only fifty-three cents. But I challenge any one of my intelligent audience to walk into any store in this beautiful little city and convince himself that this silver dollar will purchase one cent less than one hundred cents' worth of goods.")

Theme three depicted the saving of the Union, in which, besides Grant, Sherman and Sheridan, a certain Major McKinley had played a leading part. In case the delegation was from a Grand Army post the theme ran like this: "It is now thirty-two years since we, the boys in blue, fought for the preservation of the Union on the blood-stained battle grounds of Old Virginia. Bright-eyed and red-cheeked then, we are now again fighting shoulder to shoulder as gray-haired men against an enemy more menacing than secession—the enemy Fiat Money," and so on. If the delegation happened to hail from a Southern or border state, and was therefore likely to harbor a sprinkling of ex-rebels or sympathizers, the candidate's approach was: "It is now thirty-two years since you, the boys in gray, and we, the boys in blue, fought each other on the blood-stained battle fields of Old Virginia. Now, no longer bright-eyed and red-cheeked boys, but stooped and gray-haired men, we are fighting shoulder to shoulder against an enemy more menacing than mere secession—Fiat Money," and thus swing into the regular routine.

A frequent visitor to McKinley's Market Street home during the front-porch campaign was Marcus Alonzo Hanna. The cartoonists of the opposition press had pictured this Warwick of Ohio as a heavy-jowled, fat-paunched plutocrat, covered with dollar signs. Mark Hanna was nothing of the kind. No doubt a large-framed, bulky man in his prime, he had wasted away until the former jowls hung loosely on his skull, and the paunch had disappeared entirely. His countenance was deathly pale and he carried a heavy cane for support. Of the dollar marks, not a sign.

On these occasions Mark Hanna usually planted himself in the door frame to listen to the oratory of his protégé—or, more accurately, to the literary masterpieces of Joe Smith. Leaning on his heavy cane, the dark room behind accentuating the pallor of his complexion, with head cocked first to one side then to the other he would follow the speech and note its effect on the audience. When an especially telling point or happy phrase fell from the almost Napoleonic countenance of McKinley he would nod approvingly as if saying to himself, "He's doing all right today. I guess I better leave another check to help the good work along."

Compelled to listen to all of McKinley's speeches except one, I finally cast my vote for the boy orator of the Platte, whom I saw only once, and on that occasion I heard not one single word. On his way to Madison Square Garden, Bryan stopped for an address in the freight yards of the Canton depot. Two things induced me to secure a substitute clarinet player to fill my place in the band: First, I wanted to see and hear this Democratic ogre with my own eyes and ears; second, I resented the discourtesy implied in McKinley's refusal to meet his opponent on his home ground. When I arrived at the freight yard, William Jennings Bryan was orating from a flatcar, a huge sombrero in the hands of Carl Brown, a lieutenant of Coxey's Army, shading Bryan's already thinning hair. I was too far from the speaker to catch his words, especially as it appeared that every switch engine in the state was slamming and bumping more cars around than I ever dreamed could be assembled in Canton's modest switchyard. Odd, how they happened to be so busy just then. . . .

By the time the election of 1900 rolled around, my experience in helping tootle McKinley into the White House and a better insight into the workings of American politics had taught me the rule of never voting for a presidential candidate who had the slightest chance of election. The ballot is too precious lightly to be thrown away on candidates selected and financed by the "angels" and archangels of the two historic old parties which have managed my adopted country into the condition it is in today. Moreover, I had learned from my reading of history that most of the principles that defeated third-party candidates advocated were the stuff on which the next generation of politicians staked their glory and reputations as advanced thinkers and statesmen.

Anyhow, as the old saying has it, "You never know what is in a man until you put shoulder straps on him."

20

URING my periods of absence in Munich, a Chillicothe, Ohio, Lutheran preacher and fellow musician had forsaken soul saving in favor of promoting real-estate transactions in Texas. With McKinley safely elected I wended my way toward the Lone Star State. According to the letters I had received from my musician friend, Texas fell little, if any, short of all Utopias rolled into one.

Texas, as described by my ebullient realtor, contained the quintessence of beatitudes. Beauty and natural riches had conspired to make it the teeming center of future America. Its rolling prairies were strewn with flowers, longhorn steers, blooming cacti and white-faced Herefords. The climate was the kindest known to man. During a few weeks in the summer months it would, he confessed, get middling warm in the middle of the day. However, the nights, fanned by the Gulf breeze, were always cool. The winters, outside of a rare norther, were almost Maylike. If there was one spot on God's green earth where one could acquire health, wisdom and riches without the inconvenience of rising unduly early in the morning, Texas was it. And all that Texas needed to reach the acme of perfection was culture such as he and I were able to impart.

When I arrived at the Waco hotel, on the stationery of which these letters had been written, and inquired about my friend, I was informed he was not registered there and that they didn't know him at all. But when in despair I described his wavy locks, soft, flowing beard, and beautiful large blue eyes, the desk clerk exclaimed with a broad smile, "Sure, I know him. He's the German professor. He never stops here. He only comes here to write letters, and when he's through, goes up to the parlor to entertain the ladies. They go cuckoo over him playing the piano."

Had there been any lingering doubts left about the identity of the German professor, the cuckoo ladies would have dispelled them, for the ladies were both Emil's strength and his weakness.

But it developed that Emil was not only not registered in that hotel; he was not even a resident of Waco. He lived, it appeared, in a little jerkwater town some thirty miles up the cotton belt road. And when, at long last, I arrived at this unimpressive settlement and located his home, his wife informed me that Emil had abandoned realty in favor of the position of piano player with a road show. By keeping the telephone and telegraph wires hot for the better part of two days we finally located the prodigal parson and real-estate man.

Two days later he came storming into the house. Throwing both arms around me, he exclaimed, "Here again! United once more!" Then, paraphrasing the words of Schiller, "Oscar, Oscar, with thee I challenge the whole world to combat!"

As a preliminary to challenging the whole world to combat, and also to celebrate the reunion, we ordered a small keg of beer. The beer gone, the sordid question of money reared its ugly head. The keg of beer had just about broken the camel's back. Enough remained, however, to take us both to the nearest objective of our "prospecting tour," as Emil called it. This tour, he assured me eagerly, would open my eyes to the boundless opportunity of the Lone Star State.

The first halt was at Marlin. We were aiming to find a suitable berth for Professor Emil, late of the Conservatory of Stuttgart, and Professor Oscar, late of the Royal Academy of Art at Munich. We inquired for the whereabouts of a musician—any musician. There was one—a Mexican who played the bull fiddle and repaired watches for a living. The prospects of Professors Emil and Oscar didn't look so good to Professor Oscar. However, when we got to the Mexican bull fiddler and watch doctor, we were received with open arms. "Ah," he exclaimed enthusiastically, "you play the piano, the violin, the clarinet, the flute. You gentlemen are exactly what we are looking for. Great springs of boiling hot water have recently been discovered in this place. Before many moons, Marlin will be the American Carlsbad. Enterprising citizens have already erected the Arlington, a palatial hotel, in our midst. But alas, it still lacks an orchestra. There is a young lady in Marlin who plays a very good piano. You play the flute and clarinet. You play the violin. I play the bass violin. The orchestra is here."

After closing the watch repair shop, the bull fiddler accompanied us to the Arlington Hotel to see the manager. "Sure," said he, "that's what we got to have to make Marlin the leading spa of the United States. But our guests are few. The hotel and swimming pool virtually ate up our money. So if you gentlemen would be willing to work for—well, let's say the small sum of fourteen dollars a week, with room and board, we shall be happy to have you with us."

The small sum of fourteen dollars a week, plus room and board! I could not have been more agreeably surprised if I had received a wire from John D. Rockefeller or Pierpont Morgan saying, "I hope you won't hesitate to draw on me for whatever funds you may need."

Marlin also boasted a silver cornet band, whose leader was an honest tinsmith who tried his best to learn the cornet. He too received me with open arms, but would seven dollars a week for two rehearsals really be enough to assure my services? Rapidly figuring up that fourteen dollars, board and lodging, plus seven dollars, made twenty-one dollars plus, I reckoned it would. And while I was visiting the tinsmith, Emil had called on some of the better homes in Marlin and had returned with the promise of a good number of piano, violin, and voice pupils at one dollar a lesson. For all that the up-and-coming city of Marlin knew, the two of us might have been horsethieves in disguise. However, Texas was thirsting for culture, and in the opinion of the best minds of Marlin it appeared that we might fill the bill. In view of the reception received, I expressed my willingness to remain in Marlin right then and there. But not my friend Emil.

"There are," he said when I broached the matter, "hundreds of better prospects lying around Texas than the set-up you regard so highly in this air balloon of a burg, which may burst any day. I only brought you here to give you a taste of the boundless opportunities littering up Texas." And so we departed, reluctantly on my part, for of the two adventurers, I was the Sancho Panza.

Our next and—as it turned out—final stop was the town of Calvin, situated, as we soon were informed by all hands, in the delta between the Little and Big Brazos rivers, which in fertility surpassed the best of the valley of the Nile itself. The reason why we tarried in Calvin, a town of some three thousand population, predominantly black, saddle-colored, and yellow, was that by the time we reached it our combined capital had shrunk to eleven cents. This also explains why we registered in the best and only two-dollar, American-plan commercial hotel in the town.

Safely registered, and no questions asked concerning our skimpy luggage, we set out prospecting. In the second of the three blocks of Main Street we discovered a combination jewelry and piano store that seemed worth looking into. The owner at first seemed but mildly interested in our sales talk, but when, during the recital of our achievements, I mentioned the word "flute" he excitedly burst out, "Flute—flute! You play the flute! For God's sake, man, don't lie! Do you actually play the flute?" I had not lied.

"And have you got a flute?"

I had a flute.

"Where is it?"

It was at our room in the hotel.

"Then get it. For heaven's sake, get it. I play the flute, too. I got a whole trunk full of trios for two flutes and piano, and you're the first flute player that has hit this burg in the ten years I've been living in it."

When the flute and I returned, my friend Emil was already sitting at the piano; flute parts I and II were perched on two music stands. The combination piano and jewelry store owner was in his seventh heaven. Customers could wait. Dinner could wait. The whole world could wait, listening to flute duets with piano accompaniment. Finally, during a lull in the doodle storm, I brought up the subject of prospects.

"Prospects!" exclaimed our host, still in his paradise. "Why, men, you found them right here. This is the richest part of God's country. Between here and the Little Brazos two bales of cotton per acre is the rule. Our planters are lousy with money. Their daughters are dying for culture. This county sends not less than fifty thousand dollars a year to Saint Louis and Boston for the education of the daughters of its best families in art and music. That money should be kept here. The daughters should be kept here, and right here, with you two men to go on, we start a conservatory of art and music."

Before my eyes appeared the picture of the Royal Academy of Art in Munich, the picture of the Royal Conservatory of Music in Stuttgart. Here were two busted, though well-dressed, troubadors without diplomas, credentials or letters of credit. The thing seemed preposterous. But in my America of those days everything was possible. Besides, my friend, parson and pianist Emil, was as enthusiastic for launching a conservatory of art and music in this town of three thousand white and black souls as was our combination piano store and jewelry man.

That night the Calvin Chamber of Commerce met in special meeting. Two thousand, seven hundred dollars were subscribed in a wild outburst of enthusiasm for culture and town-boosting, with more to come. A few nights later, the city council met and presented us with the one-block city park on which to rear the Calvin, Texas, Conservatory of Art and Music.

A few days more and both Emil and I had gathered all the music and drawing and painting pupils we possibly could handle. Still as the days went by, the dimensions and curriculum of the Calvin Conservatory of Art and Music grew. Bit by bit, as occasion demanded, Emil had added voice culture, elocution, woodcarving, china-painting, and other cultural oddments. The prospective faculty was growing by leaps and bounds, too, though there were as yet but two of us.

While the Conservatory of Art and Music was getting under way, we moved our domicile and studio to the parlor and bedroom of the Reverend Corcoran. The Reverend Corcoran was from Ohio. Graduated from barkeeper to undertaker's assistant, thence to side-show barker, he was now the shepherd of a number of widely scattered members of the Methodist flock, to whom he ministered by horseback and buggy. "Cork," as we soon grew to call him, was, as behooves his calling, a total abstainer, but occasionally, following St. Paul's advice, he would take some wine for his stomach's sake.

The paper expansion of the faculty of the Conservatory began to worry me. Where were we to locate and, having located, how would we pay that oncoming army of renowned professors? I was brooding over this problem one day when a lanky and slightly disheveled gentleman entered the combination piano and jewelry store, temporarily left in my charge, and introduced himself in a deep, musical bass voice as Mr. J. Elias Ward from Boston. He was, he told me, a jeweler and watch maker. He had been lured to San Antonio on the promise of a lucrative position and eventual partnership in a rapidly growing jewelry and watch business, but by the time he arrived in San Antonio an unkind sheriff had closed the rapidly growing business. Now Mr. Ward was returning to Boston, under straitened circumstances. Would there be an opportunity of doing some watch and jewelry repairing to help him on his way?

"Wait a minute, Mr. Ward," I said, looking quickly around the store to make sure we were alone. "Don't you sing bass?"

Mr. Ward sang bass.

"And do you sing bass by note?" I continued.

"I ought to," replied Mr. Ward, "for I have sung bass in the Trinity choir of Boston for a number of years and would be there yet if that damn' San Antonio crook—"

"Never mind the San Antonio crook. I have more important business. While singing in the Trinity choir, Mr. Ward, did you form some acquaintances in Boston's musical circles; did you go out to dine and participate in concerts with prominent singers, musicians, and that sort of thing?"

J. Elias confessed that he was intimately acquainted with the musical circles of Boston and could reel off the names of prominent personages by the mile.

"Fine! Wonderful!" I burst out enthusiastically. "But, Mr. Ward, please now, no more words about beating your way back to Boston as a busted watchmaker. We have started a conservatory of art and music in this town. We need a faculty the worst way. Would you forget watch and jewelry repairing long enough to accept the position of dean of voice culture on our staff? Of course, we can't pay a salary until the conservatory is in operation. But in the meantime we can secure board and room for you at Parson Cork's." Mr. Ward accepted. The first hurdle was taken.

J. Elias was really a good bass singer, read notes, and knew his Boston. Beyond that, he played a fairly good string bass which would come in handy once the conservatory orchestra got under way.

Another faculty member appeared. It was on a Saturday. I was selling jewelry, on the boardwalk in front of the store, to the colored population of Calvin and surroundings. My friend and fellow flutist would not permit Negroes in his store, but at the same time, he was not opposed to accepting their money over a show-case counter on the sidewalk. His regular Saturday sales clerk for Afro-Americans had not shown up, so I was helping out.

Needless to say, I knew nothing about jewelry salesmanship, black or white; however, as I had been told that anything above ten cents was profit, I managed to get by. Just as I had sold an eighteen-karat solid-gold diamond engagement ring to a Negro for the sum of four bits, a somewhat seedy young man stepped up and introduced himself in German as Otto Ottokar, Count von Aron.

"And what can I do for you, Count?" I said, holding out the hand of welcome.

"I have been informed," continued the count, "that you and your associates are contemplating the establishment of a conservatory of art and music in this city and I thought perhaps I might secure a position in your institution."

"In what capacity?" I inquired.

His forte was violin.

We already had one competent violin professor in Emil. But could the count by any chance teach dramatic art?

The count thought he could—in a pinch—and the count joined the faculty at the residence of Parson Cork.

Soon after that our treasurer, the town's foremost banker, brought us the good news that a widowed sister of his in not the best of circumstances might make an excellent teacher of voice and elocution for us, as she had taken lessons in those fields. As far as we were concerned, there was no "might" about it. The good Samaritan held the purse strings and *Geld regiert die Welt—* money rules the world. When the lady showed up, she turned out to be an amazon with a voice so powerful and penetrating as to make the welkin ring. Her two specialties were "Psalms" and "Jerusalem, the Golden," and whenever she sang the latter the local population of Jerusalem rushed out of doors and asked where the fire was.

However, smoothly as everything seemed to progress, I could not rid myself of a premonition of impending catastrophe. Even the beginning of construction work on the conservatory building did not dispel my premonitions. As the foundation was laid down, the faculty would frequently sit on it, smoking pipes in the cool of the evening. I would often remark, "Boys, this thing is too good to last. Anything that goes up that easily is bound to fall." And so it did.

A typhoid epidemic hit town. A few years before there had been a yellow-fever epidemic which still haunted the memories of our fellow citizens. An exodus of the best families promptly followed the typhoid outbreak, and with the hegira went nearly all our students. The few that remained shut themselves up behind closed doors and drawn blinds. Needless to say, none of the faculty had saved a thin dime. When we accosted our Maecenas about advances on future earnings he was sorry, but money was getting very tight, and nobody knew what the future would bring.

It was all true. We could no longer make a living where we were, nor seek greener pastures, for that matter, because the terror-stricken planters had thrown a shotgun cordon around the town. Somehow, one dark night, J. Elias Ward made his escape. A night or so later Count Otto Ottokar von Aron disappeared, taking my gold-rimmed glasses with him for good luck. A few nights later I strolled out through the surrounding cotton fields, caught a freight train at a way station, and was gone. And finally, Emil departed both Calvin and this world. He died of typhoid in the little jerkwater town up the cotton belt road where I had found him.

Texas in the 'Nineties was rapidly shedding its wild and woolly past, but it was still wild and woolly enough in all conscience. To me, at any rate, woolly enough to make my life there a bore as prolonged as some of the sprees in which I engaged with my fellow escapists. The pulp writers are still at it, still trying to invest the drab existence of those days with romance. I suppose this is a harmless and non-exploitive way of making a living, and aside from the destruction of trees which it involves, I have no quarrel with it. Maybe, after all, there were villainous redskins, heroic cow-punchers, and noble ladies of the lariat. I just didn't happen to bump into any of them during my Texas sojourn. What I saw were folk, white, black, and red, fleeing from the dullness of small-town existence or the "rural idiocies" commented on by Karl Marx. The plains Indians who had roamed the Southwest had long since been buried, or pacified and herded in reservations. Geronimo and his braves were prisoners of war at Fort Sill, near Lawton in western Oklahoma. In later years I frequently came upon him peddling his autobiography. Not dreaming that a similar fate was in store for me, I thought gloomily how the mighty were fallen. Farther north, the Cheyennes had been civilized by a judicious application of force and violence and set down around Canton, Oklahoma. Chief Quanah of the Comanches was exhibiting himself and his numerous squaws at county fairs. Firewater, unnatural environment, slow pauperization, tuberculosis, and syphilis were finishing the civilization of the five civilized tribes, a process of deterioration begun by the manufacturers of Colt revolvers and barbed-wire fence.

That, as I saw it, was the "he-man country" now exalted by the pulps, and if there is anything more degrading in Satan's catalogue than a he-man country I've got to be shown. Respectable women were few and far between in the cow country and they frequently underscored their respectability by indulging in the most venomous gossip or by participating in evangelistic mass orgies—the psychological equivalent of the Greek bacchanalia with none of the beauty of the latter. These "respectables" were the representatives of the middle class set down in a hostile environment far from the amenities of the life in New England or the Middle West whence they had come. The genuine pioneer women stood out from this tight-lipped group of psalm shouters. The sagas that are written today about *them* are real.

The professional he-men, for the most part, liked to pose as two-fisted, hairy-chested hell-raisers who were always talking about looking any man in the eye and telling him to go to hell. I noticed that they wilted before the icy glare of bankers, bill collectors, and gun toters just as fast as those of us who possessed more sparsely covered chests. The he-man's conception of the pursuit of happiness was the chasing of skirts and firewater. In this feeble substitute for adult life I confess that I joined for a while. One day I woke with an aching head and a sudden disgust with all things wild, woolly, hairy-chested and he-man. I came back north to leave to pulp writers the glorification of those "romantic" days which I found so dull.

But before departing let me draw one more Texas sketch.

21

AT the outbreak of the Spanish-American War in 1898 I had become, of all things, the director of a military band in a small town in Texas. As extenuating circumstances let me plead that I had hit that particular town dead broke. After stepping out of a side-door sleeper, without step or porter, I was meandering up Main Street in the hope of locating something in the nature of bed, board, and smokes. I did. From the open door of a jewelry store came the wail of a tortured clarinet. On entering the place I discovered the disturber of the peace in the form of a rotund, tow-headed Swede. He was, as I later discovered, an excellent citizen, a good provider and a devout Lutheran, but he certainly couldn't play the clarinet. One of his troubles was that his instrument had a reed entirely too thin for the production of good tone.

"Come, friend," I interrupted the artist, "let me have that instrument, and I'll show you how to play it." He complied, thereby furnishing additional testimony, if such were needed, that he was not a clarinet player, for what master of that instrument would entrust its delicate bamboo sliver beneath the mouthpiece to the profaning lower teeth of a total stranger! Next I asked him if he had any more reeds. He had—a boxful. I selected one and attached it to the mouthpiece. Then I turned the pages of the instruction book until I came to one of the most difficult exercises it contained.

There was method in that madness. Not merely that I was in good practice. I knew that particular exercise by heart. I could play it backward and forward, blindfolded and with one hand tied behind my back. It was the exercise my German veteran clarinet teacher had inflicted on me every time he suffered from *Katzenjammer* or had a quarrel with his wife, which was often.

Before I was through, the store and clarinet proprietor grabbed my arm and exclaimed excitedly, "Man alive, what are you doing in this town?"

"I'm prospecting for a suitable location," I replied.

"You've found it," he almost shouted. "Watch the store, until I come back." And with that he stormed out of doors, leaving me in charge of clarinet and the jewelry stock. A few minutes later the jeweler-clarinetist returned, accompanied by an equally excited lover of culture. The two, it developed, were members of a six-man-power clarinet section of a newly organized band in which my patron occupied the first chair. Negotiations followed. Thinking seriously of the next meal, I let the twain persuade me to become the mentor of the aforesaid clarinet battery. The consideration was a dollar-fifty per week per man, making a total of nine dollars a week. In addition, they accompanied me to the best boarding house in town and guaranteed the board of the "professor." Prosperity had again turned the corner.

As it happened, there was a band rehearsal that night, and I was requested to direct. New brooms sweep clean. After an hour or so, a keen musical ear might have detected the tune the band was attacking. Would I accept the leadership of the band at an honorarium of twenty dollars a week? The band was awful. But so was the state of my finances. While my ears voted "nay," my stomach voted "aye," and the ayes had it.

It never became quite clear to me how the band had earned the prefix "military." Its members were peaceful, law-abiding citizens who, apparently, had nothing further from their minds than sticking bayonets into total strangers. We wore military uniforms, of course, but who had supplied them—or why—was a mystery to me. Also, there *was* a company of militia somehow connected with the outfit, and we served as band for these more martial spirits. But even the members of the militia gave no inkling of homicidal proclivities. Most of them were scions of the best families—clerks, bookkeepers, and counterjumpers—decent, gentle, soft-spoken men one and all. Even the privates, of whom there were a few, gave the suspicion that the murderous implements on their shoulders were purely for decoration.

The company also sported a number of auxiliary aides, recruits from the gentler sex, who looked perfectly stunning in their natty blue officers' coats, gold-braided cappies and white flannel skirts. In fact, they were so charming that they almost revived in me my youthful aspirations for the life of a soldier.

For the most part the exploits of company and band were of a social nature. When the company went on dress parade, we played the marches. When it held a dance we played the tunes. And once, when the ladies' auxiliary of the company gave the light opera *The Chimes of Normandy*, we furnished the accompaniment in a manner which, had the composer been present, might have caused him to wonder where and when he had heard something almost like that before.

All in all, it was the most peaceful and enjoyable soldiering I had hitherto witnessed. Then, like a bolt from the blue sky, came the outbreak of the Spanish-American War.

Joe Wheeler, one of the minor heroes of the Confederacy, was appointed commander-in-chief of the now happily reunited boys in blue and gray. Teddy Roosevelt was recruiting his Rough Riders. The *Maine* was sunk in Havana harbor. Lieutenant Hobson of the *Merrimac* bottled up the Spanish fleet in Santiago harbor and Hearst was yelling bloody murder. Excitement grew from day to day. Temperatures rose from warm to hot to the boiling point.

Our company drilled every evening, and the band played "Dixie" on every occasion. From "Dixie" we progressed to "The

Star Spangled Banner"—until then barred from sunny Dixie. If the turmoil had lasted much longer we might have progressed to the point of playing "Marching Through Georgia" in the very heart of Dixie. Finally, when the company marched off to the bloody slaughter, we played "The Girl I Left Behind Me"— and remained to console the girl.

However, it was not the fault of the band members that they remained behind—after all those weeks of heroic tooting. Like the rest, they had been so thoroughly fed up on Spanish atrocities, beautiful doñas languishing in Cuban dungeons, dark and dank, and the fell doings of Butcher Weyler in the lines of arson, rape, mayhem and homicide, that they were ready to exterminate Spanish mackerels themselves. Whatever deeds of glory were left undone by those bandsmen, blame on me. Whatever lives I saved from Spanish bullets and embalmed beef, may the recording angel debit to my credit.

For weeks I had argued with the boys, from piccolo to bass drum, not to jeopardize their lives and comfort in far-off Cuba.

"Boys," I said, "for all I know these atrocity tales may be true. In fact, they ought to be true, provided antiquity lends veracity, for they have been repeated in every war since Samson slew three thousand Philistines with the jawbone of an ass. But even so, Cuba is far away. It's a fearfully hot country. There are no ice houses, refrigerating plants, or breweries in Cuba. If you go there they will make you sleep on the hard ground with no other cover than the dome of heaven. You will be lousy wherever a louse can get a toehold, or find a hair to hang on. They will make you march miles and miles when it's a hundred and twenty in the shade, and the shade is over in the next county. They will feed you on hardtack that entered the last stage of petrification when Lee surrendered at Appomatox, and corned beef Mrs. Noah put up for the voyage to Mt. Ararat. If you get sick or wounded, medical apprentices will fill you full of calomel, explore your inners with post-hole diggers and remove your extremities with bucksaws; and if you die, the buzzards will get you.

"What on earth do you want to go to Cuba for? Here you are—solid, substantial citizens with businesses to take care of, wives to love, children to cherish. You sleep on box mattresses, you eat three square meals per in the bosom of your families. When you feel hot and sticky, you go under the shower. When you feel hot and thirsty, you send the boy to the corner drug store for a glass of lemonade or you go over to Bill's saloon and treat yourself to a brace of foaming schooners. If anybody has to fight those greasers, then lay your clerks, errand boys and hoe hands on the altar of your fatherland. They are raring to fight and have nothing else to fight for anyhow. So, let's content ourselves playing 'The Girl I Left Behind Me' when the boys embark for foreign shores and practice 'Home Again' in anticipation of their return."

However, I was a pacifist voice crying in the wilderness, for when war comes through the front door, reason flies out through every window. The boys voted thirty to one to go, and instructed the one to offer the services of our band to the governor of the state.

This I did. I wrote a twelve-page letter to His Excellency, telling him all about the personnel of our band, the kind of lives they led, the nice things they were accustomed to, the comforts they enjoyed, the responsible positions they occupied, the properties and enterprises depending on their managerial ability and added that in spite of all this they were willing to toot for flag and country provided he could assure them that their accustomed standards of living would not be disturbed by the warlike doings in Cuba.

Three days later I received a wire from the commander of the armed forces of Texas saying:

"SIR, WE WANT MEN TO FIGHT AND NOT TO BLOW.

"CULBERTSON, GOVERNOR."

When I read the telegram to the assembled bandmen they went up in the air and swore they wouldn't fight Spain now if the governor went down on his knees and begged them to. By the time the veterans returned from Cuba, Puerto Rico, the Philippine Islands and parts east, they had cooled off sufficiently to render "Home Again" in better tone and with more feeling than I ever thought them capable of.

And that's how it came about that when Teddy rode up San Juan Hill and down again I was among the missing; and how I escaped my part of the responsibility for paying Spain twenty million dollars for the Philippine Islands, which we have now dropped like a hot brick.

During my Texas odyssey I came as near to taking the grand tobogganslide toward what good souls call perdition as I ever hope to again. On the other hand, I hope the reader will not fall into the fatal error of accusing the bad Texas boys of leading this good little boy astray. I never had any difficulty meeting Dame Temptress at least halfway and greeting her smilingly with, "Well, lady, what can I do for you?"

After my departure from the Lone Star State, I directed the Lafayette, Indiana, military band for a summer season and then returned to Circleville, Ohio, where I had earned my first fortune as a portrait painter.

Book Five

TROUBADOR TO ATLAS

22

THE period after my return north marked a new direction in my career. I made the transition from light-hearted troubador to Atlas—the overworked uplifter who carries the world on his shoulders. There were various reasons for this inward change, among them the fact that I was married. Artists and other persons afflicted with artistic temperaments should not marry. They make brilliant lovers but darn poor husbands. . . .

At almost shockingly short intervals, three sons had made their appearances. Had I known Margaret Sanger then as well as I learned to know her later, these boys would certainly have been better spaced. However, as all three of my sons have long since happily married, have made honest livings, presented me with five splendid grandsons and one granddaughter who soon will be out of college (my youngest child and only daughter, born many years later, has only just passed from the first to the second grade), and as all of them are much better-behaved children than their dad and granddad ever was, there is no complaint on my part.

But during the period of which I write, the burden was rather heavy. I have already mentioned that my five years in Munich had ruined me as a popular portrait painter. There was, however, a still deeper reason why it had become increasingly difficult to make a living at my profession. The machine had invaded the field of portraiture. Cheap solar prints smoothed off by air brush had become so common that large portraits were found in the poorest of homes. There is, of course, no reason why people of low income should not have their dear ones immortalized. People of means and taste, however, would not tolerate these cheap portraits in their homes, but neither would they invest their money in more worthy objects of art. I have no data, but I doubt if in the closing years of the last century there were more than a few dozen portrait painters in the whole of the United States who made a decent living, drawing and painting portraits from life. The machine output had destroyed their scarcity value.

So, back to music. I organized a juvenile band, a thing common enough now but almost unknown in those days. I suspect I may have been a fairly good music teacher, incidentally, for out of that juvenile band of about twenty-five members, one became first clarinetist in a leading American symphony orchestra, another the solo trumpeter of Sousa's band, and a third the well known jazz king, Ted Lewis. In my later travels I frequently ran across the name of Ted Lewis, but how could I connect him with the Theodore Friedman to whom I had taught the clarinet in Circleville? He must have been around eight years old then; his fingers were still too short to cover the holes and keys of a B-flat clarinet, which is why I taught him the much shorter E-flat. Theodore was talented, and above that, loved music.

Besides one regular lesson and one regular rehearsal each week, I used to hold a class in ensemble playing at which attendance was voluntary. Theodore lived only a block or so from our "conservatory" in the third floor of the town hall. While holding these classes in ensemble playing, I often noticed him playing marbles on the courthouse plaza across the street. But when he heard the harmonies proceeding from the third floor of the town hall, he would pick up his marbles, disappear around the corner, and a few minutes later enter the classroom, his little E-flat clarinet in hand. Theodore couldn't stay away from music.

With the bitter memory of my military musical animal trainers still in mind, I took particular care not to overburden my pupils with scales, arpeggios and finger exercises. True, we played them, too, and as much as the youngsters would stand for. But between these absolutely necessary musical evils I provided a sweetening of such simple melodies and harmonies as the songs of Stephen Foster. Forty years later, when I heard Ted Lewis's troupe for the first time in a Los Angeles movie house, I was agreeably surprised to discover that he still employed some of these old American classics in his repertoire.

Much as I loved music, and the teaching of music, I was barely able to support my growing family. Something more substantial was required, and I began to look around for it. A friend of my earlier days was now engaged in the life-insurance business in Columbus. He invited me to join him, and to Columbus I went. Life insurance inevitably held little attraction for me, but I had to make a living, and as it turned out, I made not only a living, but considerably more. I am persuaded that had I loved either life insurance or money enough, I might well have made my fortune. The reason for this was not my superior knowledge of insurance, of which I learned virtually nothing and cared less; it was simply that I found salesmanship easy. I make friends easily, high or low. I can tell a good story and talk fairly intelligently on almost any subject. Above that, I like people; and like to be liked by people.

Thanks to my musical background, I became active in the German singing societies of Columbus. My knowledge of the German classics and painting resulted in my being elected director in chief of the pageant commemorating the hundredth anniversary of the death of Schiller. I welcomed the opportunity to try this new kind of cultural enterprise. My Munich days had taught me a great deal in that field, and the problems fascinated me. I had drawings made of groups which were to represent Schiller's great dramas—*Maid of Orleans, The Robbers, Mary Stuart, William Tell, Don Carlos, Wallenstein's Camp, The Piccolomini, Wallenstein's Death, The Muses* and *Song of the Bell.*

We secured costumes from the leading costume houses and theaters of the country. The breweries of Columbus lent us some four hundred Percheron horses. When, on a bright May day, that colorful pageant passed under the canopy of spring-clad trees, it was a thing of sheer joy and beauty. All this helped to make me known and liked in Columbus.

My life-insurance customers were largely well-to-do German bakers, butchers, grocers, and brewery owners, and there was the Catholic hierarchy—including the bishop of the diocese and Monsignor Joseph Soenthgerath of the Josephiniun Orphan Home and Seminary, of whom more later. No, I had not rejoined the church for business reasons. Whatever my faults, whatever my histrionic talents, I did not play the hypocrite. I had met these priests in the line of business, had found some well-read, highly educated, clean, upstanding men among them. None was averse to hearing a good story or drinking a bottle of wine to lubricate the tongue while the two of us were warmly discussing (and usually disagreeing on) some problems of the times.

Yes, I might have become a very successful insurance agent, perhaps even an insurance magnate, but something happened. Tom Lawson had written his *Frenzied Finance*. The leading magazines, the *American, Harper's, Everybody's, McClure's,* broke out in a spate of muckraking articles by Ida Tarbell, Lincoln Steffens, Ray Stannard Baker, Charles Edward Russell and others. Insurance scandals were aired in the courts of New York before future Supreme Court Justice Hughes. Of course I read all of it, and reading all of it I became ruined as a future insurance magnate. As I have said, I could sell almost anything by selling myself. But before selling myself I had to believe in the immaculate conception of the thing I sold. And judging by my reading of the muckrakers, life insurance and high finance were a hell of a way from being immaculate.

Another thing happened about that time. Some well-meaning world saver had handed me Henry George's *Progress and*

Poverty. And did I eat it up, and having eaten it up, did I preach single tax to all who would hear or could not think of some excuse to get out of hearing! In an ill-fated moment I even preached single tax to an intelligent socialist doctor by the name of Addel, who got even with me by handing me Bellamy's *Looking Backward*.

But before getting too deep into *Looking Backward*, I ran as single taxer for the legislature of Ohio. I was one of Tom L. Johnson's young men. Newton Baker, later Woodrow Wilson's Secretary of War, was another of them. Peter Witt, the iron molder, and for a third of a century one of the leading lights in the municipal government of Cleveland, was another. Frederic C. Howe, who ended as a New Dealer and who was as clean and sincere as they make them, was still another.

Sure, I got beaten. Who wants world savers to make laws for a world that refuses to be saved? I did, however, get one more valuable political lesson out of that campaign to cap the one I had learned by tooting my clarinet in McKinley's front yard. The Democratic boss of Franklin County, in which Columbus is located, had patiently explained to me that while my political and economic views were all right, and he was all for them, it would require some money to have me elected.

My friend, Tom L. Johnson, who wanted to see me elected the worst way, was many times a millionaire. The boss's advice was for me to see Tom L. and pull his leg for a contribution to the campaign fund of the Democratic party of Franklin County, Ohio. So I went to Cleveland to see Tom L. There was nothing wrong in pulling his leg for such a worthy, even world-saving cause as the single tax. However, I did not go alone. The Democratic sheriff and the probate judge of the county accompanied me in the capacity of spiritual advisers. When we got to Johnson's palatial residence on Euclid Avenue, my two advisers advised me to see Tom L. alone. He was a single taxer and friend of mine. He would do more for me than for the whole Democratic party of Franklin County.

Tom received me most kindly. The first question he asked me after I stated my mission was, "Did you come by yourself?" No, I said, the sheriff and probate judge of Franklin County had come with me, but had decided I'd better see him alone.

"I thought so," mused Tom L. "They were afraid to face me. You are already doomed, my boy. The deal is made. The county offices are to go to their Democratic friends, the state offices, including your office, to their Republican friends." I was thunderstruck. But when the returns were in, the election had gone as he forecast, and I was out in the cold.

What about Edward Bellamy and his *Looking Backward?* Yes, yes, *Looking Backward.* A great book. A very great book. One of the greatest, most prophetic books this country has produced. It didn't make me look backward, it made me look forward, and I haven't got over looking forward since I read *Looking Backward.* Neither did *Looking Backward* cure me of the single tax. It did worse than that by bringing on the complication of single taxer and socialist from which I am still painlessly suffering.

Unable to usher in the combination of single tax and co-operative commonwealth before the next month's rent fell due, I went back to music, became leader of the Liederkranz capelle, started another juvenile band, and preached my complication of economics to bandsmen, pupils, audiences and passers-by. Through my connection with the musicians' union I became delegate to the Trades-of-Labor Assembly, and as the most eloquent, scholarly and best-qualified prophet of that proletarian body finally became editor in chief and publisher of my first paper, *The Labor World.* This was in 1903. Years later I was to write, from a long and tempestuous experience as editor of successive but by no means successful labor papers: "Running a labor paper is like feeding melting butter on the end of a hot awl to an infuriated wildcat."

In those May days I had, of course, no intimations of the *Sturm und Drang* to which a labor editor is constantly subjected.

Liberal-minded youngsters with a commendable itch for expressing themselves on the subject of this cockeyed world, with special
reference to the plight of the workers therein, are always asking
me how to break into what, with a slight tone of awe, they speak
of as "labor journalism." I can only tell them what I did with
my *Labor World*, which is, sit down and write pieces presumably
of interest to workers and then try to get labor to read them.
I go on to inform these eager novitiates that the various tasks
set for Hercules were child's play compared with the job of
getting a laborer to read his own labor paper. In most cases members of a union are forced, willy-nilly, to subscribe to their official
paper since the subscription is included in their dues. But this
does not imply that they read it. Neither is this neglect wholly
the fault of the union member. A worker coming home at night
pooped out by his day's occupation of putting nut three hundred
and eighty-six into hole seven hundred and seventy-seven is not
exactly in the mood to read fulsome accounts of the junketings
of his union officials, adorned with flattering pictures of these
same officials and their families enjoying themselves at the expense of the local union treasury.

Skipping rapidly over this routine front-page "must" material, the worker is next confronted with so-called "educational"
items consisting of a mish-mash of boiler plate of the sort contained in the inside pages of a small-town weekly, conveying the
exciting statistics of the number of quadruplets born annually in
Borneo, or the amazing performances of a whistling pony in
Arizona. Following this inspiring section is one supposedly devoted to the interest of women. This consists of excerpts from
the syndicated writings of Emily Post and her imitators, and
keeps the wives of coal diggers, boiler makers and organized
steam-shovel operators *au courant* as to the approved method of
answering an invitation to a débutante's coming-out party or
arranging a dainty luncheon for twelve at the country club. There
are also patterns for sports clothes and evening gowns upon which

the workers' wives, clad in their latest-model day dresses, gaze with tired eyes.

The back page of most labor papers is devoted to editorials. These are usually pieces of sales promotion for the union which is subsidizing the sheet in which they appear: Under the beneficent aegis of the present union administration (which it is to be hoped will be unanimously re-elected at the next convention), significant gains, the worker learns, have been made for the rank and file all along the line. It is true that in view of the current economic depression the officials *were* obliged to accept a slight cut in wages and lengthening of hours for their membership. But this retreat, if retreat it can be called, is purely a strategic one and is really but the preliminary to a general forward march. If, as sometimes happens, the radicals in the membership are stirring uneasily, an editorial referring—in the days of my youth to "anarchists," later to "socialists," and in the days of my old age, to "Stalinists"—blisters hell out of the leftists in a style which a *Saturday Evening Post* editorial writer might well envy.

Is it any wonder that the weary worker hands the labor paper over to his wife for shelf lining or other more intimate uses and turns to the pulp magazines or the sports pages of the local capitalist "kept press"? Is it any wonder that the weird journalistic offerings of William Randolph Hearst, labor-baiter and yellow reactionary that he is, are still the favorite reading matter of millions of American workmen?

"But," say my inquiring youngsters, "isn't it true that the labor press is freer than 'the kept press'? Can't you write pretty much what you please?"

To my deep regret I am forced again to shake my head. "No, sonny," I answer. "The labor press is like any other court organ. With some honorable exceptions, I have found that the union officials regard their editor as no more than a subsidized plugger for the songs which the officials sing. The union hierarchy looks with the darkest suspicion upon any deviation on the editor's part from the accepted rôle of court jester and press agent. Though the editor is invariably the lowest-paid of all the union's official family, evidence of independent thinking or a tendency to indulge in frank criticism of any phase of union policy serves to separate the editor from even the meager pay envelope that is his."

If by this time my questioner is still with me, he then asks: "How can a journalist who wants to write as he pleases and at the same time line up on labor's side get a job that will at once keep him free and fed?"

I then tell him of my lifelong ambition to establish a genuinely free paper with a national circulation and a grass-roots, rank-and-file appeal which would attract just such alert-minded youngsters as himself, and tell him to go to it. But—and here I scratch my dolefully wagging head.

"You must know," I say, "that although the authors of the Bill of Rights assured us that the freedom of the press could not be abridged by any act of Congress, they neglected to state that it could and would be abridged by every conceivable act of impervious advertisers, paper and ink manufacturers, printing-machinery makers, distributing agencies and other sordid minions of the capitalist system who refuse to accept declarations of journalistic independence in lieu of non-bouncing checks. Just take that single item of advertising, which of course is the sole reason for the existence of our commercial, or if you like, 'kept' press. After all, advertisers have an understandable aversion to committing suicide and a disinclination to aid and abet those who are urging them down the path to self-destruction. It is a man-sized job to persuade an advertiser, let's say of privately owned public utilities, to pay space rates for his advertisement in a paper that is telling its readers that the owners of these utilities are a bunch of conscienceless pirates who should be hanged, drawn, and quartered for the public good. If the prospective advertiser happens to have a product well outside the realm of controversy, he still hesitates to use a paper whose readers are so admittedly poverty stricken as to be unable to buy a bag of branded prunes. He will pick up your paper and read an article proving conclusively that the purchasing power of the farmers, laborers and liberals who are your subscribers is not only being steadily whittled down by the 'system,' but is likely to disappear altogether. If he has any brains, and some advertisers do have agents with some brains, he will then assure you that, while all that your editorial says may be true, he is not spending his appropriation to advertise automobiles, cigars or snappy clothing to the potential tenants of a collective poorhouse."

When I see how low the mind of my young questioner is becoming, I admit that there are some exceptions to this black picture. I tell him the story of the solicitor for a socialist paper who was attempting to persuade a hard-bitten Republican owner of a widely advertised cathartic to use the "radical rag," as the Republican put it. All the stock arguments failing, the socialist finally exclaimed: "What the hell! Socialists get just as constipated as Republicans or Democrats." And that got him the order. But that was a rare exception. The important advertisers, of cigarettes, packaged foods, household accessories, automobiles, and so on, are not only indifferent to the advertising solicitors for left-wing papers; they are generally, and understandably, hostile. Which pretty well eliminates advertising as our chief source of revenue.

"But what about circulation?"

"Now, sonny, you're getting warm. But here again the sordid matter of cold cash insinuates its slimy presence, because circulation costs money, as a great many well-heeled promoters of purely commercial enterprises have found to their sorrow. My old editor buddy, Charles Ervin, likes to quote the saying, 'Get circulation, and all things shall be added unto you.' But getting circulation on a national scale is no peanut-stand job. It means an outlay for promotion by direct mail, national advertising, and word of mouth that usually sinks the promoter by the time the first issue of his paper is on the stands. It means organizing a bunch of loyal followers who will, at the cost of great sacrifice, go out after their day's work is over and sell subs. It means—"

"Oh, well, skip it," says our discouraged youth, preparing to depart before any more cold water is poured over his dream of a free press.

"Hold on," I say. "All that I have said does not mean that it can't be done. In fact it has been done right here in the United States of America and in the face of the tremendous odds that I have been describing." And then I tell him a little of the success of *The Appeal to Reason,* the socialist weekly that flourished so lustily before the war, and of the triumphs of *The Milwaukee Leader* in the early days, and of the heroic achievements of the socialist *Call* in New York in the darkest of the war days.

"But," says my no longer starry-eyed lad, "all that is old stuff. You old-timers just sit around like Civil War veterans mumbling your gums about Antietam. You tell us what a great movement you had 'before the war.' You tell us what a great press you had 'before the war.' You tell us how up-and-coming everything was 'before the war.' We're sick of this 'before the war' stuff. We're living after one war and maybe, who knows, before another. But we're living in this present, this here and now, and when we propose doing anything about things here and now you set your nostalgic tear ducts watering. You trot off to your G.A.R. wailing wall. I'm going to start something—here and now."

And hearing the echoes of my own youthful protests against the defeatism of the ancients of my own days, I suddenly realize that there is more to that youngster than a naïve enthusiasm. Maybe, after all, he will go and do as I did in 1903, sit down and start writing and let the chips fall where they may. And here's hoping these here-and-now kids will have fewer of the headaches and all of the sheer joy that was my lot when I started pioneering in that fantastic world of labor journalism.

At this juncture some long-memoried reader may want to know why I didn't take up my former connection as humorous contributor to *Judge* and *Puck?* What an idea, to play around with amusing trifles designed for patrons of saloons and barber shops when the world was so obviously out of joint and no one but me to set it right! Life, for me, had become earnest, at least, and rather more real, too.

My new seriousness was not wholly due to Henry George and Edward Bellamy. There was another man who influenced me toward socialism and reform. That one was none other than a Catholic priest, Monsignor Soenthgerath, whom I have already mentioned. Monsignor was widely read, a profound thinker, and sympathetic to the aspirations of the great unwashed. When discussing my pet theories, he would often say, "You are talking quite enthusiastically, but what you don't know about the subject is appalling. Come on, let me give you this book or that book to read. It will clarify your mind."

Among the books he gave me was *Socialism and the Socialist Movement in the Nineteenth Century* by Werner Sombart. I still have it. Another was a small volume, *The Quintessence of Socialism* by Dr. Schaeffle. Neither author was a socialist. Sombart at that time was professor of economics at the University of Breslau. Dr. Schaeffle had been minister of finance of the Austrian Empire. In one other book, the *Impossibility of Social Democracy*, he had outlined a program of social legislation as the best method of combating socialism à la Marx. Bismarck had borrowed that program from Schaeffle. So did the New Deal, eighty years after Schaeffle had supplied the inspiration.

But while neither Sombart nor Schaeffle were believers in socialism, they were both clear thinkers and intellectually honest. They gave me a better understanding of both the strength and weakness of the socialist movement, by which Sombart, especially, understood the trinity of the labor union, co-operatives, and political organizations of labor, than any other socialist work has done.

The smallness of the dent made by the labor press upon the public as a whole, even in the days of our "before the war" glory, is illustrated by the manner in which the industrial-union program of the C.I.O. was covered by this latter-day generation of newspapermen. Most of the news stories and editorials treated the concept of industrial unionism as though it were something thought up one night by the active brain of John L. Lewis. It had, however, been a subject of violent controversy years before the present Socialist Party was founded by Eugene Debs, Victor Berger and Morris Hillquit in 1900. The Knights of Labor, the first large-scale organization of the workers in this country, had industrial unionism as opposed to craft unionism for one of its central aims. Socialists advocating industrial or mass organization were abused by Sam Gompers and his hierarchy as vehemently as communists now are abused by William Green, Gompers' successor as head of the American Federation of Labor. Yet all this far-flung fighting received the scantiest notice in the capitalist press, which first paid any really serious attention to the matter as late as 1935, when the Committee for Industrial Organization started.

I had early aligned myself on the side of the industrial unionists and one of my first editorials in *The Labor World* was on this subject. Because it attracted the attention of the Brewery Workers Union, the first large-scale industrial union in America, and because it took me to another of my Americas, namely, New Orleans and the industrial South, I am reprinting that editorial here:

"UNION SCABS"—AND OTHERS

There are three kinds of scabs—the professional, the amateur, and the union scab.

The professional scab is usually a high-paid, competent worker in the employ of strike-breaking and detective agencies. His position is that of a special officer in the regular scab army.

The amateur scab brigade is composed of riffraff, slum dwellers, rubes, imbeciles, college students, and other undesirable citizens.

Professional scabs are few and efficient. Amateur scabs are plentiful and deficient, and union scabs are both numerous and capable.

The professional scab knows what he is doing, does it well, and for the sake of the long green only.

The amateur scab, posing as a free-born American citizen who scorns to be fettered by union rules and regulations, gets much glory (?), little pay, and when the strike is over he is given an honorable discharge in the region where Darwin searched for the missing link.

Traits of the Union Scab

The union scab receives less pay than the professional scab, works better than the amateur scab, and doesn't know that he is a scab. He will take a pattern from a scab pattern-maker, cast it into a union mold, hand the casting to as lousy a scab as ever walked in shoe leather and then proudly exhibit a paid-up union card as testimony of his unionism.

Way down in his heart he seems to have a lurking suspicion that there is something not altogether right in his actions, and it is characteristic of the union man who co-operates with scabs that he is ever ready to flash a union card in the face of innocent bystanders.

He doesn't know that a rose under any other name is just as fragrant; he doesn't know that calling a cat a canary won't help make the feline sing, and he doesn't know that helping to run a shop while other workers bend all their energies in the opposite direction is scabbing. He relies on the name and seeks refuge behind a little pasteboard card.

Must Tie Up Plant

When a strike is declared it becomes the chief duty of the organization to effect a complete shut-down of the plant. For that purpose warnings are mailed, or wired to other places, to prevent workingmen from moving on the afflicted city.

Pickets are stationed around the plant or factory, or harbor, to stop workers from taking the places of the strikers. Amateur scabs are coaxed, persuaded, or bullied away from the seat of the strike. Persuasion having no effect on the professional strike-breaker, he is sometimes treated to a brickbat shower. "Shut down the plant; shut it down completely," is the watchword of the strike.

Now, while all these things are going on and the men are stopped in ones and twos, a steady stream of dinner-pail paraders pour through the factory gate. Why are they not molested? Oh, they're union men, belonging to a different craft than the one on strike. Instead of brickbats and insults it's "Hello, John; hello, Jim; howdy, Jack," and other expressions of good fellowship.

"57 Varieties"

You see, this is a carriage factory, and it is only the Amalgamated Association of Brimstone and Emery Polishers that are striking. The Brotherhood of Oil Rag Wipers, the Fraternal Society of White Lead Daubers, the Undivided Sons of Varnish Spreaders, the Benevolent Compilation of Wood Work Gluers, the Iron Benders' Sick and Death Benefit Union, the Oakdale Lodge of Coal Shovelers, the Martha Washington Lodge of Ash Wheelers, the Amalgamated Brotherhood of Oilers, the Engineers' Protective Lodge, the Stationary Firemen, the F.O.O.L., the A.S.S.E.S. Societies have nothing to do with the Amalgamated Association of Brimstone and Emery Polishers. The whole thing is like beating a man's brains out and then handing him a headache tablet.

How Men "Scab"

During a very bitterly fought molders' strike in a northern city the writer noticed one of the prettiest illustrations of the workings of plain scabbing and union scabbing. A dense mass of strikers and sympathizers were assembled in front of the factory waiting the exit of the strike-breakers. On they came, scabs and unionists in one dark mass. Stones, rotten eggs and other missiles began to fly, when one of the strikers leaped on a store box and shouted frantically: "Stop it, stop it, for God's sake stop it, you are hitting more unionists than scabs."

That's it! Whenever scabs and union men work harmoniously in the strike-breaking industry all hell can't tell the difference.

To the murky conception of a union scab, scabbing is only wrong when practiced by a non-union man. To him the union card is a kind of scab permit that guarantees him immunity from insults, brickbats and rotten eggs.

After having instructed a green bunch of amateur scabs in the art of brimstone and emery polishing all day, he meets a striking brother in the evening and forthwith demonstrates his unionism by setting up drinks for the latter.

Union scabbing is the legitimate offspring of craft organization. It is begotten by ignorance, born of imbecility and nourished by infamy.

"My dear brother," said the sheriff, "I am sorry to be under contract to hang you, but I know it will please you to hear that the scaffold is built by union carpenters, the rope bears the union label, and here is my union card."

23

THE strike I had come to conduct was a jurisdictional one, and those are the most ruinous of all strikes. The contract of the brewery workers with the local brewery owners had expired, and the union submitted a new agreement containing minor changes. The owners no doubt would have signed the agreement submitted. But now the A. F. of L. demanded that the employer enter into separate contracts with the craft organizations over which the Federation claimed jurisdiction. There were about half a dozen of these craft unions. The largest among them were the teamsters, engineers, and firemen. Among the smaller ones were the electricians, coopers, machinists, ice pullers, and ash wheelers. From the viewpoint of the Brewery Workers Union, all these people were engaged in the manufacture and delivery of beer and consequently all were brewery workers. Moreover, they had been organized by the Brewery Workers Union and had been members of it since its inception in 1884.

To me, the attempt to tear up one of the oldest, cleanest and most progressive unions in the land appeared criminal. There had been no demand for separation on the part of the craftsmen over whom the A. F. of L. claimed jurisdiction. They fought against separation from the Brewery Workers Union to the bitter end. The brewery owners, on their part, had become reconciled to the industrial form of organization in their establishments.

193

Instead of a dozen contracts expiring at different times, there was only one contract. Once signed, the brewery workers lived up to it religiously. The racketeering which curses so many craft unions was absent in the industrial organization of the united brewery workers. So were graft and bribe taking.

Multiplication of unions in the same plant multiplied points of conflict and therefore meant more strikes. The brewery owners would have preferred no union at all, of course. But if union there must be, one was better than many. Besides, they were making money hand over fist. Beer, selling at five cents the pint, cost them around seventy cents the barrel. Whatever small increase of wages was demanded in the new contract could easily be offset by improved machines and processes or the simple expedient of putting more water in the beer. There was no end of water in the Mississippi, flowing right past New Orleans. So, on the whole, the brewery owners were willing to sign up with us.

But now the brewery owners found themselves between the devil and the deep blue sea. If they signed with our organization, the A. F. of L. would boycott their beer. If they signed with the craft unions, who, by the way, didn't have a single member employed in their breweries, we would strike against the plants.

The strike started in the Columbia brewery, adjoining the Elysian Field—a mass of railroad tracks and switches. The president of the Columbia was the very opposite of the typical brewery lord as popularly pictured then. Instead of being fat, he was slim. Instead of being red-faced, he was pale-faced. Instead of swilling beer, he devoured books. Instead of associating with lowbrows, he craved the company of highbrows. He was, in brief, a gentleman, a scholar, and what would be called, nowadays, an enlightened employer. He told me afterward that when his employees walked out of the brewery on his refusal to sign the agreement they had submitted, both he and his brewmaster felt a powerful urge to call after them, "Come back, boys. Let's quit that foolishness, we'll sign up." The opportunity of settling the strike right then and there was missed. The employees of the other New Orleans breweries walked out in sympathy with those of the Columbia. Thereupon, the employers formed an ironclad mutual protective association, pledging themselves individually not to sign with us unless all signed together.

The fat was in the fire, and what might have been settled in a few minutes of calm deliberation became one of the most bitter jurisdictional strikes in the annals of American labor. It tore up the entire labor movement of New Orleans, and at the end of eleven months had inflicted such damage on both brewery industry and brewery workers that neither has recovered to this day.

The brewery strike became the signal for other strikes. Following the brewers' example, the union of pile drivers walked out. And as New Orleans is built on wooden piles driven into the silt of the Mississippi delta, the pile drivers' strike tied up the entire building industry. Next the telegraphers went out, followed by a sympathetic strike of telephone employees, between them crippling the communications system of one of the largest ports of the country. Next the dock unions went on strike. Since shipping is the largest industry of New Orleans, all business was tied up. Then, as the dock workers were tied up with the brewery workers, and I was the fighting editor of the brewery workers' *Labor World*, I became tied up with the whole strike movement, regardless of A. F. of L., anti-A. F. of L., or innocent bystanders.

Work in breweries is slack in winter, heavy in summer; work on the levees, or docks, is heavy in winter and slack in summer, so many dock workers found employment in breweries during the summer, while many brewery workers were to be found at the docks in winter. Out of this situation developed the exchange of union cards. By simply depositing his dock worker's card with the Brewery Workers' Union, the dock worker became a brewery worker in good standing and entitled to all the rights. By the same token, brewery workers who deposited their cards with dock unions became dock workers in good standing.

Such exchange of cards had been in vogue among the industrial unions of the Old World, almost from their inception. The Old-World unions were international: the union card of the Frenchman was good in Germany and Italy, as was the German card in England and Holland, and so on. Most American unions also call themselves international, but their internationalism is usually confined to members of the same craft and quite frequently does not extend as far as the next county. Members of the American Federation of Musicians, for instance, must be readmitted to their own union when they move to other cities, and the initiation fee is often high and in some instances prohibitive. The same holds true of many other "international" A. F. of L. unions.

The Brewery Workers Union, true to its international faith, admitted Negroes, although up to then all A. F. of L. international unions, except the United Mine Workers, barred them. There was one other exception. On the docks of New Orleans, Negro unions affiliated with the A. F. of L. had reached a working agreement with white unions affiliated with the A. F. of L. They had, after many bitter struggles, been driven together by the inexorable law of survival. At one time the whites had owned virtually all the jobs on the docks. The all-white port bosses had broken one of their strikes by the importation of Negro strike breakers from cotton and sugar-cane fields of the Delta. Thereafter Negroes held the dock jobs. Now Negroes certainly have stomachs just like white folk, and these stomachs, strange as it may seem, preferred chicken to swine's bosom. So when the blacks had established their near monopoly on dock jobs they banded together in unions and struck for chicken.

When the Negroes struck, the cry went up from the white man's sanctum, rostrum and pulpit: "White men, assert your supremacy, rescue your jobs from the niggers," and the white dock workers asserted their supremacy by scabbing and breaking the strike. This went on until both whites and blacks got down to sow-belly wages. In one of the last of these affairs, the white-

supremacy strikers killed some ninety black strike breakers, whereupon the white-supremacy militia of white-supremacy Louisiana
shot hell out of a similar number of white-supremacy strikers.

The upshot of the shooting was that whites and blacks agreed
to quit scabbing on each other, to recognize one another's unions,
and go fifty-fifty on dock jobs.

Now the united black, white and yellow brothers were striking for chicken by way of a minimum wage of five dollars a day.
The all-important task in this situation was to preserve the newly
gained solidarity of the strikers. And as I, the red-hot interna-
tionalist, had no prejudice against the black brethren, but, on the
contrary, liked them, the board of strategy delegated to me the
task of keeping the black boys in line.

What a book, what a whole library of enlightenment that experience was to me! It gave me my first insight into the true nature of the thing called the race problem. Among the many, many
things I learned was that these black men were men even as you
and I. Beneath their black skins beat the same hearts, gnawed the
same hunger, circulated the same blood. Below their kinky hair
lodged the same dreams, longings and aspirations. Like you and
me, they sought pleasure and evaded pain. What they asked from
life was living. Happiness within four walls, a loving mate, children, and the chance to rear them better than they had been
reared. Health, laughter, beauty, peace, plenty, a modest degree
of security in sickness and age.

Some were good, some bad; some stupid, some crooked. They
were wise and foolish; there were heroes and cowards. Most of
them were a combination of all these faults and virtues. Each
had inside him his inherited angel and devil warring for supremacy.

The Negroes were more easily moved to song and laughter
than their white fellow slaves. Beneath their monkeyshines was
the wisdom born of suffering. For the submerged, it is wiser to
amuse than to assert. Mentally they were the equal of the white

strikers, and by the way, let me caution the reader that the poor whites of the South are not mentally inferior to other people. They often lack the balanced and sufficient diet to develop the energy and health required to withstand languor and disease, but mentally they are no more inferior to the average American than Swedes are to Norwegians, or vice versa. In some respects the blacks even surpassed the whites on their own economic level. Rules of the union required recipients of strike benefits to sign their names beside the amount stated on the books. And on those books I found a smaller percentage of "his mark" among the black strikers than among the whites.

As strikers, there could be no better. I saw some of those boys lose the shine of their skins, grow thinner as the weeks went on, but they stuck. Their women, too, proved themselves staunch helpmates. Many of them worked in white men's kitchens, and the supplies they carried home at night under their aprons contributed greatly toward holding out. One of them, black as midnight, was a veritable Spartan mother. Someone had paid her fifteen-year-old boy four dollars for driving a dray loaded with a single bale of cotton some five blocks to the docks. The big idea behind the dray and bale was to show the strikers that things were moving again. Well, they moved. When the mother of the boy spotted him she dragged him off the dray and almost stomped daylight out of him.

Next day, in police court, she explained to his honor: "Yessa, jedge, I tried to kill the little nigger. I'se carried him under my hea't. I'se nussed him on my breast. I'se set up with him at night. I'se washed an' scrubbed fo' him. They's nobody got mo' right to kill him than I, his mother. An' if I catch him scabbin' again, I'll kill him, sure as hell. Now, jedge, do as you please." The judge dismissed her.

One of my duties was to visit the Negro union in their own labor temple and urge them to hold out until victory was achieved. There was, let me say, considerably less danger of the Negroes deserting the whites than of the whites deserting the blacks. However, the white end was in other hands.

The Negro unions were conducted on the pattern of secret lodges. There was a great deal of ritualism to be observed. Coming to the door, behind which the union was in session, I would rap three times. A shutter would open. Through the round opening, two large white eyeballs and a husky voice would inquire who was the stranger knocking at the door, and what was his mission? The stranger was not a newcomer. The large white eyeballs had often beheld him through the same round opening.

There followed some sharp knocks on an inner door. More mysterious whispering. By and by, someone gave a little marble-topped table a number of sharp knocks with a wooden gavel, and shortly thereafter, four guards armed with long spears appeared at the outer gate and escorted me into the inner sanctuary. On my arrival in front of the presiding high mogul, the congregation arose. The mogul ceremoniously introduced the visiting brother to the audience for the ninth time, and I started to speak.

As the audience warmed up, there came responses such as "Now he's talking, now he's talking. Tell 'em. Tell 'em." Their responses were harmonized somewhat in the manner of Negro spirituals. An eerie picture, these chanting black men, their white eyeballs shining under flickering gas jets. But once I heard them chanting, I knew they would stick for another week. Their unionism was far more than a matter of hours and wages. It was a religion, and their only hope of rising from the depths of a slavery more cruel in many respects than chattel slavery. For dock work is back-breaking work. It wears men out rapidly, is extremely seasonal, and at the wages these black men received before unionism came to their rescue, their standard of living was but little, if any, above that of the chattel slave. What emancipation had given them in mobility it had taken from them in security.

It was a good strike, as strikes go. There were a few breaks on the part of the white men; none on the Negro side. The railroad companies hauled in strike breakers in great numbers, but as fast as the railroad companies brought them in on the cushions, the railroad workers sent them out in box car and caboose on passes secured from the strike committee. Passes bore the inscription, "This is to certify that the bearer of this card was brought to New Orleans on the promise of a legitimate job. Discovering on his arrival that he was to act as strike breaker, he refused. We kindly ask all good union brothers to assist him in returning to his home in ——."

Most of the strike breakers came from the slums of northern cities, mainly Chicago. They were recruited from the human flotsam around the cheap employment agencies, in flop houses, Salvation headquarters and jails. There were some professional thugs and strike breakers supplied by the Thiel, Pinkerton, and Burns detective agencies, but the bulk of them was composed of unfortunate men to whom most any job anywhere held out the promise of three meals per.

The method by which some of these people were hired is illustrated by the following case. The I. C. railroad had brought in a large consignment of "American heroes," as President Eliot of Harvard had termed the most miserable of all Americans. In order to prevent contact between the new arrivals and the strikers, the "heroes" had been interned on a steamer anchored in the middle of the Mississippi River, and after some days of confinement they got out of hand and were landed under police protection. Among that terrible, ragged, ill-smelling, unwashed rabble I spotted a small, delicate man, wholly unfit for dock work. He stank to high heaven, and his face had not seen a razor for some days, but his clothes were whole and there was no question but that they had been made by an excellent tailor. I was interested in the prospective dock walloper in tailor-made clothes, and asked him how he happened to get mixed up with that crowd.

"How did I get mixed up with that bunch of bums?" he burst out in broken English. "That's what I want to know. I'm from

Chicago. I'm a respectable married man, with a wife and three kids. I own my own home. I'm a cutter in the most fashionable merchant-tailor establishment in Chicago, and here I am with that lousy, stinking bunch of hoboes to do what? Work on the docks loading ships—to break a strike? Me loading ships—me a strike breaker! Me, secretary of my union! Me, a class-conscious proletarian member of the Socialist Party! Me breaking a strike!"

The indignation of the good fellow was refreshing. As I pieced his story together in the nearest restaurant, the man had attended a birthday party. He must have drunk a little too much, as he put it. Something must have happened to him on his way home, for when he came to, he was in jail. Then, before he could collect his badly befuddled wits to ask for a lawyer or notify his people, the cops had loaded him and his jailmates into a closed van, pushed and jostled them into a waiting train, and here he was. In the process, somebody, in all likelihood the Chicago cops, had relieved my socialist comrade and union brother of purse, watch and chain. He gratefully accepted the few dollars I offered him for a shave and bath and to wire to his no doubt distracted spouse for transportation. He waited at the telegraph office for the reply, identified by the name and address he had luckily sewed in the breast pocket of his tailor-made coat, repaid the few dollars, and we parted *auf baldiges Wiedersehen.*

In spite of the dimensions of the strike, and the feeling it aroused, there was astonishingly little violence. This was largely due to the neutral attitude of the city administration headed by Mayor Baerman, and to the political influence wielded by the unions.

Meanwhile the great port of New Orleans was completely tied up. Fruit steamers from the tropics could neither coal, nor discharge their cargoes. Thousands of tons of bananas and citrus fruit were dumped in the river. Thousands of workers not connected with the strikes were thrown out of work. Business of all kinds suffered tremendously. Nevertheless, the sympathy of the overwhelming majority of the city remained on the side of the striking men.

Other and more drastic methods than hunger and want had to be employed to break the strike, the employers decided. Not the least effective of them would be to frame the leaders. And I had become one of those leaders.

24

LATE one evening an official of our union came to my rooms on Camp Street, accompanied by two strangers, whom he introduced as "crowbar men" with a proposition to make. They offered, for the small sum of ten dollars, to kill the scabs camped out in the breweries. Some of the scabs would occasionally leave their combination working and lodging places at night to visit the red-light districts. There the crowbar men would get them with the short bars employed by dock workers.

The price was reasonable, but how was I to know they had crowbarred the right men? Easy. They would restrict their operations to certain red-light streets. Any crowbarred man found in those streets after midnight was theirs. Payment was not to be made until the coroner had pronounced the corpse crowbarred beyond hope of recovery. Attractive as the proposition was, I declined. Much as I despised scabs, I could not and would not have them cold-bloodedly murdered.

When the union official who had introduced the two crowbar men heard my unqualified refusal, he became insultingly wrathful. So that was the kind of strike leader I was? Too damned yellow to have scabs killed by men who assumed all the risk and only asked ten bucks per killing! If this strike was lost, it was nobody's fault but mine. But just wait, he'd see to it that the crowd up in Cincinnati (the national executive board of brewery workers) would get me off the job, and so on.

After the trio had departed, slamming the door, I fell to pondering over that emotional eruption. Ordinarily the man was unemotional, quiet-spoken, almost too calm for a striking brewery worker. True, he had often counseled violence, and some of the boys who had followed his advice had got into trouble. There might be something unnatural in the violent outburst of the fellow. There was.

Meantime, the Louisiana brewery on Chapatoulas Street, paralleling the levee, had secured a flock of strike breakers through the Thiel agency. These Thiel men ate and slept in the brewery and between eating, sleeping and drinking, brewed beer in Thielmen fashion.

The boss of the Thiel men, or "the scab herder," as we called him, was the nerviest man I've ever met—before or since. He was tall, lank, and hatchet-faced. Regularly at twelve noon and at six in the evening he would leave the brewery, two six-shooters in his belt, walk calmly through our picket line, enter a restaurant, select his pet table, his back to the corner, pound the table with one of his six-shooters, and command, "Come on, fetch the grub. I'm in a hurry." It took a great deal of courage, or bravado, for a man in his position, even heavily armed as he was, to invade that strong-held union territory. Virtually all the men in and around that particular restaurant were striking dock workers. They hated scabs like poison. And there is nothing meek or ladylike about dock wallopers. The scab herder aroused my admiration. There was something in the fellow worthy of a better cause. I had learned his name from one of our own undercover men: it was Becker. His original home was Berks County, Pennsylvania. The man was worth looking into.

One noon, as Becker emerged from the main entrance of the brewery, I left the picket line and met him halfway. "Your name is Becker," I said, when we were face to face.

"Sure," said Becker, "and what of it?"

"My name is Am—"

"Ameringer," cut in Becker. "And what do you want?"

"I have a business proposition for you," I said.

"Shoot."

"But I can't make it here."

"Sure," said Becker. "But first tell me, any money in it?"

"Sure," I said. "Come to my room between ten and twelve tonight. I live at—"

"Nine-thirty-two Camp Street," said Becker.

"And I'll tell you how to make a piece of money—on the side."

"Good," said Becker. "I'll be there, but remember—" patting an ugly six-shooter, "—if there is any monkey business, you're the dead monkey."

That night, around the appointed hour, there came a rapping at the closed shutter of my room. I opened the street door leading into the hall. "Turn up that gas," said Becker. I turned up the gas. "Now walk into that room, hands up," he ordered. I walked in, hands up. "Now sit down on that chair at the window." Then, taking in the whole room with swift, experienced eyes, he grabbed another chair, planted himself and the chair in the corner of two brick walls, and said, "Shoot."

As a preliminary I wanted to know how much the agency paid him to chaperon his bunch of scabs.

The agency paid Becker twenty-five bucks a week and keep.

Wasn't that rather low pay, considering the low company he had to keep and the risk involved?

"Hell, yes, but the brewery pays me another twenty-five bucks."

"Oh," I said. "You are a brewer."

"No," said Becker. "I'm not even a half-assed brewer, but they want to go through the motion of operating the brewery to scare you fellows into going back to work."

"How's the beer you're turning out?" I asked.

"The slop ain't fit to drink. Got any real beer in this dump?"

I had real beer and real Milwaukee Dutch lunch on the covered back porch outside my bedroom.

"Fetch it," said Becker. "But, remember, no monkey business."

Eating Milwaukee rye bread seasoned by Usinger sausage, washed down by Milwaukee union beer, was not monkey business to Becker. He enjoyed it. After the lunch, I brought the subject back to beer.

"You say the beer, or rather slop, you fellows turn out isn't fit to drink?"

"No," replied Becker, full of real beer and Dutch lunch.

"But," I questioned, "does it look and smell like beer?"

"Oh, it does that all right."

"Well, in that case," I wanted to know, "is there some way of doctoring that beer so that it doesn't even look and smell like beer?"

"Sure," said Becker, "drop a cake of naphtha soap in the kettle."

Becker really knew more about the art of brewing beer than I had expected. We discussed the chemical relations between naphtha soap and beer a while longer, and finally agreed that twenty-five dollars a week would be about right. But how could I make sure he would deliver the goods?

"Hell," said Becker. "When I sell out, I sell out. That's my business, and if anyone hires me to sell you out, too, I sell you out. Get me?"

Reassured, I asked him how I could get his weekly honorarium to him. "Don't try getting it to me, I'll come for it. I like your beer and lunch, and I think you're on the level." Thanking him for the compliment, I saw him to the door.

From then on, at the appointed day and hour, Becker would come to my room for his weekly beer, Dutch lunch and honorarium. In one of these sessions he told me he had once been a staunch union man himself. He had led a bitter strike that had landed him in jail, and while in jail, the company and his union had made a compromise, leaving him out in the cold. Since then he had had no use for "the yellow union hounds" and made his living on the other side.

At a later visit I described my experience with the two crowbar men, omitting, of course, the name of the union brother who had introduced them to me.

"I bet I can tell you who the guy was," and to my astonishment Becker gave me the correct name. When I nodded assent, he exclaimed, "Why didn't I warn you about that son of a bitch before! He's a Pink (Pinkerton), I'm telling you, and one of the rattiest of that whole rotten outfit."

"But," I faltered, "this man is an old member of our organization. He has held important union jobs in other places."

"Yep," replied Becker, disgustedly, "and wherever that guy worked, a strike followed some time later, and somebody regularly got framed, and if you don't believe what I'm telling you, I'll tell you where the skunk mails his reports and you can find out for yourself."

We found out that he was telling the truth, and revealing still a spark of unionism in an otherwise pretty black heart. Besides, he had delivered the goods in connection with soap and beer.

The rooming house in New Orleans in which I had rented a parlor, bedroom and covered back porch was run by an old lady and her daughter, both of whom had seen better days. One day the mother remarked how much she missed sitting at the front window of my parlor and watching the people pass, and how dreary it was to be cooped up in the little back sitting room in the rear of the house.

"Why," I said, "how stupid of both of us. You can have your seat at the front window any time you want. I am away a good part of the day and when I am writing you won't disturb me in the least. Besides, your black silk dress with the white lace collar and your silvery hair please my eyes, which see little that's pleasing these days." The old lady accepted, and from then on was a steady visitor in the parlor.

The beer and Dutch lunch I kept in the large ice box on the covered back porch were there largely for the benefit of my newspaper friends. Newspaper Row was only a few blocks from the house. Partly because we were colleagues, and partly because of the beer and lunch, the boys from the *Picayune, Item,* and *State* were frequent visitors to my rooms. In return they often presented me with passes to shows and other places of entertainment and amusement. As my evenings were fully occupied with union meetings, I could not avail myself of such opportunities, and usually presented the passes to my landlady and her daughter, thereby winning such part of their hearts as was not yet mine.

In the knock-down and drag-out fight between the A. F. of L. and my own union, with the brewery owners in the rôle of more or less innocent bystanders, I had, in my paper, accused an official of the teamsters' union of being so low that he would steal pennies from the tin cups of blind beggars, and so crooked that he had to sleep in a copper coil. The gentleman was all that and worse, and when suit was brought against me, I stood ready to prove it. But unfortunately, under the libel laws of Louisiana it was not sufficient to prove that the plaintiff in the case was low enough to do the things I had accused him of. I must prove that I had made the accusation "for the good and well-being of the great State of Louisiana," an assignment difficult for a northern agitator who had come to the great State of Louisiana for the purpose of tying its principal industries into a wet, hard knot.

During the long trial, considering the stakes and personages involved, my landlady had repeatedly urged me to let her testify in my favor. The fact, however, that I had paid my rent on the dot, permitted the dear old lady to monopolize the rocking chair next to her front window, and had presented her and her daughter with free passes, could not wipe out the other part of calling the plaintiff what I had called him. Nor would it contribute anything materially to the plea that I had called him all that for the good and welfare of the great State of Louisiana, whose best people, by then, would have gladly seen me in hell in place of

New Orleans. According to the law I was guilty, and guilty I was found by Judge Baker. The penalty for criminal libel was anything from thirty days in jail, a fine of one hundred dollars, or both, to four years in the penitentiary, which in Louisiana meant four years on the levee.

Visualizing her star roomer pushing a wheelbarrow in company with "niggers," my landlady decided to call on Judge Baker, persuade him of the error of his ways and, that failing, give him a piece of her mind concerning judges who condemn perfect gentlemen to pushing wheelbarrows on the levee in company with "niggers." She did not inform me of her intention.

Another gentleman, Covington Hall, poet of forgotten men, escorted the dear lady. Covington, at that time, was the handsomest young man in all New Orleans. On top of that, he was its best-dressed man, who set the fashion for the male population. On top of that, he was adjutant general of the Sons of the Confederacy. And on top of all that, he was a member of the Covington and Hall families, two of the oldest and most honored families of the old South.

However, some time previous to our meeting, Covington had resigned the post of adjutant general of the Sons of the Confederacy of Louisiana, on the ground that he was tired of advertising the fact that his father had made an ass of himself fighting for slaves he might have sold to the Yanks and still kept as sharecroppers. This was true enough, but it gave an awful jolt to the best families. Not content with that, Covy, with his poetical vein and sympathies for underdogdom, had written poems of the "arise and throw off your chains" sort. He had aided me both by word and pen during the strike. To him, the perfect Southern gentleman, more than to me belongs the credit for welding the black and white dock slaves of New Orleans into the solid body that raised them from the depths.

Judge Baker, I learned later, was not hostile to me personally. But I was a fanatic, an agitator, a socialist, and also a dangerous character. He would not give me the limit of the law—but, and so on. Just as the seekers of mercy were about to depart in despair, my good landlady mentioned that she never had expected a Baker could be so mean, she herself being a Baker from Tennessee.

"You, a Baker of Tennessee, too? Why didn't you tell me that in the beginning? Well, well, a Baker of Tennessee, too, and you assure me that that wild-eyed guest of yours is a perfect gentleman—well, we'll see."

What the good judge saw when he read my sentence a few days later was thirty days in parish prison, or a fine of one hundred dollars. We paid the fine. God bless the Bakers of Tennessee!

In the interval between my verdict and sentence I called upon the sheriff in charge of the parish prison. My lawyer and I felt that my limit would not be more than a short while in jail. From what I had heard, arrangements could be made for eating at the sheriff's table for the extra sum of a dollar a day. The sheriff, largely elected by union votes, received me most hospitably.

But besides board, could I secure a decent room, preferably with south exposure, at his hotel? "Well, let's shop around and see what we've got." The room I finally declared to be satisfactory already contained a guest. The sheriff, however, assured me that being a deadhead, as contrasted to a dollar a day guest, he would be moved to other quarters. There was one more request. The room was painted in an obnoxious yellow, deepening toward the bottom into a most unappetizing grayish brown. Could the room be redecorated? And if so, luna green was my favorite color. That, too, could be done. There was a house painter downstairs who was incarcerated for wife beating. The sheriff would see to it he did a satisfactory job of painting the room.

Room and decoration settled, I explained to the sheriff that, not being used to confinement, I would like to know if there would be a chance of getting out of the hotel occasionally. The sheriff reckoned that could be arranged by appointing me foreman of a chain gang. I thanked him for the honor but explained

I had made many friends of high respectability in the city who would be greatly embarrassed to see me on the chain gang. The sheriff, respecting the feelings of my many New Orleans friends, thought a deputy chain-gang foreman might substitute for me and give me the opportunity of entertaining my many friends in a more agreeable manner. The same satisfactory arrangement was made for both day and night. That New Orleans parish prison would have been superior even to the Bürgerstube in Munich, in which I had served ten days in twenty installments for contempt of court. Thanks to the two Bakers of Tennessee, however, I was not compelled to accept the sheriff's hospitality.

During the course of events, a beer driver and member of our union had been convicted of defalcation. The penalty was a number of years on the levee.

The man was only technically guilty. Beer drivers were agents of the breweries; the saloon keepers were theirs, not the brewery's customers. The desire of the breweries to hold both agents and customers had led to a system of permitting these drivers to get in debt to the brewers. When the driver went on strike, the brewery threatened him with a suit for defalcation unless he returned to work. The man refused. The union, knowing both the man and the system, offered to make the defalcation good, but the brewery instigated suit and the man was found guilty.

One of his daughters had just passed her teacher's examination; another held a secretarial position with a large firm. The family was frantic. Father on the levee was more than they could bear. Would I, a friend of their father, and knowing he was innocent, go to Baton Rouge and persuade the governor to change the levee to parish prison?

I would.

The state house in Baton Rouge was built under the influence of *Ivanhoe*. It was of gray stone, very narrow, with high Gothic windows, moss-covered, overgrown with ivy, and totally unfit for the purpose for which it was built.

The governor—who, I noticed idly, had a French name—invited me to have a seat and listened attentively to my recital of the troubles of the innocent friend of mine waiting in the parish prison of New Orleans for commitment to the levee. At the end of my plea, he informed me he could do nothing about it. A jury of his peers had heard the testimony, found the prisoner guilty, and the judge had passed sentence.

Bent on missions of this character, one should never accept the first no as final. I didn't. I tackled the governor from new angles. No use. A jury had heard the evidence. The judge, an honorable man, he knew, had passed sentence. The governor could not and would not change the sentence from penitentiary to parish prison.

Hope almost gone, I watched the last glow of the setting sun over the broad Delta, through the Gothic ivy-framed windows of Ivanhoe, and exclaimed, with no thought of the governor, "Look at that! What a magnificent subject for Millet!"

The governor almost hopped out of his seat. "You are—you are an admirer of Millet?"

I *was* an admirer of Millet, painter of the "Angelus" and the "Man with the Hoe." I still believe no painter before or since has caught more of the soul of the things he painted. The governor was more than an admirer of Millet. His life's hobby was paintings—old and new. He had repeatedly visited the principal art galleries of Europe. He knew every school of painting; knew more about schools of painting than I, an ex-painter. But at the same time I knew enough to make an intelligent listener, and intelligent listening is quite frequently more effective than intelligent talking.

It was pitch dark in the room by now. Every so often the governor's secretary in the outer office had gently opened the door a few inches and, satisfied that the governor was not exposed to the dagger of an assassin, had quietly closed it again. I had resigned all hope of bringing the unfortunate beer driver into the conversation, when suddenly the governor exclaimed: "Apropos of that beer-driver friend of yours. You understand I can't change the penitentiary sentence to parish imprisonment, but I *can* give him a pardon," and pressing a button, the governor dictated one on the spot.

Shortly afterward I caught a train, and by midnight my brother beer driver was back in the bosom of his overjoyed family.

25

THE agreement between the black and white dock unions stipulated an equal division of jobs. This included equal wages and working conditions for both races. But the white and black unions still met in separate places, and out of this developed misunderstanding and friction. A unifying central body was needed in which both races were represented. Thus the Dock and Cotton Council came into existence, a representative body composed of an equal number of white and black delegates.

The seventy-two delegates, half white, half black, represented thirty-six unions of dock workers. And just as jobs on the docks had been divided fifty-fifty, between the races, so the offices of the Dock and Cotton Council were divided fifty-fifty. Delegates addressed each other as "brother." The division of officers was on the following order: President—white; Vice-President—black; Financial Secretary—white; Corresponding secretary—black; and so on. At each annual election, the rotation of officers was reversed. From which it may be gathered that everything was done to preserve the equality and solidarity of the central body and to prevent friction between the two races. This was not a question of either social or political equality. Its basis was economic equality. The driving force was neither idealism nor sentimentalism, it was necessity. The two races could fight each other and go down together; or help each other and rise together. They preferred to rise together. The eternal urge for life, liberty and happiness had driven these men together and wiped out the Jim Crow law in the chief centers of their lives—working place and union hall.

Somewhere in the second month of the nine-week dock strike the legislature of Louisiana appointed a committee of eight to meet a committee of eight to be selected, or elected, by the Dock and Cotton Council, to find a basis for settling the strike. The legislative committee was composed of four members of the lower and four members of the upper house. The committee finally elected by the Dock and Cotton Council was composed of four white and four black brothers.

The hue and cry that followed the announcement of the make-up of the workers' delegation came near to bringing the stars in their courses to fall on Louisiana.

"What! Meet with niggers in the same room, around the same table, discussing a problem concerning the superior race exclusively?" Was it not terrible enough to meet common dock wallopers, water rats, white trash, in the same room, around the same table, to discuss as equals—well, almost equals—the weal and the woes of an industry in which the workers had not invested a red cent? Was it not terrible enough that men could no longer run their own business as they saw fit? Now that riffraff had the effrontery to ask white gentlemen, honorable law makers of the great State of Louisiana, to meet with "niggers" in the same room, around the same table!

The real purpose of this turmoil was to destroy the solidarity of the two races. With sixteen white men behind closed doors and thousands of unrepresented Negroes on the outside, what could be easier than to make a deal on the inside leaving the blacks on the outside for keeps? What could be easier for the emissaries of the employers than to spread the idea among the blacks on the outside that they were being sold out by the conspiracy of white men behind closed doors? Isn't the Negro always sold out when white men put their heads together? Don't be fools, black men. Get your jobs back before those white men behind closed doors take yours. And hurry—hurry!

The Dock and Cotton Council stood pat. It had learned by bitter experience that once the two races permitted themselves to be divided, their strike was lost.

In an effort to persuade the council to withdraw the four Negro delegates, Mayor Baerman had appeared at one of its meetings. Mayor Baerman was well liked in labor circles. He had been fair to Labor. He made a subtle approach in this speech. To begin with, he had not come as the representative of the harbor bosses. He spoke for the city of New Orleans, at large. The whole population was suffering grievously on account of the strike. Tens of millions of dollars had already been lost to capital, labor and business in general. The great port of New Orleans was in danger of losing its position of importance in the United States. Shipping was being diverted to other ports. The loss inflicted might well cripple New Orleans for all time to come.

He had no prejudice against Negroes. (I believe Mayor Baerman spoke the truth. He was a Jew, and there are no other people, unless it be the French, less susceptible to that particular aberration.) It was not the fault of the Negroes, the Mayor went on, that they were in this country. It is not their fault that they worked on the docks. White men had imported them in previous dock strikes to break the strikes of white dock workers. They had as much right to make a living as other people. They were hardworking, law-abiding folk and entitled to the same wages and working hours as white men performing the same labor. He was not asking the white delegates of the Council to withdraw the four black delegates. He asked the black men present to sacrifice their representation temporarily, in order that the peace, tranquillity and prosperity of New Orleans might be restored.

The audience listened attentively to the plea of Mayor Baerman, and at its conclusion warmly applauded the speaker. A Negro delegate arose, asked for the privilege of the floor, and moved to reconsider the previous action, that is, the selection of the four Negroes. Another Negro delegate seconded the motion.

In the discussion that followed, every white speaker declared himself opposed to the withdrawal of the four Negroes. Only a few Negroes had spoken in favor of it. There was no need for a roll call. The motion for reconsideration was almost unanimously defeated. All white men present had voted nay, and only a few Negroes had voted aye, some of those merely as a matter of confidence in the sincerity of the white brothers.

Shortly after this amazing exhibition of solidarity, the committee of eight selected by the legislature met with the committee of four white and four black dock workers elected by the Dock and Cotton Council.

In the capacity of editor of *The Labor World* and chief scribe of the great strike, I attended most of the meetings of the Committee of Sixteen. The outstanding personalities at those meetings were three: Ellis, a mulatto; State Senator Cordell; and Dan Scully, president of the longshoremen's union, a red-headed Irishman in every sense of the word.

Ellis stood no more than five-feet-five and weighed about a hundred and ten. In his youth he had been a jockey and in that capacity had seen much of the world. When he had become too heavy for jockeying, a disaster which overtook him during a European tour, he secured a job on one of the boats of the Hamburg-American Line. His intention had been to desert after landing in God's Country, but liking his job, and having no other in prospect, he had stuck. Later he had become a member of the German Seamen, the reddest of the German unions, had acquired a fair smattering of German, and more than a fair understanding of the Communist Manifesto. He had swallowed whole the theory of the class struggle and uncompromisingly regarded the Gompers notion of the identity of interest between capital and labor as high treason to the proletariat of the world.

Dan Scully's outstanding characteristics were a good dash of Irish wit coupled with an uncontrollable temper and an ingrown hatred of bosses, irrespective of race, nationality, religion, and state of moral turpitude.

Senator Cordell was the composite portrait of the Kentucky Colonel seen in whiskey advertisements. He was topped by a shock of beautiful silvery hair. He sported a silvery mustache and goatee. He had a florid complexion, suffered from high blood pressure, fell frequently into the rôle of Shakespearian hero, such as Mark Antony declaiming over the body of Caesar, and for the balance had a temper as uncontrollable as that of Longshoreman Scully, though somewhat more culturally restrained. The scene most frequently enacted by the three leading characters was something like this:

Senator Cordell, violently rising from his chair at the conference table, violently tearing his hair, and violently striding around the conference room:

"The ideah! The ve'y ideah! White men conspirin' with niggas against the honoah and prosper'ty of the gre-at po't of N'yo'l'ns; against the honoah and prosper'ty of the gre-at State of Louisianah itself! The ideah, the ve'y ideah, white gen'lemen of honoah compelled to heckle like penny-pinchin' tradas ovah a few pennies mo'h'less with a pa'cel o' watah rats and niggas. Ah shall not continya this disgra-ceful, shameless bickerin' fo' anotha second. I am leaving . . ."

Ellis: "Please sit down, Senator. We're not here to save the honor and prosper'ty of the great State of Louisiana. We is here to settle the strike. That's what they sent you down here for. Your job is to see to it that we work the longest possible hours at the least possible pay. Our job is to make your crowd pay us the highest possible wages for the lowest possible amount of work. Now let's get down to business. What's more, we've won the strike already, else you gentlemen wouldn't be here to talk compromise, honor, and prosperity."

Dan Scully: "Oh, we're water rats, are we? And white trash, are we? But you can't run your goddamn port without us. Can you? I guess before long you'll call us nigger lovers, too. Maybe you want to know next how I would like it if my sister married a nigger? Well, go ahead, ask me. But take it from me, I wasn't always a nigger lover. I fought in every strike to keep the niggers off the dock. I fought until in the white-supremacy strike your white-supremacy governor sent his white-supremacy militia down here and shot us white-supremacy strikers full of holes. You talk about us conspiring with niggers against the honor and prosperity of the state. But let me tell you and your gang, there was a time I wouldn't even work beside a nigger. You got 'em on the loose. You made me work with niggers, eat with niggers, sleep with niggers, drink out of the same water bucket with niggers, and finally got me to the place where if one of them comes to me and blubbers something about more pay, I say, 'Come on, nigger, let's go after the white bastards.' "

During the strike, President Schlosser of the Columbia brewery (where it had started) and I had become warm personal friends. This was the more astonishing because I had done everything in my power to put his business on the blink both by picketing and boycott. We first met at one of the conferences of the Brewers' Association. In these conferences Schlosser had become the dominant moderating influence. He had, from the start, advocated that the Association renew its contract with the Brewery Workers Union on the ground that it had organized the industry, that the relations between union and industry had on the whole been beneficial to both, and that the craftsmen employed in their plants over which the sundry A. F. of L. unions demanded jurisdiction were bitterly opposed to being separated from the Brewery Workers Union. Finally, it was his conviction that one big union was preferable to many little unions, each of which was capable of paralyzing the whole plant. A very sensible man, and what a tragedy that the leadership of the A. F. of L. was far from sharing the good sense of that brewery plutocrat.

The main stumbling block in the road to industrial peace was the threat of the A. F. of L. that if the Association entered into an agreement with the Brewery Workers Union, it would boycott its products, even though they would still have been a hundred-per-cent union made. As far as New Orleans proper was concerned this would have mattered little, because the dock unions who made up the overwhelming majority of unionized labor in the city, though affiliated with the A. F. of L., stuck loyally to the brewery workers to the bitter end. However, these New Orleans brewers sold their beer all over the South and most of it in cities where we had no dock wallopers to support us. Hence these conferences always ended in stalemates.

There was one other obstacle, insignificant in itself, and yet more responsible for the eventual defeat of our forces than the threatened boycott of the A. F. of L. That obstacle was a pair of cut traces. In the early days of the strike, someone had cut the traces on the harness of a team of horses attached to a beer delivery wagon. The wagon belonged to the Louisiana brewery, in which my friend Becker was herding scabs and spoiling beer. The owner of the concern was an old German named Betz, and the traces, which might easily have been repaired, had become an obsession with Betz. In the conferences he would usually say, "*Ja, ja. Das ist alles verdammte Dummheit* (it's all damned foolishness). We are losing hundreds of thousands of dollars, our men are losing even more than we are. The only people who are gainers are the Milwaukee and St. Louis breweries who are stealing our markets while we are cutting each other's throats. Sure we ought to settle." All this was very true and sensible, but at the word "settle," something cracked in the round skull of the sensible Mr. Betz, and instead of putting his Betz on the dotted line he would bang his fist down on the table and shout, "But I be *verdammt* if I settle with people who cut traces."

The traces could have been made as good as new by being sewed together by any good harness maker at a cost of seventy-five cents. In the end, that seventy-five cents cost us the loss of our strike. The members of the Association had pledged themselves to sign only by unanimous consent, and Mr. Betz would not consent.

The rational attitude and calm manner he exhibited at these

dramatic conferences had drawn me to Schlosser. The attraction was mutual, and after the adjournment of one of the earliest of those futile meetings, he had invited me to Sunday dinner. In doing so he smilingly added that we would not be alone. Two other gentlemen whom he was sure I would be glad to meet would be present.

The home to which I had been invited was near Tulane University. The two other guests at Sunday dinner were James Dillard, who later became the directing genius of the Rosenwald foundation, and U. O. Nelson, a manufacturer of bathroom fixtures and pioneer of profit sharing between capital and labor. Dillard was a professor at Tulane and one of the finest Southerners I have met, with deep sympathy and a broad understanding of Southern problems. I was delighted to find him a single taxer. Of the other three, Nelson was a philosophical anarchist, cooperator and large-scale employer of labor; Schlosser, a brewery lord and lover of books; myself, socialist and strike leader. Four men of more divergent background, rearing, and culture could hardly be imagined. Yet it was this very divergency that made our discussions so interesting, and to me so profitable. In this, and many following confabs, we discussed almost every problem under the sun, each from his own viewpoint. Discussion often grew warm, for each of us was strong in his particular faith. But they never exceeded the bounds of reasonableness.

Toward the end of the strike it had become more and more apparent that we would lose, and another problem emerged. That problem was, what are we going to do with Oscar? In his *Labor World* and by word of mouth, Oscar had written the bitterest invectives against the American Federation of Labor and its high priest, Sam Gompers. There were indications that the Brewery Workers Union would make peace with the A. F. of L. Oscar would not make peace with the A. F. of L. Hence, Oscar would be out in the cold. And with the financial support of the Brewery Workers Union gone, his *Labor World* would join the grand

army of dead and forgotten labor papers. Something, the majority
of the meeting felt, would have to be done for Oscar.

The scheme my friendly enemies eventually worked out for
the salvaging of Oscar was this: A wealthy Quaker lady by the
name of Jeans had left some millions to be devoted to uplifting
the poor whites and Negroes of the South. Dillard had become
secretary of the Jeans foundation, later merged, or federated, with
the Julius Rosenwald foundation. Nelson was its treasurer;
Andrew Carnegie and Charles Taft were associated with it—and
would I accept the position of field organizer?

It didn't look so good to me. I was past the uplift stage.
Getting tangled with such shining exploiters as steel-king
Carnegie, and Charles Taft, the corporation bonanza farmer,
grated on my proletarian class consciousness. On the other hand,
in my own way, I was a sort of uplifter, too. I liked the poor
whites and blacks of the South and, God knew, they needed lots
of uplifting. Lastly, or perhaps, firstly, I soon would be out of a
job, with no other in hailing distance. I accepted the position
tentatively.

Then another problem arose: where to commence uplifting?
Dillard, who, as a Virginian and lifelong resident of the South,
knew that section a hundred times better than I, who had only
skirted the edge of it, was in favor of starting work in the heart
of the old South, while I, the hundred-per-cent amateur, advocated starting the work in Oklahoma. The reason I sponsored
Oklahoma was that I wanted to work along lines of less resistance
to white and black uplift than in the deep South. Another reason
I gave was that a live socialist movement had developed in Oklahoma, a fact which indicated to me a high degree of intelligence
on the part of its population. As for myself, I had only passed
through Oklahoma on my way to Texas in the fall of 1896. All
I knew about the state was what I had read in the papers, as
Oklahoma's Will Rogers was later to remark of his general
information. But foremost among those papers was *The Appeal
to Reason,* the lively socialist organ, whose authority could not

be doubted. In the opinion of my friends, uplift and politics were poor bedfellows, and so the matter stood when Nelson departed for LeClair, Missouri, where his profit-sharing manufacturing plant was located.

A month or so later, after all the calamities predicted by my friends had duly happened and my job and paper had gone glimmering, I followed Nelson to LeClair to settle the question as to where the uplift should be started: Old South or the brand-new state of Oklahoma? Had he been in LeClair when I arrived there, it is quite possible that I might have become a social worker and eventually one of the shining lights of the New Deal. However, when I got there, Nelson was on a tour of Ireland with his fellow co-operator, Sir Horace Plunkett. In my harum-scarum way of doing business, I had failed to make an appointment. Why are people with whom I have important business to discuss almost always some place else when I call at the place they ought to be?

It was too far to follow Nelson to Ireland. Besides, by the time I got there, he might have returned to the United States. On the other hand, Oklahoma was only six hundred miles from where Nelson was not. I had recommended Oklahoma as the most promising field of uplift. Why not get the lowdown?

And so to Oklahoma I went.

Book Six

SAVING THE WORLD

26

I CAME to Oklahoma City in the early spring of 1907, the year Oklahoma entered the Union as a State. On my arrival I went first to the state office of the Socialist Party of Oklahoma, on Main Street. The state secretary was Otto Branstetter, later national secretary of the party, and there were various reasons why I called on him so promptly. In the first place, I was a member in good standing of the Socialist Party. Second, the secretary should be qualified to give me the low-down on Oklahoma. Lastly, I meant to give him my opinion on the fallacy of a socialist movement almost exclusively composed of farmers. I knew farmers like a book. I had slept in their beds, eaten at their tables, had even painted farmers in the Pickaway plains of Ohio. They were fine enough people, but they certainly were not the kind to whom Marx had addressed his clarion call: "Proletarians of the world, unite! You have nothing to lose but your chains. You have a world to gain." Besides, had not Marx written about "the idiocy of rural life"?

Farmers were not wage earners. They were capitalists, exploiting wage labor. They owned the means of production. They had a great deal more to lose than their chains. They had acres of land, thousands of dollars' worth of farm implements, fine homes and big barns to lose. And before they'd give them up, they'd fight. I explained all this to Otto Branstetter, sparing him none of my opinions on this vital point.

227

The secretary confessed there wasn't much of a proletariat in Oklahoma to build a proletarian revolution on, and with. Further east in Indian territory, he told me, there were ten thousand coal miners. A fine, fighting bunch, and a good number of them members of the Party. The conservative building-trade workers of the larger towns were fairly well organized, but on the whole, a poor crowd to work on. If anything was to be done in the line of social revolution, there was no choice but to enlist the farmers who formed the overwhelming bulk of Oklahoma's population. But was I really sure that all farmers owned large farms, and commanded the implements of production and exploitation? Above all, what did I know about Oklahoma farmers? Was I sure they were the same kind of farmers I was acquainted with back in Ohio? If not, and since I had come to Oklahoma to study its social and economic conditions, how would I like him to arrange a speaking tour for me? It would give me a close-up of Southwest farmers and farm life. The Party didn't pay salaries to its missionaries. I would have to take up collections to pay my fare from place to place. However, in most instances the comrades would haul me, and in all cases entertain me at their homes. What did I think of the idea?

I thought it was a first-rate idea.

The initial speaking date which the obliging state secretary arranged for my benefit was in Harrah, a hamlet of some two hundred souls twenty miles east of Oklahoma City. I had difficulty in reaching Harrah by train. There was a flood. Creeks and rivers had overflowed their banks. Culverts and bridges had been washed out. All roads leading to Harrah were under clay-colored water. It took the train the better part of the day to make the twenty-odd miles.

The meeting was in a one-room schoolhouse, unpainted on the outside, unceiled on the inside. I was late. The audience had already assembled, and what an assemblage! All hands were soaking, sloppy wet. Puddles of water had formed on the floor. A few stable lanterns supplied the illumination. Babies were sleeping on the speaker's platform. More babies slept, nursed, or cried on the breasts of their mothers, uncomfortably wedged into school seats designed for ten-year-olds. All were wretchedly dressed: faded blue jeans for the men; faded Mother Hubbards and poke bonnets for the women. These people had trudged in soaking rain, or come in open wagons or on horseback or muleback, to hear a socialist speech—and they were farmers! This indescribable aggregation of moisture, steam, dirt, rags, unshaven men, slatternly women and fretting children were farmers! Ghost of Dan Hitler—they were farmers! I had come upon another America!

The chairman of the meeting, who looked as if he had just been dug out of a wet clay bank, apologized for the small attendance. (It wasn't a small attendance. It was an outpouring of the masses, considering the night and road condition.) The main trouble, he explained, was that most of the comrades lived in the Kickapoo country across the Canadian River, and the bridge was washed out.

Further questioning revealed that my chairman lived over the river in the Kickapoo country, too. When I asked him if he had come across in a skiff, he replied, "No, I hitched my team on the other side and swam across. I feared you might get sore, not having a chairman."

Great Jehoshaphat! He had swum the swollen North Canadian in the only suit to his name. No question but these people were American farmers, but not the kind I had known in the Pickaway plains of Ohio. These people occupied an even lower level of existence than the white and black "water rats" of New Orleans.

During the days of opulence on a rising labor scale, I had acquired a certain standard of comfort and decency. The brewery workers had been especially liberal toward me: "Don't sit up nights in day coaches. Take the sleepers. Don't eat cold lunches. Eat in the diner. Don't stop at cheap hotels. Stop in good hotels and see that there is a bathroom handy. You need all your strength for the work you are doing." Such had been the advice of the officials of the Cincinnati headquarters. My weekly salary had been fifty-four dollars and all expenses, plus five dollars a day "treating money." And as I had made it a rule to stay away from saloons as much as possible during strikes, that extra five was largely mine.

Green as I was in my new America, I knew enough not to expect a room with bath in Harrah. As it turned out, the town contained no hotel of any kind. A comrade would entertain me in his house. The comrade was waiting. He had already loaded his wife and flock of children in the wagon bed. He and the honored guest mounted the wagon seat and started out in the pitch black night and pouring rain. The oil in his wagon lantern had given out; we jolted over blackjack stumps and roots, sumped into ruts, slushed through young lakes, had our faces caressed by wet blackjack branches. At last we came to the house, the typical tenant shack I was soon to know so well, and hate so deeply.

Actually, this was one of the better tenant shacks. The comrade was not a share cropper. He was a managing tenant. There were three whole rooms and a lean-to kitchen, as I found out the next morning. There were glass windows—with most of the panes out—in every room, but no screens on either doors or windows.

My host had replenished his wagon lantern and shown me my room and had departed with a pleasant "Good night," and an ominous admonition, "Don't let the bedbugs bite." There was no furniture in the room other than a sagging steel cot. There was not even a nail in the straight up-and-down board of the walls on which to hang my clothes. I undressed, deposited my clothes on the floor, put on my nightgown, and lay down on the cot. I had suspected a mattress under the faded gray cotton comfort, oozing cotton from a thousand holes. There was no mattress. But there was a faded brown blanket at the foot of the cot. I was too tired from the experiences of the day to take out a book from my suitcase to read myself to sleep in the light of the smoking stable lantern.

I was lying in the dark, thinking how heartily I should kick the posterior of a certain person who had known all about American farmers the day before, when I heard the whine of an oncoming army of mosquitoes. I had encountered mosquitoes in the flats of New Jersey and the swamps of the Delta, but these Oklahoma mosquitoes were the bitingest I had met so far. Either their auger bits sank deeper, their appetite was sharper, or the hungry man-eaters had at last discovered the man of their dreams. I pulled the faded brown blanket over my rapidly swelling face. It was a horse blanket, and from the powerful ammonia odor it exuded, had served oftener under than on the back of the horse.

Presently things began biting me under the horse blanket. They seemed to care specially for my neck, wrist and ankles. At last I caught one of them and investigated. I had met bedbugs, too, before, but not these famished baby turtles.

The moon was peeping through a yellow ring of clouds. I thought I saw something like grass out of the window. It was glistening wet, but anything was preferable to that axis of mosquitoes and bedbugs!

Lying on the wet grass, I had escaped the baby turtles, but the mosquitoes still pursued me. The nightgown, wet as it was, still offered some protection for the unexposed portion of my anatomy, but now something new was feasting on me under the nightgown, something small and wingless. I was being introduced to chiggers, and they seemed to be exceedingly fond of itinerant socialists.

How I survived that long night is beyond me. When breakfast was announced I was still too full of lumps, bumps, and itches to mumble more than "Good morning." Breakfast consisted of fat meat, corn bread, molasses and black "coffee," made of chicory and minus cream and sugar. The cow had gone dry and they had forgotten to bring home sugar from town. . . .

The home in which I was entertained the following night was

not quite so luxurious. It lacked board floors and glass windows. But the mosquitoes and bed turtles were a little bigger, hungrier, and more numerous than at the first place. I didn't try the chiggers. From the look of things they might prove to be saber-toothed tigers the size of woolly mastodons.

I am not exaggerating. As the days grew into weeks, I found worse than what I have described so far. I found toothless old women with sucking infants on their withered breasts. I found a hospitable old hostess, around thirty or less, her hands covered with rags and eczema, offering me a biscuit with those hands, apologizing that her biscuits were not as good as she used to make because with her sore hand she no longer could knead the dough as it ought to be. I saw youngsters emaciated by hook-worms, malnutrition, and pellagra, who had lost their second teeth before they were twenty years old. I saw tottering old male wrecks with the infants of their fourteen-year-old wives on their laps. I saw a white man begging a Choctaw squaw man who owned the only remaining spring in that neighborhood to let him have credit for a few buckets of water for his thirsty family. I saw humanity at its lowest possible level of degradation and decay. I saw smug, well dressed, overly well fed hypocrites march to church on Sabbath day, Bibles under their arms, praying for God's kingdom on earth while fattening like latter-day cannibals on the share croppers. I saw wind-jamming, hot-air-spouting politicians geysering Jeffersonian platitudes about equal rights to all and special privileges to none; about all men born equal with the rights to life, liberty and the pursuit of happiness without even knowing, much less caring, that they were addressing as wretched a set of abject slaves as ever walked the face of the earth, anywhere or at any time. The things I saw on that trip are the things you never forget.

What those people needed, what they need today, is not pious soothing syrup and political Castoria. What they needed was not uplift from above, no matter how well meant, but upheaval from below that would give them a big and good enough share of God's footstool on which to work, rear their children and restore to themselves the dignity of human beings. Goethe says youth is revolutionary, maturity conservative, old age reactionary. Well, I am nearing seventy, but I still regard a social arrangement in which some possess thousands of acres of life-giving earth, while millions of children are born without enough earth to plant their little pink bottoms on, a black betrayal of democracy, and an insult to Christianity.

The Grapes of Wrath, by John Steinbeck, has shocked tender-skinned sisters and sensitive brethren who wouldn't lift a finger to wipe the foul blot off the face of America. They have called the book vile, vulgar, and indecent. It is as vile, vulgar and indecent as the condition of the people whom Steinbeck saw and I saw years before him.

For myself, the die was cast. Up to then I had been a part-time world-saver. Now I was a professional, on full time, and in every fiber of my being. This thing was too terrible to be tolerated. I would arouse these people, so much lower in the scale of life than New Orleans dock wallopers, black and white, at the end of their nine-week strike. They were worse fed, worse clothed, worse housed, more illiterate than the Chicago packing house wops and bohunks Upton Sinclair described in his *The Jungle,* and whom I had seen with my own eyes while doing my bit in one of their strikes. The Oklahoma farmers' living standard was so far below that of the sweatshop workers of the New York east side before the Amalgamated Clothing Workers and International Ladies' Garment Workers Unions had mopped up that human cesspool, that comparison could not be thought of.

But these people were not wops and bohunks. They were not Jewish needle slaves, escaped from the ghettos and pogroms of Czarist Russia and Poland. They were Americans almost to a man. Their forefathers had been starved, driven, shipped and sold over here long before and shortly after the Revolution. They were Scotch, Irish, Scotch-Irish and English with only a few exceptions. They were more American than the population of any present-day New England town. They were Washington's ragged, starving, shivering army at Valley Forge, pushed ever westward by beneficiaries of the Revolution. Pushed out of Tidewater Virginia, and out of the fertile Piedmont, and the river valleys of the Central Atlantic states, into the hills and mountains of the South Central states. They had followed on the heels of the Cherokees, Choctaws, Chickasaws, Creeks and Seminoles, like the stragglers of routed armies. Always hoping that somewhere in their America there would be a piece of dirt for them.

Now they had settled down in the hills of the Indian Territory, tenants of white land hogs, Indians, squaw men and Afro-American freedmen. A quarter of a century later, burned out and tractored out, they pulled up stakes for the last time until they landed in ramshackle trucks and tin lizzies in California, as ragged, hungry and shivering as their ancestors at Valley Forge.

They had hoped the Homestead Act would be applied to the Indian Territory. That Uncle Sam would have farms for them, too. Uncle Sam had presented quarter-sections of virgin prairie land to millions of Swedes, Norwegians, Danes, Germans. Why should he deny a forty-acre, two-mule farm to Americans stemming from Valley Forge and Yorktown?

The Indian Territory was not thrown open for homesteading. It had been given to the Indians under a sacred treaty, signed by the Great White Father in Washington, providing it should be theirs "as long as water flows and grass grows green." By that time the bulk of North American Indians were safely cornered. But their hunting grounds had woefully shrunken; buffalo almost exterminated and other game greatly diminished. Fire water, white man's diseases, a new, and to the Indian, unnatural mode of living, had undermined his resistance, pride and constitution.

Somebody had to support poor Lo. He could not be supported by taxes levied on the whole of the United States, all of which had been taken from him. So what more natural than to let poor Lo keep his land and the poor hillbillies work it? And so we have the interesting spectacle of white, native, Protestant Americans working as the land slaves, tenants and share croppers of the aboriginal Indian.

The Indian was not a bad landlord. He still labored under the heathen delusion that land belonged to the Great Spirit who had made air, rain and sunshine. So long as his superior Anglo-Saxon land slave could supply him with a hog or a jug of fire water now and then, in addition to the meager dole he received from the White Father in Washington, he was contented. Later on, when the Office of Indian Affairs assumed the rôle of rent collector, poor Lo's income went up as his white tenant's went down. Still later, when squaw men, usurers, land sharks, and Eastern insurance companies had come into possession of most of poor Lo's inheritance, to have been his "as long as water flows," the position of the tenants and share croppers hit rock-bottom. So at last they pulled out onto Highway Sixty-Six on their final journey to Gethsemane.

I wish someone would look up the names on the roster of Washington's army at Valley Forge and trace the bloody footprints of their descendants across the North American continent until they were washed up and washed out on the shore of the Pacific. What an all-American Odyssey it would make! What a great history of the Rise and Fall of American Civilization. And I, a social worker—hell! I had a real job on hand.

27

O N my first tour of exploration, I penetrated deeper and
deeper into the Indian Territory, the tenant and mining
sections of Oklahoma. I traveled on foot, horseback, by
buggy and covered wagon. I was sometimes carried in the cabooses
of freight trains by friendly trainmen, on the strength of my
union card. I ate hog belly, corn pone, baking-powder biscuits,
poke greens, and New Orleans molasses until my stomach cried
for mercy. I slept in tenant shacks with kids across the foot of my
bed and one on either side. I was watered and irrigated until I
learned the technique of turning their sweet little faces in the
opposite direction to my slumbering self. I slept in wagon yards,
miners' tents, tenant shacks and farmer hotels, the worst in the
land, and wherever I slept, the bedbugs were always with me.

I am mentioning bedbugs first because no matter where I went
I invariably found them waiting for me. True, I seem to be unusually attractive to every critter that crawls, flies, bites and bores,
but above all, I am the first choice of bedbugs. Before retiring I
would examine every crack, chink, seam and knothole in and
around my bed without detecting a solitary bug. Hardly had I
stretched out before one would bite my ankle or wrist, then blow
his bugle to notify his friends and relatives that he had discovered the choice morsel of his young life, and the stampede was on.

I had been told pennyroyal and citrus oil would keep bedbugs
away. In my case, they only seasoned poor me. I would examine

every fiber and seam on the blanket or comforter before stretching it on the board floor of some miner's boarding house or farmer hotel. I would load my trusty bedbug gun with insect powder up to the snozzle, draw an insect-powder ring around the blanket or comforter wide and high enough to discourage the most enterprising. All in vain. Hardly had I closed my eyes when they were upon me, growing more numerous and more vicious with every beat of my pulse.

I never found out how these lowly creatures managed to get over that barrier of insect powder. Are there hopping bedbugs, winged bedbugs? Or did they, on discovering my barricade of insect powder, simply turn around, climb up the wall, cross the ceiling fly-fashion, and parachute down on me? I saw bedbugs emerging from pine boards that had left the saw mill the day before. I saw them lying in ambush for me, hanging from trees and shrubs head down and ready to spring. I saw them crawl out of exhumed coffins, pale as death, transparent as glass, and ask for breakfast. And if there was one in even the best of hostelries that couldn't follow the bellhop and me fast enough to my room, he would look my room number up in the regular fashion and follow at his leisure.

I saw so many bedbugs on that tour, and so much of them, that I finally got to the place where the sight of a bed made me start scratching and wish I were dead. Certainly this is a "vulgar" subject. But it suggests, I think, the unspeakable living conditions of some of our fellow citizens.

Two of us were going to an afternoon meeting on horseback. I was not a good equestrian, but in my Texas days I had learned enough of the art so that I could fall off almost any horse without hurting myself. On the way to the one-room schoolhouse in which I was to hold forth, we fell in with a bunch of Choctaw Indians, and they were by far the drunkest Indians I had ever fallen, or hoped to fall, in with. They were armed with two gallon jugs of oh-be-joyful, each still a quarter full. They knew my companion. He was the best friend they'd ever had. He must take a good hard swallow of their oh-be-joyful. He did. I did. The jug kept going round and round. It was the vilest stuff I ever drank, but how can you refuse to go along with a bunch of very drunken Indians?

The Indians decided they would accompany us to the powwow. I was stumped. It would never do for Messiah Oscar Ameringer to enter that schoolhouse with a bunch of drunken Choctaws. And how drunk they were! Even their ponies reeled in an effort to keep under their riders. My companion and I exhausted our stock of arguments to dissuade the noble red men. At last, I hit on a brilliant idea. The schoolhouse was rather small and no doubt already overcrowded. But that night I would preach in a large church some eight miles up in the Kiamichi mountains. Would they come to that church and bring many more of their friends and relatives with them? I would deliver a sermon on the problems of the North American red men at large, and point a way out of their trials and tribulations. The Indians promised to be there with bells on and so we parted. When they had gone whooping down the road I turned to my companion and said, "Gosh, how lucky that we got rid of them."

"Rid of them," replied my companion. "You mean how deep you got your foot in it."

"What do you mean?"

"Didn't those Choctaws promise to be at your meeting tonight?"

I agreed they had.

"And didn't they promise to be there with bells on and bring a lot more Indians with them?"

I acknowledged it was even so.

"Well," he answered, "don't worry. They'll be there with all the Indians they can scare up, if they have to drag 'em there by their scalps. Whatever may be said against them, their word is better than most white men's bond." And in verification of that statement, he told me the following story:

Some years past, an Indian had stopped at his shack and asked for a drink of water. When handing the Indian the dipper, he had inquired where he was bound for. The Indian replied he was going to a certain town to be shot. He had been found guilty of murder by a territorial court, had received permission to return to his people to get his affairs in order and bid them farewell. Now he was on his way back—all alone—to be shot.

A railroad tie buyer from Pennsylvania, whom I had inducted into the faith at the afternoon meeting, offered to take me in his buggy to the church in the Kiamichi. I gladly accepted. Shortly after nightfall we reached the place, a dilapidated, barnlike structure, minus doors and windows, and the Indians were there with bells on. There were at least three times more than we had invited, and all of them twice as drunk. Besides our Indian friends there were some fifty tie-hackers from a near-by lumber camp, all of them as drunk as the Indians. Other people had come. Earnest, sober, determined people. I saw their horses hitched in a circle of trees around the clearing in which the church stood, and I saw the glitter of Winchesters on their saddles. A rumor had gone around that the Democrats had sworn to lynch the first "socialist agitator" who came to that neck of the woods. The riflemen had come from far and wide to protect their comrade speaker.

I was not lynched, for barking dogs don't bite. But what a meeting! The only light in the barn was the dash lantern of my convert. Every time I took my breath, thunderous applause, Rebel yells and Indian war whoops shook the rafters. Every humorous allusion was met with a veritable tidal wave of uproarious hilarity. But I was not lynched. The sober, determined comrades at the door in the rear of the church attended to that. Everything went off peacefully. A good time was had by everybody. Without other mishap than an empty dash lantern and a broken doubletree we reached the valley settlement just as morning painted the eastern sky rosy gray, and early breakfast smoke ascended from cabin chimneys.

How miserable those cabins were, ventilated by chinks, cracks, knot and woodpecker holes, and yet how beautiful they often looked in such settings. How beautiful and inviting when one passed them on winter eves, smoke pouring from stick chimneys, the glow of their fireplaces in their windows, the sweet fragrance of fried bacon and boiling coffee floating from the door. How little it would take to make these people secure, healthy and happy, and even that little denied by the greed and stupidity of their "betters."

This story was told to me by a young coal miner. Later on it was corroborated in person by the hero of the story.

The Oklahoma miners had tried to organize ever since the coal lands of the Indian Territory had passed into the hands of the railroad corporations. Some years previous to my arrival there had been a bitter strike. Federal regulars had invaded the valley stretching from McAlester to Wilburton on the Arkansas line and beyond, and made short shrift of the striking coal diggers. They evicted them from the company shacks, loaded them on box cars, plus wives and children, and shipped them to Arkansas and Texas—whichever happened to be more handy. A miner's wife gave birth to a child on a flat car; she told me about it herself. If, in that process, families became separated, it was just too bad. But it certainly was no concern of a government of, by and for the people.

Later there was another strike. This time there were no evictions. The company imported Negro strike breakers from the sugar-cane, tobacco and cotton fields of sunny Dixie, and protected them with white thugs and gunmen. It lodged these beauties in a string of box cars along a siding, surrounded by a board fence crowned by barbed wire. The drunken, degraded rabble of thugs and gunmen found amusement at night by discharging revolvers and rifles in the direction of the sleeping mining camp. Bullets penetrated the walls of the flimsy shacks. No one had been hurt yet, but something had to be done.

A small body of volunteers agreed to do whatever had to be done. In the dead of night they crawled toward the protecting board fence, each with a bundle of dynamite sticks stolen from the company's powder house under his arm. Their leader was Sam, peace to his ashes: he was laid to final rest in Illinois only a few years ago. Sam was a preacher and miner. He preached salvation until he became too drunk to preach; then he worked at digging coal until he had sobered up sufficiently to save souls again.

The volunteers pried a board loose from the board fence and were ready to enter when a whisper from parson Sam bid them pause.

"Brothers," he said, "let us not enter this battle without asking the blessing of the Lord."

They all knelt down, each with his bundle of dynamite sticks properly primed with fuse and cap, and preacher Sam told the good Lord above why it was his duty to help the miners, rather than the dirty coal operators who were robbing them in their company stores and shanty towns. According to my young informant, and later verified by parson Sam, a few minutes later it rained box cars, strike breakers, and thugs from heaven. The miners' prayer was answered.

Raw, sordid, beastly? Yes, as raw, sordid, beastly, and brutal as life in American mining camps before the United Mine Workers put an end to it—in part.

I had struck a two-by-four hamlet on the mountain fork of the Little River. I had eaten sow belly, corn pone, and molasses until my stomach had gone on the warpath. I had to have a change of diet, no matter what, or pass out. I purchased cane pole, line, and spinner in the general store of the two-by-four hamlet, and walked into Little River with blood in my eyes and cold murder in my heart.

A bass struck. This was no occasion for playing with a bass. I walked out on the shore dragging the bass behind. He was a beauty. Perhaps a three-pounder. I stuck my knife in his neck, pulled out his entrails, built a fire on a flat rock and waited for two centuries for the rock to heat up. Then, the rock heated, I placed the bass on top, covered it with ashes and glowing coals, waited another eternity and finally devoured the half-done bass minus bread and salt. He tasted better than any food I had ever eaten.

From the standpoint of bodily comfort and spiritual tranquillity, the two months I spent on that research tour belong to the worst of my experiences. They taught me that there can be abject feudalism in a democracy. And that a democracy in which millions of its people are denied access to mother earth, or other means by which to gain their living, is pure and unadulterated eye wash.

My last stand on that tour was in Wilburton, a good-sized mining camp near the Arkansas line. I was out of kilter in every organ of my body. My blood had gone to the cause by way of chiggers, mosquitoes, bedbugs and ticks. I was so weak from malaria that I was compelled to sit on the wagon seat from where I addressed my audience of coal miners. After the meeting the boys had put me to bed in a miner's boarding house, and when I staggered out of bed next morning I found eighteen dollars in change on the dresser. They are the salt of the earth, those miners, the bravest, most intelligent and scrappiest set of America's wage earners, not even excepting the Jewish needle-trade workers, who, in my opinion, stand next to the miners. With that eighteen dollars I took the train to Oklahoma City, where I purchased soup meat and vegetables, and went on a vegetable-soup debauch such as the world has never seen. It cured me of malaria. Of my notion that all American farmers were capitalists and exploiters I had long since been permanently cured.

28

FORT TOWNSEND is a small sawmill town in the southern part of what was once Indian Territory. It was from this place that Sam Houston had started for Texas to bring the plains Indians into the confederation of Indian nations he had launched some time previously on the Seven Bull River in northeastern Oklahoma. He was later to be the "liberator of Texas." On the occasion of my first visit to Fort Townsend I was unaware that I was the second liberator who had honored the place with his presence. Perhaps some day the Daughters of the Revolution will affix bronze tablets on some suitable walls bearing the legends:

"Near here, Sam Houston, the Liberator of Texas, took a long drink of redeye out of a three-gallon jug fastened to his saddle horn, and lit out for Texas."

"On this identical spot stood the soap box from which Oscar Ameringer, the immortal agitator and pamphleteer of the social revolution, spilled Marxist dialectic all over the place."

At that particular time I did not feel like a liberator. Fort Townsend was an aggregation of unpainted shotgun shacks straggling out from a center section of unpainted, straight-up-and-down board stores. D.A.R.'s, of either brand, aspiring to place bronze placards on those walls, would have experienced considerable difficulty locating a wall capable of supporting anything more weighty than circus bills or Battle Axe tobacco signs.

The town was hot and sticky. It must have been a hundred and ten in the shade, and no shade. There was nobody to welcome me. I was the only socialist in the place, and socialists were not welcome in that rock-ribbed Democratic neck-of-the-woods. Once I had a sizable crowd before me, speaking came easy enough. To be my own chairman and in that capacity ballyhoo the crowd together for the main event was always painful to me.

However, I had my trusty clarinet. "Music hath charms . . ." So presently I found myself on a soap box dispersing such classics as "Turkey in the Straw," "Arkansas Traveler," and "Everybody Works but Father," which were the latest song hits of that day, age, and locality. Gradually an audience assembled—a few white men, some Negroes, two or three Indians and a respectable number of mongrel dogs thirsting for knowledge and water. By sandwiching my discourse between slices of melody, I built the crowd until there must have been not less than ten hearers before me. My minimum for shedding the clarinet was twelve, but the missing twain remained missing. However, succor was near.

I had noticed a small, black-eyed and black-haired, well dressed young man in the audience. He carried a roll of copper wire in one hand and apparently had something on his mind he was trying hard to convey to me, for he made sundry gestures indicating something of that nature. Finally, during one of the pauses that every good orator makes as an invitation for uproarious laughter or tumultuous applause, the well dressed young man (well dressed because he wore store clothes in contrast to the regulation blue-jean overalls worn by the regimented assembly of American peasantry and proletariat before me) stepped up to the soap box and whispered, "What's your graft, bo?"

I scented and resented the implication. I did not regard myself as a grafter. I was the humble herald of a new epoch in civilization and plainly told him so.

"Oh, go on," said the young man with the piercing black eyes and the copper wire. "I only want to know what you're driving at. What's your spiel? What are you trying to sell the boobs?"

"I'm making a socialist speech; I'm a socialist, if you want to know," I replied sternly, still smarting under the implications.

"Fine," said the young man. "I'm a hypnotist, mind reader and phrenologist, and if you let me have that soap box I'll get a crowd that'll make your eyes pop out, and we'll work it together."

The two missing disciples were still missing, so I surrendered the soap box.

The young man understood his business. He had "it," "oomph," personality, and magnetism that spluttered and crinkled from his very finger ends. He asked candidates for phrenological experiments to step forward. They did. He felt the lumps and humps on their cranial topography and explained their significance. He took his copper wire and measured the width, depth, and circumference of their skulls, and told the virtues and skulduggeries concealed therein. If not a great phrenologist, he was at least a great psychologist, for his findings were often met with such exclamations of approval as, "Say, can you beat it? If that ain't Jasper to a dot!"

Having delivered his opinions of the skulls and their bearers he continued, "And now, ladies and gentlemen, I will give you a demonstration of mental telepathy, popularly known as mind reading. I therefore ask this large" (and by that time it was large) "and intelligent audience to select a committee of two responsible men, in whom all of you have confidence, to purchase and hide a cigar, agreeing between themselves who shall smoke it. I in turn agree to find that cigar blindfolded and stick it blindfolded between the lips of the man the committee has agreed upon."

"Some chore," I said to myself. However, the committee of two was duly elected, purchased the cigar, and proceeded toward the outskirts of Fort Townsend. Soon the two returned, to blindfold the young man's eyes with a handkerchief he had providentially brought with him for that purpose. Then, folding his arms across his breast, he requested each of the committeemen to grasp the wrist nearest to him. That done, he uttered the command, "Forward march!" The migration, accompanied by myself, clarinet, and dogs, got in motion. After considerable zigzagging, we landed in the rear of a blacksmith shop, before a junk heap of broken wagon wheels, superannuated farm implements, and discarded horse shoes such as only a blacksmith shop can produce. The young man, still blindfolded, commanded the committeeman to the right of him to grasp his right wrist. That done, he groped with said hand in the junk pile and extracted the cigar, among the surprised cheers of the audience. Then, again requesting the gentlemen of the committee to grasp the wrists of his folded arms, he started the procession in the general direction of the mouth of the man who was to smoke the cigar. We found him dozing on the counter of the Busy Bee General Store.

"Now my right-hand guide, kindly grasp the wrist of my right hand," commanded the young man, and after some fumbling he inserted the cigar between the very teeth of the person the committee had agreed should smoke it.

By that time the population of Fort Townsend was at the feet of the young man with the piercing black eyes, and when on returning to the soap box he announced that he would give a lecture and demonstration on the mysteries of hypnotism, mind reading, mesmerism, and phrenology at the schoolhouse that night, admission fifteen cents for adults and ten cents for children, there was no doubt in my mind that Fort Townsend would be there en masse.

Having delivered the invitation he continued, "And now, ladies and gentlemen, permit me to introduce to you a man you all know, a man who has spoken before all the crowned heads of the old and new worlds, a man who requires no introduction." Turning to me he whispered, "Say, guy, what's your name?" "Ameringer," I whispered back. "And now I take great pleasure in introducing to the citizens of this beautiful little city the world renowned orator, Mr. Hammerslinger, who will speak to you on the mysteries—say, fellow, what did you say your spiel was?"

"Socialism." "Who will speak to you on the mysteries of social-ism." I did.

At the end of my discourse I threw my hat in the sand and requested all those who had enjoyed or, perhaps, even profited by my lecture to assist the international brotherhood of man by depositing their contributions therein.

There was no rush toward the hat, although a few made certain gestures indicating a modest degree of financial sympathy with the ideas I had expressed. The net result was thirty-five cents, which induced the following disgusted comment from the young man with the piercing black eyes:

"Thirty-five cents! Can you beat it! You," addressing the audience, "are the worst aggregation of cheap skates and dyed-in-the-wool pikers I ever heard of. I know nothing about this socialism of his, but it surely sounds good to me. What's more, he talked in your interests, you boneheads. If you listened to him, you might get somewhere. If he had sold you chill-and-fever medicine of aqua pura flavored with a bad smell, you would have bought his last bottle. That's the kind of spieler that man is. And you hand him thirty-five cents! Get out of my sight, or I'll throw a spell on the whole outfit of you—you—you!"

Had my new-found friend worn a ten-gallon hat and carried a six-shooter on his hip, or possessed less occult powers, there might have been trouble, but as it was the audience dispersed somewhat sheepishly, and left the field to the two of us.

It still was a hundred and ten in the shade, but the sun was getting lower, painting the Winding Stairs Mountains with violet. We were sitting on the soap box and resting on our laurels. "Buddy," commenced the young man with the piercing black eyes, "I like your spiel; you got a good line, and there's a heap in what you're preaching. But take it from me, you'll never get anywhere preaching horse sense. You've got to humbug 'em, and the bigger the humbug, the better they like it.

"Take that mind-reading stunt of mine. In the first place, they haven't got minds to read. In the second place, it's as easy as

rollin' off a log if you know how. You noticed after I was blindfolded I crossed my arms across my chest and asked the boobs
to get ahold of my wrists. That gave me a guide on each side.
Now look at this high-ridged nose of mine. Properly blindfolded,
and you may have noted I folded the handkerchief myself, I can
see neither sideways nor straight out. But I still can see straight
down, which is more important, because when I give the command, forward march, those guides of mine invariably turn their
toes in the direction in which they hid the cigar. If I let 'em, they
would lead me smack to it, and that would spoil the suspense.
So, to make the feat look harder and gather a bigger crowd, I
always zigzag around a bit, knowing full well that the involuntary tug of their hands on my wrists will keep me on the right
course. You also noted, when we finally got to the junk pile
behind the blacksmith shop, I asked one of them to hold my
right wrist. He's the baby that guides my hand to the cigar and
renders the same indispensable service when it comes to sticking
the cigar between the teeth of the man they agreed should smoke
it. As far as mind reading is concerned, I couldn't find a haystack blindfolded without the assistance of these boobs. They are
leading me to the cigar, not me them. But just watch the crowd
that shabby trick will pull tonight.

"What we two ought to do is to strike up a partnership: I humbug 'em and you teach 'em. Not that I'm all humbug. I'm as
good a hypnotist as they make; you'll find out tonight. Besides,
I always wanted some music to improve my act. You play that
whistle of yours while I make my hypnotized gang go through
their stunts, and we'll go fifty-fifty."

Bless his heart, and what a tribute to my persuasive powers.
He had heard only one speech of mine, and was already willing
to divide up. How could I resist? And that's how it came about
that hypnotist and socialist struck up a partnership.

That night the elementary seat of learning of Fort Townsend
was crowded to overflowing. Every seat, window sill, and square

foot of standing room had somebody sitting on it. Broad-hipped
matrons, with babies on laps or breasts, crowded two strong behind
school desks designed for seven-year-olds, and flowed over the
edge. Through every opening, chink, crack, and knothole peered
glittering eyes, and children everywhere.

True to his word, Mooney—Jim Mooney was my new partner's name—was a real hypnotist. He made his victims go
through the customary stunts of swimming on the floor, pulling
gigantic catfish out of imaginary fishing holes, throwing rocks
at nonexistent hornets' nests and battling the enraged insects.
Then he climaxed the performance by a skit in which three sleeping lumberjacks combated hoards of visionary bedbugs. It
brought down the house, and it deserved to. No aggregation of
Broadway stars could have acted their parts as naturally as those
hypnotized lumberjacks did. Nor could any Broadway audience
have been as appreciative of the fine points involved. A great
hypnotist was my partner, Jim Mooney. He must have had even
me hynotized, for when I heard something snap before my nose,
I was sitting cross-legged, clarinet in mouth, on the teacher's
desk, giving an imitation of a Hindu snake charmer soothing an
enraged cobra with the lullaby from *Il Trovatore*. Then I heard,
"I now take pleasure in introducing to you the world-renowned
orator, Mr. Hammerslinger," and my act started. . . .

Sitting on the step of the schoolhouse, counting the receipts of
the night in the moonlight (the audience had brought its own
implements of illumination and had returned home with them),
we toted up seven dollars. The partnership of hypnotist and
socialist was a howling success.

As the days went on, our joint act improved. I was still supplying incidental music with a Marxist finale. But Mooney was
taking on more and more of my educational cargo. He had become a rip-roaring socialist determined to convert this unbeliev-
ing world to the only true faith. So hypnotism made a united
front with socialism. Selecting three of the seediest and lowliest

of his subjects, he would address them in the commanding voice
of a born Svengali:

"You are John D. Rockefeller. You own all the oil wells,
refineries and tank wagons in the country. You," he would
thunder, pointing to a one-button overall, "are Pierpont Morgan.
You own all the banks, railroads and insurance companies in the
country. And you over here are Andy Carnegie, you own all the
steel mills and libraries in the country. All of your pockets are
bulging with money. Up at your palatial residences are bales of
bonds and slews of stocks. Now do business."

Thereupon, short and chunky John D., garbed in ventilated
work shirt, patched blue jeans and leaky brogans, would thrust
peaked chest and bulgy stomach out and address lean, hungry,
six-foot Carnegie, out at knees and elbows:

"Now, Andy, I'll give you a hundred million dollars for that
second-hand railroad of yours, but not a damned cent more. Take
it or leave it, it makes no difference to me. You haven't got the
only railroad to sell in the United States. There are plenty of
folks who'd be tickled pink to sell their railroads for good, hard
cash. John D. Rockefeller don't have to stand off nobody. When
I say a hundred million cash I mean it—and if you don't believe
I've got the kale here"—extracting bags of imaginary gold out
of imaginary pockets—"here's the stuff. Now take it or leave it.
I ain't begging nobody to take my money."

Or Pierpont Morgan, sadly in need of a haircut and shave,
but affluently removing ghostly Havanas from his snaggle-
toothed mouth, would solemnly answer six-foot Carnegie:

"If you think I'm gonna buy your steel trust for a measly
five hundred million smackers you better get out of here right
now. The house of Morgan ain't running a peanut roaster or a
hot-dog stand. We never buy anything for less than a cool billion.
So you either take a cool billion for your junk or the deal's off."

During these transactions it frequently happened that the
larger share of America's natural resources, industrial equipment
and fluid assets passed from calloused hand to calloused hand.

The hands were as empty as the minds of their owners. But what of it? Man is as he thinketh, even if someone else doth the thinking for him. At the end of the act my partner would bring Rockefeller, Morgan and Carnegie back to earth by snapping his fingers. Then, addressing the hilarious audience, he would continue:

"Funny, isn't it, to make these poor devils imagine they are rolling in money? But just as I had them hypnotized, so the capitalists have got you hypnotized into believing that all of you can become Rockefellers, Morgans and Carnegies if you work hard and save your money." Then, turning to me, "Now, Mr. Hammerslinger, snap your fingers at the rubes and wake 'em up." Whereupon my act started.

The combination of hypnotism and socialism with clarinet obbligato was literally a howling success. The fame of our team spread all across the corner where Texas and Arkansas slobber over into Oklahoma, as the saying goes. Audiences and financial returns mounted steadily. There is no doubt in my mind that had the partnership continued, the path of the co-operative commonwealth would have been shortened by many weary miles.

But alas, as so often happens, the profit motive reared its ugly head and broke up our team. In a small town in the Pushmataha country we came upon the worst smell that ever assailed the human nose. Closer investigation revealed that the smell emanated from a spring of yellow sulphurous water, flavored with decadent hen fruit and glue-factory perfume. On smelling that water I moved to adjourn to the leeward, and at the greatest distance.

"What!" exclaimed my partner, with an acquisitive glitter in his eyes. "Run away from this water? Why, man alive, there's millions in that stinkhole. Anything that smells as bad as all that must have no end of medicinal virtue in it, to say nothing of profitable returns. There isn't a germ, microbe or bacterium that could live within a mile of it. Right here we stay, bottling and jugging that water. We will advertise it as the Famous Pushma-taha Pain Killer, and make our pile."

I was not averse to making a pile. With a pile of money I could launch the dream of my life—a socialist daily. But try as I would, neither my nose nor my stomach could stand the fearful odor of that health-giving fluid, and so partnership between hypnotist and socialist broke up.

Years later, speaking at a socialist encampment in Texas, I met my former teammate again. He had not extracted the million from the waters of Pushmataha. Lack of capital had prevented the spreading of its therapeutic fame. He had, though, accumulated a comfortable competency by adding fortune telling, and imparting the art of finding hidden treasures, to hypnotism, mind reading and phrenology. In the process he had become a "tired radical."

29

THE state secretary of the Party had written me to meet a certain comrade at a certain date and hour at the depot of Hugo, Oklahoma, county seat and capital of Choctaw County and Nation. The comrade was to convey me to a sawmill town on the Red River bearing the euphonious name of Frogville. The purpose of my mission was the reorganization of a socialist local that had gone to pot.

When I reached Hugo I found the comrade waiting with the conveyance, a dilapidated Studebaker wagon propelled by a sway-backed mare and a blind mule. The comrade himself was a second-degree tenant farmer, meaning that, as the possessor of tools and animal power, he paid one-fourth of the cotton and one-third of the corn he raised for rent, whereas first-degree tenants or share croppers, possessing nothing outside of their own labor power, worked on halves.

He was the most pessimistic and dour-looking mortal I ever happened to run across. As we creaked over the sandy near-road toward Frogville, I turned to him and inquired, "Tell me, comrade, what happened to the Frogville local?"

"Gone to hell," he replied in sepulchral tones and with the mien of an undertaker burying his last corpse preliminary to making application for voluntary bankruptcy.

"Gone to hell! But why?" I asked.

"Capitalism," he replied in a voice of ultra-indigo.

"But what has capitalism to do with the Frogville local?" I persisted.

"Capitalism," he replied, "will make a crook and a thief of the best of men. No man can lead a straight life under capitalism any more than a rattlesnake can sleep straight in a copper coil."

"Quite right," I confessed, "but please tell me how capitalism manifested itself in the Frogville local."

"We had forty members in our local. It was the biggest local in the whole Choctaw Nation, and we got along swimmingly until we had three dollars in the treasury."

"And then?" I asked.

"And then," he replied in a melancholy voice, summing up all the accusations hurled at capitalism and the total depravity of man in general, "the secretary's house burned down."

"And the money burned up?"

"That's what he said," he replied with a disdainful and decidedly wry grin, "but the next day we caught him lugging a fifty-pound sack of flour, a gallon jug of molasses, a ten-pound sack of sugar, and a ten-pound slab of sow belly to the new place he had rented."

"Just so, but what has that got to do with the three dollars of Frogville local that burned up?" I wanted to know.

"Well," he replied, "figure it out yourself: fifty pounds of flour costs a dollar, a gallon of molasses, fifty cents, ten pounds of sugar, fifty cents, and a ten-pound slab of fat meat, another dollar. And there are the three dollars of Frogville local that went up in smoke."

It didn't seem reasonable that a man would burn his house down to come into possession of three dollars. However, after my pessimistic comrade had explained that the house of the guilty treasurer was not a house at all, but a mere tenant shack, and that it was not his property, but belonged to a squaw man, and that by pulling his stove and bed out of the shack and striking a match to the remainder the faithless secretary would make a net profit of three dollars out of the transaction, I saw the light. And that night I reorganized Frogville local.

Mindful of the bitter experience the membership had had with a profit-minded share cropper, and to re-establish the confidence of the assembled ex-and-prospective members in the integrity of the international socialist movement, I decided the next secretary of the Frogville local must be a genuine proletarian.

I found such a man. His name was Nickel, and he was a saw filer in the town's only sawmill. Before that he had been a member of the United Mine Workers of America, in which he had served as corresponding secretary of one of the locals, which suggested that he could both read and write. The obvious man for the job, I figured, and at the meeting that night he was elected over considerable opposition. Next morning I was on my way to the depot of the Choctaw Nation, a passenger on a profit-motivated lumber wagon. The pessimistic comrade had refused to haul me back on the ground that I had rigged up the election of Comrade Nickel. I had.

That fall there was a socialist encampment near Hugo, the county seat and capital of Choctaw County and Nation. The battery of speakers were Gene Debs, Walter Thomas Mills, Caroline Low and myself. These encampments usually lasted a week and attracted thousands of people who often came in covered wagons, cooked, slept, and ate right there on the camp ground. Meandering through the encampment one day, shaking hands with friends and making new acquaintances, I spied my pessimistic comrade from Frogville.

"Hello," I cried, with all the cheer and buoyancy I could muster, "and how is Frogville local getting along?"

"Gone to hell," he replied, extending a cold, limp, and anything but comradely hand.

"And why?"

"Same old thing, capitalism," he replied in a voice shaking from suppressed emotion.

"How did capitalism manifest itself this time?"

"Well, I told you capitalism makes a crook and a thief of the best of men and that no man can go straight under capitalism any more than he could lay straight in a copper coil."

"You did," I said, "but what happened?"

"Well, you remember the fellow, Nickel, that saw filer who said he had been secretary of a Mine Workers' Local up McAlester way."

I confessed.

"And you thought he was a pretty good man, didn't you?"

I confessed that such was the case.

"And you kinda pulled the wires and had him elected over our protests, didn't you?"

I had.

"Well, he was a good man, a mighty good man until we had a dollar and eighty cents in the treasury."

"And then?" I inquired, all needles and pins.

"And then," came the crushing reply, "he ran off with the treasury and took a comrade's wife with him."

All of which goes to show that the profit virus had already destroyed the moral fiber of the nation to such an extent that even proletarians could not be trusted any more.

The Party had established the policy that speakers and organizers must alternate between Indian Territory and old Oklahoma. The two are roughly divided by the Santa Fe Railroad, which traverses the state from north to south. The eastern part was almost exclusively populated by people from the Old South. The tenant system along with the social conditions described in earlier pages were a replica of Southern agricultural life.

Oklahoma proper was settled under the Homestead Act. By fulfilling certain formalities, the homesteader received a hundred and sixty acres of land, free; the only conditions were a filing fee of three dollars, and the requirement to put up a habitable shelter, live on the land and work it in person. Having complied with these terms for seven years, he "proved up," whereupon his claim became private property, to be sold, bequeathed, and, alas, mortgaged, at the will of the owner.

The outstanding feature of the Homestead Act was that until the settler proved his use and occupancy, his presence constituted his only claim to the land. Or, in other words, the title remained with the government while the settler enjoyed the usufruct thereof. Relinquishment of claims could be sold, but only to purchasers who agreed to live on and work the claim. Thus, only farmers who farmed the land could possess the gift of Uncle Sam. Under this form of land tenure, which, so far as I know, was a purely American invention, absentee ownership was excluded. The tragedy of American farm life is that the Homestead Act was not made perpetual. If its principle had been extended in perpetuity, American farmers who farm would still own those farms. Neither would it have been possible to crush them under a mortgage burden which by now has reached the staggering sum of nine billion dollars, a sum, by the way, so vast that if the interest on it were paid in full, the annual payment would be large enough to buy the entire annual wheat crop at current domestic prices. When the homesteader had established satisfactory evidence that for seven years he had worked his claim, lived on it, and built a habitable shelter thereon, this beneficial and vigorously American form of land tenure went into the discard as far as those particular hundred and sixty acres were concerned. With the possession of a title deed in fee simple, ownership and farming of farms could be separated. The farmland remained where it always had been, but the title to it could be in the safe of a county-seat doctor, lawyer, merchant or banker, or a New York insurance company. The same held true of mortgages. If the deed and mortgage holder had had to live on his property and work it in person he would, in nine cases out of ten, have run from the holding like the proverbial devil from holy water. Under the seven-year provision of the Homestead arrangement, farmland would have remained the collective property of farmers, each farm in undisturbed possession of the man who

lived on it and worked it. The farmstead could not be mortgaged because the title would rest in the collectivity of farmers.
And yet, any farm could still be sold, but only to farmers who
would work it. By the same token, it could be bequeathed, but
only to children who occupy and farm farms.

Under such conditions absentee ownership would have been
virtually impossible, and with that evil absent, farm tenantry
and crushing mortgage burdens would have disappeared. As it
was, the same separation between ownership and labor came about
in American agriculture that characterizes modern industry. The
title deed in fee simple, instead of assuring the tiller of the soil
of unabridged occupation and use of the soil, becomes the very
implement by which farmers are separated from their farms.

Even in cases where the homesteader remained in unencum-
bered possession of the farmstead until death, his farming children were beset by another menace: division through inheritance.
To illustrate this, let us say that Father had homesteaded and
proved up a quarter section of fine wheat land in any one of the
northern counties of Oklahoma, and that by the time of Father's
death, the value of the quarter section had reached thirty thousand dollars. The increase of land value from the original filing
fee of three dollars neither increased the yield of the land nor the
price of the farm products. The only things that did increase
with mounting land value were taxes. And as taxes are paid out
of proceeds from the sale of the product of the farmer's labor,
increasing taxes are reflected in lower farm incomes. As far as
the working farmer is concerned, other things being equal, the
lower land values are, the higher, not relatively, but actually,
his income.

In our assumed case, there are six heirs. One hundred and
sixty acres divided among the six would give each less than thirty
acres. But thirty acres of wheat land will not, even under the very
best conditions, support a farm family. Both parents and children
have recognized that fact long ago. Only two of them, therefore,
now remain on the homestead; four others move to town. So

instead of dividing the land we divide the value of the farm. The share of the heirs who have moved is five thousand dollars apiece, or twenty thousand all told; the share of the two heirs farming the homestead is ten thousand. The farming heirs are now called upon to pay the non-farming heirs twenty thousand dollars for the land Father acquired for three dollars, and as they haven't got the cash, they put a mortgage on the farm. In addition, they pay taxes on a property which is only one-third theirs. Beset by interest, taxes and mortgage-lifting, accompanied in most instances by soil depletion, the farming heirs give up the struggle. The mortgage is foreclosed. The two become tenants, farm hands, wage earners, or members of the army of the unemployed.

These details are presented to make clear what I believe to be the principal cause for the decrease of farm ownership among the actual tillers of America's soil. I am fully convinced that, unless a new farm tenure somewhat along the lines of a perpetual homestead act is put into effect, the farm freehold upon which American democracy is based is doomed, and with that democracy itself. I believe, further, that all attempts to solve the troubles of American agriculture without first settling the fundamental problem, land tenure, is at best well meant but futile. However, this is not a thesis on farm economics, so on with my story.

Partly as a reward for having stuck it out the full seven lean weeks in the tenant, bedbug and Indian country, and partly to fatten me up for future ordeals, the Party's secretary sent me to proselytize in the free, homestead-land country. And there I found still another America. The population was of many states and many types. From Texas had come cowmen and cotton farmers; from the Old South, share croppers and other poor whites. From the north and eastern states had come corn, cow, hog, and wheat farmers and a good percentage of former wage earners.

Oklahoma was opened for homesteading in 1889. The eight-

hour movement of 'Eighty-six definitely defeated, during the following two years many of its most active champions had forsaken
shop and factory to find freedom and sustenance on the free soil
of Oklahoma, America's last frontier. In 1894 the Cherokee
Strip was thrown open for settlement. In the same year, the
American Railway Union strike led by Eugene V. Debs had
broken out, been crushed, and Debs had landed in Woodstock
jail, from which he emerged to become leader of the newly
formed Socialist Party. So the land-rush into Cherokee country
brought not only many northern farmers, but among them a good
sprinkling of the defeated A.R.U. strikers.

I have called Oklahoma the "last American frontier," though
there was still another up in the Pacific northwest. But while it
was a frontier in America, its frontiersmen were mainly Scandinavians, Germans, and Irish from the old sod. The frontiersmen
of Oklahoma were almost exclusively of old American stock, and
they were radical Americans. The American frontier had always
been radical, since the days of Shays's Rebellion, and the presence
of a large number of disgruntled Knights of Labor and A.R.U.
strikers lent additional radicalism to the Oklahoma scene.

Like most western and southern farming states, Oklahoma had
been swept by Populism, but unlike the other states, Oklahoma's
Populists had not fused with the Democrats when, in 1896, the
Boy Orator of the Platte led the aroused farmers into the dismal
swamps of Sixteen-to-One. The Oklahoma Populists were irreconcilable foes of Wall Street, by which they understood the
united front of industrial and finance capitalism. Now that the
Populist Party had vanished, this seething mass of discontent had
nowhere to go. And there was plenty of cause for discontent.

The rolling prairies of the staked plains were brought under
the plow much more easily than the timberland east of the Mississippi. On the other hand, they lacked the basic building materials
for homes, barns, and fences. The herds of buffalo, deer, and
antelope had disappeared, soon to be followed by winged wild
life; jack rabbits and prairie dogs still supplied a modicum of

fresh meat, of a kind. The time was gone when farmsteads produced, and also consumed, the bulk of their owners' requirements. Reapers and threshing machines cost a great deal more than cradles and flails.

Money is always scarce on the frontier, and interest high. I have seen notes bearing ten per cent interest per month. Bulky farm staples, such as wheat, corn, broom corn, and raw cotton frequently had to be hauled to markets fifty and even a hundred miles distant. Arrived at the market, often over almost impossible roads, there was no haggling over the price. The farmer took what was offered, and what was offered was far below the market price announced on the market pages of Kansas City, Chicago and New Orleans papers. Instead of escaping industrialism and finance capitalism, as they had hoped, the last frontiersmen had brought it with them, sticking like cockleburs to their blue-jean breeches and flowing Mother Hubbards.

When I arrived in the free homestead land, virtually all of the homesteaders had proved up, meaning that they had acquired the means by which most of them would lose their homesteads in the not-far-distant future. However, many of the original settlers still lived in their dugouts, or sod houses, or the regulation fourteen-by-fourteen homesteader shacks. Even the worst of these dwellings were often preferable to the sharecropper shacks and cotton-picker breeding pens I had found in Indian Territory. Bedbugs in dugouts and sod houses were fewer; whether they prefer frame shack to earthen shelter, or were chased away by the centipedes that frequented the latter, I never learned. But beds were cleaner, and more numerous.

And the food, oh, so much better! Poor as these people were, they had at least a quarter section of dirt under their feet. Virtually all of them had cows, chickens, hogs, sheep, a vegetable garden, and had planted some fruit trees. All this meant a better balanced diet, explaining the greater energy and higher degree of health and education of the population as compared with that of the tenant population of Indian Territory, and those who lived further east and south to the Atlantic and Gulf of Mexico. But only once in all my years of wandering through the western part of Oklahoma did I find a bathtub in a farm home. It was only a tin tub, and the water was out in the cow lot and had to be carried in buckets. But to me at that time it was the marble bath of a Roman epicure.

Our meetings were usually held in schoolhouses which also served as churches. There was usually only one room and it was always illuminated by the stable lanterns and coal-oil lamps supplied by the audience. I still remember with pleasure the sight of those lanterns swinging on distant rambling wagons or from the hands of pedestrians, twinkling like lightning bugs for miles over the dark prairie, all converging toward the meeting house.

As a rule, families appeared in a body. Sleeping babies were deposited on the platform. For the orator, striding around the platform was ill advised. There was the danger of stepping on a future socialist voter and, the Lord knows, socialist voters were difficult enough to make. Young children from toddlers up crowded into the front school seats by twos and threes. Women with babies on their laps or at their breasts took the seats farther back in ones and twos. There was always at least one crying baby in the audience. If nursing, or a drink of water dipped from the common water bucket, failed to silence him, I usually would allay the embarrassment of the mother by saying, "Now, folks, don't let that baby worry you. Someday he will make a great speaker, like me, but I still can outtalk him. Accordingly . . ." and so on. This sally always restored peace and tranquillity, and for some reason usually put baby in better humor, or to sleep.

These frontier people constituted the most satisfactory audience of my long experience in "riling up the people." They were grateful for anything that broke the monotony of their lonesome lives. Of more than average intelligence, they followed the main arguments easily and caught even more subtle points quickly. Humor appealed to them immensely, for they belonged to the tribe from which America's great humorists—from Mark Twain down to Oklahoma's own Will Rogers—have derived their inspiration. One reason why these frontier people were even easier to address than my favorites, the coal miners, was because they were homogeneous, and they all understood English. Even my English.

As the movement developed, we added summer encampments to schoolhouse meetings. These encampments were lineal descendants of the religious and Populist camp meetings of former days. They usually lasted a full week. The audience came in covered wagons from as far as seventy miles around. We furnished water, firewood, and toilet facilities. The pilgrims brought their own commissary, cooked, ate and slept on the ground or in their covered wagons. Besides a large circus tent, we carried cooking and sleeping tents for the crew. Expenses were defrayed from collections taken at meetings and funds raised by the chambers of commerce in the nearest trading centers, the local bankers usually heading the list.

What? Chambers of commerce, merchants, bankers, supporting such subversive activities as socialist encampments? Why not? A good number of them were members of the faith. I remember a Socialist local in the Kiowa country composed of the town banker, lumber-yard owner, druggist, and blacksmith. And as Party regulations called for five members to constitute a local, these four leading citizens paid the dues of a nearly blind hamburger stand operator. There is, indeed, nothing to prevent people with a reasonable earned income from being good socialists. As the French say, "Money doesn't stink."

These encampments were attended by an average of five thousand people, and they meant business. Furthermore, they were welcome because they brought customers together and stimulated business. In those days, every town and trading center saw in itself a future metropolis of teeming millions. Each was competing with other towns for business and population. I remember one town, Elk City, in which our own co-operative hospital is now located, where the chamber of commerce had decorated the lamp and telephone posts on the line to the camp ground with red flags. On that memorable occasion, the show windows of the merchants displayed the red banner of international brotherhood.

In the course of the encampment we often arranged horseback parades through the town proper. Many of the younger people had arrived on horseback. Others rode the horses and mules of their covered wagons. A few thousand men riding through a town of perhaps not twice that many inhabitants looked like the migration of nations. Or at least, it looked as though the social revolution were just around the corner. . . .

As I have remarked, nearly all of the local agitators and speakers were ex-middle-of-the-road Populists, and all of old American stock. One of them was "Herdlaw" Johnson, so called because he had been instrumental in causing the cattlemen to fence in their grazing land, thereby protecting the crops of nesters, "Sooners" and all early settlers. Back in Arkansas his father had been a Union sympathizer during the Civil War. A band of jayhawkers had come to their clearing one morning and, in full view of the wife and children, had hanged the father on a tree. Subsequently, Herdlaw had pushed on to New Mexico, where the Apaches of Geronimo were on the warpath. He had pitched his tent on a rocky elevation overlooking a broad valley, and for protection had built a little stone fort. All one day he had seen the smoke of burning homesteads and heard the war whoops of the Indians; by nightfall, the Apaches were starting toward his fort, whooping and yelling their war cries. But still whooping and yelling they swept past Herdlaw, snuggled in his little stone fort, finger on the trigger of his Winchester, while from the tent behind came the first cry of a new-born babe.

A brave folk, courageous, yes, and above the average in intelligence, these Scotch-Irish "white trash" were capable of fighting their battles against men and nature, if given a Chinaman's chance.

"White trash!" There is good stuff in those people. If many of them are now below par it is not their nature that made them so, but the greed and stupidity of their so-called betters. On the free soil of the West the children of Ohio, Illinois, Indiana and Iowa farmers, many of them, in turn, sprung from down-east Yankees, and of Old South "white trash," could not be distinguished. Of course there is something to inheritance, breed and blood. But far more important in the shaping of men is environment. What I set down here holds equally true with Negroes. I have seen them at their lowest, in the land of share cropping and in the Negro slums of northern cities, and I have seen the very same people as hard-working, intelligent, law-abiding farm owners on free soil. But back to our encampments.

On the morning of the first day a mixed chorus was organized and rehearsed in Socialist songs, usually of Populist origin, sung to familiar melodies. After singing school we conducted economic and historical mass lessons. They were exceedingly informal. The instructor planted himself in the chair or store box on a raised platform, then urged the audience on the ground or pine planks to ask questions. Our most effective educator was Walter Thomas Mills, the author of *The Struggle for Existence*, our principal textbook. Both in history and economics we employed economic interpretations which have only recently and reluctantly been adopted by the centers of higher education. From high school down, our public school system still teaches the historic and economic fairy tales handed down from the eighteenth century. Charles Beard had not yet written his important *Economic Interpretation of the Constitution of the United States*, nor his even more important *The Rise of American Civilization*. We did have J. Allen Smith's *American Government* and Turner's epoch-making contribution, *The American Frontier*. But what we didn't have we simply made up ourselves. My personal contribution to America's enlightenment was *The Life and Deeds of Uncle Sam, A Little History for Big Children*. Up to America's entrance into the World War, some half million copies of that monumental

historic work of seventy pages had been sold. And today, enlarged
to a hundred pages, it is still going strong. Besides the English
edition there were some fourteen translations in other languages,
and even a re-translation from German back into English. The
German translator had done an excellent job. He had credited
me as author of *Unter dem Sternenbanner*. The only thing he had
overlooked was stating that it was a translation from the English.
Later on it was published as a translation from the German in a
student publication issued in New York, the capital of America's
brain belt.

Dinner over, and dishes washed, the two o'clock meeting started
under the big tent with singing and instrumental music. Singing
was led by our choir, recruited on the ground. The instrumental
music was supplied by myself and three sons, and we played only
the best, so far as the best can be played by a brass quartet augmented by piano. Before our instrumental concert, I usually gave
a short lecture on classical music, which I defined as Bill Nye had
defined Wagner's music: "it is a helluva lot better than it sounds."
I also explained how to acquire the appreciation of good music
by simply listening to it with all your mind and heart. Believe it
or not, we played arrangements of Beethoven, Mozart, and
Schubert quartets, chorals of Bach, songs of Mendelssohn, Wagner's "Evening Star" from *Tannhäuser*, the "Bridal Chorus"
from *Lohengrin*, and of course gems from Stephen Foster, America's own sweet singer. They loved it. Those simple people took
to good music like ducks to water. Their minds were not yet corrupted by the Tin Pan Alley trash that later was a music for
profit. Besides, "classical music" is folk music clarified, inter-
preted and ennobled by the great masters, and these were folk
people. As there was a demand for "something quick and devilish," we added a talented young lady violinist to our outfit, who
gave them Wieniawski's Hungarian dances, and abstracts from
Liszt's Hungarian rhapsodies, selections as quick and devilish as
the reels and jigs of the hearers' forgotten Scotland and Ireland.

At night we held another meeting with singing and music.

AT A SOCIALIST ENCAMPMENT, THE AUTHOR IN THE CENTER

ANOTHER ENCAMPMENT GROUP—WITH OTTO BARNSTETTER AT
EXTREME LEFT, THE AUTHOR FOURTH FROM THE RIGHT

SPEAKERS AT THE ENCAMPMENT

Left to right: CAROLINE LOW, OSCAR AMERINGER, EUGENE V. DEBS, AND WALTER THOMAS MILLS

After the night meetings, discussions around the glowing camp fire continued on into the small hours. For to these people radicalism was not an intellectual plaything. Pressure was upon them. Many of their homesteads were already under mortgage. Some had actually been lost by foreclosure. They were looking for delivery from the eastern monster whose lair they saw in Wall Street. They took their socialism like a new religion. And they fought and sacrificed for the spreading of the new faith like the martyrs of other faiths.

The speakers at the encampments were Eugene V. Debs and the beloved Walter Thomas Mills. There was also Kate Richards O'Hare, reared and educated on the sunburned, wind-swept plains of western Kansas, and later to be an honored guest at Ft. Leavenworth, where she served some years for trying to prevent America's entrance into the most hare-brained and disastrous adventure of history, the great madness complimentarily alluded to as the World War. Caroline Low, another speaker, hailed from near Kansas City, where she had been a high-school teacher when the religion of socialism captured her sweet and noble soul.

Gene Debs, always our star attraction, was not only a great orator. He was more than that: he was a great soul. People loved him because he loved people. Children used to flock to him as they must have flocked to the Carpenter. I remember graybearded farmers, who as American Railway Union strikers had followed him to defeat, rushing up to their Gene, crying, "Gene, Gene, don't you remember me any more?" And Gene remembered them always, threw his long arms around them, pressed them to his heart until their eyes moistened in love and gratitude to the leader who had lost them their strike, their job and their home.

Gene Debs was the dreamer, poet, and prophet of the weary and heavy-laden. He was of the stuff of which the prophets of Israel, the fathers of the Christian Church, the Ethan Allens, Nathan Hales, Abe Lincolns, and John Browns were made. He

was a riler-up of the people by the grace of God. It didn't matter
what Gene said or how he said it. He won men by the force of
his magnificent personality and the power of faith within him.
The people heard him gladly because he believed in them, was
for them, would give his life for them, and they knew it.

Gene Debs was the only thorough-going Christian I have met
in the flesh in my three score years and ten. Money meant absolutely nothing to him. Whatever he earned went back into the
cause of his heart, provided someone more needy didn't get it
first, which happened often and often. Here's a story told me by
Dan Hogan, the father of Freda, my second wife:

"We had paid Gene the customary hundred dollars honorarium
and expenses for addressing one of our weekly encampments. I
know it was one hundred because I often had handed him the
roll of bills myself. I accompanied Gene to the depot, where a
woman was waiting for him on the platform. She was the widow
of one of his former American Railway Union strikers, and to
Gene she poured out her troubles. Whatever they were I never
learned, for Gene gently led her out of my hearing, and when
he returned after bidding the troubled soul good-by all he said
was, 'Dan, will you lend me five bucks to pay my fare to
Girard?'"

Some ten years later the champion of "The New Freedom"
and savior of democracy in Washington presented Gene with a
retreat in Atlanta's Federal hoosegow behind iron bars, as punishment for having opposed America's entrance into the World War.
Just as if saints could be punished, be it by imprisonment, gallows,
faggot or cross! Just as if ideas could be killed by locking their
possessors behind bars, hanging, shooting, starving or deporting
them!

Walter Mills was not only a brilliant teacher, but also a
brilliant speaker. His logic was keen as a razor. His speeches were
built from the ground up, first the foundation, then stone on
stone, side walls, supporting pillars and arches, and finally the
roof topped by mast and flag. In looks and manner, Walter was

one of the last Victorians of the Spencer, Tyndall and Huxley breed. And to me he was a marvelous teacher of logic and public speaking.

My main function at these gatherings was acting as master of ceremonies, supplying music and the rough humor so sadly lacking at most radical meetings. How effective it is in breaking down opposition and making friends of the cause—any cause! Kate Richards O'Hare was a close second to Debs as a riler-up of the people, while Caroline triumphed through her womanly sweetness and sympathy.

At the height of the movement, the Socialist Party commanded close to one-third of the total vote of Oklahoma, elected six members to the state legislature, and a number of county officers. All this in strictly agricultural districts in which the percentage of foreign born was practically nil, although there was one exception to the dominant native character of the population. In some of the northern and central wheat counties were large settlements of Russian Mennonites. The ancestors of these people had lived originally in Switzerland, Holland and Germany. The founder of their religion was one Menno Simons, whence the name Mennonite. Like all the religious sects that had arisen after the official reformations of Zwingli of Switzerland, Luther of Germany and Wycliffe of England, their faith was rooted in the communism and pacifism of primitive Christianity. The Mennonites are spiritual kin to the Moravians and Bohemians, brethren to the Taborites and the Quakers, Shakers and Levelers of England.

The communistic character of the Levelers is clearly indicated not only by their name but even more by their slogan: "When Adam delved and Eve span, who was then the gentleman?" All these sects had arisen in opposition to the aristocratic reformation, whose economic basis was the desire of the princes and merchants of that time to rid themselves of the tribute Rome was exacting, and were almost exclusively the affairs of the peasants and craftsmen of the towns. When the princes, nobles and merchants had successfully relieved themselves of the "spiritual" yoke of the papacy, they naturally received their reward from the lesser freemen by collecting and keeping all of the loot in place of going fifty-fifty with Rome. Hence the peasant wars in England and over a good part of continental Europe. Hence also the terms Quaker and Shaker, rooted in the fact that when one of the poor fellows fell into the hands of an official soul warden and tribute collector, he naturally would quake or shake. All these minor sects were cruelly persecuted by Protestants and Catholics alike; later on, while seeking religious freedom in the New World, they were cruelly persecuted by the Calvinists and Puritans who had preceded them in search of religious freedom.

Persecuted in Germany for their primitive Christian communism and pacifism, the Mennonites had accepted an invitation of Catherine the Great of Russia, herself a German princess, to settle on the rich black earth of the Volga basin, where, in the course of time, they became rich kulaks. In the early Seventies, when compulsory military service was introduced in Russia, many of the Mennonites migrated to America, having been promised exemption from military service by President Grant, a promise faithfully kept until America's entrance into the World War, when the selective draft law made a scrap of paper of it.

When I first met these Mennonites they were prosperous, hardworking, frugal, law-abiding farmers. Being deeply religious as well, they made poor material for us to work on. Later, when title deeds, and persecution during the World War, had educated them, we gained many supporters among their people. In the course of events, they even allowed socialist agitators to preach in some of their plain, simple churches, so much like the meeting houses of Friends, whom I have learned to love and respect as the most Christian of all Christian sects.

I don't know why I have wandered so far from America's last frontier, unless it be to indicate how deeply American life is rooted in the sins, crimes, and virtues of the Old World. How and why an American manifestation of free democracy such as our Oklahoma socialism was eventually defeated shall be told in another chapter. By the time that happened, many of the homesteaders I first met at the summer encampments were living under the roofs of mortgaged farmhouses. Their women had grown sick unto death sweeping the dust floors of dugouts, removing the dust and living things eternally falling and crawling from the roof and walls of sod houses. And who will blame them? But to achieve the dreams of their dreary, lonely lives, money must be borrowed. And so the mortgage, the thing that, along with drought and tractors, eventually made them the miserable Okies described in *The Grapes of Wrath*.

One of their outstanding characteristics was hospitality and natural, social democracy. No matter how poor the stranger was, he was always welcome. "Come in, come in. Put up your horse and stay overnight," was the regulation greeting. "There is always room for one more. We haven't got much to eat but if we can stand it all year round, you can stand it for a few meals," were other expressions. For the rest, one man was as good as the next. The only people looked down on were snobs who pretended to be better than others. Where all are equally poor, all are equal. And the frontier is always poor. American democracy was a gift of the frontier, and not of the bewigged and bepowdered gentlemen in knee breeches and silver-buckle shoes who are worshiped by the D.A.R.

As indicated by the name, the dugout was actually dug out of a convenient rise or hillside. Its walls were that part of the hillside which had not been dug out. The roof was made of sod slabs laid over cedar poles and branches hauled from the nearest canyon, which in many instances was miles away. In ordinary dugouts, God's footstool supplied the floor; in the better-class ones, the floor was a composite of gypsum, salt and wood ashes. Ventilation and illumination were secured by leaving the door open. Better-class dugouts boasted a front window or glass door. The narrative I am about to relate took place in one of these, with both composition floor and glass door. In addition it had a storm door, slanting, cellar-door fashion, outward and downward from the glass door.

My host of the night before was taking me in his buggy some ten miles to my next meeting place. He was an Indiana man who had brought some money from his native state, with which he had built an honest-to-goodness four-room cement-block house on his homestead and had purchased the buggy we were riding in. He was a rich farmer, as riches went in that age and place, and I was a lazy agitator, fattening on the pennies of the poor. Even before we left the house we had debated the advisability of the trip. Black clouds were piling up on the western horizon. It looked as if before long it might rain "pitchforks and nigger babies," as the saying went. However, there was another saying in the future dust bowl to the effect that "the blacker the clouds, the surer it ain't gonna rain." And so we took the risk and for once got fooled. After traveling some five or six miles it rained not only pitchforks and nigger babies, but water spouts. It was too late to return, impossible to go on. However, Spence, my companion from Indiana, knew a North Carolina man who had a "good dugout" not far from where we were. We lit out for it and made it. The slanting outer door was clamped down, pouring a little Niagara out into the yard. After getting through both outer and inner doors we were greeted with the customary "Come in, come in, and make yourselves at home. There's always room for a few more. We ain't got much to eat, but if we can stand it . . ." and so on.

Regarding the room for more, I had my serious doubts. True, it was a good dugout, composition floor, glass door and all. Better still, it was large, measuring, I judged, around twelve by eighteen feet. The roof was high enough so that a not overly tall person could stand. But there were eight in the family, father, mother, three sons and three daughters, and the youngest was well over ten.

After a supper of side meat, corn pone and molasses, fortified by fried potatoes and milk in coffee, it came time to turn in. "Turning in" with four women in the same room requires a special technique, for these frontier women were rather prudish. "Time for bed," father would yawn, and casually remark, "I guess we might all go out for a drink before turning in." On that well-understood signal all the males would go outside, congregate around the well or windmill, take a drink, and do any other requisite chores before turning in. Then, after the required intermission, we would re-enter the dugout. In the meantime even the hands and shoulders of the women had been hidden beneath the bedclothes. Whereupon the males undressed in the dark and turned in.

I can't yet make out how the ten of us slept in the dugout that night. There were only two beds. The four women were stowed away in one of them, and the family insisted that we take the other. I suppose the other males slept on the composition floor. Spence and I had to take that second bed. No sooner had we stretched out than bedbugs started their pernicious activities. In anticipation, I had hung my vest, containing my trusty citrus vial, on the bedpost. I was rubbing oil on my ankles, neck and wrist, their favorite hunting grounds, when Spence, smelling the citrus oil, by rubbing my wrist gave me to understand they had located him too. I handed him the bottle, and the bedbugs hunted more hospitable quarters, but by then the air in the dugout had reached the density where it might have been cut with a sawtooth cheese knife. I stepped out of bed and sought refuge in the space between the inner and outer doors. Spence followed. We sat in the narrow space with water trickling down our necks from the little Niagara washing over the outer door. When the deluge had reached the limit of human endurance, we lifted the door and went out into the blinding rain. Surely there must be some roof on that homestead. But search as we would, there wasn't. Mule team and family cow were protected by barbed-wire enclosures; the only near-shelter we were able to discover was a wagon loaded with bales of broom corn.

When we located ourselves under the wagon there was already some four inches of water under it; the level rose to eight inches before daybreak, and in that water we sat like two bullfrogs, until sunrise and the cessation of rain delivered us.

One method for garnering the socialist sheaves was protracted meetings patterned after those of religious congregations. They were held in country schoolhouses, village churches, and more rarely in the courtrooms of county courthouses, and usually lasted a week or two, according to the attendance and the results obtained.

Having selected a promising school district or village, I secured the permission of the proper wardens or directors to use their church or school. Then gathering my little flock together, I started preaching Marxism. As the meeting proceeded, attendance grew so that toward the end there was usually only standing room left, and quite often not even that. In the latter instances, the more faithful would do the standing, or listen to the speaker through the windows from outside. This was done in order to give new converts, or the not yet converted, a chance to hear the message with the least degree of discomfort. What an earnest, self-forgetful bunch those American farmer comrades were!

At every meeting pamphlets were sold, subscriptions and applications for membership taken. On the last night, and as a sort of climax and initiation into the faith, we frequently held box socials. The young ladies of the flock would bring boxes filled with sandwiches, cakes, pies and other delicacies. Then the boxes were auctioned, sight unseen, to the highest bidder. When the young lady was unusually attractive or popular her suitors often bid her box far above its intrinsic value. For box holder and box purchaser were to eat its contents together.

These meetings were usually better than self-supporting. Expenses were low: there was no rent to pay; advertising was done by giving "general ring" calls over the party lines, which were free; the speaker was boarded and bedded by one of the comrades.

The salary of the preacher was catch as catch can. Speakers and organizers of the Party, as strong advocates of unionism, had organized a union of their own, providing a sliding scale of from twelve to eighteen dollars a week. As one of the stars, I received the top. Any money left over the union scale went to the cause.

Small pay. Plenty of inconvenience and hard work. But please don't waste any sympathy on world savers. Their reward is the joy they get out of saving the world, even if the world stubbornly declines to be saved.

30

IN one of the central Oklahoma wheat counties was a hamlet—
call it Omega. It was next on my list for political salvation
by socialism, so I arrived one day ready to rally the faithful.
The enterprise began in the usual fashion. Permission for use of
the schoolhouse secured, the next problem was illumination. Of
course there were the inevitable stable lanterns and coal-oil lamps
to count on, but this was almost plutocratic territory and perhaps
we could do better. Someone told me the proprietor of Omega's
pool hall had two fine gasoline lamps of the pump and mantle
type. I approached this establishment and stated my case.

"Well, I guess I got to let you have one of my lights. They're
the only two lights worth a shuck in all the country around," was
the pool-hall man's reply. "But I hope you won't treat me as
ornery as the last preacher that borrowed one."

"What did the last preacher do to you?" I inquired sympathetically.

"There ain't any saloons and whorehouses around here to
preach against," the pool-hall man told me sadly, "so this fella
preached how sinful it was for people to play pool. While pool
playing might look innocent enough, it was one of the devil's pet
ways of leading boys to perdition, and breaking up families. He
went on preaching that way until 'most everybody around here
was converted. I was all alone in this pool hall of mine. I didn't
mind losing the money; I don't need much money, nohow. I'm a

276

bachelor. I own the pool hall. I have a jim-dandy milk cow, a little truck patch, all the Rhode Island Reds I need for meat and eggs. But I got so dodgasted lonesome I almost died. I would have gone up to the schoolhouse and listened to that preacher, if he hadn't singled out my pool hall and me to preach against. Nobody wants to sit in a crowd and be bully-ragged by a preacher. You wouldn't either, would you?"

I confessed I had had that sort of punishment inflicted on me as a boy, and consequently knew exactly how he felt. In addition, I told him that the socialism I was preaching had nothing against pool halls. But, I wanted to know, how did it all end?

"That preacher didn't even bring my lamp back. And when I went after it the chimney and mantle were broke, and there was nary a drop of gasoline left in it. It was almost full when the preacher borrowed it!"

"Pretty ornery," I admitted, "but how about your customers?"

"As I told you," the pool-hall owner replied moodily, "everybody got religion up at the schoolhouse and stayed away from the pool hall. Some of them even got so they walked on the other side of the street and let on they didn't hear me when I hollered 'howdy' at them. About a day after the preacher had gone, one of the boys came in and sat down on a chair.

"I was awful lonesome, so I said, 'Dave'—Dave was his name —'Dave,' I said, 'would you like a game of pool with me just for passing the time away?' 'No, thank you,' said he. 'I joined the church and I'm never gonna play pool any more.' Well, that was all right with me. Even if Dave didn't play pool, at least I had somebody to talk to.

"Next day Dave came back and sat around on first one chair and then on the other, like he was sorter fidgety, or had ants in his pants. Then he sat on the edge of this here pool table, and started spinning balls around. You know, not playing pool, just kinder spinning the balls around. So by and by, I said to him, 'How about a little game of pool, just for the fun of it?' 'Well,' said Dave, 'I guess one little game of pool won't hurt.' So we played until Dave said he'd better go home.

"Next day he came back again and we played some more. Then another fella comes traipsing in. But he said he wasn't going to play pool any more. He had made peace with Jesus. He said he had just stepped in to watch us play pool and maybe show Dave how wrong it was for him to backslide as quick as all that. The next day, Dave and the other man came back, and we all played pool. More and more of the others came dropping in.

"But"—still smarting under the wrong inflicted on him by the ungrateful preacher—"it was all of two weeks before I had the last of 'em back again."

Something more than schoolhouse meetings, encampments and soap-box preaching was needed if the world was to be saved before it went plumb to hell. (At the rate it's been traveling recently, it will get there, too, although not as fast as we socialists were predicting back there in 1910.) One thing that was clearly necessary was a Party newspaper. So I started the *Industrial Democrat*.

John Chamberlain, in his book *Farewell to Reform*, has given me credit for inventing the term "industrial democracy." I am not so sure I am the inventor. But it's a good term, a much better term than socialism, for what it really means, but falls far short of saying, is "industry of the people, by the people, and for the people."

I had begged and borrowed the money to start the paper from the ever-willing comrades. In addition, one larger and quite respectable sum was contributed by a well-to-do farmer, a founder of the Populist Party, who had the interesting name of Steuben deKalb Wham. Another contribution came from a small-town banker in the Seminole country who might be a multimillionaire by now if—but of that, later. His name was C. B. Boylan.

The *Industrial Democrat* had come to fill a crying need. Its chief trouble was it never got over it. Before it finally folded up, however, it contributed materially to the defeat of an initiative measure sponsored by a railroad corporation. This choice piece of legislation was intended to wipe out a clause in the Oklahoma constitution which provided that the "fellow servant and contributing negligence" act should have no standing in Oklahoma courts. That clause is still in the Oklahoma constitution, even if the *Industrial Democrat* is no more.

Its demise, though, did not keep me out of the radical newspaper field for any real time. My next paper, *The Oklahoma Pioneer,* lasted a little longer than the *Industrial Democrat.* Eventually it, too, went to whatever place fundamentally radical publications go when they suspend publication. But before it turned up its toes it also rendered a service to the cause of democracy and decency. The state's Democrats had initiated a measure infamously and undemocratically known as the "grandfather clause," intended to rob the Negroes of Oklahoma of the franchise. *The Oklahoma Pioneer* was the only paper in the state that fought that measure with all it had. What it had wasn't much to brag about, but it was enough to keep the vicious clause out of Oklahoma's constitution. The lily-white Republicans didn't have courage enough to fight for their own voters, so I wrote a twenty-five hundred word argument against the adoption of the grandfather clause. This document was printed and distributed by the state in accordance with a clause in the state constitution which provided that each side to an initiative be granted a twenty-five hundred word argument setting forth its position.

After the election the good Democrats—and Democracy, what crimes are committed in thy name!—declared the grandfather clause carried. But the thing was so rotten it stank to heaven. The Democrats—in full control of the state then as now—didn't have the nerve to put their own child into the constitution. So the Negroes still vote in Oklahoma. Of course they get nothing at all for their votes, but even so, they fare no worse than their white brethren, the farmers, wage earners, and common people of the United States, in general. After all, the ballot is but a means to an end. One may grab at the end of a rope and with it climb out of a well. Or tie one end to the limb of a tree, tie a noose in the other, stick one's neck through the noose and jump. So far, the popular way of using the ballot has been the noose and jump act.

By this time a number of things had been happening which resulted in my leaving, for a while, the turbulent young state of Oklahoma. But before I recount them, it is only fair to the reader to point out that I hadn't confined all my political activities to camp meetings and newspaper columns. I had actually run for a number of offices; at one time, indeed, for the high office of Congressman-at-large. Well, I remained, and still am, at large. Also, I ran for mayor of Oklahoma City, and came within a few hundred votes of being elected. That was a narrow escape both for Oklahoma socialism and for me, personally. Had I been elected, I would have been just in time to take office on the eve of the collapse of the Oklahoma City boom, and that event would have been blamed on me instead of the other fellow.

As for my fellow Socialists, my defeat was a disguised blessing. I am not a politician, and still less an executive. They were fortunate in not having to sponsor me as their mayor. I might have shaken their faith. . . .

Book Seven

MILWAUKEE AND THE FIRST WORLD WAR

31

IN the spring of 1910 the Socialists of Milwaukee had elected their city ticket and a majority of the city council. Naturally, this was a Party event of the first magnitude. It was to have a profound effect on me as well as the Party, for by this time I had acquired a nation-wide reputation as a Socialist speaker and writer. The circulation of my pamphlets had gone well over the million mark, not counting the translations. And so the Milwaukee Socialists had invited me to help in the approaching county and Congressional elections. Victor Berger was running for Congress in the Third Congressional District of Wisconsin, which, besides the northern half of Milwaukee, embraced the strongly Republican county of Waukesha. In the municipal election, the Socialists had carried the city and part of the district with a safe majority. But unless the Republican majority of Waukesha County were materially reduced, Berger's chances of carrying the district were doubtful. As Waukesha County contained only a very small industrial population, this meant converting a good number of farmers to Socialism. . . .

Most of those farmers were second and third generation Germans whose forebears had settled in Wisconsin after the collapse of the '48 revolution in Germany. Their fathers and grandfathers had been republicans, as contrasted to monarchists. When the Republican Party was organized in Ripon, Wisconsin, which is only a short distance from Waukesha, these German exiles joined the new movement almost to a man, for besides being antimonarchists, they also were violent Abolitionists. On the other hand, the descendants of those Forty-eighters had become prosperous farmers and consequently poor prospects for the gospel of Socialism. They had, however, retained the German language, for reasons to be explained later. So, to make inroads on these people, any Socialist proselytizer had, first, to know how to talk to farmers, and second, how to do it in German. Which explains why the Party management of Milwaukee had selected me to stump Waukesha County on behalf of Victor Berger. That their selection might have been worse was witnessed by the fact that in the ensuing election the Republican majority of Waukesha County was reduced by some thousand-odd votes, resulting in the election of the first Socialist Congressman in the United States, Victor L. Berger.

Of course, I didn't do it all. While there were few wage earners, and still fewer confirmed Socialists, in Waukesha County, there was and always had been a strong undercurrent of political and economic radicalism in that district. Before the Civil War the same district had elected one of the first Abolitionists to Congress. His name was Bowie-Knife Potter, and he had operated a station on the underground railroad for runaway slaves. After the Supreme Court, in the celebrated Dred Scott decision, had legalized the recapture of runaway slaves in free states, one of the poor devils was in the Milwaukee county jail awaiting the arrival of the duly constituted authority who would take him back to his master in sunny Dixie. Before the arrival of the majesty of the law, the enraged Milwaukee citizens freed the slave, and just to let the world know their sentiments on the subject of chattel slavery and Supreme Court decisions, they burned both the jail and the courthouse. Later on, the same district sent a Populist to Congress.

Election over and victory won, the Milwaukee comrades labored under the delusion of having caught a world beater. They persuaded me to accept the position of state organizer, from which I rose to county organizer of Milwaukee County, editor of the *Voice of the People,* editorial writer and columnist of the *Milwaukee Leader,* official organ of the Party, and finally candidate for governor of the great and progressive state of Wisconsin. Oscar, what a candidate you have been in your time!

Nowadays Milwaukee has the reputation of being the best-governed city in the United States, and deservedly so. Its finances are in apple-pie order. It is the only large municipality in the country operating on the cash and carry basis. In a few years "red Milwaukee" will be entirely out of the red, while nearly all great municipalities are going still deeper into debt. Its tax, crime, fire- and burglar-insurance rates are the lowest in the country. Almost next door to Chicago, Milwaukee is free of political scandals, racketeers and gangsters. And if the forces of darkness had not ganged up on the Milwaukee Socialists, it is quite possible that the city would by now be free of all taxes.

As I look back over the years, it seems that in all my wanderings I never found a cleaner, more idealistic and self-sacrificing aggregation of men than those Milwaukee Socialists. During the decade I was one of them, those forgotten men and women contributed hundreds of thousands of dollars to the cause of their hearts, and the overwhelming majority of them were wage workers, who had little time and money to spare.

Reader, no matter what your political convictions may be, those Milwaukee Socialists are worth remembering. They made their city a fine, safe, clean, and progressive place in which to live. At the end of their days they were as poor as when they went into Milwaukee politics and socialism, and often poorer. How seldom that seems to happen in either of the two "great" parties which get all but a handful of American votes! Those were people who didn't talk endlessly about "the American way," but instead devoted their energies to making it a possibility for the citizens of their city. They did not trade upon inherited political ideals which they were interested only in pawning in return for office.

Instead, they believed and lived the great American ideals, enriching them with work, and labor, and sacrifice, and practical accomplishment. They aren't in the history books we give our children, but it's barely possible that they are a nobler monument to democracy as well as socialism than all the plutocrats we have found it so fatally easy to admire.

There were thousands of them, of course, and you would have had to know them to read the whole roster and have it mean something. But some of their names belong here, if for no other reason, because you may not have heard them before.

Victor Berger, of course. A man who was a solid block of integrity. All the money in the world could not have purchased him. Meta, his wife, for thirty years an indispensable and leading member of the Milwaukee school board, who was his equal in every respect. Elizabeth Thomas, a modest Quakeress, author of children's stories and poems in her girlhood, who lived in and for the cause. C. B. Whitnall, father of city planning in America and later treasurer of Milwaukee County, founder of the first co-operative bank, which he is still serving as president, though well in his eighties. Edward Melms, for decades secretary of the Milwaukee Socialist Party, a working man with little schooling but possessed of tremendous energy and organizing ability. Emil Seidel, first Socialist mayor of Milwaukee, pattern maker by trade, lover of men, and honest as the day is long. Bob Buech, ex-saloon keeper, during the World War High Sheriff of Milwaukee County, a tireless worker, with heart and purse ever open to saint and sinner alike. And Daniel W. Hoan, for a quarter of a century mayor of the best-governed city in America.

When the Socialists captured Milwaukee its government was just as corrupt as any of the municipalities described by Lincoln Steffens in *The Shame of the Cities*. Its press was just as vile; its educators just as cowed and kotowing; its preachers, with rare exceptions, just as subservient to the almighty dollar. Its slums were just as festering, its red-light district as foul, its justice as uneven-handed. Its banks and public-service corporations were as greedy, debauched and rapacious as that of the city's neighbor, Chicago. At best the municipal government was a milk cow; at worst a criminal conspiracy to rob honest men. Gold coast and red-light district, bankster and blackmailer, pickpocket and parson, during the campaign all of them were united in the holy crusade against the "godless Socialists."

Of course there were exceptions to this indictment even in the ranks of our opponents, just as there are white crows and two-headed calves. But omitting those few honorable variations from a revolting pattern, the picture was precisely as it is described here. Political and social poison had corrupted both business and people. When we got control of the municipal department of weights and measures, for instance, we discovered there was not a pint, quart, gallon, peck, bushel, foot or yard measure in the whole city that didn't fall short of the amount described thereon! Even the city scales were doctored. When we took charge of the city water department we found that "respectable," million-dollar corporations had stolen city water through eight-inch water mains for years. When we got hold of the fire department we found it a medium through which private contractors who were in the know secured cheap horses. When we moved into the city hall we discovered that outgoing "servants of the people" usually took the people's typewriters and furniture with them. Milwaukee was as rotten as every other large municipality of that day and age—and as most of them still are.

As I look back on what Milwaukee was then and contrast it with Milwaukee today, I marvel not only that the Socialists have achieved so much in the field of political house-cleaning, but that they themselves have remained unsullied until this very day. There is not space to tell the whole story of the redemption of Milwaukee. The best I can do is to present the following sample.

The Socialists captured Milwaukee under the slogan, "Make Milwaukee a better place in which to live." Now, to make any city a better place in which to live requires city planning. In the pursuit of this goal our administration had, under the direction of C. B. Whitnall, worked out a city plan. The Milwaukee river, flowing almost through the center of the city, had become an open sewer. Its banks were littered with dilapidated ice and slaughter houses. The places between them harbored offal, ashes, tin cans and rubbish. The river stank to heaven from the sewage of half of the city. There was also danger that some day the banks would be lined with factories, the smoke of their towering chimneys destroying the beautifully wooded heights framing the valley. The plan worked out by the Socialists was to buy the river valley and the high land adjoining it, then to convert the open sewer, along with ice and slaughter houses and dumps, into a city park. The cost of all this was to be defrayed by the sale of building sites made valuable by the park they overlooked.

Here at last was a plan that every good citizen could conscientiously back. Here was something that benefited everybody and cost nobody a cent. But do you imagine our opponents would admit that? No. Oh, no. The old crowd sandbagged the first step toward making Milwaukee the city beautiful.

First it became "Berger's million dollar park" in the local press. Why Berger's million dollar park? Berger had no million dollar park to sell, no million dollar park to buy. The crime Berger had committed was to appeal to the local pride of the old Milwaukee families who owned the property and to ask them either to deed or sell it to the city at reasonable prices. These old families did not like Berger's politics but they respected the man. The price of the property totaled a little over nine hundred thousand dollars. By now I dare say it is worth ten times that figure. The argument against Berger's million dollar park ran something like this:

"Little taxpayers, small home owners! Aren't you burdened enough with taxes without having Berger's million dollar park foisted on you? And just between us, how much rake-off will there be in it for Berger?"

The little property and home owners lined up against Berger's million dollar park.

"Saloon keepers! Parks are fine things for the people who own carriages and these new-fangled gas buggies to drive out to them. Well, let them have their park. But a park right in the heart of the city, do you realize what that would do to your business? Working people, the kind of people you make your money from, instead of patronizing your saloon, will spend their leisure time in the park with their families. Then where do you come in?"

The saloon keepers, even some of the professed Socialist saloon keepers, lined up.

"Bawdy-house and dive keepers! Oh, so the damned goody-goody Socialists are gonna have a big park only a few blocks from our red-light district! People walking to that park with their wives and children almost have to pass the doors of our places. They may not like it, and if they don't, they'll raise a row. Besides, ain't those goody-goodies already talking about cleaning up River (principal red-light street), only a block from their city hall? Well, we'll show 'em about their million dollar park."

Bawdy-house and dive keepers lined up against the plan.

"Holy men of all denominations, excepting rabbis! Certainly parks are fine things. People must have recreation, fresh air and that sort of thing. But a park almost in the middle of the city! A million dollar park at that. Very dangerous indeed, for young people strolling around in it at night, making love on park benches. How many poor girls have been started on the primrose path by moonlight and park benches? It must not be. Lord, lead us not into temptation!"

The parsons lined up.

"Real-estate sharks! Sure, Berger's million dollar park would raise real-estate values on the wooded heights overlooking it. There is nothing more conducive to good business than rising land values. But why can't those damned Socialists stick to laying out that million dollar park and let us realtors handle the lot sales on the heights? What's the world coming to anyhow, with politicians going into the real-estate business on the pretense that since the city creates the land values the city might just as well get the benefit instead of private enterprise?"

Real-estate sharks lined up along the opposition fence.

"Bankers! So the Socialists propose to finance Berger's million dollar park by going into the real-estate business? How preposterous! If a park they must have, and of course we are all for parks, let them finance it by the approved method of floating twenty-year bonds. The credit of the city is not any too good, it must be admitted. Nevertheless, local patriotism will compel us to handle the bonds."

The bankers lined up with the proprietors of whorehouses, the keepers of saloons, the real-estate operators, the ministers, and the small property-holders.

"Public-service corporations and big business in general! We realize, of course, that anything that makes Milwaukee a more desirable place in which to live will enhance real-estate values, increase population and swell the number of our customers. But if the Socialists succeed in the real-estate business the next thing they'll demand is the public operation of public utilities for the benefit of the people of Milwaukee instead of the poor widows and orphans of our demised stockholders in Boston, New York, Philadelphia and Baltimore. Aren't those subversive demands already in their platform? And while we fully realize that political platforms are bait wherewith to catch suckers, isn't there grave danger that these wild-eyed agitators don't know what political platforms are made for? No, it must not happen. Once these people have entered the public-utility business, in which they are naturally bound to fail, how soon will it be before they tackle other legitimate private business enterprises?"

Public-service corporations and big business in general lined up, bringing their mercenaries of the press along with them.

The propaganda that this united gangland conducted against

"Berger's million dollar park" resulted in the defeat of the Socialists in the next election.

How well I remember that election night of the spring of 1912. We had assembled in one of the larger halls of the city to hear the returns. The people making up that sea of faces—working people almost to a man—had given their time and meager earnings for the redemption of Milwaukee. How well I remember those faces growing ever more tense as the evidence of defeat mounted. How well I remember that when we left that hall I heard church bells ring and saw the bawdy houses across the Milwaukee river illuminated by red flares to celebrate the defeat of the Socialists. If Milwaukee has today the merited reputation of being the best-governed city in the United States, it was the common people who made it so, not their "betters."

There is one more associate in the glorious enterprise of making Milwaukee famous whom I must mention. Today his name is well known in every household the world over in which good books are at home. But at the time of which I speak he was the humble labor reporter of the Milwaukee *Leader*, and an emerging poet on the side.

Now labor reporter in the Milwaukee of that day was a prosaic sort of a job. The labor movement was almost indecently clean, matter-of-fact and peaceful. Strikes were few and harmless. The social revolutionists and the minions of the law usually addressed each other by their first names. Moreover, at some of these almost disgustingly ladylike strikes it was at times difficult to tell whether the pickets acted as bodyguards for the cops, or vice versa.

All this was naturally hard on a labor reporter suffering from poetic complications. So in order to put pep, thrill and red blood into the job, my reporter-poet pulled off a one-man street-car strike. I say one-man strike because as I remember only one street-car employee was pried loose from his post. And he was largely propelled by the physical force and none too poetic language of our emerging young poet.

As for that poetry, there was all too much reason, sense, and even force, in it. But of rhyme and neat rhyme words, nary a sign. In place of writing about nightingales and lovers under moon-silvered bowers and the blooms and flowers in the spring tra-la-la, this young man wrote about such sordid subjects as belching smokestacks, sooty boilermakers, ill-mannered dock wallopers, sunburned prairies and red-necked clod-hoppers. Instead of sighing "On the wings of love I flee to thee," he rumbled and grumbled about horny-handed overallers tearing down and rearing up Chicago streets, and perfectly normal people in new cars driving all Sunday long from Bloomington to Jacksonville and Jacksonville to Bloomington all Sunday long.

People were shocked by his verses. It's perfectly proper to harp about Apollo's harp or the harp that hung in Tara's hall, but why harp about such common everyday things and occurrences? Besides, this emerging poet, while he wore his hair rather long, was usually cleanshaven (well, almost, and some of the time), when all the great American poets from Longfellow, Whittier and Bryant down to Markham wore the regulation poetical whiskers.

It was not until many years after, when I heard the by then fully arrived versesmith recite some of his own stuff, that I caught the tremendous, coal-born, lightning-endowed energy and futility of my own age. Long before that, the young labor reporter and poet had advanced to the high position of private secretary to Emil Seidel, first Socialist mayor of the best-governed city in America. It was a fine team, ex-reporter Carl and ex-pattern maker Emil, for both were poets. One dreamed about the city beautiful, the other about the beautiful life. One drafted tree-lined parkways and playgrounds with the loving hand of the craftsman. The other coined words which bespoke their souls. And so, when telling of the brave men and women who helped to make Milwaukee famous, I must not forget America's foremost living immortal— my old friend and sidekick, Carl Sandburg.

32

A T this point, let me say something more about my friend, Victor Berger. Friend? Victor and I were far more than friends. We loved each other as did Damon and Pythias or David and Jonathan. The dark days I have just described had drawn us closer and closer together. When we walked through the streets of Milwaukee, we walked arm in arm. When we occasionally visited a movie for a temporary respite from the madness around us, we often sat hand in hand. I stood at his side during the tragic days of the World War, when he was persecuted and prosecuted by the shallow-pated politicians, judicial mountebanks, and grafting merchants of death into whose hand an inscrutable Providence delivered the destiny of the nation in its most critical days.

Victor was a powerful editorial writer and a most skillful editor. I never knew a man who could so tremendously strengthen a piece of writing by striking out a word here and there and, more rarely, adding one. He wrote English and German with equal fluency. His library of some thousands of volumes contained the best works of the ages. He had read it all and remembered it all. His knowledge of history was phenomenal. Never having had systematic training, forced to pick up wisdom wherever I stumbled on it, I never could give verse and chapter. He could, together with date and background.

Victor cared no more for money than Gene Debs. As he had it, so he gave it. I used to tell him, "Small change with you, Victor, starts at five dollars." He gave not only freely, but also delightfully indiscriminately.

"Do you know what that comrade who just left had the gall to ask me for?"

"What was it, Vic?"

"Sixty dollars," replied Vic.

"And what did you do?"

"Gave it to him. The fellow told it so artistically, his story alone was worth the sixty. Besides, he promised to pay it back as soon as he got out to Seattle where his people live."

"Better kiss it good-by," I told him disgustedly. But I was fooled. The comrade actually returned the money some weeks later.

Victor could tell a humorous anecdote excellently, but only on a rare occasion would humor creep into his editorials and speeches. Nor was he a brilliant speaker. He won his audience by the sheer force of his character and integrity. On the other hand, in print his speeches read as if prepared with utmost care, although he usually employed only notes and frequently spoke extemporaneously.

At the convention of 1912 in Indianapolis a rather bitter controversy had broken out among the simon-pure Marxists and the revisionists, to which latter group both Victor and I were adherents. In one of his usual brief remarks he had pointed out the folly of separating ourselves from the body of the nation. "Don't," he warned, "be like the ancient Hebrews who, when going on a journey, carried a bundle of hay to sleep on so as not to come in contact with a place on which a Gentile had previously slept."

That afternoon, Tad Cumbie, "the Gray Horse of the Prairie," and one of our irreconcilables, who was to become commander in chief of the Green Corn Rebellion, appeared with a tiny bundle of hay pinned to his flaming red shirt.

"Well, Victor," said Tad, "here is my bundle of hay."

"Well, well," replied Victor. "I see you brought your lunch with you."

Victor was not a Marxian socialist in the sense that he championed the forcible overthrow of capitalism or the dictatorship of the proletariat. One of his favorite expressions was "Socialism is coming all the time. It may be another century or two before it is fully established." IIis definition of socialism was "Anything that's right." By right, he meant the greatest good to the greatest number, and with that the greatest good to the country at large.

But evolutionary socialist as he was, Victor was fully convinced that an unarmed people is an enslaved people. To him the most important clause in the Bill of Rights was not the first amendment guaranteeing the right of free speech and press, but the second amendment reading: "A well-regulated militia being necessary to the security of a free state, the right of the people to keep and bear arms shall not be infringed." Toward this end he had introduced a bill in Congress contemplating the reorganization of the American militia on the Swiss basis. Every able-bodied man in Switzerland is a member of the militia, and on return from service takes his rifle and munitions home with him.

Wise Victor. He knew the futility of paper constitutions in cases where the unarmed majority is confronted by an armed minority. For details on this point, see Italy or Germany or the U. S. A. during the World War. He believed that the mighty forces unchained by the industrial revolution were either driving mankind to destruction through war and bloody revolution or forcing it to adopt the co-operative system of production and distribution. He regarded enlightenment expressed in political action as the handmaiden of social evolution, through which the new order might be achieved without the chaos which heretofore has accompanied every great transformation. He saw in the organized working masses, disciplined in social production, the main but not the only bearers of the new order. His appeals were never exclusively addressed to the proletariat. "A socialist," he would often say to me, "is anyone, irrespective of class, who places the common good above his own."

Like Marx, Engels, Lasalle, Jaurès, Vandervelde and Lenin, Victor was not himself a member of the working class. He came from a well-to-do family, had a university education, and had been a respected high-school teacher up to the time when sympathy and intellectual conviction had converted him to the cause of the lowly. And to that cause he had devoted his life, his magnificent intellect, and his inheritance. Had it not been for a little stack of accident policies of the dollar-a-year, newspaper-premium type, he would have died virtually penniless after a street car had given him the blow resulting in his death. And it was not only Victor's life and fortune that had gone into the cause; that of his Spartan wife, Meta, was as generously devoted to it.

The only term I can think of that embraces the whole of Victor's character is that of intellectual aristocrat. He would appeal to the reason, intelligence, heart and obvious self-interest of the many, but never to the passions and prejudices of the mob, an appeal which is the chief stock in trade of the majority of the politicians. Victor never stooped either in word, speech or action. Dignity personified, he was dignified to others, never looking up or down, but eye to eye to rich or poor. Hand-shaking, back-slapping, and baby-kissing were completely out of his line. I frequently had to pull him into a saloon at election time. He always was afraid he was stooping to Milwaukee's most popular electioneering method.

You have heard the saying that a man couldn't be bought with all the gold in the world. Well, Victor couldn't be bought with all the gold plus all the honor and flattery in the world. During the free-silver campaign of 1896 he had written in his *Daily Forward* a powerful argument against the fallacy of bimetallism. The argument was so devastating to the Bryan forces that the Republican National Committee, with millions to spend, had offered to purchase a large edition of the *Forward* for national distribution at his own price. Victor refused. He was no more interested in the success of McKinley than in that of Bryan. And that, dear reader, at a time when, as his treasurer, Louis Bayer, told me, Victor was so hard pressed for money that he paid the printers in nickels and dimes whenever they became too unruly. I myself saw the letter in which Hearst offered Berger fifteen thousand a year to write a weekly editorial for the Hearst chain. He turned that offer down, at a time when I know he came a darn sight nearer *owing* than owning fifteen hundred.

One Sunday, Victor, Meta, and I were sitting on the porch of their First Street home. This was after the War. Harding was President, but Victor's appeal from a twenty-year sentence for obstructing enlistment in the armed forces of the United States was still pending before the Supreme Court. Victor was under a million dollar bond. None of the multitude of other indictments against him, good for fifteen hundred years' imprisonment, had been quashed.

Two gentlemen left a limousine and walked up the front steps. One of them was a prominent Milwaukee banker, whom I knew merely by sight. The other was a stranger to me. I subsequently learned he was a Washington emissary of President Harding. After some preliminaries the two visitors expressed the desire to see Mr. Berger—alone. Victor must have given us the signal, for if I remember rightly, both Meta and I accompanied the three of them to the library on the third floor. Arrived there, I soon realized that the visitors were rather reluctant to tell the purpose of their mission in my presence. I therefore stepped to the rear of the library, then, after browsing among the books, I descended to my place on the porch. Meta must have remained with the others, for it was both from her and from Victor, some hours after the visitors had departed, that I heard the story, and here it is.

Bob La Follette was running again for United States Senator. In the election of two years before, Victor had come within twenty thousand votes of becoming the junior Senator from Wisconsin. The proposition the two prominent callers had made was this: if Victor would run against La Follette for the Senate, he would perhaps not be elected, but at least would take enough votes from "fighting Bob" to permit his stalwart Republican opponent to step into office. In return for this favor, the Administration in Washington would (a) supply the necessary funds for conducting an active campaign, (b) see that the twenty years' sentence was thrown out by the supreme tribunal, (c) quash all pending indictments, (d) lift the million dollar bond.

Is it necessary for me to add that Victor declined that most generous proposal? Of course he did, although there never had been any love lost between Victor and old Bob, whom he regarded as a scrapping but rather superficial statesman—an opinion, by the way, which I never shared.

This was the man whom Judge Kenesaw Mountain Landis condemned to twenty years in prison for high treason to his country because he was farseeing enough to oppose the war crowd in Washington and Wall Street, and brave enough to stand up for his convictions.

In all of the indecency and war-drunk lunacy of that trial, the prisoners before the bar, their witnesses, and their attorneys were the only just and sober men in the courtroom. Victor closed his plea with the words, "From my early youth, I have surrounded myself with the best and noblest minds of the ages. I am the sum total of the impressions they have left on me. I am what I am. I cannot be otherwise."

That was my friend and comrade, Victor Berger. I saw him for the last time in the rotunda of the city hall of Milwaukee, walled in by flowers. I could not join the hundred thousand who had passed his bier the two days he rested there. I was alone up in that gallery. But down below, in that mass of floral wealth, there was a sword of flowers that Freda had sent from Oklahoma

which said more than the eulogy I delivered the following day.
The flowers bore the words of Heine:

> "When I die, lay a sword on my bier,
> For I have been a brave soldier in
> Humanity's war for emancipation."

His ashes are scattered among the pines and oaks which he
had planted on the shores of Lake Michigan to make his Milwaukee, his country, the world, a better place in which to live.

33

IN June, 1914, England withdrew its navy from Mediterranean waters for maneuvers in the North Sea. Shortly thereafter, Crown Prince Francis Ferdinand of Austria and his wife were murdered by a Serbian patriot or assassin, depending on where one is located. Then came Austria's war-provoking ultimatum to Serbia. There was still talk of a localized war, to be stilled by Berlin's blank check to Vienna. Wires flashed the news of Russia's mobilization. The war the world feared, prepared for, and made inevitable, was about to break loose.

I was on my way to Europe when I read in a Washington paper that the *Vaterland* (later the *Leviathan* of the United States line), on which I was to sail, had postponed its departure. This could only mean that Germany would enter the war on the side of Austria, while England would join Russia against the Central Powers. Some hours later, in the home of Morris Hillquit in New York City, I met my fellow delegates to the international socialist congress which was to convene in Vienna on the twenty-second day of August, 1914. Among these delegates were Victor Berger, Emil Seidel, Charles Edward Russell, the well-known writer; George Lunn, then Socialist mayor of Schenectady, New York; Morris Hillquit, our host; and myself. Meyer London, Socialist Congressman from New York, who was also a delegate, had left for Europe the day before.

Needless to say, as international socialists we were bitterly opposed to war. In common with our comrades of all countries we had agitated against militarism, preparedness, and nationalism in favor of peace and understanding. To us the war meant the mass slaughter of the innocent, the tearing of the thread that had woven even the competing nations of the earth into a semblance of a co-operative texture. We knew from history that every war had been a rich man's war and a poor man's fight, and we knew that in a world which science, inventions, and discoveries had welded into one single workshop, field, and market, a world war would be as destructive as the attempt to separate the organs of the human body.

But now the thing we had predicted, feared, and that no one wanted, was upon us. The heap of artificially stimulated mistrust, hatred, lies, diplomatic chicanery, powder, oil rags, and matches, exploded. A rat had bitten into a match head in an obscure Serbian village.

In the discussion which followed, the majority agreed it was our duty to proceed to Vienna. The question was how to get there and what to do after we got there. If, as seemed evident, Austria was the first to attack, Vienna would be the center of a social brainstorm such as only war can provide, and there is no place for peace in social brainstorms. I was in favor of remaining at home, to await developments, for it seemed to me that if the powerful labor unions and socialist parties of Europe, with their millions of members and votes, could not stop the war, it would be futile for our little group, which had neither millions of votes nor members behind it, to make the attempt.

While we were still discussing the pros and cons of our problem, a cable from the international secretary of the Party advised us to remain at home and await instructions. The following morning another cable informed us that the meeting of the international socialist congress had been shifted to Brussels, Belgium, and to await further instructions. The third and final wire informed us that the congress was called off.

A few days later, the field-gray hordes of the kaiser poured into Belgium, while the gray-green hordes of the czar poured into East Prussia. The red-blue hordes of France poured toward the Rhine and Austrian artillery poured shots on Belgrade.

Then followed blow on blow. The Reichstag representatives of the German Social Democratic Party, our guide and model, had, with few exceptions, voted for the war credits. French socialist members of the Chamber of Deputies, not knowing what their comrades across the Rhine had done, did the same thing at almost the same time. Jean Jaurès, the foremost socialist and peace advocate of France, was assassinated. English labor and socialist leaders, long honored for their opposition to war, accepted ministerial posts in the War Cabinet. Ramsay MacDonald was not among them. Destiny reserved him for a more cruel fate.

Vandervelde, of Belgium, one of the most brilliant leaders and writers of the international socialist movement, joined the war party, for which we may forgive him, because his country was invaded. But not so Plekhanov, the Russian Marxist, who joined the czar in the holy crusade which, later, was "to make the world safe for democracy."

We in America still had one great consolation. Three thousand miles of salt water separated the hell over there from God's country. Surely, surely, there was no reason why the United States of America should get mixed up in the bloody mess on the other side of that blessedly deep and wide ocean? We had traded peaceably with all of Europe since the birth of the republic, and warred only with England. In our veins flows the blood of all European nations, and all of them had made their contribution toward building the New World. Europe's quarrels were old quarrels, antedating the discovery of America itself. Some of them reach back to the slave raids of the noble Romans. Some had their origin in the folly and greed of princes, popes, potentates dead a thousand years. The ground they fought over had been drenched with blood a hundred times. The markets, trade routes, coaling stations, and territories they fought about were on the other side of the world. We desired none of these. Our real market was the North American continent. Burning our fingers on the Philippine Islands in a youthful outburst of imperialism was enough. It was nice to trade with these people, but in a pinch we could get along well enough without them. Surely, no people as intelligent, practical and antimilitaristic as we, could possibly get mixed up in family rows three thousand miles from our doorstep.

There was still another good omen. The head of the nation was not an ex-general, as so many of its heads had been. He had not entered the White House by the way of drill grounds and battle fields. He was not a fire eater and saber rattler, as one of his immediate predecessors had been. He was a scholar, savant, a doctor of law and history, who had stepped from the ivied walls of Princeton almost directly into the White House. Let the bloody waves rage and thunder on the other side of the Atlantic; with such a man at the helm, peace was assured to our people. When shortly after the outbreak of hostilities, that man cautioned his countrymen to remain neutral even in spirit, he not only expressed the true feeling of the American people; he also laid down the policy which would have kept his country out of the war.

Neutrality of spirit is not enough unless it results in neutrality of action. What the good doctor of law and history overlooked is a passage in his father's Bible which reads to the effect that where a man's purse is, there is his heart also. We could not supply only one side of the conflict with the wherewithal of war and still maintain American neutrality. We could not say to the people of the Central Powers, "Our hearts bleed for you as they bleed for your opponents. Were we able to reach your shores with the clothing and murder material we are selling your enemies, we would gladly supply you with the same goods, so if some of the steel-jacket bullets and shrapnel splinters we are supplying the Allies happen to find their way into the breasts of your sons, kindly remember we are still neutral in spirit."

America's declaration of war against the Central Powers was not written on a White House typewriter on April 6, 1917; it was written when the house of Morgan floated the first Anglo-French bond issue with the consent of the American government. It was sealed when the first boatload of war material left Hoboken for Liverpool. What followed was rationalization, coupled with a forlorn hope of recouping values that had gone up in smoke.

Wilson is often accused of having "bamboozled the American people into the World War." This is only true in so far as he condoned the first step that inevitably led on to its successors, and even on that score there are extenuating circumstances. Besides being President, Wilson was the head of the Democratic Party, whose success in the election of 1912 was largely the result of a split in the opposition. Now, it has been the experience of American parties that they never survive hard times. The American people have a notion that good or bad times are pulled out of silk hats, as conjurers extract rabbits. If the rabbit happens to be a nice fat animal called Prosperity, people thank God for the conjurer in the White House and he is retained; if, on the other hand, he pulls out a very skinny rabbit called Hard Times, he and his assistants are cast out into utter darkness by a rather foolish, but nevertheless sovereign, audience.

In present-day society politicians perform very much the same service to business that whipping boys once rendered to princes. The prince, being God's anointed, could not be spanked when he was naughty enough to deserve it, so a whipping boy was attached to the prince who took the thrashing for him, and justice was appeased. When business ascended the throne, the politician became its whipping boy. When business goes bad, nowadays, the people express their wrath by throwing the "rascals" out, while business continues to maintain its prerogatives, and posterior, undisturbed.

In the spring of 1913, when Woodrow Wilson was inaugurated, hard times were already on the way. Shortly before the outbreak of the World War there was a catastrophic fall in farm prices and employment. If the flow of goods to Europe, which soon followed the outbreak of hostilities, were to be stopped, the country would be facing a major depression.

It was in order to save the country, and with it his own administration, from the effects of a serious business slump that Woodrow Wilson sanctioned the huge loans and shipments of war materials to the Allies. The rest followed as the day follows the night. As the old business motto goes, "The customer is always right."

On my return from New York to Milwaukee I resumed my work as organizer of the Socialist Party and part-time editorial writer on the Milwaukee *Leader*. Soon afterward the *Leader* began to get into hot water. Under the influence of the War, public opinion in the city was crystallizing along nationalist lines. The Poles of South Milwaukee, many of whom we had captured for the Socialist Party, were now fighting the battles of Poland in the twelfth and fourteenth wards of Milwaukee, Wisconsin. The large German element of North Milwaukee, under the leadership of *Germania*, a hundred-per-cent German daily published for revenue only, had taken up the cudgels for the Fatherland, while the third- and fourth-generation American sector of the population was fluctuating between nowhere and what-the-hell-now? The Milwaukee *Leader*, standing between the devil and the deep blue sea, tried its level best to retain the socialist position that this was a capitalist war caused by the commercial and financial rivalry of European hijackers and consequently was of no concern to the good people of Milwaukee and to the country at large. One of the first slogans the *Leader* published was "Starve the war and feed America," a most excellent slogan which the rulers of today might well take to heart if they love America and have sense enough to keep out of the rain.

But while the *Leader* controlled its own editorial policy, it could not control the news agencies that supplied it with news and they, as such agencies are wont, specialized in sensation and exaggeration: The gray hordes of the kaiser had dispatched, the day before, a hundred thousand Allies; the victorious Allies had dispatched a hundred thousand Germans. Both sides advanced so many miles into enemy territory that, had the news bulletins been true, the German army would soon have been fighting in the middle of the Atlantic, while the Allied forces would be almost in sight of the Ural mountains. Without reporters of our own in the field of carnage there was nothing left to do but to print the mess of lies furnished by the news agencies, whose war correspondents knew no more of what was going on than we did. As a result, the local Germans called us pro-Russian, the Poles called us pro-German, while the old American stock allowed we were just plain liars. The *Leader* lost prestige, circulation, advertising, and more money than usual.

One of my duties as organizer was to see to it that the official organ of the Party wasn't buried along with the hundred million soldiers already slaughtered by the news agencies. The technique I developed in that particular sphere was to send out an S O S to the most faithful and best heeled of the comrades to come to my office without fail that night on a matter of life and death to our *Leader*. When they got there I explained to them that unless the carload of paper standing on the siding of the Chicago & Northwestern was taken out of hock, or this or that of our multitudinous promissory notes in the claws of this or that bourgeois-minded banker was not paid at the bank opening next morning, the last hope of America's free press was lost forever.

The faithful souls responded to the best of their ability. However, there is a limit beyond which even the most faithful cannot go. Toward the end they became fewer and fewer until only Bob Buech, ex-saloon keeper and future High Sheriff of Milwaukee County, showed up. I had cried "Wolf, wolf!" so often that had the wolf been in my hearing he would have taken to the woods for fear I'd ask him to sign a note too. But just as things looked blacker than printer's ink, a brilliant idea hit me.

Brilliant ideas, as the discerning reader may have observed, are my specialty. The particular one that hit me at that moment was to throw up my organizer's job, go back to Oklahoma, and start a daily paper as a branch of the Milwaukee *Leader*, of which the latter would be the parent company, though it had so much trouble of its own that I had to borrow the railroad fare to Oklahoma. In the meantime the *Leader*, as the parent company, would have the use of the money I raised in Oklahoma. Somebody may tell you it was Banker Whitney, Pierre Du Pont, Samuel Insull or Pierpont Morgan, who invented the first holding company. But don't let 'em fool you. It was I.

34

B Y the time I started promoting the Oklahoma daily I had
learned that it takes lots of money to launch a newspaper and still more to keep it going. Formerly I had
undertaken the job rather lightly: I used to proclaim the glad
tidings that I was about to fill a long-felt need and asked for
subscriptions. When enough subscriptions at one dollar per year
had been gathered to pay for the first issue I brought out the
first issue. When enough money had accumulated to pay for the
second issue I brought that out, and so on until about the fourth
issue, when the flow of money began to dwindle and I owed my
subscribers forty-eight issues which I could not publish. About
that time I started to stand off the printer and defer the salary
of ye editor, publisher and general manager. When the printer
refused to be stood off any longer and the editor-publisher had
exhausted his credit with butcher, baker, and grocer, he would
make a swing around among the faithful to raise money, and
keep it up until there were no more faithful to corral. Soon
thereafter appeared a boxed notice in the paper to the effect that,
due to the insidious opposition of plutocracy and certain financial
difficulties, the paper would suspend until further notice.

I didn't want any more of that kind of business. This time,
I would do things up right. I asked the leaders of the Party in
convention assembled for their consent to raise a quarter of a
million dollars to launch the proposed daily and see it safely into

the harbor of prosperity. The boys didn't think there was that much money in the whole state of Oklahoma, but they reckoned that if I was fool enough to think otherwise, I had their permission to go ahead. I went ahead.

In reality the venture was not quite as harebrained as it seemed. This was in the second year of the World War. War prosperity had reached the farmer, and what a magnificent term for war prosperity the Germans had coined when they called it *Blutsegen,* that is, blood blessing. Wheat was nearing the three-dollar-a-bushel mark. Cotton had gone up to forty cents the pound. Corn sold at two dollars per bushel, hogs around twenty five cents a pound. All other farm products were in proportion.

In the election of 1914, some fifty-six thousand Socialist votes had been cast in Oklahoma. There were almost as many registered Socialist voters in the 1916 primary. At the regular election following, many of them voted for Woodrow Wilson, who ran on the slogan "He kept us out of war." I didn't blame them for voting for Wilson. Neither they nor the American people at large wanted this country mixed up in the slaughterfest three thousand miles across the pond. After all, the co-operative commonwealth was still a few years off, while war was already pounding at the gates. The slump in votes put a damper on our enthusiasm, but we understood, and, understanding, carried on.

The meeting at which final plans for the daily were worked out was held in a Greek restaurant in the town of McAlester. Present were just three conferees. One was Emil Marianelli, American born, educated in Italy, then trapper boy in a Pennsylvania mine and then a rising young lawyer. The second was Marianelli's partner-in-waiting-for-clients, a Delaware Indian, graduate of Carlisle, celebrated football player and coach. His name was Exendine. I was the third. The formation of our plans hadn't progressed to the point of incorporation; it had gone as far as my purchase of a ten-cent receipt book. The rest would follow.

What did follow wasn't unduly encouraging. Everyone to

whom I talked was pessimistic. Sure, the comrades wanted the daily. How could we hope to capture the state without a daily paper? But wasn't it rather utopian to think that a quarter of a million dollars could be raised? Somehow I usually managed to talk the doubting Thomas out of a fiver or a ten spot, enough to keep me going. And the going was mostly by foot. I walked from mining camp to mining camp, addressing miners' locals and soliciting money for the daily. Of course the miners responded. Miners always respond to anything going forward.

It took me almost three weeks to accumulate the first three hundred dollars. Then something terrible happened. Hoofing from McAlester to a mining town some twelve miles distant one Sunday, a railroad corporation cinder managed to sneak into one of my shoes. A serious infection set in. I was laid up for weeks on a cot in the Marianelli-Exendine bedroom. When my foot got so I could stand on it I purchased a second-hand Ford. It took all of the three hundred dollars' capital, reserves and un- divided profits of the unborn daily. However, even a second- hand Ford is capital, defined as wealth employed in the produc- tion of more wealth. The Ford lived up to that definition. I got around quicker, saw more faithful ones. Money came faster. What I still lacked was a prospectus. Home without mother is sad enough, but sadder still is a prospective corporation without a prospectus. My prayer was answered. A local of electrical work- ers in Oklahoma City voted the seven hundred dollars in its treasury for the proposed daily. Better still, it paid the seven hundred in cash on the barrel head.

Now for the prospectus. I had it printed on glazed paper in three colors, then used the rest of the spectrum to describe what the proposed daily would achieve in the line of curing mankind of the evils of the flesh, the devil, and capitalism. I sent that prospectus to the thirty-eight hundred precinct committeemen of the Party, asking each one to raise a hundred dollars in his precinct. According to Hoyle, one hundred times three thousand eight hundred makes three hundred and eighty thousand dollars.

According to Heck Sinclair, the state secretary of the Party and by now my financial secretary, it was too much to expect to get all of that, but he was pretty sure we'd get at least three hundred thousand, and began to worry what we'd do with that extra fifty grand.

I wasn't quite so optimistic. I had launched papers before. I told Heck that if that magnificent prospectus and appeal brought in only two hundred thousand, I would be well satisfied. The rest I would raise easily by personal solicitation. When the returns were all in we got exactly twenty dollars. No, that is not a misprint. We took in twenty dollars. Let me immortalize the cheerful giver of that twenty. He was an American-born Bohemian drug-store owner, a petty bourgeois named Jimmy Kolachney, who is still living in Ponca City, Okla. When I visited Emil Ludwig a few years ago, while he was lecturing in Ponca City, I took him to see Jimmy Kolachney. Ludwig had interviewed about all the great ones of the earth, but I wanted him to see the real thing.

With the capital of the proposed daily gone, I couldn't stop without being accused of having criminally wasted the money, or worse, be charged with having obtained it under false pretenses. So I kept going. Money was still coming in slowly. It takes a huge amount of two, five and ten dollar bills to make up a quarter of a million dollars. But right here my pagan patron saint, Goethe, stepped in and saw me through. I had read in his *Faust:* "Upon the smallest point devote thy greatest strength; that is, my son, what brings success to thee." That bit of wisdom had stuck in my head. I forgot all about the quarter-million dollars and concentrated on the two, five, and ten spots concealed in the jeans of my prospects. It was slow work. But when a fellow waits and keeps going long enough all kinds of things can happen, good and bad. This reminds me of another valuable piece of wisdom I had picked up: "All things happen in life, good and bad," my old friend Sidney Hillman, of the Amalgamated Clothing Workers, and one of America's greatest labor statesmen, told me one day. "The trick is living down the bad things and the good things will take care of themselves." Well, I had lived down a goodly collection of bad things when a really good thing showed up.

A banker comrade in the Seminole country had sold his land holdings and invested the proceeds in the Bartlesville oil field, where he presently accumulated a sizable fortune. Had he remained where he was he would have become a multimillionaire. For it was in this same Seminole country, where my banker friend had sold his extensive holdings, that one of the largest and richest oil pools in America was discovered shortly afterward.

At any rate, banker comrade C. B. Boylan had made enough money to promise me he would match every dollar I raised up to twenty-five thousand. Now whenever I solicited a prospect I could show him that every dollar he contributed meant two. That helped. However, by the time I had raised my twenty-five thousand and had come for Boylan's, something else happened that wasn't so good. Feeling that the nations of Christendom over in Europe were hell-bound to exterminate one another, Boylan thought he might help them by going into the lead and zinc business, which he shortly proceeded to do. Then something still worse happened. America got itself into the war, or rather was got into it. This in itself wasn't bad for Boylan's enterprise, because it actually increased the demand for lead and zinc. But the Guggenheim dollar-a-year men serving on the National Council of Defense made the astounding discovery that only Guggenheim lead and zinc contained the necessary metallurgical qualities for the proper extermination of mankind. As a result my banker comrade lost his lead and zinc property and fortune, along with the twenty-five thousand he had pledged.

"Well," I told myself, "keep on going."

I kept going until I tumbled to the fact that the ill wind that had brought the war had also brought something good for me and my venture. Liberty bonds! How these Liberty bonds were sold and what their purchasers thought of them, I will relate later. What is important now is that they came in denominations of fifty dollars and up. The other important thing is that our comrades hated the very sight of them. They weren't going to spend their hard-earned money in killing their brothers across the sea; not if they could help it. However, they hadn't been able to help it, so it was easy for me to separate them from the bonds, the very sight of which was a reproach. Contributions began coming not in two, five, and ten dollar bills, but in Liberty bonds of fifty and up.

Better still, it wasn't only my Socialist comrades who hated war and Liberty bonds. Republicans and Democrats hated them. Holy Rollers, Seventh-day Adventists, Mennonites, hated them. Yes, even hundred-per-cent war-shouters hated them, as I soon discovered when talking to some of them behind the barn, and I often left with their Liberty bonds. I got so busy picking up Liberty bonds I either had to have help or succumb to Liberty-bond-pick-up cramps. In fact I was so tuckered out picking them up that if Freda hadn't come along to help me I might have thrown up the sponge and called quits.

Freda will appear again and again in this roughneck Odyssey. For the present I will explain only that she came from a small mining camp in Arkansas where she and her father, Dan Hogan, had operated a small labor weekly. What with hard work, close confinement in a stuffy print shop, and worry about paper and ink bills, Freda had got herself down to ninety-six pounds. The doctors pronounced her condition incipient T.B., and urged her to seek health and livelihood in God's fresh air. So Freda was helping me pick up Liberty bonds in the wide open spaces.

What a salesman that ninety-six-pound girl was! Almost anyone can sell almost anything once. But to sell 'most anything to anyone three and four times over and be cordially received the fifth time—that's real salesmanship. And when the 'most anything happens to be but a piece of paper representing something that isn't yet, and may never be—that, I submit, takes a supersalesman like Freda. Freda was such a marvelous salesman that if De Lesseps, the Panama Canal promoter, Sam Insull, or the Van Sweringen boys had got hold of her before that ill wind of threatened sickness blew her into my arms, I'm certain they would all still be in business. And so we kept going until eventually we had picked up a quarter of a million dollars in Liberty bonds. Then our real troubles started. But before I come to that painful subject—back to Milwaukee for an episode that makes much grimmer reading.

35

THE First Amendment to the Constitution of the United States reads: "Congress shall make no law . . . abridging the freedom of speech or of the press." But when the forces of righteousness, aided by the author of *The New Freedom,* elected on the slogan "He kept us out of war," were making the world safe for democracy, that amendment apparently ceased to apply to any of us who did not participate in the hysteria of wartime.

Victor Berger wired me one day that a very serious situation had developed in Milwaukee, and that my presence was needed. When I arrived, I learned that Postmaster-General Burleson had revoked the second-class mailing privilege of the *Leader,* on the ground that it had not complied with the postal regulation providing that a daily paper must be mailed every day. It was true that one issue of the *Leader* had not been mailed on a certain day. The reason why it had not was that the postal authorities had destroyed it.

With the second-class mailing privilege revoked, the *Leader* could be mailed only by affixing a two-cent stamp on each copy. Putting a two-cent stamp on each of the eighteen thousand copies of the national edition would have bankrupted the paper in short order. Victor Berger had decided that under these circumstances the best thing to do was to shut down the plant and wait until the storm of emotional insanity had blown over. But what was my opinion?

My opinion was to nail the flag of international brotherhood to the mast and, if need be, go down with flying colors. Berger personally was inclined to accept that policy, but would our readers remain with us? I proposed that we find out by calling a mass meeting at the auditorium in Milwaukee by the end of the week. The main and side halls of the auditorium held some twelve thousand people. At seven o'clock of the night of the meeting the police closed the doors because the auditorium was filled to capacity. By speaking time, the crowd had overflowed the streets outside.

We told our story of the suppression of the *Leader* to the crowd in and around the auditorium. At the end of our recital I came out on the stage with a washtub slung over my shoulder. I told the audience that whatever its decision was, to say it not with flowers, but with money. The answer was several washtubs full of bills and coins totaling some four thousand dollars. The audience had told us to carry on. Among the offerings of that night was a quart of ladies' rings, earrings, and bracelets, which spoke louder than the cash itself. By next morning lines of women, some with shawls on their heads, brought more money along with pledges of Liberty bonds and War-savings stamps their husbands had been compelled to buy. Democracy had given its mandate. We carried on.

Not having succeeded in killing us then and there, Postmaster-General Burleson revoked our letter privilege. All letters addressed to us or in care of the *Leader* were stamped "Undeliverable under the Espionage Act" and returned to the sender. Friends and sympathizers who sent us money became marked persons. Creditors who had sent us bills appeared in person to collect them. We still could send bundles of papers destined for rural subscribers by express to agents and creamery stations, where they were delivered or handed out. Pressure from Washington finally stopped even that. However, our circulation in the city itself, delivered by carriers, mounted. With circulation mounting, our advertisers stuck by us and the paper. In order to deprive us of our advertising income, the crusaders for democracy instigated a boycott against the *Leader*. The Fuel Administration gave business concerns who advertised in the *Leader* to understand that if they didn't withdraw their patronage, they couldn't secure fuel. The Food Administration hinted to breweries who still employed the *Leader* as an advertising medium that unless they ceased they might experience difficulties in securing malt, hops and sugar. A well-known motorcycle manufacturer was told that unless he put pressure on a certain hardware dealer to withdraw his advertising from the *Leader*, the motorcycle he supplied to the government might not pass inspection.

Under the terrific pressure exerted by Washington we even lost the advertising patronage of persons and firms that were in full sympathy with the policy of the paper. One of them was Oswald Yaeger, of the well-known Milwaukee bakery of the same name. As a young man in Germany, Yaeger had become a Social-Democrat. His greatest pride was his collection of party dues-books, testifying to his fifty years of unbroken membership. When the *Leader* was launched he contributed a thousand dollars to the venture. When we were financially embarrassed we always could depend on Comrade Oswald Yaeger's help. Now even that devoted friend had canceled his advertising in the *Leader*.

Victor Berger and I called at Yaeger's home one Sunday morning to learn why he, too, had forsaken us and, if possible, to change his mind. We learned that, well, a man had a right to advertise where he wanted to. It was useless to combat one's government in wartime. Why not be sensible and accept the inevitable?

Victor and I realized the good comrade was shamming. He was, for presently he slumped down in a chair, covered his eyes and, with tears streaming through his fingers, sobbed, "My God, I can't help it. I can't advertise in our own paper. They told me if I didn't take my advertising out they would refuse me the flour, sugar and coal necessary for operating my bakery. And that is all I've got in the world."

"They" were the Fuel and Food Administrations—the latter directed by the ex-Quaker and future President, Herbert Hoover.

A well-known Milwaukee brewery had canceled its advertising contract with the *Leader*. I called on its president. No, he was not opposed to our war policy. On the contrary he was in full sympathy with it. We were right. We were the only sane people left in bedlam, and true patriots, if patriotism means love of country. He had never agreed with our economic and political views. In labor controversies we had always defended the interests of his employees against his own. But we had fought a clean fight on all occasions. It was largely due to Mr. Berger that labor racketeering had not gained a foothold in Milwaukee. Besides, whatever might be said against us Socialists, it would be foolish to deny that our influence had made Milwaukee a better place in which to do business. But advertise in your paper? Impossible! How can I operate my brewery without fuel, corn, barley, rice and sugar? Perhaps, though, if I called on his wife she might help. She was as much in sympathy with our anti-war position as he himself. Her private income was quite satisfactory and she had no financial interest in his brewery. I acted on the hint. The lady helped.

Ultimately the postal authorities even deprived us of the right to send first-class letters through the mails. We would at times deposit thousands of properly stamped and addressed letters in the main post office, not a single one of which was delivered. After we learned that mail robbery had become one of the functions of the Post-Office Department of the good old U. S. A., some of us, among them always Mrs. Meta Berger, would drive over the city at night distributing small numbers of letters in mailboxes, hoping and praying that they might escape the Argus eye of Postmaster-General Burleson.

Besides holding the position of mail-robber number one, Burleson filled the office of censor-in-chief. During the War he decided what the free American people might print and read. And as virtually everything printed and read in this great democracy must go through the mails, he exercised his censorship by denying the use of the mails to publications which expressed notions contrary to his own. The first publication barred from the mails was *The Rebel*, the official organ of the Tenant Farmers Union I had fathered in Oklahoma some years before.

There was a good reason why Burleson should select *The Rebel* as the first of his many hundreds of victims. My poor baby, the Tenant Farmers Union, had crossed the Red river into Texas, where it grew lustily. The editor of *The Rebel* was a sharp-tongued Irishman, Tom Hickey, who besides his Irish wit, had brought a large dose of inborn hatred of landlords and landlordism from the auld sod.

About the time Tom established *The Rebel*, Uncle Sam began to get worried that all was not quite as it should be, and appointed a commission headed by Frank P. Walsh to find out what might be wrong. Among the revelations dug up by the Walsh Commission was the testimony of a group of Texas tenant farmers evicted from their old homes on the Valley Steiner farm of the Lone Star state. Doctor Steiner had been a good landlord as landlords go; at any rate, the tenants lived more or less happily on the Valley Steiner farm for many years. However, the good man had gone to his reward, and the farm had passed, by way of his daughter, into the hands of a Southern gentleman, her husband.

The husband, in his turn, was not a good landlord, even as landlords go. He conceived the idea that more money could be made off the four-thousand-acre farm by operating it with prison labor than with share croppers who, the Lord knows, are cheap enough. The gentleman, being also one of the leaders of Texas Democracy, pulled the proper wires. And so it happened that one Christmas morning there appeared on the Valley Steiner farm a number of men in striped suits escorted by dignitaries with gats, rifles, and chains. The men in stripes, under the eyes and rifles of their guards, threw the group of tenant farmers and their belongings, along with their old, sick, halt, lame, blind, and babies, out in the festive, frosty Yuletide air.

At the hearing of the Walsh Commission one of the evicted tenants testified in the vocabulary of an eight-year-old and with the dramatic power of a Shakespeare how they wept when they were passing for the last time the little school and church of the farm, their only social center, where they had held their spelling bees, pie socials, literaries, and singing rehearsals; where so many of them were married, saw their children baptized, and were laid out in death. Tom Hickey, Clan na Gael, Sinn Fein Irishman, who hated landlords and landlordism more than any devil could possibly hate holy water, printed abstracts of that testimony in his *Rebel*, which explains why of all the many hundreds of American publications, *The Rebel* was the first to walk the plank. But what has all that to do with Postmaster-General Burleson? That riddle is solved by the simple and factual explanation that the Southern gentleman behind this human drama was none other than the sterling champion of democracy, chief censor, and mail robber, Burleson.

Perhaps I should not be too hard on Burleson. It is quite possible the unreasonable demands of the Tenant Farmers Union had annoyed him greatly. Among these demands were three-room tenant houses with glass windows and wooden floors, two-room schoolhouses, and six-months schools, and, to cap the climax, payment for improvements made on the landlord's property in case of surrender or eviction. I know these unreasonable demands well, for I wrote them myself. . . .

36

WITHOUT advertising, denied second-class mailing rights, deprived of the privilege of receiving and sending letters, it might appear that to continue to publish the *Leader* was a hopeless task. It just couldn't be done. Yet we did it. And because all that hadn't killed us, Washington indicted our editor in chief, Victor Berger, on so many counts that, had he been found guilty on all of them, it would have meant fifteen hundred years in the federal penitentiary. The accumulated total of Berger's bail bonds reached one million dollars. The million dollar bond, moreover, stipulated that Berger must not write a line in the paper of which he was the chief editor. Then, to relieve us of some more of our burdens, they confiscated our files, books, and whatever else could be hauled or carried away.

There were at that time some 700,000 paid and unpaid spies assisting in saving democracy. Apparently about 678,347 were keeping 1,356,694 eyes on our little group. Our roost was so infested with dictaphones that we couldn't say "Pop goes the weasel" without causing the poppies in Flanders to pop. When Berger and I had something very important to discuss we used to climb into my little Ford and drive some twelve miles up the Milwaukee river to a spot where it was only two feet deep and had a smooth stone bottom. There was one slight inconvenience connected with that conference place, because I always had to step out into the water to crank my Ford. Victor, with all his marvelous learning, couldn't crank a Ford.

How often during that tidal wave of emotional insanity did the words of Schiller come to my mind:

> "Dangerous to rouse the sleeping lion,
> Destructive are the tiger's fangs,
> But the most terrible of terror
> That is man ensnared by error."

And why, oh, why, didn't I follow his advice contained in "Against stupidity even the gods battle in vain"?

I am not talking here about how the American people were swept into the World War. Every intelligent person knows by now how that was done, why it was done and by whom it was done. I am talking only about what happens to a normally decent, intelligent people when the dogs of war are turned loose. I was well aware that if the Central Powers had triumphed they would have comported themselves just as viciously as the victors. I knew then what Woodrow Wilson discovered afterward, that it was a war of commercial and financial rivalry here and over there. The gang over here had thrown America into the World War when the first Anglo-French bond issue was floated by the house of Morgan—with the consent of Wilson. What followed after that was merely rationalization.

The leader in that national self-deception was Woodrow Wilson. His cocksureness, and magnificent talent for phrasemaking— "neutral even in spirit," "too proud to fight," "benevolent neutrality," "peace without victory," and finally, "war to make the world safe for democracy"—made him the mouthpiece of the very forces which in the beginning of his career he had denounced as the "invisible government" and threatened to "hang higher than Haman." In the end the man hanged himself and his country, the peace of the world, and became the godfather of Mussolini, Hitler and Stalin.

As I understood and understand the temper of those war years, the great mass of Americans had no desire to get mixed up in the bloody welter. They had given their mandate for peace when they cast their votes for "the man who kept us out of war." They had expressed their innermost feelings when they refused to buy the first three-per-cent war bonds floated with the blessing of their government. They expressed it again in the poor response to Wilson's call for volunteers, most of whom enlisted in the hope of securing swivel-chair jobs. They expressed it again when nine million out of the total of ten million youths drafted under the selective draft law gave all the reasons they could think of why they should be excused from going over there. They showed their true feelings again when on the false alarm of the armistice they poured out of homes, offices and factories in joyous delirium.

I am not afraid of democracy. I have seen enough of life to realize that the only way to mislead the voting masses is to overwhelm them with lying appeals to their innate sympathy, decency, and sense of justice. That was what so successfully swept America into the World War. Nor am I afraid of the rank and file. As my old friend, Carl Sandburg, once said, the common people have hung around for a long time. And I presume they will continue to hang around unless the stupidity and cupidity of their "betters," in conjunction with the tremendous forces of production and, alas, also of destruction, that modern science has awakened, do not blow both them and their betters off the face of the earth.

How my mind is wandering! Please excuse me, young readers. Reminiscing is the curse of advanced age. Besides, I only want to tell you what certified historians and history textbooks don't tell you. Those were the sweetless, wheatless, meatless, heatless, and perfectly brainless days when your fathers broke Beethoven's records, boycotted Wagner's music, burned German books, painted German Lutheran churches and Goethe's monument in Chicago the color of Shell filling stations today; strung up a

Mennonite preacher in Collinsville, Oklahoma, by his neck until he fainted, repeated the process until he fainted again, and then graciously relented; hanged another to the limb of a tree in Collinsville, Illinois, until he was dead, and later, ransacking the room of the corpse for pro-kaiser evidence, the executioners found that their victim had been refused service in the American army for physical defects.

Those were the days when your mothers collected old casings and prune kernels for Belgian babies, or knitted sweaters for doughboys engaged in saving Morgan's dough; when anti-cigarette and white-ribbon sisters collected "coffin nails" for poor Serbian swineherds and Montenegrin goat-thieves; parsons of the Gentle Carpenter made recruiting stations out of His temples and lied like Munchausens about German atrocities—such as cut-off baby hands, Canadian soldiers nailed on barn doors, women's breasts cut off by bloodthirsty Huns. I know of sincere followers of Christ—Russellites, Mennonites, and Seventh-day Adventists tortured to death in those war years—hanging by their thumbs suspended from cell doors. I have no sympathy with talk about the moral uplift engendered by mass murder, or with the superiority of the pious and intellectual bellwethers who led their flocks to slaughter.

37

YES, it was a considerable chore running a daily newspaper under the circumstances I have described. But, by and large, our crowd stuck. While we lost eighteen thousand outside readers, the *Leader's* circulation kept on mounting in Milwaukee. Some advertisers eventually returned. Money came in from many unexpected sources. A West Virginia coal operator sent the paper a check for a thousand dollars. A well known cigarette manufacturer sent more than one thousand dollars: Wood Axton, of the Louisville firm of Axton-Fisher, manufacturers of Clowns, then one of the few union-made cigarettes. Many other people who loved liberty hastened to our rescue with cash, checks, and Liberty bonds.

But how did we receive their letters, deprived of mail as we were? Freda managed that. We asked her to drop her Liberty-bond-collecting campaign in Oklahoma, and come to Milwaukee. No one would suspect that slip of an Arkansas girl—with the non-German name of Hogan—of trying to stop the World War. We installed her near one of the main branches of the Milwaukee post office, where she carried on her subversive activity as our underground depository of whatever mail our friends among the postal employees could snitch and deliver after working hours.

Our greatest help, however, came from the Huns of Wisconsin, the descendants of the "Forty-eighters"—immigrants who had pulled the eternal stumps from Wisconsin's cedar swamps, reared the marvelous stone fences with boulders dug out of the five- and ten-acre fields they still surround; in short, converted the waste land of Wisconsin into the smiling countryside it is today. These people were not kaiser lovers. Their republican, revolutionary fathers and grandfathers had been defeated by "Shrapnel Prince William," grandfather of William II. They had found asylum in the wilds of the new state of Wisconsin. Up to my meeting with them they were still called *Lateinische Bauern,* Latin farmers, a term derived from the fact that many of their ancestors had been university students.

Besides being republicans in the true sense of the word, these original settlers became violent Abolitionists. When Old Abe called for volunteers, the West-side Milwaukee Turnverein of some twelve hundred members enlisted in a body. By the second year of the Civil War, pioneer Wisconsin was virtually depopulated of men. I have been told by widows of some of these men that while their husbands were at war they had walked thirty miles for a sack of flour, worrying all the way that strolling Indians might do something to the children they had left at home. In the township of Rhine, Sheboygan County, stands one of the first soldiers' monuments erected after the Civil War, bearing the inscription:

"Erected in memory of the twenty-nine sons of the Town of Rhine who gave their lives for the preservation of the Union." Think of twenty-nine lives contributed by one thinly settled frontier township, then ask yourself if these German immigrants were good Americans.

Linguistically they were not good Americans. They had retained their German speech. The language was still taught and preached in their neat brick schoolhouses and churches. In many instances the third generation still spoke and read German as well as English. There were old German books around their homes, which father or grandfather had brought from the fatherland that had driven them out. I found yellowed volumes of German classics in their bookcases. For some reason the command of the two languages had not prevented the offspring of these Latin farmers from acquiring a much better English than I have found in many hundred-per-cent American localities. Perhaps a larger percentage of their children had passed through high school and university than from any other stratum of the Wisconsin population. Quite possibly they might also have had something to do with the fact that Wisconsin University had become one of the most progressive state universities in the nation.

There were many reasons why the German tongue endured so long among these people. When the Forty-eighters settled in the Wisconsin wilderness they found no English-speaking white men from whom to learn English. The few Canadian voyageurs who penetrated the territory spoke only French. Of course, there was a small population of native Americans already in the territory when the German immigrants arrived. These natives had coppery skins and spoke Indian dialects. So when the Latin farmers organized their school there was nothing else to be done but hire German teachers whom they and their children could understand. When they established churches they employed German ministers for the same reason. When they laid out townships and counties they elected only Germans to office on the poor excuse that there was nobody else to vote for. Then, because all the officials were Germans they naturally kept the township and county books in German. Why should anybody be so dumb as to keep books in a language nobody else could make out and the bookkeeper himself can't sabe? Once started, these people kept going in the same old beaten path. That's how people are.

However, by the time the World War came around, quite a number of foreigners, such as down-east Yankees, had settled among the descendants of these German Forty-eighters. I say "foreigners" because those Germans regarded themselves as the aborigines of Wisconsin. The late-comers didn't belong.

When war came it was the small-town and county-seat people that became the "real patriots," while the old-line German farm-

ers were decidedly hostile to the mess. This situation provided
the late-comers with a fine opportunity to show the original
settlers who the true Americans were. In the pursuit of this
worthy aim the riff-raff of the towns organized themselves into
"Home Defense Guards," "County Councils of Defense," snoop-
ers, and Liberty-loan strong-arm squads. The leaders in these
patriotic drives were the bankers, naturally. It is said that the
mortality rate of bankers during that war was even lower than
that of generals, and that's saying a lot, because only one of our
generals was wounded in action—by the premature explosion of
a champagne bottle.

Now the Teutonic ruralists were not against licking the kaiser.
Licking kaisers was in their blood. Nor did they offer opposition
to having their boys dragged three thousand miles over there.
Of course they were too intelligent to swallow the whoppers engendered in Wall Street, on Capitol Hill and Pennsylvania Avenue. They even suspected it was against the Constitution's phrase
"repel invasion" for the United States to send American soldiers
against their own will outside of the territory bounded by the
Atlantic and Pacific oceans, the Canadian line and the Gulf of
Mexico. In the matter of Liberty bonds they always bought their
quota and better. You see, the patriotic bankers who headed the
Liberty-bond drives knew almost to a penny what those hyphen-
ated Americans were worth.

They'd say, "Mr. Spiegelmeyer, you are down for five hundred dollars. So no back talk. I looked up your account before
I came out here." Or, "Mr. Scheibenschieber, your share is seven
hundred dollars. I know you haven't the cash on hand, because
you have just bought the forty adjoining your place. But don't
let that worry you. Just sign this six-per-cent note for the seven
hundred dollars and I'll keep your four-per-cent Liberty bond
for security. I know you are perfectly good for the note and so
are the Liberty bonds." Or, "Mr. Rauschenbauer, your quota is
three hundred dollars. I know you've only got a hundred dollars
in my bank. So give me your check for one hundred and sign

this six-per-cent note for the balance and I'll see to it the bonds are safe in my safe." In the latter instance, if the balance of two hundred was not paid, as happened in many cases, the banker had the three-hundred-dollar bond and the hundred-dollar down payment of the buyer. In case the buyer had paid in full for the bond or bonds and got hard pressed for money, the bankers would always accommodate the customer by taking his bond or bonds back, at first for sixty-five cents on the dollar and toward the end at ninety-six cents on the dollar. It pays to be a patriot.

In cases where the prospect refused to buy Liberty bonds he would be visited by strong-arm salesmen who brought ropes with them to help the prospect see his duty toward his government. Quite frequently his house was painted yellow to proclaim just what kind of a dog lived there.

Perhaps the German-Americans might have become reconciled to that method of salesmanship, which I must admit was duplicated in every factory, store and township of the land. But there was one thing they couldn't stand for, and that was being called "Huns," "baby-killers," "kaiser-lovers" and "alien enemies."

What, alien enemies?

Until shortly before the World War, very few immigrants took out naturalization papers in Wisconsin. When the Latin farmers settled in the wilds of Wisconsin there was nobody else around except Menominee Indians. They, as native Americans, would have been the proper people to issue naturalization papers to later arrivals. But somehow the Indians never got into the habit of issuing naturalization papers, whereupon the Forty-eighters simply "naturalized" themselves. There was nothing else for them to do if they wanted to organize their township and county governments. So they just voted and let it go at that. And so the matter stood with any number of the older settlers.

The local saviors of democracy would ask one of these old-timers: "Where were you born, Mr. Laubenheimer?"

"I was born in Germany."

"Aha, Germany! And how long have you lived in this country?"

"I've lived"—it might be sixty or seventy—"years in this country."

"Oh, that long? And when did you take out naturalization papers?"

"Naturalization papers? I never thought of taking out naturalization papers. Nobody around here ever took out naturalization papers. We just voted when election time . . ."

"What? Why, you are an alien enemy and an illegal voter to boot! Come along, we'll teach you what true Americanism is."

I will limit myself to three examples of how some of the old settlers were taught true Americanism.

The old gentleman I had called on for his Liberty bonds was in ill humor when he told me his story. He had left Germany when not quite sixteen. Two years later he answered Lincoln's first call for volunteers, was severely wounded in the battle of Lookout Mountain, but on recovering, returned to the front, where he served to the end of the war. Then he received his honorable discharge with the rank of major. Like his neighbors, he had never taken out naturalization papers. He said he had been under the impression that serving Uncle Sam in four years of war had automatically established him as a citizen. However, a few days previous to my visit, a committee from the county seat had come to his house and demanded to see his naturalization papers. Ignoring his honorable discharge from the army, they had taken the old man to the county seat and declared him an alien enemy. Then for good measure they took his photograph, front and profile, gave him a number, and took his fingerprints.

As I say, the old gentleman was a bit peeved. "Take my fingerprints, mug me like a common burglar, me who never broke a law. I, who fought four long years in the Union army and the so-and-sos mug and fingerprint me like a common burglar! Of course you can have my Liberty bonds. I was about to burn 'em up along with my honorable discharge from the army. Sure, take

'em along, and if the rats make me take more you can have them,
too!"

John Barsch was another. When I drove up he was sitting on
the fence, whittling a stick with an ugly-looking knife corresponding to the ugly look he gave me when I said "Good morning,
Mr. Barsch."

"Well, what do you want?" grunted Mr. Barsch of the ugly
look and knife. Before I could state my mission he growled, "I
suppose you want to sell me more Liberty bonds?"

"No, Mr. Barsch, I've come . . ."

"Or maybe War-savings stamps?"

"No, Mr. . . ."

"Well then, I suppose you come for my firearms?"

It took me quite a time to get Mr. Barsch sufficiently mollified
to tell him I had come to ask for his Liberty bonds.

"Well," he grumbled at last, folding his ugly knife and climbing down from the fence, "come up to the house. You can have
'em. I want to pay a fine for having been an ass all my grown
years. And I'd rather pay it to you than anybody else I can think
of. Your Milwaukee *Leader* bunch are the only people left in
this God-damned coward country who have guts enough to sass
back."

At the house, with a mug of hard cider between us, Mr. Barsch
explained how he had made an ass of himself. He had come to
this country a baby in his mother's arms. His dad had not taken
out naturalization papers. Neither had he. He had just voted at
elections like everybody else around there. However, he had been
more than a mere voter. He had risen to the high position of
Republican boss of his township. In that capacity he had seen to it
that no Republican jumped over the traces into the Democratic,
or worse still the Socialist, camp. Mr. Barsch had never aspired
to public office; boss of the township was honor enough for him.
He said he felt mighty proud when the big shots from the county
seat visited his house, and, between eating chicken and drinking
his good hard cider, discussed the fortunes of the Grand Old

Party with him. He had, he said, entertained Congressmen at his house, where they discussed such weighty subjects as high tariffs and the gold standard. One time he had even received a letter from a United States Senator, asking him in the name of God, flag, and country to bring out the full Republican vote of the township if the country was to be saved.

"See that schoolhouse, creamery and saloon down there?" he asked me, pointing through the window to a cluster of buildings a little over a mile off. "That schoolhouse used to be right between the creamery and the saloon. But the fellows up in Madison passed a fool law that saloons must not be permitted within fifteen hundred yards of a schoolhouse. So we moved the saloon fifteen hundred yards from the schoolhouse, and that puts it just over the one-mile limit."

"One-mile limit of what, Mr. Barsch?"

"Wait, I come to that later," said Mr. Barsch. "Well, around election time the candidates would come to my house. After chicken supper and hard cider we'd go down to that saloon, electioneering. We'd fill the bellies of the sovereign voters with cold beer, and their pockets with nickel cigars. We'd shake hands, slap backs and ask whether the little woman at home had got over her lumbago yet. I'd set 'em up as much as the candidates, even if I was running for no office and wouldn't take one if they gave it to me. All I wanted was for my neighbors to know who was boss of the township and how much the G.O.P. was dependent on me.

"Well," he continued in rising indignation, "some boss I was! I wasn't even a citizen of the country, as I discovered when that damned committee of highbinders came out from Sheboygan and asked to see my citizenship papers. Of course I had no citizenship papers. Nobody around here ever thought of taking out papers until this damned war came along. Well, when they saw I had no papers, they took me up to the courthouse, where some of the skunks I helped to elect, mugged and fingerprinted me, John Barsch, Republican boss of this here township! Take a look at this card with my picture, fingerprints, and number on it. Right here it says I must not be seen out of my house after nine at night, and no further than a mile from it in daytime, and that saloon down there is just over the mile limit. So I can't even get beer any more. Sure you can have those damned Liberty bonds. I want to pay a fine to somebody and you boys earn it, sticking up for your convictions. Oh, yes, and before I forget it, yesterday I got an order to deliver my firearms. Look at that old single-barrel muzzle-loader over there. That's my arsenal. The only time we ever used it was to shoot a rooster, when company came unexpectedly. Now the damned crooks demand I give up that old fowling piece, and next time they come around I'll have to run my legs off trying to catch a rooster for them."

A fine upstanding man, Mr. Barsch, though easily peeved.

When I met Grandma Pfeil she was nearing four score, but she was as lively as a cricket and chipper as a wren. She was a remarkably well-read woman and as witty as they make them. In all the reunions and old settlers' meetings, Grandma Pfeil was the center of attraction. She would recite poems about early days which she had "made up out of her own head." She'd tell stories about the time when most of the country between Kiel and Milwaukee, sixty-five miles off, was cedar swamp, stumpy pine clearing, rock piles, and log houses. She'd tell what fun she had with the Indian children who used to come with their squaw mothers to her dad's house, and how sorry she felt for the little papooses who were strapped on wood frames their mothers had leaned against the log walls of their house. Grandma Pfeil had a good right to shine at those social doings. She was the first white child born in Sheboygan County, Wisconsin.

However, she had made a fatal slip when she married George Pfeil. George had come with his parents from Germany when he still couldn't say "da-da." Neither his father nor he had taken out citizenship papers. Caught red-handed minus these documents, George Pfeil was declared an alien enemy, mugged, and fingerprinted. If the patriots had stopped then and there, they might be forgiven. But they did not stop there. They hot-footed after

Grandma Pfeil too, for she was married to an alien enemy, which made her one as well. So they took Grandma Pfeil, the first white child born in Sheboygan County, to the county seat, where she was properly entered in the rogues' gallery

Her alien-enemy permit stipulated that she must not leave her house after nine P.M., or be seen at any time further than a mile from it. And she always carried that permit tied round her neck, in fear of losing it, she claimed. On her rounds of the spotless little town of Kiel she would ask all kinds of foolish questions: "Johnny, are you sure it isn't nine o'clock yet? Seems to me the sun is trying to lead me into a trap, hanging around eleven A.M." "Willy, are you sure I'm not over a mile from my home? I wish you'd measure it off. I forgot my yardstick." (The village of Kiel covered one half of a square mile.) "Sammy, maybe you'll get to hear I was signaling the kaiser again last night from our second-story bedroom window. But I swear to you I was only hunting for my glasses. I found 'em pushed up on my forehead. But it took almost half an hour before I felt for them and saw where they were. . . ." These anxious remarks Grandma reserved for the local patriots and home guard; with normal people she acted quite normally.

What a crazy time! Fortunately for us, the resentment the democracy-savers roused in those Wisconsin sons of the Forty-eighters made it easy for them to sacrifice their Liberty bonds and savings certificates on the altar of Liberty. We, in this case meaning Bob Buech, the high sheriff of Milwaukee, and I, must have picked up well over a hundred and fifty thousand dollars in bonds. All of which goes to show that it's no trick at all to publish a daily paper that can't go through the mails, send or receive letters, has no advertising to speak of, and whose editor in chief is under a million dollar bond stipulating that he'll not write a line for the duration of the War. Easy, maybe, but the job certainly kept us hopping. I used to get through with my daily column of six hundred words around noon, then spend the time between noon and two in the morning with Bob Buech, idling around the land o' lakes absorbing its beauteous moonlight and Liberty bonds.

There were other ameliorations. Outlaws as far as Washington's new-freedom dealers were concerned, we had captured the county government in 1917. Bob Buech was high sheriff of Milwaukee County. Comrade Leo Krzycki, now member of the executive board of the Amalgamated Clothing Workers of America, was undersheriff. Not all the deputies were members of our church, but the dictum is "tell me whose bread you eat and I'll tell you whose song you sing," and they behaved accordingly. With the majesty of the law on our side, the dregs that crawled out from the social dump heap when war stirred things up were kept in check. For good measure, Bob appointed many of us deputy sheriffs, myself included. There was no salary attached to this position, but we were entitled to carry murderous six-shooters, and wear the shining star of the majesty of the law. I did not avail myself of the privilege of lugging the six-shooter. I did, however, affix the star where it might come in handy, as it did on several occasions.

The police of the city were not under our official control. They were headed by Chief Janssen, appointed by the Republican governor. There was little love lost between Janssen and our crowd, we had done everything in our power to get rid of him. Nevertheless, he did maintain law and order in Milwaukee during the great madness; he even protected our meetings.

One day we called a mass meeting in the auditorium. A rumor started that it would be broken up, and some of our people spread the word around to come with railroad spikes and iron nuts wrapped in handkerchiefs to defend paragraph one of the Bill of Rights. Chief Janssen got wind of the nuts and railroad spikes. He telephoned Berger and asked him to please call off the nut and railroad spike brigade. There would be no meeting broken up while he was chief of police of Milwaukee and he assured Berger that if any rough-house was started by the other side, his police would be there to squelch it pronto. The police were there, and there was no rough-house.

Another possible outbreak of mob rule was nipped by our high sheriff. Milwaukee possessed one of the best German theaters of the country. In the early days of the War some hooligans placed a machine gun in front of the German theater, threatening to shoot up the "Hun" actors and audience. The play to be given that night was Schiller's *William Tell,* the most antiautocratic and fervently pro-democratic of all German classics. But what do hooligans know about classics? The police promptly dispersed the mob; however, the director of the Pabst Theater, home of the German thespians, deemed it advisable to close the house. The German actors were now in the street and most of them in desperate circumstances. They decided to give a benefit performance for themselves. The play selected was a harmless farce comedy that had no more to do with the War than circus clowns with moral philosophy. In searching for a place to give it, the actors came to me. I was then a director of the *Freie Gemeinde* and its hall, that is, the hall of the Freethinkers Society, and the hall contained a fair-sized stage. Of course I told the applicants they could have it.

As the day of the performance approached, rumors reached us that selectively drafted recruits from Fort Sheridan, some fifty miles south of Milwaukee, had threatened to break up the "Hun" play. Just as the curtain was about to rise the budding democracy saviors arrived. This was a new sort of mob, a mob dressed in Uncle Sam's uniforms, equipped with drums, bugles, and flag. We too were well prepared.

Bob Buech, master of ceremonies for the day, stepped up to the ringleader of the uniformed mob and said, "Tell me, young man, what your crowd expects to do in this city."

"We are going to break up this 'Hun' show."

"Well," replied Bob, drawing himself up to all of his five-feet-seven, "I am the high sheriff of Milwaukee County. I am responsible for preserving law and order. What's more, I am fully prepared." Then gently turning the young hero by the lobe of his ear toward the opposite side of the street, he pointed. "See those roughnecks lining the sidewalk over there? They are deputy sheriffs, sworn to uphold the majesty of the law, if you know what that means. Each one has a six-shooter in his hip pocket and a riot club behind his back." Then gently turning the head of commander in chief in the general direction of Fort Sheridan, he perorated, "Now get yourself and your mob the hell out of here before you land in our hospital."

And they got.

Kier Hardie, leader of the Scotch miners, used to say in one of his speeches, "The majesty of the law is like a burro. Pull it by its tail and it'll kick your block off. Pull it by the ears and it carries your load." On the whole Milwaukee's population and government remained a sort of tranquil oasis in the elsewhere universal madness. A voice of calm reason amid the raving bedlam all around. Outside of Milwaukee County there had been considerable patriotic mob violence. Bob La Follette, one of the six Senators who voted against American entrance into the European fracas, had been burned in effigy by a college mob on the campus of Wisconsin's progressive university, to whose prestige he himself had so greatly contributed.

38

WHEN I ran for Congress in the Second District of Wisconsin, which lay outside of Milwaukee, patriotic partisans were breaking up meetings and instilling love of country in the hearts of the people by making them kiss the flag. I never found out how Old Glory enjoyed those shotgun weddings. The night before one of my meetings, the saviors of democracy had thrown a doctor in a river and held him at intervals under water until he decided to kiss Old Glory rather than drown.

I was holding forth in a dance hall in the rear of a Sauk County saloon. I had explained to the assembled multitude the platform I was running on. It was not an anti-war platform. I had accepted the war as an accomplished fact and accepted it with the same grace any normal human being might accept a carbuncle. All I asked in that platform was that Washington should state the conditions for our entering the War, then, having stated them, induce the party of the second part to sign on the dotted line and give bond for the faithful carrying out of contract.

It's true that I wasn't a doctor of history and law. But some time before that I had built a barn. After showing the contractor a sketch of what I wanted, he reckoned the cost would be around five hundred dollars. Of course it might cost a few dollars more or less, but I could depend on his doing the right thing by me, whatever it was. When the barn was finished it cost me fifteen hundred. With that experience in mind it had struck me that before the sapient gentlemen in Washington delivered the wealth and youth of America to the democracy builders over in Europe, it might not be a bad idea to submit blueprints and specifications and give bond for faithful performance.

Just as I was winding up, the door flew open and, behind drums, bugle, flag and guns, in marched the procession that had conducted the affair of the doctor and the flag the night before.

To quit in that situation would have been impossible. I would have invited the doctor's fate, and besides, I had learned by then that so long as the speaker kept his ground, looked his foes—no matter how hostile—boldly in the eye, and continued speaking, there was little danger of assault.

I got this valuable piece of wisdom from dogs. Repeatedly I had noticed how a dog rushes toward another with every hair of his body and tail saying, "Now, watch me make that dog's fur fly." Then the threatened dog turns toward its would-be exterminator, bares his dental work and says, "Well, stranger, what can I do for you?" Whereupon the would-be exterminator wig-wags with his tail, "Please excuse me, mister. You aren't the dog I thought you were," and suddenly remembers something he has forgotten.

With that profound observation in mind I bade my visitors welcome, and announced that as they apparently had come a long way to hear me speak I felt myself duty-bound to make my speech all over again. This I did, but while speaking, I felt out the pos-sibilities of the legs of the old beer table forming my pulpit. I was fully determined that at the first manifestation of violence I would break off one of its legs, and sail in. I am not a hero. But on that occasion I would rather have died fighting than kiss and insult Old Glory under duress. However, nothing happened, except that my original hearers gradually departed, leaving me alone with the visitors. At the end of my speech, the leader of the patriotic mob, a manufacturer from a near-by town, upbraided me for my unpatriotic conduct at "such times." I replied that inasmuch as I was running for Congress I owed it to him and to all my future constituents to apprise them of my position, and so we parted.

A few minutes later, when I left the hall, I discovered that my original audience had not deserted me as I had feared. Although it was long after haying, a good number were waiting around outside, equipped with pitchforks. Perhaps the latter had more to do with my peaceable conduct and departure than had my "brave" stand. Mobs are always cowardly, and those pitchforks really looked mean. This was the only one of my meetings where mob violence threatened. My others were sandbagged by due process of law. The flu epidemic was raging. All over the country meetings were forbidden by health authorities. Wisconsin followed suit, but due perhaps to the progressiveness of the Badger State, only my meetings were prohibited. The audiences of my opponents were presumably immune to flu germs.

The difficulties under which I carried on my campaign undoubtedly contributed to my defeat at the election. Not only were my meetings hamstrung, but my campaign posters were torn down. I could not even reach the sovereign voters of the Second Congressional District of Wisconsin by first or second-class mail, for the reasons already related. The chief cause, however, was that I was indicted for obstructing recruiting in the United States army.

Indicted and arrested with me were the other Socialist Congressional candidates, six all told, among them Louis Arnold, state secretary of the Party, now and for the past twenty years tax commissioner of the best-governed city in the United States, and the treasurer of the Milwaukee *Leader*, Miss Elizabeth Thomas, the Quakeress I have mentioned before, who spent her Sabbaths hunting poor little birds in the parks of Milwaukee, murderously armed with camera and spy glass.

None of us was ever brought to trial. The idea behind the sensational arrests was to destroy us politically. Victor Berger, elected in the previous Congressional election by a majority of over five thousand, had been denied the seat to which the sovereign voters of the Third Congressional District of Wisconsin had elected him. The ground on which our defeat was based was that, in the event of election, we would not be seated either, which was true enough, as the experience of Berger had demonstrated. Why in the name of common sense and democracy should people throw their votes away on candidates who would be thrown out of Congress? So why not vote for somebody they didn't want and be sure they were seated?

Well, it worked. There was no possible way by which we could escape from that legally concocted campaign maze. I was defeated by a few hundred votes, which, under the circumstances, was a remarkable showing. I knew if I were elected to Congress I would not be seated. And if seated, I would certainly have been the most miserable of all mortals, for with all my slips from grace, I always have been careful with whom I associated, and that War Congress was no place for a peaceable fellow like me.

When, on a Friday morning in November, 1918, the forces of law and order of the U. S. A. appeared in Brisbane Hall to escort us to the federal hoosegow, there was one gent among them who I am sure had his whole heart in the task. At that moment clothed with the authority of a deputy United States marshal he was no other than the would-be building trades racketeer whom Victor Berger had forced to resign from his union for attempted labor extortion. What joyous satisfaction that grafter must have derived from hauling us as prisoners from the very building from which we had driven him.

The indictment against me contained only four counts, to wit:

One: I had inserted or caused to be inserted in the Milwaukee *Leader* an article captioned: "A.M. Patriots, P.M. Pirates." The author of the article was none other than Amos Pinchot. He had sent it to the entire American daily press, pointing out how the dollar-a-year men of the National Defense Council handed out millions of dollars' worth of contracts in the morning in their capacity as counselors, and in the afternoon as shining lights of the corporations they represented, graciously accepted these contracts for their firms. In the body of his article Amos Pinchot had used the term "A.M. patriots and P.M. pirates." Unable to think of anything more fitting, I slapped that on top of the article and signed it at the bottom, "Amos Pinchot."

Somehow the printer's devil had dropped that last line, and I became the author.

Two: I had inserted or caused to be inserted an article in the Polish language appearing on such and such a date in the *Voice of the People*. What that Polish article contained I never found out, as I can't understand a word of the language. But whatever its contents, I, as editor of the *Voice of the People*, had failed to submit an English translation to the postmaster who, under the Espionage Act, also fulfilled the high function of censor of the foreign-language press. Under the provisions of the Espionage Act, all foreign publications had to be submitted in English translation to the eagle eye of the postmaster of the place of their publication. The viciousness behind this count lay in the fact that the *Voice of the People* had never been sent through the mails. It was always distributed from house to house by our devoted bundle brigade.

Three: This was made up of abstracts from my historic masterpiece, *Life and Deeds of Uncle Sam, A Little History for Big Children*, published in 1909.

Four: I had composed, inserted, or caused to be inserted in the issue of the Milwaukee *Leader* of a certain day in November, 1914, a poem entitled "Dumdum Bullets."

In regard to that epic, the Department of Justice really had something on me. True, it had been written two and a half years before America's crowning folly, but also it had kept drifting from paper to paper until a few days before America's dive into the World War. Contrary to all newspaper experience, my name had stuck to "Dumdum Bullets" to the bitter end. The last time I had seen the poem was in a small country weekly up in Vermont, with my name still on it. The inspiration for this masterpiece had come to me one Sunday morning in late October, 1914. As older readers may remember, in those early days of the War both sides accused each other of using dumdum bullets. Personally, I have no objections to dumdum bullets. If the nations of Christendom are hell-bound to exterminate one another I want them to make a good job of it, and the sooner the better. In brief. I am violently opposed to civilized or Christian warfare.

DUMDUM BULLETS

A working man, a little dumb,
Made for his boss a little gun,
A cartridge and a bullet
With point sawed off to dull it.

Another worker, just as dumb,
Made for another boss a gun,
A cartridge and a bullet
With point sawed off to dull it.

One day the poor, dumb workers met,
Aimed at each other's wooden heads
And each one sent a bullet
With point sawed off to dull it.

Two bullets fled and said
"Dumb dumb,"
Two dummies tumbled over dead—
Never knew what the bullets said.

Our cases, as the reader already knows, were quietly dropped by the Department of Justice after the War. In the meantime, however, it had deprived the Congress of the United States of one of its most intelligent members since John Quincy Adams. Am I proud of the four counts that definitely connect my name

with the greatest thinkers and finest minds of the great madness?
Well, not exactly proud, but when posterity erects a monument
to this unknown hero of world-wide lunacy, please, Posterity,
don't forget to put on that monument:

> "He tried his damnedest
> To keep his country out of war."

Book Eight

THE AMERICAN GUARDIAN

39

THE War over, the world made safe for democracy at long last, freedom of the seas established, big and little nations enjoying the blessings of self-determination, Austria beheaded, quartered and drawn, the kaiser exiled, Germany made helpless for all time to come, I returned to Oklahoma for more punishment.

Many things had happened during my absence. The worst of these was the Green Corn Rebellion, so called from the green corn, or roasting ears, which constituted the principal diet of the rebels.

I have already sketched the character and living conditions of the people of the former Indian Territory, in which the rebellion occurred. To this picture I should like to add a very truthful description of the people and locality. This description is taken from a thesis submitted to the Graduate Faculty of the University of Oklahoma by Charles D. Bush:

> "Participants in the revolt were almost wholly native Americans. A few Negroes, usually coerced into joining the disaffected party, and a very small number of irreconcilable Snake Indians made up a minority racial group, but the vast majority of the people were white American citizens. Hardly a foreign name appears in the list. They could truthfully claim to be 'one-hundred-per-cent Americans.'
>
> "A majority of these people were from the hill country

of Arkansas, Tennessee, and other Southern states, migrating from the poorer sections of these older communities. These people were generally lacking in education. Actual illiteracy was common, and even a grade-school education was very rare. A man was locally considered well-educated if he was able to write a little and read the columns of the weekly paper.

"Their schools, for the most part, were poor and attended by the children only during the seasons when the crops were 'laid by' in July and for a brief period in winter. Frequently, they did not attend at all. Good schools could not be brought to these people because the districts were poor.

"Religion was the great outlet for pent-up feelings and stifled emotions. Camp meetings were the great events of the summer months and the tabernacle or rustic brush arbor was the focal point and mecca of a wide area. Shrouded in superstition, and frequently in a peculiar mysticism, their religion was intolerant and often wildly demonstrative. The most extreme religionists affiliated with the 'Holy Rollers,' various branches of the Holiness, Nazarenes, Saints, and other sects. The more conservative elements were advocates of the Baptist, Methodist, Presbyterian and other Protestant faiths— usually of the 'hard-shell,' 'free' or 'shouting' type. A Catholic was regarded with extreme suspicion, and anti-Catholic lecturers and agitators invariably had a wide and believing following.

"Economically these people were generally very poor and chronically in debt. They were too restless to stay long in one location and consequently they accumulated little property. Practically all were tenant farmers. Farm improvements, provided by absentee owners, were of the very poorest kind. Untutored even in agriculture, they generally depended on one crop—cotton—and measured their prosperity or poverty by the price of cotton and the prevalence of the boll weevil.

"In many respects these men were little more than serfs or peons, slaves to a 'cash crop' demanded by their landlords. Yet they did but little to help themselves. When they did have money, they spent it freely and often foolishly. The practice of saving was generally neglected, and they lived from crop to crop, year to year, vaguely dissatisfied, always dreaming of a new country somewhere.

"In common with the majority of American citizens, these people acquired their political beliefs mostly from their antecedents, but partly from the political spellbinders who harangued their meetings. Originally the Democratic Party claimed the allegiance of the great majority, but economic conditions exerted more pressure than precedent, and many turned to Socialism as a sort of gospel of despair.

"The finer tenets of Socialism were undoubtedly but faintly understood by these people, but it offered a hope that neither of the major parties promised, and a recognition that had long been denied them except during the hot days of the summer primaries. Socialism gained rapidly in strength. It not only became a real third party but it also had its third of the total area vote and its share of county officers, at the time the world was plunged into the Great War."

All that Mr. Bush has set down in the foregoing paragraphs is the truth. The rebels were hundred-per-cent Americans. The overwhelming majority of them did not own a square foot of their country. I am dead certain that many of these people's family names are emblazoned on the regimental lists of George Washington's army at Valley Forge; that the great bulk of them could barely read and write, and a very large per cent of them could do neither; that the ninety and nine of them had never eaten a well-balanced meal, slept in a decent bed, or taken a bath in a bathtub; and I know that they lived in shacks no European peasant would keep his cows in. There are only two points on which I disagree with the findings of Mr. Bush. These people did not spend their money foolishly. In the first place, they had no more than a few dollars a year to spend, and if they had been foolish enough to save that little their landlords would have taken it by raising the rent. My second objection regards their alleged ignorance.

Illiterate, poorly schooled, doped with all the mental poison their "betters" could pour into them, yes; but ignorant, no. There is a great deal of native intelligence among these people. Their state of illiteracy protected them, partially at least, against the flood of lying propaganda with which their "betters" of press, pulpit and rostrum deluged the country, while their native common sense allowed them to see through the pretensions of the war-mongers far better than could many a Ph.D., LL.B., or D.D., for that matter.

Why should these people tear their shirts wresting the Hamburg-Bagdad railroad from the Huns over there? Why should they get excited over menaced democracy across the sea? What had democracy ever done for them over here except to rob them of the first requirements of democracy, the opportunity to make a living without paying tribute to others? It had delivered them and their state, with its wealth of oil and gas, into the maws of eastern corporations, and deprived them and their children of education, health and bodily vigor.

Why should they break their hearts over the woes of Belgian women while their own women crawled like beasts on all fours between cotton rows, dragging nine-foot-long bags behind them, with the youngest baby on the end of the sack? Why should they get excited over poor Belgian children three thousand miles away while their own rickety hookworm-infested children shivered in the cotton field sucking their bleeding fingers, cut by cotton burrs in the cruel November and December winds?

Now that the price of cotton had risen to where, for the first time in their miserable lives, there might be enough left on settlement day to supply themselves and their families with shoddy clothes, shoes and schoolbooks, the crowd in Washington demanded that their grown sons be shipped over there and leave the struggle for existence to be borne by the old, the women and children.

Of course they protested. Besides native intelligence, they had a fairly well developed sense of humor, permitting them to see the irony of the situation. To me, the grimness of that situation was not that these people were so naïve as to think they could stop the great madness by means of the few rifles, belts of cartridges, and few hundred sticks of dynamite in their possession. They did burn down a few railroad bridges, blow up one or two pipe lines, before they were dispersed by the sheriffs they had elected, augmented by posses composed of the electric-light town parasites who feasted on them. The total damage inflicted in the Green Corn Rebellion would not defray the cost of a single torpedo or bombing plane. The total loss of life was three, and one of them was killed accidentally by a member of his own posse.

No, the most appalling aspect of the Green Corn Rebellion was not the naïveté of these people, but the effrontery of the rabble on top, so ignorant and conceited as to believe that these simpleminded folk would swallow their blah. The opposition to America's entrance into the world slaughter was not restricted to the Indian Territory section of Oklahoma. It was just as strong in the western half of the state. And there the bitterest opponents of Wilson's policy were not the Socialists, nor the Republicans, but the Democrats, who had cast their ballots for the man who "kept us out of war." The only difference was that, being better situated and educated, they saw the futility of opposing the war by force. However, even in that territory I know of many honest farmers, who, years after the armistice, still shot jack rabbits with the Marlin rifles and cartridges they had purchased for an entirely different purpose.

My own connection with the Green Corn Rebellion was that of an advisor whose advice was not followed. I had heard rumors of an intended putsch, but knew nothing definite about it until I was invited to attend a meeting of a small group of extreme Left-wingers. In this connection I should add that farmers are naturally given to direct action, or self-help. This trait is primarily due to their isolation and the strong individualism arising from that fact. To these extreme Leftists, the policy and tactics of the Socialists, as expressed in education, organization and political action, were too slow. They were the true Reds; we of the center and right wing were "compromisers," "opportunists," and "yellows."

In order to secure speedy action they had organized the Working Class Union and the Jones Family. Both of these were secret societies, as contrasted to the open and above-board organization of the Socialists. The members of the groups that invited me either belonged to those two secret organizations, or were in close touch with them. The real leaders of the two organizations were not present at that meeting for the simple reason that they knew well enough that we "yellows" had done everything in our power to destroy their influence among our people. After the customary preliminaries, we got down to business. They had, I was told, sent for me to give me a chance to change from yellow to red.

"And what, precisely, have you boys in mind in relation to my changing color?"

"We are going to stop this damned war the gang out East has foisted on us."

"But how?"

"On a given signal we'll slam the bankers, county officials, and newspaper owners in jail."

"And . . ."

"That will give us the money, government and press of our counties."

"And then?"

"We'll burn railroad trestles, bridges and blow up pipe lines."

"But how can your little group achieve all that?"

"We are not a little group. Our organization has penetrated into every state of the Union. There are seventy thousand of us in

Colorado. More than twice as many in Texas. One hundred and ninety thousand I.W.W.'s in Chicago alone are waiting for the signal to break loose. What's more, we are fully armed with high-powered Marlins and ammunition. Out in the coal fields there is enough dynamite to blow up the whole country."

"But," I inquired, "if there are so many hundreds of thousands of you, how have you managed to keep all this secret from the government?"

"Because we are a secret organization."

"Oath bound?"

"Sure."

"Passwords?"

"Sure."

"High sign?"

"Why, certainly."

"Well, then," I said, "if all that is true, then let me say, scatter, and scatter right now. If there were only one thousand instead of hundreds of thousands of you, then at least a hundred of that thousand would be informers, planted among you. Rest assured, enough have already blabbed to inform the authorities of every move you make. What's more, from what I know about conspiracy, I wouldn't be in the least surprised if one of these informers was in this room right now. So for his benefit, and for that of the party at the receiving end of the dictaphone hidden behind some object in this room, here is where I stand:

"I am convinced beyond the slightest shadow of a doubt that the American people did not want this war, that it is not a war to make the world safe for democracy, nor a war to end war. I believe this war was foisted on the American people by their lying press, politicians, warmongers and munitions manufacturers, and by the bankers who are making billions out of the agony of mankind.

"I believe that the American people will bitterly rue the day when they permitted themselves to be swindled into the most harebrained and futile adventure of their long history. I further believe that America's participation in the mess will only prolong the war and eventually father more and more devastating wars. All this I said before we entered the war. All this I still believe. But now that the gory die is cast, the only thing any one of us can do is to work for a speedy peace through all the legal and constitutional means still open to us. This is what I am going to do. This is what I advise all of you and your followers to do. You talk about a hundred and ninety thousand I.W.W.'s in Chicago alone. Why, there are not as many as nineteen thousand I.W.W.'s in the whole of the United States, and most of them are up in the timber country of the Northwest. If your information concerning the other hundreds of thousands, or rather, millions, you claim, is no better than in the case of the Chicago I.W.W.'s, your combined forces could be better measured in thousands than in hundreds of thousands and millions.

"All you will do is destroy the splendid Socialist movement we have built up in Oklahoma at such a high cost of labor and sacrifice. Some of you have been, may yet be, Party members. The whole force of the terror following your worse than childish attempt to stop the war will fall upon us Socialists who have so stubbornly opposed America's entrance into the slaughter. Our movement will not recover from that blow for many years. Perhaps never. As for you and your following, you will all be hounded like wild beasts. Some of you will be killed. The bulk of you will land behind the bars. For I am sure your names are already carefully filed. You are marked men, so scatter, while the scattering is still good."

All in vain. Their hearts were in the right place. Their heads were not, yet they were still superior to the important people out in the brain belt whose hearts and brains were both off the base —the American base at that. I was voted "yellow" by the good fellows, but I also received a vote of confidence that I would not inform on them. Needless to say, I would not.

A few days later I was given my last opportunity to change from yellow to red. I had addressed a farmers' picnic near Fort

Reno, Oklahoma. I had made my plea for money and support for the big daily we were to launch as soon as the emotional insanity had blown over. At the end of my address a young school teacher, whom I had met, took me aside and said, "Why all that hog wash about raising money for a paper to educate voters and eventually capture the powers of government? Why, in a week from now we will have both the press and government of this country in our hands. This picnic is only a blind. Tonight the general staff of the eastern, central and western armies will meet in a canyon a few miles from here to make final plans. The boys have sent me to invite you to that meeting. They want to give you one more chance to show you aren't yellow."

"Young friend," I answered. "Do you see the yellow dust-covered tin lizzy under that jack-oak tree? Do you see that yellow road winding toward Fort Reno? Well, in a few minutes you will see me in a yellow dust cloud traveling over that yellow road as fast as this Ford can make it. And now, for God's sake, tell the boys back in that canyon to scatter—scatter as far and as fast as they can scatter." The boys didn't scatter. And at the Ardmore trial of the Green Corn rebels, my young school-teacher friend was the chief witness—for the state!

When the Green Corn Rebellion had fizzled out, as we "yellows" predicted, a veritable white terror swept Oklahoma, and of course, we were on the receiving end. The Socialists had opposed America's entrance into bloody bedlam. We were the outstanding pacifists of that day. All through our history we had advocated international brotherhood, peace on earth, good will to men. Long before the outbreak of the World War, we had predicted it as a necessary consequence of industrial and commercial rivalry. And now it was upon the bloodied but unbowed heads of the Socialists that the war-crazed mobs high and low spewed their venom.

Though not a single official of the Party was connected with the Green Corn Rebellion, thousands of our members were arrested. Jails were so overcrowded that four hundred prisoners were shipped to the state penitentiary for safe-keeping. Thousands sought safety in the Winding Stairs Mountains, in adjoining Colorado, Texas and Arkansas.

Of the Green Corn rebels convicted, some thirty-odd went to Leavenworth, the Federal prison, from which the last of them were released after Kate Richards O'Hare had marched their wives and children to Washington, where they picketed the White House. This was during the Harding administration. And while mentioning President Harding, may I add that, with all his faults, the man had more milk of human kindness in his make-up than Messiah Woodrow Wilson. Some of the kind comrades of that time accused Kate O'Hare of being more interested in personal glory than in the fate of her imprisoned comrades. To me it seemed then, and still does, that this lone woman, herself released from prison only a few months before, with practically no funds, leading hundreds of women and children two thousand miles to Washington and bringing all of them safely back—and liberating their husbands and fathers for good measure—constitutes one of America's great epics.

Shortly after the trial of the Green Corn rebels an emergency convention of the mortally wounded Party was held in Oklahoma City. It was at that convention that Patrick S. Nagle, one of the leading attorneys of the rebels, sponsored and succeeded in passing a resolution disbanding the Socialist Party of Oklahoma. I was not present when that step was taken; had I been, I most likely would have supported that resolution for the following reasons.

During the trial of the rebels, another trial was taking place in Chicago. The prisoners before the bar were Victor Berger and the entire national executive committee of the Socialist Party. The charge was conspiracy to obstruct the prosecution of the war. The persecution established the proof of conspiracy by defining conspiracy as the collusive action of persons toward a definite purpose, though said persons had never actually met. But proving conspiracy by definition was not enough; it was necessary to prove that the conspiracy had resulted in an overt act. The overt act was influencing one or more persons to oppose the selective draft law.

Toward the end, the persecution—I say persecution deliberately, because that Chicago trial certainly did not come under the category of due process of law—did everything in its power to produce at least one witness willing to testify that he had refused service in the armed forces of the United States while at war with the Central Powers because of something the defendants had said or written.

They brought Carl Haessler from Leavenworth prison where he was serving his term as a conscientious objector. Before that he had been an employee of the Milwaukee *Leader;* he was also a member in good standing of the Socialist Party. What more could the persecutors desire?

They marched this clean, upstanding Oxford graduate and teacher of philosophy into the courtroom, dressed in prison uniform and handcuffed, and placed him on the witness stand. Carl's testimony was a blow to the court. No, none of the defendants had influenced him to refuse to serve in the armed forces of the United States. No one had to tell him that it was a war, not to make the world safe for democracy, but rather one caused by commercial and industrial rivalry. He knew enough of history, economics and the forces that drag nations into war without asking the advice of others.

But while this was taking place in Chicago, down in Oklahoma thousands had opposed the draft act by force and violence. Among them were Socialists and readers of the Milwaukee *Leader.* It was the fear of establishing the connection between overt acts in Oklahoma with the defendants in Chicago that had caused Patrick S. Nagle to advise the disbanding of the Socialist Party in Oklahoma. I am making this record clear because in later years

Pat was accused of destroying the Socialist movement of Oklahoma. Pat was not a coward. He was as courageous as they make them, and, in my opinion, acted wisely.

In the meantime, we had raised our quarter of a million. The building of the *Leader* plant was finished, the machinery installed, and so out with the first issue of the Oklahoma *Leader*. Had we known the almost insurmountable difficulties that confront publications such as ours, we certainly would have awaited more favorable circumstances. What we babes in the woods didn't know about operating a daily paper would have filled a sizable library. I was the most experienced in our crowd, but I was never, am not yet, an all-around newspaper executive. I am at best an editorial writer. Moreover, management of things and men had always been, and still is, a book with seven seals to me. I am an excellent agitator, salesman of ideas and promoter. But once that work is done, somebody else must carry on, although when it comes to raising money for one of my brain babies, I will stick it out until the baby dies or stands on its own.

For our manager we selected Comrade John Hagel, a good Socialist, bookkeeper and manager of a string of lumber yards: experience which hardly qualified him as managing editor of a daily. For editor in chief we imported a gentleman from Springfield, Massachusetts. The Springfield *Republican,* for which he had worked, had the reputation of being one of the best-edited dailies in the United States. For all we knew, he may have been responsible for the good repute in which the *Republican* stood in American journalism, but he certainly didn't know anything about Oklahoma and its people. That he was a good man is testified to by the fact that later he became one of the shining lights of the New Deal. In addition to the chief editor from Massachusetts we imported a number of journalists from New York City, the metropolis of the brain belt. Good men, all of them, no doubt. At least two of them have made their mark in American journalism, one as art critic on a slick-paper magazine. But what all of

THE AMERINGER QUARTET
THE AUTHOR (*second from right*) AND HIS THREE SONS

The "Leader-Guardian" Building

them knew about Oklahoma, its people and their problems, could have been safely stowed away in a snuff can.

Our circulation manager was a red-headed, overgrown newsboy. For advertising manager, we selected an ex-life-insurance agent, who didn't even possess the saving quality of being a comrade world-saver.

Under the policy we had adopted, the daily was not to be a Socialist Party organ. It was to print all the news worth printing, and steer clear of scandals, crimes, murders, sensations. Further, it was always to tell the truth, though the heavens fell. It was to promote the general welfare and avoid all tendencies to lower the intellectual and moral level of its readers. Under no circumstances must it truckle to advertisers or print questionable advertising. The good it must diligently work for must be the greatest good to the greatest number. If, in this laudable aim, wage earners and farmers got a little the best of it, it was not our fault that there are more farmers and wage earners than bankers, merchants and plutocrats. We would make some concession to the prevailing sport craze, print a few carefully selected comic strips for the children, but under no consideration would we print pictures and detailed descriptions of brutal prize fights, or give our young readers anything tending in the general direction of slapstick and low-brow humor. In brief, this journalistic paragon was to be everything an American daily can't be and get away with it.

But naïveté, inexperience, and mountain-moving faith in the eternal justice of things, bolstered by the inherent goodness of man, were not our only troubles. After all, faith does move mountains. The Red scare let loose by A. Mitchell Palmer, Attorney General for the author of *The New Freedom,* was still in full swing, and, much more significant, war prosperity had evaporated, almost overnight. The glorious victory over there was followed by a catastrophic fall in farm prices and employment over here. Wheat slumped from two dollars and twenty, to sixty cents, cotton from forty cents to five, hogs from twenty-five cents to three, and everything else in proportion.

Sam Gompers' partnership between capital and labor was dissolving. It had worked marvelously during the War because the "ten-per-cent-plus" clause in government contracts did not worry about cost: in fact, the higher the cost, the greater the plus. As to how ten-per-cent-plus had harmoniously united the interests of capital and labor, these two examples will suffice.

I called on a friend employed by a plumbing firm doing work at Fort Sill. When I located him, he and another plumber were painting a small radiator. One held the small tin can of paint; the other held a half-inch brush. Both moved with the deliberation of the slow-motion movie. When I said, "Why don't you fellows use at least a two-inch brush on the job?" the answer was, "Oh, yeah? And get bounced by the boss?"

On the same occasion I saw a carpenter acquaintance cut out two feet from the middle of a twelve-foot board and throw the two ends on the handy scrap pile. When I asked him why he hadn't sawed the two feet from the end of the board, his reply was, "Say, where have you been living? Don't you know that the more we waste the bigger the profit for the boss? Do you think I'm going to be bounced for being stingy with Uncle Sam's dough?"

But now that ten-per-cent-plus had joined the other sweet memories of wartime, the open-shop movement was in full blast. Wage cutting had become the order of the day. Strikes broke out all over the country. The railroad shop crafts were on strike. The coal miners were on strike. The building trades had gone on strike. All of Oklahoma seemed to be on strike, and as these were our people, and as our policy was the greatest good to the greatest number, we just naturally took up the fight for the greatest number. This netted us the boycott of the local open-shop committee, of which our banker was the head. But of him, later.

While we supported the greatest number, the greatest number could no longer support their champion. The farmers were going broke, the proletariat was on strike, and we were in the soup. With never enough advertising to speak of, circulation income hitting zero, and not a thin dime of working capital to go on, we were what is called in polite business parlance, financially embarrassed.

Being one of the conservatives on the right wing of America's socialist movement, and having had at least some newspaper experience, my preliminary calculations for success had included a hundred thousand dollars of working capital. However, the War had raised prices to the point where, by the time we were all ready to go, there was nothing left to go on. Our building and equipment had swallowed our quarter of a million. Even some of the equipment was not yet paid for. And now we had a deficit that at the height of its glory reached four thousand dollars a week, including one pay day.

Some of my other conservative calculations had miscarried. Before the Great Madness there had been some fifty-six thousand Socialists in Oklahoma. Most of them, I reasoned, must still be living. Perhaps the War had added quite a few more, in the light of those Liberty bonds which good Republicans and Democrats had given me to start our daily. Even if the Party had gone, these people must still be hanging around.

Of course I was not so optimistic as to think that all of these people would subscribe to our daily. But I had expected that at least twenty thousand out of the fifty-six thousand Socialists would subscribe to our paper. The subscription price of the daily was six dollars a year. Multiplying that by twenty thousand subscribers makes a hundred and twenty thousand dollars; before such a titanic sum was spent, I still reasoned, all kinds of things could happen. The first thing that happened was that instead of twenty thousand subscribers, we secured only two thousand. One reason for this decline from our great expectations was the fact that by the time we started, most of our potential subscribers had gone broke. Much more damaging, the Green Corn Rebellion and the Red scares frightened the very lives out of our supporters. People who had given us hundreds of dollars for launching our paper were afraid of having it delivered to their homes, afraid of being marked Reds.

Under these circumstances any sane businessman or firm would have welcomed bankruptcy with open arms. But world-savers are not good businessmen, which may explain why they have outlived so many sets of cool, calculating businessmen, both crowned and uncrowned, and still carry on. How we managed to stave off involuntary bankruptcy remains to me still the eighth wonder of the world. We used to hand out two to three thousand dollars in pay checks three minutes before noon, Saturdays (banks closed at twelve on Saturdays), and then frantically rush for the already cranked Ford in a wild scramble to get the money in the bank before it opened at nine o'clock Monday morning. My companion in these wild sallies was Freda. Freda knew every one of the faithful in the state. If there was still a Liberty bond at large, she knew exactly where it was.

Once we left the office on a Friday evening. Almost anybody could be trusted to hand out pay checks three minutes before twelve on Saturday. The real job was to get the money in the bank before nine o'clock on Monday. And on this occasion we had to get no less than thirty-five hundred dollars together to meet the deadline. By Saturday sunrise we had reached Medford, close to the Kansas line. Freda was sure Comrade Tharp of Medford had held out a thousand-dollar Liberty bond on her. Comrade Tharp confessed his guilt and promised to get the bond out of the bank before we returned. In the meantime we should see So-and-so, who, he suspected, had also held one out on Freda. On the way to So-and-so's, Freda saw a comrade she knew standing at a new oil derrick. No, he didn't have any more Liberty bonds, Freda had gotten the last of them, but would a five-hundred-dollar check help out? Would it help out! The next prospect had gone to visit relatives in Missouri, another had driven off some place, and his wife, not being a comrade, didn't know where. A third wasn't at home. We finally located him in a cornfield. Yes, he still had a thousand-dollar Liberty bond. If we would drive him to town, he would get it out of the bank.

The banker, as bankers will, knew lots better places for our comrade's bond than losing it with us. This was no time for speculation. If the comrade had money to invest, he'd better put it in something conservative, something he could see, such as oil leases, or wells, or refineries. There also was, the banker happened to remember, a threshing-machine company selling stock in that vicinity; some other people were promoting an automobile company, the Geronimo Automobile Company, to be precise, in nearby Enid, the capital of Oklahoma's wheat belt; some very responsible parties, he happened to know, were promoting a packing plant in El Reno, a candy factory in Oklahoma City, and a glass-coffin factory some place, where sand especially adapted for glass coffins could be secured for the hauling. To the credit of the banker be it said that he didn't try to sell his depositor Peruvian bonds, German marks, or eight-per-cent, gilt-edged debentures of the Leipzig City Hall. You see, he was only a small-town banker. Local blue-sky stock was as high as he could reach.

However, our good comrade was not converted. He was of age and knew his own mind. It was nobody's damn' business what he was doing with his money. Incidentally, none of those conservative enterprises the good banker had spoken rather highly of ever got over the promotion measles. Every dollar sunk into them was lost, along with the bank of our conservative banker.

By the time we had rescued that particular bond it was close to three o'clock. We still had some twenty-odd miles to drive to Medford, where comrade Tharp had promised to get his bond out of his bank. What if the Medford banker had talked him out of letting us have that thousand-dollar bond? There was no time to lose. Then, as we were ascending a long rise, with Medford a mile beyond, our tin lizzy stopped dead. Out of gas. I rushed toward a farmhouse a quarter of a mile from the main road, praying to heaven that the farmer owned a car and was at home. Before I got there, I heard a frantic tooting and shouting behind me. Freda and the Ford were slowly crawling and coughing up that long ascent. Before they reached the summit I had crawled over the door of the tin lizzy—often the contrary thing flew open of its own accord and was correspondingly almost impossible to open when one tried to—and from that summit we rolled down the long descent, landing smack in front of the bank, where good Comrade Tharp was waiting with bond in hand. There wasn't a drop of gas left in the tank of the lizzy. I still don't know what made it start. But don't tell me there isn't a guardian angel who takes care of children, drunks, and world-savers.

One five-hundred-dollar check and two one-thousand-dollar Liberty bonds make two thousand, five hundred dollars. We were still one thousand dollars short. Freda remembered another comrade some sixty or seventy miles south of Medford, Fred Coulter, bachelor and farmer, who, she felt, had bonds or cash. We got to his place long after pitch dark, but he had no Liberty bonds. Fred didn't even have a dollar in the bank. He didn't trust bankers any farther than he could see them. "But over there, right under the floor, in a tin box, let's see what I can find for you, comrades." What Comrade Fred dug out for us was the missing thousand dollars. The world was saved for seven days more.

Toward three, Sunday morning, with Freda sleeping exhausted on the back seat, I drove into Oklahoma City. I thought of the many good people and also of the still more numerous crooked people who were accusing us in those days of keeping going by means of Moscow gold. It was gold that kept us going, all right: gold smelted in the crucible of a noble ideal and by the fire of faith. But it didn't come from Moscow.

40

TROUBLE, trouble, no end of trouble. The evil spirits roused by the War refused to dissolve in the dawn of peace. People had been taught to hate, taught by school, college, newspaper, politician, and statesman; they had been taught to hate even by the churches of the gentle Nazarene who had come to bring peace on earth and good will to men. But the end of the War meant that the evil spirits it had aroused needed new objects for hatred. Trade unionists, Reds, radicals, pinks, foreigners, Negroes, Jews, and Catholics were at hand, and along with them, an organization perfectly adapted for persecution. In Oklahoma, the Klan became the militant instrument of all these hatreds. . . .

We declared war on the Invisible Empire of the Imperial Wizard of Atlanta, Georgia. The multitude of our other troubles had not left us much ammunition for the fight, but with what little we had we did our best. We fought the Klan with reason and ridicule. A talented draftsman, son of a wealthy oil operator, one-time partner of Doheny, supplied our cartoons. They were extraordinary. That young oil man might well have become a second Art Young, had not his father's fortune prevented him from choosing cartooning for his life work.

The struggle against the Klan made us, besides a few friends whose friendship never was translated into financial support, a vast number of enemies who commanded both money and influence. During the height of the battle I received many letters in which the writer promised to knock my brains out, perforate my black heart with leaden bullets, or cut out my lying tongue. At last, tired of reading the letters, and fully convinced that barking dogs don't bite, I announced meetings in the five towns from which the most vicious of these threats had been mailed.

The first town was Clinton, Oklahoma. When I arrived there, on the Saturday for which I had advertised my anti-Klan meeting, I discovered that a good-roads meeting had been advertised for the same afternoon in the pavilion of the municipal park, the only meeting place suitable for my purpose. I thereupon went to the highest authority of that, or any other western town of that day, namely, the principal banker, and explained my predicament. Would he, I suggested, let me use the municipal pavilion after the good-roads meeting had adjourned? In return I would, if requested, add my oratory to the good-roads movement.

The banker knew both me and the road I had in mind. It was to connect the up-and-coming metropolis of Clinton with the good farming district of Dewey County, and as Dewey County had been captured by our forces, the request was graciously granted. At the good-roads meeting I made by far the most eloquent appeal for the new road. I had my heart in that speech, for the simple reason that I had traveled the old road often. I had traveled it when winter storms had howled through the two strands of barbed wire that separated the north pole from Oklahoma. I had traveled it when the soil-laden air of the future dust bowl had cased my eyes in silt; when it was a hundred and ten in the shade and the nearest shade was in some canyon ten miles away; I had traveled it when it required from ten to twenty hours to make the twenty-five-mile journey from the heart of Dewey County to Clinton, a town which I had known since its early days, when the sign on the Rock Island track reading "Clinton, the Hub of the West," still covered the whole of the Hub of the West.

At the close of my good-roads speech I announced that I

would now give the gentleman who had written the letter post-marked "Clinton," an opportunity to knock my block off, per-forate my black heart, or cut out my lying tongue, whichever he might prefer. There were many Klansmen in that audience, as I could easily tell by the scowling faces when I mentioned the Klan.

My subject for the day was rule by majority. I developed the theme that in the days of yore I had patiently suffered the rule of the majority in spite of the fact that the majority was always wrong. I showed how in the long ago I had advised the farmers to let Uncle Sam keep the title to their land. The majority had voted me wrong, and now the majority had lost their land or were on the way to lose it. I showed them how not only I but all of us socialists the world over had ceaselessly pointed out that industrial and commercial rivalry coupled with militarism must inevitably lead to a great war. The majority of the world had voted us wrong. I showed them that when war had come we Socialists had valiantly fought to keep our country out of it, how we had consistently warned our people that supplying one side of the struggle with the wherewithal of slaughter would inevitably drag us into the slaughter on the side of our good customers. Our reward had been scorn and persecution. And the country was dragged into the War.

I showed them how, the War over, I had warned President Wilson in an open letter to stay away from Versailles. "Stay home, Mr. President," I wrote. "If you go over there those hard-boiled highbinders will steal the very gold fillings from your teeth. Only you and the country back of you have the economic power to make them sign on the dotted line below the fourteen points you have borrowed from the Socialists' St. Louis platform. Tell them, from over here, not another American dollar, sack of wheat, pound of bacon, or ounce of copper, cotton, iron, zinc, or lead, until they sign on the dotted line, seal it, and give security for faithful performance." Well, Wilson went over there and see what a peace he brought home with him.

"And now," I continued, "the Ku Klux craze is sweeping the country. From the awful racket the boys are making it sounds as if the majority is on their side. Peace made with the Huns, democracy and civilization saved, we are now told to make war against Negroes, Reds, labor unions, Jews, Catholics, and foreigners in general. 'Unless these people are driven out of the country or are shown their proper places, the Reds will raise the red flag of Socialism over the Capitol in Washington, the Negroes will marry our sisters, the unions wipe out what little business peace is left us, the Jews foreclose the mortgage they hold on the United States, and the Catholics install the Pope in the White House.' To me the whole thing looks just silly. Especially so in this state. Our total foreign-born Jewish and Catholic population is less than two per cent. If that two per cent is going to walk away with the ninety-eight per cent of native-born Protestant Americans, and take Oklahoma with them, I want 'em to have the whole shebang. For I believe in the survival of the fittest and from what the Klan brethren tell us about these people, they certainly must be the fittest.

"Just see what this latest lunacy is doing to your town. Catholics are boycotting Protestant stores, Protestants are boycotting Jewish and Catholic stores. Everybody is afraid of everybody else. Everybody is looking under the bed at night for bolshevik Reds, Socialists, papists, klansmen and landsmen of Jesus Christ.

"The worst sufferers of this Klan craze are your merchants. You want a good road built to bring the trade of the Dewey County farmers to your door. Well, I am for that road. But I have talked with many of those Dewey County farmers. The majority of them are Socialists, as you know. They carried Dewey County before the election of 1916, when so many of them deserted their cause to vote for the man who was to keep us out of war. The comrades there have told me that your town is lousy with Kluxers. And that even if the good road materialized they would rather send their money to Sears, Roebuck, or Monkey Ward, than let you have a thin dime of it. Besides, the head of Sears, Roebuck is a Jew by the name of Julius Rosenwald, a man any race, nationality or religion would be proud of. He has given his money to help the kind of people from whom he got it, which is a darned sight more than the Jew-baiter of Dearborn is doing. Why bite off your own business noses to spite the Jews? What's more, I want to know whatever have the Jews done to us good Christians that we should hate them? They have given us Moses, the prophets, Christ and his disciples. If it were not for the Jews, hell-fire would be our future. Besides all that, you can't down God's chosen people. Always remember Moses died, and the Jews are still in business, and I've got a hunch they will be in business for many years after this Klan craze blows over."

All the time that I had been speaking, I had been, like every experienced platform man, carefully scrutinizing the faces of my audience. As I went along, mixing in a bit of ridicule to give the speech flavor, scowls and tenseness had gradually given way to smiles, laughter, and finally applause. So, judging that the psychological moment was at hand, I continued:

"However, I'm tired of always being in the minority. Somebody is crazy, either you or me. Now let's settle the question for keeps. Whatever the decision of the majority present, I shall faithfully abide by it. Now, all of you who believe I am crazy, so signify by raising your right hand." An old gentleman on the hard-hearers' bench in front raised his right hand. When he heard the uproar of laughter behind him he turned around, and seeing no other right hand raised, pulled down his own.

"And now all those of my audience who believe they are crazy, please so signify by raising their right hands." And believe it or not, that audience voted itself crazy without a single dissenting vote.

I hope my description of the Klan has not left the reader with the impression that its sole cause was the hysteria of the War. No doubt that was a contributing factor; the real cause, however, lay deeper: the hard times following on the heels of the Armistice. "Hard times," says a Chinese proverb, "bring hard deeds." Crime, homicide, insanity, divorce, go up and down with bankruptcy. Crimes against property increase as the temperature goes down; the struggle for existence is more difficult in winter than in the summer. Crimes against the person increase in summer and decline as it grows colder. All this is known to science, but remains to be learned by the jurist.

The Klan started in Georgia, which has the lowest per-capita income of all the States in the Union. Even in normal times the great bulk of its population lives on the lowest possible subsistence level. When hard times come, these people are forced below the level of brute existence and the brute takes command of them. In unconscious compliance with this iron law, Imperial Wizard Simmons had located the capital of his empire in Atlanta, Georgia. From there the Klan infection spread to the weakest parts of our social body—the States of the Old South. As hard times increased, the Klan moved westward and northward. The localities least afflicted were New England and California—three thousand miles apart.

Are the people of the New England States and California morally superior to the people of Georgia and of the Old South in general? It is at least debatable. There is no question, however, but that the per-capita income of the people of California and that of the New England States is six times higher than that of the people of Georgia, four times as high as that of the people of the Old South as a whole, and more than twice as high as that of the American people generally.

Another characteristic of Ku Kluxism was that its greatest strength was neither in the industrial centers nor in the purely farming districts; it was in the county-seat towns and smaller trading centers of the South and Middle West. Is the population of these county-seat towns and small trading centers of different character than that of the surrounding rural population? No. Population is virtually the same in character, with this exception. While there are few foreign born among the surrounding farm population, and no Jews at all, there is, in almost all of the smaller towns of Klan territory, a sprinkling of Greek, Italian, and Jewish merchants who compete with merchants of second- or third-generation Americans.

Rinaldo Rinaldini, for instance, came to town as a peddler of bananas and oranges. Now Rinaldo Rinaldini owns the Sanitary Grocery. Polonios Aristoteles opened a shoe-shining and hat-cleaning stand when he first arrived. Now he owns the All American Restaurant. Isidore Rosenthal came to town with a pack on his back peddling notions. Now Isidore owns Rosenthal's National Clothing and Dry Goods Emporium. When hard times exert pressure, mere tolerance easily turns to envy and open hostility. If we could get rid of those goddam Jews and foreigners, we superior, native-born Anglo-Saxon Protestants would fare better.

The Catholics are in a somewhat different category. Fewer Catholic merchants are found in the smaller towns of the South and Middle West. But whatever their number, they depend largely upon the trade of their coreligionists. Minority religionists are always more or less clannish. And so, wherever we find a Catholic church and school in some rural district, there usually is a fair-sized general store close by, and that store is almost invariably operated by a good Catholic. From what I have observed, the cause of Ku Kluxism, as of most social diseases, lies in rivalry which, under pressure, breaks out into open warfare. There is always someone ready to serve as the leader of such outbreaks; the point is that they are not the cause but the effect of an underlying cause, which is usually economic. When a herd of cattle go on a stampede it's the whole herd that is stampeding and not this or that bull or lead cow which the stampede pushed forward. Moreover, give a herd of cattle all the green grass and water it needs, and not even Adolf Hitler or Mussolini could make it stampede.

If anyone thinks that man in the mass is in any way different from the cow in the herd, he has had scant experience with human group behavior. If Adolf Hitler had come to my Munich in the early Nineties, all his eloquence would not have pried a baker's dozen of Bavarians loose from their beloved steins, *Rattisches* and *Hausbrot*. Coming after the defeat of 1918, augmented by the trial by hunger that followed on its heels, and after the world depression had lowered its resistance still further, he was able to walk away with the whole of Germany.

If there had been no Hitler in 1932, when unemployment had passed the six-million mark and the German birth rate had fallen below that of France, someone else would have taken his place. It might have been someone worse or better than Hitler, but he would have appeared, of that be sure, for leaders, good or bad, are the products of their times. The more desperate the times, the more desperate and ruthless the leader.

And so it also came about that when the sun of prosperity smiled once more on the great and intelligent people of this nation, Ku Kluxism melted away, until the cold winds of the 1929 crash brought it back again, as may be observed in the sundry colored-shirt movements and the popularity of Father Coughlin.

To further the human in humanity, make lighter the struggle for existence. To bring out the worst in humanity, lower it to brute existence. If it is within the province of man to lighten the struggle for existence, of which there is no doubt in my mind, then well and good. But unless that is done, the brute will hold sway. And all the preaching and denunciation in the world will not change one iota of this fact.

41

THE struggle against the Klan almost cooked our goose, but worse was to come. When it finally dawned on us that there was no hope of resurrecting the Socialist Party in Oklahoma, someone in our group had a brilliant idea. A farmer-labor coalition had forced the initiative and referendum into the constitution of Oklahoma. The referendum end of direct legislation had been badly whittled down by the Oklahoma founding fathers, who, be it recorded, had no more love for majority rule than other, more celebrated founding fathers.

Measures passed by both houses and signed by the governor became law only after the lapse of sixty days. This was to give the sovereign voters a chance to nullify an obnoxious law by a referendum vote. The exception was a clause providing that in case of emergency the law would go into force immediately. Since then, every law passed by the Solons of Oklahoma has carried the emergency clause. The initiative, however, was still intact. Why, then, should we not achieve our aims by way of the initiative?

If, let's say, the progressives—the farmer and labor forces of the state—could unite on some four or five measures of interest to all, and then get whole-heartedly behind them, there was no reason why they should not be adopted by a majority of the voters. A conference was called.

It was attended by the state president of the Farmers' Educational and Co-operative Union, the president of the Miners'

Union of Oklahoma, the president of the State Federation of Labor; the representative of the railway brotherhoods, and two representatives of the Socialist Party: Dan Hogan and John Hagel, manager and editorial writer, respectively, of our rapidly sinking daily. A five-point program was adopted. Some time later a larger meeting ratified the five-point program of the smaller meeting. Finally, a mass ratification meeting was held to give the five-point program the blessing of the multitude and the proper send-off.

At the ratification meeting in Shawnee, Oklahoma, 751 delegates appeared, each paying his own expenses. The bulk of the delegates were anti-Wilson Democrats, and Socialists. The remainder were disgruntled G.O.P.'s. The enthusiasm of the meeting was boundless. None of the individual members had expected such a gathering of the underdogs. The original five-point program was elaborated into an eighteen-plank platform. The platform almost unanimously adopted, the natural sequel was the nomination of a full state ticket. Why stop at initiating measures? Why not also elect the men to carry out these measures?

So a new political movement arose from the ruins of the Socialist Party. Its name was the Farmer-Labor Reconstruction League. The League was modeled after North Dakota's Nonpartisan League. Its aim was to capture the Democratic Party of Oklahoma in the forthcoming primary election. In pursuit of this aim, the convention had nominated its full state ticket. The labor unions offered the name of one J. C. Walton ("Our Jack") as banner-bearer of the embattled farmers and workers. "Our Jack" was a friend of labor. While serving as mayor of Oklahoma City he had always closed both eyes when an infuriated striker poured his wrath onto some obnoxious scab. As further proof of his devotion to the horny-handed sons of toil, he carried a card in one of the railroad unions. Brother Jack received the enthusiastic and almost unanimous support of the assembled League.

The liberation of the great and sovereign electorate of Oklahoma from the clutches of Wall Street seemed to be just around the corner. With Our Jack in the governor's chair, and myself adjutant general of the armed forces of the state, the abdication of the plutocracy was only a matter of hours. True, I had not sought the position of adjutant general of the state militia; it was thrust upon me by the inner council of the soviet of peasants, farmers and ex-service men. The boys felt that only a tried and true revolutionist like my humble self could be entrusted with the task of combating the counter-revolution which the forces of darkness were bound to stage after our victory at the polls. . . .

Unfortunately for our embattled legion, and democracy at large, it takes more than enthusiasm, numbers, and purity of motive to elect the servants of the sovereign American people. This is especially true whenever the great majority is fighting a compact, well-oiled machine energized by powerful forces from far beyond the state boundaries—as was the case in Oklahoma. There is no data to show the cost of electing Oklahoma governors. Based upon painful observation, I should say it comes to well over a hundred thousand dollars. Lesser posts are in proportion. Engaged in a holy crusade against the state's four politico-economic parties—oil, asphalt, cement, and the privately owned utilities— we could and would not besmirch our cause with filthy lucre contributed by the special interests. On the other hand, our own crowd was cleaned out. Eventually we mooched some fifteen thousand dollars of clean money for our campaign funds. Of this, nine thousand came from the four railroad brotherhoods, smaller amounts from the farm and labor organizations, the coal miners leading as always. The rest was made up from the nickels and dimes of our destitute but deserving following of hungry share croppers, jobless wage slaves, near-bankrupt little shopkeepers and mortgaged-to-the-hilt dirt farmers.

Among the collection of "chicken feed" were three dimes which Our Jack claimed had been sent to him by a hard-pressed widow with seven small children, as her libation on the altar of liberty. Jack put these three dimes to good use during that memorable campaign. "My campaign funds," he would declaim from stump and rostrum, "do not come from the strong boxes of the blood-sucking bankers, monopolists, and oil corporations who are backing my opponents." Then, holding high for all to see the three dimes of the widow, he would thunder with the holy fervor of a prophet of Israel, "This is the kind of money that pays my campaign expenses. The money of the poor and heavy-laden. No tainted money, but the money earned by calloused hands and sweating brows. May my right hand wither and my tongue cleave to the roof of my mouth if I desert the honest farmers and laborers who so loyally support my candidacy with their dimes!" It was a most effective oration and always brought down the house, though one of our "Reds" had composed it for him. And so, while Our Jack made the welkin ring, we rattled tin cups all over the rolling prairies of the Sooner State.

The Democratic State Convention, following the nomination of Our Jack by the comfortable plurality of thirty thousand votes, gagged a bit on our eighteen-plank platform and on Our Jack as well. But in the end it swallowed both.

Re-reading that old platform the other day, I was profoundly puzzled as to why anybody, including both its opponents and proponents, should have become unduly excited about its demands. They were mild indeed. By now most of them are incorporated in the statute books of this great democracy without either ushering in the millennium or causing the heavens to fall. There was a plank demanding the establishment of a state bank. Another demanded the abolition of a shirt factory operating for private profit in the state penitentiary. A third demanded a bonus for the doughboys, mainly designed to drive a wedge between the new-born American Legion and its Wall Street sugar daddies. Another plank (for some reason the most strenuously opposed by the oil interests) demanded an increase in the tax on oil taken out of the state by "foreign" corporations, such as Royal Dutch Shell, Magnolia, and the Standard Oil of New Jersey.

As so often happens in political battles fought so largely with sound and fury, the paramount issue was not even mentioned in the platform, but emerged in the heat of the campaign. Back in 1912 a School Land Commission had leased some 118,000 acres of school land to E. W. Marland, one of the state's leading oil men, for the magnificent sum of fifty dollars. If oil was found on that land the educational institutions of the state were to receive an additional royalty of eight per cent of the value thereof. Largely because of the generosity of the School Land Commission (servants of the sovereign people), beneficiary Marland was able to announce ten years later that through the exercise of thrift and stern frugality he had accumulated a nest egg of sixty-three million dollars on his original investment of fifty. From this it is evident that Mr. Marland had quite an interest in the personnel of Oklahoma's state government. It also may explain why Oklahoma, at that time the seventh richest state in the Union, was forty-seventh in educational standards, Mississippi alone ranking below it.

The "foreign agitators" of the League alleged that oil-man Marland had acquired the 118,000 acres of school land by methods reminiscent of Teapot Dome, and we demanded the restoration of the land to the school children of the state.

Oh, yes, our opponents raised that monotonously inevitable cry of "foreign agitators." Foremost among these foreign agitators of ours was Paul Nesbit, who had been private secretary to the first governor of Oklahoma, and was later Speaker of the Lower House of Oklahoma, and George Wilson, who had surreptitiously sneaked into Oklahoma during the run of 1889 where, in the course of events, he rose to a professorship in the Oklahoma Agricultural and Mechanical College. It was, incidentally, the same George Wilson who climbed with me onto slow-moving coaches, ate hamburgers three times a day and stopped at dollar hotels on the crusading quest to secure three thousand dollars from the conductors' union for Our Jack's campaign fund. We got the money and returned with it, comforted by the thought that we had cut expenses to the bone, and no ham bones at that, in the arduous course of its collection.

In spite of the most violent barrages from Wall Street stooges, from the state press, and from all "right-thinking people," the uprising of peasants, workers and ex-service men swept Our Jack into the governor's chair with the healthy plurality of sixty thousand votes. His inaugural was celebrated with a barbecue such as a wondering world had never seen, and most likely will never see again. The heady odors of that Gargantuan feast were wafted throughout the nation by the press stories of amazed correspondents who had come from every important news agency in the land. They became lyric about the "last of the frontiers." They described cow-punchers, Indians, share croppers and miners tottering through the streets of Oklahoma City, gorged with slabs of whole steers, cross-sections of titanic hogs, Paul Bunyan helpings of sizzling mutton. And all on the house, the house that Jack built on our grass-roots foundations. Be it said for our candidate that here, at any rate, was one campaign promise which he gloriously fulfilled.

For days, all comers were served with all that they could get away with. The dark shadows of Prohibition that lay upon the land were lifted for the time being and the state capital became the Mecca for boot-legging pilgrims from all the Southwest. Old-timers who were present at that barbecue today wipe the water from their aged mouths and tell you, "Jack Walton promised us a free-for-all if we would elect him, and by God, he made good."

Childish as the wild enthusiasm of the barbecue may appear to the sophisticated denizens of the Atlantic brain belt, to me it signified the dawn of a new epoch in American history. Again, as so often in the tragic past, the frontier had risen against the forces of the invisible empire that had developed within the framework of our political democracy. Soon representatives of the toiling masses of Oklahoma would join the farm bloc in Washington represented by Frazier and Nye of the Dakotas, Shipstead and Magnus Johnson of Minnesota, Norris and Robert B. Howell of Nebraska, Brookhart of Iowa, and fighting Bob La Follette of Wisconsin. Without money to speak of, with virtually the entire press of the state and all the spokesmen and spellbinders of the financial and monopolistic interests against us, we had triumphantly elected Our Jack, destined to become the Andrew Jackson of the Nineteen-twenties.

Naïve as we were, we realized that the winning of the first battle did not necessarily mean the winning of the war. Many more battles would have to be fought to restore the government of Oklahoma and the wealth of mineral resources to the people of the state. But even if we failed to overthrow Wall Street and its minions completely at the first onslaught, the start had been made. We had put our hands to the plow. There was one state institution in particular which we were determined to capture and hold, come what may. That was the Oklahoma Agricultural and Mechanical College. A pitifully small number of its graduates returned to the shops and farms from which they had come. Instead, this institution of learning had been turning out, to the vast disgust of our farmers and miners, a pedigreed collection of potential life-insurance, lightning-rod, patent-fence-gate, and oil-burner salesmen, prepared to bite the paternal hands that fed them. Older heads among our crowd figured that it might be a good idea to give the youngsters some idea of the economic time of day. Nothing wild, mind you, but merely a look at how we get this way and where we're going, in the nature of what the Eastern professors call "orientation courses."

We had a rich vein to mine. The best professorial brains of the nation were in those post-war days quartered in academic doghouses. The New School for Social Research had just started in New York. Today schools provide a shelter for exiles from Mussoliniland and Hitlerdom. Just after the War, fugitives from the chain gang of Nicholas Murray Butler, and others, as distinguished as Professors Charles Beard, John Dewey, and the many-times-exiled Thorstein Veblen, were putting new life into old academic bones.

We assigned the job of writing the curriculum for courses in economics and sociology to one of our *Leader* reporters, Ernest Chamberlain. He got in touch with educational leaders all over the country. He turned out as thoroughgoing and scholarly a job as one could wish for. Best of all, he adapted it to the needs of our young people. I don't know what's happened to that trail-blazing work of Chamberlain's, but I do know it was a model for a genuinely democratic school of the people.

Next we picked George Wilson to be president of the A. and M. As I have said, George had been a teacher and a good one. To be sure, he had no Ph.D., and that was used against him by the oil gang who fought his appointment. There was a touch of irony in that. The distinguished members of that oil gang could, by and large, barely spell out their own names in the local telephone book. Furthermore, the fact that George had no Ph.D. did not keep Our Jack awake at night. Ph.D.'s to Jack were as primroses to Peter Bell. As far as I was concerned I had met some Ph.D.'s (and as I shall relate later, I was to meet more), so I lost no more sleep than did Jack over George's presumably lamentable inability to write these mystic letters after his name.

In spite of the opposition, one of the first official acts of the governor, our governor, was to appoint George as president of the A. and M. We saw George and his family off to Stillwater and I've rarely seen as happy a human being as was Wilson that day. He was beholding the dream of his lifetime come true—the chance to hand on his great-hearted and gentle philosophy of civilized living to the boys and girls of his own people.

So now we had a college, a curriculum and a man who could be trusted to carry on our program of peace, plenty and security. To hell with the state political plums. If we could bring up a cross-section of the next generation of Oklahoma farmers and workers to a real understanding of the world about them, we could let the political ward heelers wallow in the troughs, confident that the future was ours. For a little space we enjoyed the most roseate of visions. With Our Jack in the State House, our George at the A. and M., and myself slated to be adjutant general of the state militia, ready to put down any counter-revolution headed into Oklahoma by way of Wall Street, we had the forces of darkness definitely on the run. Or so we thought.

42

HARDLY had Andrew Jackson II been seated in the governor's chair when disturbing rumors reached the ears of his victorious army of farmers and wage slaves. He had, said Dame Rumor, taken a trip to the palm-shaded island of Cuba, accompanied by a gentleman suspected of oil connections and illicit relations with Mme. Fortuna. That trip alone must have cost Our Jack the equivalent of ten bales of cotton, eight hundred bushels of wheat, a carload of Berkshire hogs, or the average annual wage of a jobless proletarian at the prevailing scale of 1922. Soon thereafter, items appeared in the opposition press describing Our Jack dining and wining with such counter-revolutionary organizations as bourgeois booster outfits and open-shop chambers of commerce where he assured his hearers that the revolutionary upheaval forecast by his deluded followers was now indefinitely postponed, and that irrespective of what certain irresponsible persons had said during the campaign, any attempt to overthrow the government of the State of Oklahoma by force and violence would be speedily suppressed by the armed forces under his command.

"Armed forces," good grief! I was still waiting for my commission as leader of those very forces. It is unnecessary to add that I never had a chance to try on the uniform of Adjutant General of Oklahoma. Worse and more of it. As the days went on, Our Jack applied additional coats of red paint to the public reputations of his "deluded followers," myself preferred. The very editorials, speeches and interviews which we had composed in his campaign as the champion of the forgotten man were now quoted as evidence of the subversive intentions of his former, now definitely repudiated, intellectual general staff.

Our Jack even reversed the oldest and most honored American political tradition, "to the victors belong the spoils." All the key positions in the State House, state, and county governments were presented to our vanquished foes. The highest honors which Our Jack bestowed upon his erstwhile comrades in the soviet of farmers, workers and ex-service men of Oklahoma were the ignominious positions of fish-and-game warden, auto-tag dispenser, and assistant cuspidor custodian in the state capitol. Nor, in other respects, did Our Jack make even a gesture toward speeding on the new dawn. The ancient régime of oil, cement, asphalt and privately owned public utilities that had governed Oklahoma since President Taft gave his left-handed blessing to the constitution of the state, back in 1907, reigned as supreme as of yore. The platform manifestoes and demands of the Farmer-Labor Reconstruction League joined the collection of broken Indian treaties moldering among the exhibits in Oklahoma's new Museum of Ancient History.

More dark clouds lay along the horizon. Among other things, Our Jack had been the anti-Ku Klux Klan candidate. Now Klansmen strutted through the marble halls of the capitol in broad daylight. Kleagles, Dragons, Titans and Klaligators picked the plums of victory in every county of the Oklahoma dependency of Emperor Simmons, reigning in Atlanta, Georgia, while we dazed anti-Klanners scratched our puzzled heads, mumbling, "How come?"

Harder blows descended upon our bloody but still unbowed heads. Reliable eye-witnesses testified they had seen Our Jack garbed in tasseled knickers and silver-buckled sports shoes playing golf on a Muskogee links surrounded by oil derricks and their owners. Worse still, according to our spies, Our Jack had even employed a little boy to carry the leather bag containing the fancy shinny sticks with which he knocked little white balls around the exalted cow pasture. Think of Moses leading the Children of Israel out of bondage dressed in tasseled knickers, silver-buckled brogues, and with a little Aaron lugging a bag of sticks to be turned into snakes or used to knock water out of rocks, as occasion may have required! That may give you some faint notion of the breaking hearts engendered by the mental picture of Our Jack in his golf togs parading as an employer of child labor.

Then came another blow. During the campaign we had raised the slogan: "War of hut and shack against mansion and palace!" Now the triumphant champion of hut and shack had bought himself a forty-eight thousand dollar mansion in the very heart of Oklahoma City's most exclusive residential district, reserved for the palaces of Oklahoma's oilocracy. There was nothing rumorlike about that. I saw it for the first time one gloomy night from across the street, with bleeding heart, moist eyes, and whirling brain. I even saw the undaunted champion of the lowly and heavy-laden leave the chauffeur-controlled limousine presented to him by his moneyed friends and admirers. I actually beheld the prospective protector of the poor nod solemnly to his hired man in butler's uniform as he disappeared through the doors of the forty-eight thousand dollar mansion.

Too much. Too much. We were naïve, unsophisticated folk. We still believed in Santa Claus, fairies and democracy. Some of us even believed the Biblical story of the loaves and fishes wherewith a certain multitude were filled in the long ago. But this was too much like the "conspicuous waste" spoken of by Thorstein Veblen. There was something rotten in the State of Oklahoma. By no stretch of the imagination could that forty-eight thousand dollar mansion of Our Jack have been purchased by the three dimes of the widow.

There was, however, one consolation left. We had George Wilson at the Oklahoma A. and M. There would be no worshipping at the shrine of Mammon while George was there. Of course the announcement of Wilson's appointment had set the opposition into a blind rage. The oil interests and their allies ordered their clerical kept men, their educational mercenaries, and their journalistic procurers to gang up on gentle George Wilson on the ground that he was an ignoramus, having acquired no Ph.D., a "stirrer up of the people," and a dangerous Red. But even so, it was inconceivable to us that Jack Walton, who had known Wilson well, would pay any attention to such obviously oil-smeared libels.

We were licking our raw wounds in the lobby of the Egbert Hotel in Oklahoma City where we had our headquarters when George Wilson came in, a few short weeks after his appointment. The look on the man's face startled all of us. It was the stricken look of one who had just received his death sentence. "Boys," said Wilson, in a low, thick voice, "I'm through. Look at this." He fumbled blindly in his pockets and at length drew out a telegram. It was from the governor, notifying Wilson of his immediate discharge. There was no explanation of any sort. Walton was kicking Wilson out as unceremoniously as a bartender would kick a bum out of his saloon.

We stared at the slip of paper in George's trembling hand. There was nothing we could say. A farmer friend of George's reached out to pat him on the arm. A big miner swore bitterly. But there was nothing we could say to take that dazed look from the face of a man whom all of us loved like a brother. We just stood there for a little, and then George turned, picked up the bag he had brought along from Stillwater, and started to walk slowly up the worn stairs to his room on the second floor. He walked like an old man, bent over, beaten. We drifted out under a night of mocking stars. A few weeks later we read, in the very paper that had slandered George for columns on end, that Wilson had accidentally killed himself while cleaning his revolver in his home. . . .

George Wilson was dead. And with him died the last hope any of us held to make our state a decent dwelling place for civilized men and women. More than that, for some of our people it was the death of all faith in the democratic processes. To what avail this sacrifice and suffering, this scraping together of hard-won dollars and cents, at the end to elect a man like Walton who could so treacherously betray us and the cause for which he had stood? If there had been a real Red agitator anywhere in the state in those dark days he would have found willing converts in our disillusioned ranks. But as it was, the most bitterly disillusioned turned to cynicism as an escape. Never again would they answer the summons of any rank-and-file movement. The defeatism that was born of the Walton betrayal still hangs like a black cloud over the progressives of the state. But I understand that the young men of the Oklahoma A. and M. have a good basketball team, and that's what really matters, isn't it?

The future historian of what Henry Adams called "The degradation of the democratic dogma" will do well to consult the record of the impeachment hearings of Our Jack, now on file in the state capitol. For sure enough, Our Jack was impeached, ten months after he had set up his business, and a big business at that, in the governor's office. But he was not impeached by us. We had no heart left for such an involved procedure. No, the country's outstanding anti-Klan candidate was impeached largely through the efforts of a right-wing faction inside the Klan with whom he had fallen out. For of course, as we suspected when we saw the rush of Kleagles to the State House right after the inaugural, Our Jack had become a Klansman too, even as he raised his unwithered hand on high against the nightshirted brethren. Just how far he had penetrated into the higher circles of Klandom is made sufficiently clear by the following letter, of which I still cherish a photostatic copy:

1640 Peachtree Road
Atlanta, Georgia

September
Tenth
Nineteen-Twenty-three.

Hon. J. C. (Jack) Walton,
Oklahoma City, Okla.

My faithful Klansman:—

In just recognition of your constant loyalty, unwavering devotion and splendid service to the Knights of the Ku Klux Klan,

I, by authority possessed by me as Emperor of the Invisible Empire, have conferred upon you the lofty honor of Life Membership in K-UNO, and same dates from August 1st, 1923.

Your certificate will be duly engrossed and forwarded to you at an early date. This letter will be your authority in claiming and proclaiming the fact of your Life Membership.

"Let him who serves best be honored most."

Faithfully yours in the Sacred
Unfailing Bond,

(*Signed*) William Joseph Simmons

EMPEROR

INVISIBLE EMPIRE

The sorry tale of corruption unfolded at the impeachment proceedings is far too long and complicated for retelling here. If I pick out highlights from these lower political depths I do so, not in retrospect, but with my eyes firmly fixed on the current political scene of the year 1940. In this year of nation-wide nominations and campaigns, a year so fateful in the history of the Republic, the story of Walton may have a certain significance.

The sworn evidence at the impeachment hearings arrived at an estimated two hundred and fifty thousand dollars as the sum contributed to Our Jack's campaign, largely from the oil groups led by Marland affiliated with the Royal Dutch Shell on the one hand, and Harry Sinclair on the other. Though ostensibly these two groups were in cut-throat competition, when a common danger such as our proposal for oil taxes threatened, they could get together quickly enough (which I may add is more than our present-day liberals and radicals can do in the face of the current reactionary drive). Alongside the united-front contribution of Royal Dutch and Standard, how pitiful appeared our clean-money jack-pot!

No sooner had Walton moved into the forty-eight thousand dollar mansion than, not only the representatives of the oil men, but agents of the paving ring, the sweatshop shirt factory, and other interests as well, moved right in with the governor. Needless to say there was no governmental interference with the operations of the shirt factory at the state pen. The school children didn't get their land back. No tax on oil such as we had proposed was even hinted at. In rounding out his educational program, initiated by the discharge of George Wilson, Walton announced that he contemplated cutting five million dollars from the state's educational appopriations. Among the institutions which would be affected by the cut was a state school in Tonkawa. Alarmed over this threatened menace to higher education in the cultural center of Tonkawa, two well-heeled citizens of that metropolis journeyed to Oklahoma City and there conferred with the paving member of the Walton brain trust. The visitors left behind some six thousand dollars in thousand-dollar bills. Twenty days later the governor, according to the testimony, deposited six thousand dollars in Liberty bonds in a bank in Kansas City. Coincidentally the Tonkawa state school received its usual appropriation in its entirety.

It must be admitted that such a transaction as this was a departure from the normal routine. To Walton's credit be it stated that, fired by local pride, he usually deposited his honoraria in the banks and trust companies of his own home town. It developed that one of these institutions held Walton's notes on the purchase of the gubernatorial mansion to the amount of thirty thousand dollars. Although Marland had gushed mightily during the campaign, with the thought that there might still be some oil in that well, Walton sent an emissary to the oil man suggesting that Marland might like to take these notes off the embarrassed hands of the governor. At first Marland intimated that it might be better for Walton to try his luck on the stock market with inside tips provided by the inside oil men. Walton complained bitterly about Marland's ingratitude and the latter finally capitulated, putting up the thirty thousand in cash, which, considering previous contributions of some seventy-three thousand, made the Walton affair quite an investment for Marland.

Let it also be recorded to the credit of Our Jack that as an entrepreneur on a large scale he let no lucrative by-products go to waste. The pardon and parole enterprise, for example. Among the numerous pardons granted by the great-hearted governor was one to Virgil Hollingshead, a young man who was serving a long sentence in the state penitentiary. His parents were industrious and respectable farm people, but they had not thought of the chances of obtaining a pardon for their errring offspring until they were visited by a former convict who had been appointed a special officer by Walton. That worthy suggested to the Hollingsheads that there was a good possibility of obtaining a pardon if they could raise five thousand dollars on the sale of one of their farms. Acting on this subtle hint, the farm was sold and forthwith a pardon, signed and sealed by the fine Italian hand of Walton and delivered by the ex-convict, arrived at the Hollingshead home.

Remember the proletarian barbecue? Well, brothers and sisters, even that good-will gathering was turned to gold at the Walton touch. Nobody knows what it cost. For although most of the material and food was donated, Governor Walton's inside bagmen began a campaign for donations to cover an undisclosed deficit, soon after the last mutton chop sizzled away. This campaign continued unabated until the impeachment of the governor ten months later.

All the calculations of investigators and the expertness of expert public accountants failed to reveal the grand total of the Walton take. Only his Maker and Our Jack are qualified to speak on that subject, and from both there has been a prolonged silence. Whatever it was, it was plenty.

Very naturally, this sordid business not only meant the end of our movement, but the end of the Oklahoma *Leader* as a daily. We kept on as a weekly with such remnants of support as we had left, until I changed the name of the *Leader* to *The American Guardian*. Of this weekly, with its not-to-be-sneezed-at national circulation and, in all modesty, national influence, I am, at the present writing, still the proud editor.

In our last issue of the *Leader* we bade farewell forever to Our Jack, and ran the quotation from Browning's "The Lost Leader": "Just for a handful of silver he left us, Just for a riband to stick in his coat." Walton was in the governor's mansion when a copy of our paper was left on his desk. He rang for his secretary. "Go and find out," he commanded, "who this son-of-a-bitch Browning is, and give him some sort of a job that will close his mouth."

43

WHEN I tell the story of Walton to my radical friends in the East they say, "Of course, that's Oklahoma. After all that's a raw, crude state you have. From what we read in the papers the most fantastic things are always going on down there. Things that would be impossible in any civilized community."

Maybe so, but I doubt it. I am completing this narrative in a suburban home in New Jersey, set down in a countryside over which Washington's rabble in arms fought and bled. Before the Revolution, early Dutch settlers built their sturdy stone and wooden homes here, with their long gambrel roofs sweeping down almost to the ground. This county and this state have been long in the essential American tradition. Yet no less than twenty years ago Victor Berger, Congressman-elect from Wisconsin, and I enjoyed the distinction of being among the first of those "dirty Reds" to be thrown out of young Frank Hague's Jersey City on the grave charge that we were causing a crowd to collect to hear us discuss with our fellow Americans the state of the nation.

Today, in this same suburb in which I am writing, the younger set of bond peddlers, oil-burner salesmen, and assorted parasites from eastern institutions of higher learning are exchanging smutty stories about the President of the United States and his gallant wife, swapping hoary hate-wheezes about Jews, repeating outworn lies about the racketeering of C.I.O. leaders, and in the next breath boasting of their one-hundred-per-cent Americanism. Today in Jersey City, not so many miles from here, hard-driven women and children are still working in quarters that are paralleled only by the squalor of the shanties of share croppers in the Deep South, and at the same time the local papers announce that the ineffable Frank Hague has gone to Florida for the winter, there to play golf with the Honorable James Farley. Today in south Jersey a handful of devoted men and women organized into the Workers' Defense League are fighting an under-dog fight on behalf of persecuted Negro potato pickers, whom night riders have been flogging. Today the ten richest counties in the State of New Jersey pay tribute to the ironically named Public Service Corporation of New Jersey, the Morgan-controlled holding company which monopolizes the gas, electric, and transportation services of the state in these counties. By the same token, these counties send as sorry a collection of rubber stamps to the legislature as can be found in the governing body of any other of the forty-eight states of the Union. Today a trail of corruption extends from Haguetown to the stronghold of Republican Enoch Johnson in Atlantic City. Local and state governments are making a hideous farce of every democratic dogma. Bundists, Coughlinites, Night Riders, runaway sweatshop proprietors, race-track gamblers and public-payroll robbers, with the consent of the overwhelming majority of the Jersey press, pulpiteers, and professors, have made a state endowed by nature with a host of natural beauties, a stink in the nostrils of all liberty-loving Americans. Oklahoma, with all its faults, still has a long way to sink to reach the low political level of the "Garden State" of New Jersey.

I don't go in for morals, but if I did I would draw from the miserable tale of our Jack Walton the moral that to fight such entrenched interests as reign over Oklahoma—and New Jersey—more is needed by the representatives of the people than a proletarian front. It takes courage, patience (worlds of that), intelligence, and most of all integrity and more integrity to beat as ruthless a gang as ever scuttled the ship of state. That it can be done, however, is testified to by the fact that my friend and comrade, Dan Hoan, is still serving as mayor of Milwaukee.

Brothers and sisters of the rank and file, always remember to look over your potential candidates with as much care as you would exercise in choosing a wife. In the last issue of our daily paper, which was done to death by Walton's treachery, I wrote these words about politicians of Our Jack's school:

"Politics is the art by which politicians obtain campaign contributions from the rich and votes from the poor on the pretext of protecting each from the other."

I still stand on that.

My experience with Our Jack left me politically so limp that I haven't voted for an Oklahoma governor since. No doubt most of Oklahoma's governors and statesmen in general have been good men and true to the Eastern corporations who greased their way into office. However, I am strenuously opposed to absentee ownership, and that includes Oklahoma governors. The latest one of that species has just called out the militia to prevent the waters of an Oklahoma river from accumulating in sufficient volume behind a federal dam eventually to drive turbines for the manufacture of electric juice in competition with private enterprise. The good man is a great enthusiast for little dams, and the more the merrier, but he'd be damned if he'd stand for dams high, wide and long enough to drive turbines, and New England public-utility corporations out of Oklahoma.

By the way, and apropos of nothing in particular, just when my faith in democracy and my personal fortune had hit rock bottom, came a wire from Moses Annenberg, then one of *die Hauptmacher* of the Hearst organization, asking me to come to New York. Well, I went to New York, because just then I was so low in mind and cash that if his Satanic majesty had invited me to his summer resort, I would have thumbed my way in that direction.

The proposition Messrs Moses Annenberg and Arthur Brisbane laid before my still watery eyes was to become a Hearst scribe at an initial salary of one thousand dollars a month (yes, $1,000), to be raised to twenty-five thousand per annum if I made good. When I declined the flattering offer on the grounds that I could not desert my Oklahoma *Leader* baby while it was about to give up its ghost, the twain offered to buy our plant at a price that would get me outright. The big idea behind buying my baby was the publication of a Hearst Sunday paper. However, hard-pressed and sorely tempted as I was, I felt the good people of Oklahoma had suffered enough from absentee ownership ministered by their native sons without having William Randolph Hearst inflicted on them. On parting, Arthur Brisbane ruefully shook his head, as if to say: "This kind of impractical person would sell America short," while the less philosophical Moe called me a damned fool.

Well, I wasn't. Arthur is dead. Moe became a multimillionaire, which is worse yet. On the other hand, I'm still alive and kicking, and happily so poor that no self-respecting income-tax ferret would dream of snooping into my financial affairs. Besides, as the Good Book says, "What shall it profit a man to gain the whole world and lose his soul?"

44

THE coal fields of Illinois were my next America.

The Illinois miners and I were not strangers. During their strikes in 1910-11 I had spoken on their behalf in virtually every mining camp in Illinois. What renewed my acquaintance with them was something that happened in Kansas. During the open-shop drive following the Armistice, the legislature of Kansas, under the leadership of Governor Henry Allen, passed the Industrial Court law. Its purpose was the prevention of strikes. Under its provisions a court of three men, appointed by the governor, would conduct a hearing to which both parties of the controversy were cited. If, after such a hearing, the court decided that the strike was not justified, both strikers and union officials were subject to fines and imprisonment for violation of the law. The decision would, of course, depend largely upon the personnel of the court chosen by the governor, and in the event of its being unfavorable, the would-be strikers could do nothing but obey the law or go to jail. The miners, justifiably, regarded the Industrial Court law as an attempt to deprive them of their only weapon—the strike.

The dominant personalities among the miners were Alexander Howat, president of the Kansas miners, Frank Farrington, president of the Illinois miners, and John L. Lewis, national president of the United Mine Workers of America. All three were strong, resourceful men, who rose to be leaders in the rough-and-tumble fighting characteristic of the organized labor movement. Howat, called the "stormy petrel" of the Southwest miners, called a strike against the Kansas Industrial Court law, thereby violating the existing collective agreement between the coal operators and the miners of the state. Frank Farrington came to the support of the striking Kansas miners with all the resources of his Illinois organization, then the strongest and financially best-situated of the districts composing the United Mine Workers of America. John L. Lewis, on the other hand, declared the strike to be in violation of the contract—that is, an outlaw strike—and had threatened to revoke the charter of the Kansas miners and place them under a provisional government of his own selection.

In course of time, Lewis carried out his threat. Governor Henry Allen also carried out his threat, so that for a time there were three governments active in the Kansas coal fields: the Industrial Court, appointed by Governor Allen, the provisional government of the Kansas miners, selected by Lewis, and the elected government of the miners, composed of President Alexander Howat and the executive board, for the larger part of the controversy in the jails of Cherokee County.

I do not here pass judgment on the personalities or tactics involved in the Industrial Court law. Henry Allen is dead. So is Frank Farrington. The Industrial Court is dead. I have long ago forgiven what trespasses John L. Lewis may have been guilty of on that occasion, while Alexander Howat, still hale and hearty, has given no indication of digging up old bones. So why should I, whose only connection with the Kansas Industrial Court fight was that of leading literary light and spokesman of the Kansas miners?

While the battle raged in Kansas, my *Leader* baby in Oklahoma was passing from crisis to crisis. Now a crisis of crises had appeared, imperatively demanding father at the bedside of his barely breathing child. The situation was that, in order to secure working capital, we had issued a hundred thousand dollars' worth of first-mortgage bonds bearing the customary six per cent interest. There had been no time to peddle these bonds among our own friends. However, our bank had graciously lent us twenty thousand dollars on two notes of ten thousand each, secured by our entire bond issue of a hundred thousand. Now one of these notes would be due in two days, and not a dime in the treasury. Worse, and more of it, the president of the bank holding that menacing ten thousand dollar note was the chairman of the open-shop committee of the Chamber of Commerce of Oklahoma City. If that note was not paid, pronto, the bank could, by "due process of law," walk away with our quarter of a million dollar plant. Or, preferably, take the plant and tell us to walk away.

But where to get ten thousand dollars in a hurry, when every experienced money raiser knows that there is nothing that slows up money raising so much as hurry? We talked ourselves into a veritable labyrinth of vicious circles, all ending where they had started. At last, no more circles showing up, I said to our ever resourceful Freda, "Let's drive out to Northeast Lake, sit under a tree, and meditate in nature's peace and tranquillity over the possibility of where, and from whom, we are going to get that ten thousand."

Under that tree, by the yellow waters of Northeast Lake, Freda received the inspiration that saved not only the immediate situation, but the future of our newspaper. "Go to Springfield, Illinois," said Freda. "See Frank Farrington. Tell him our situation and Farrington will help."

"What! Expect Frank Farrington to come to our aid? Preposterous! The man is a dyed-in-the-wool Republican, an all-around conservative. All my friends among the Illinois miners tell me he hates Socialists worse than poison."

"Go and see him," Freda insisted. "Farrington is supporting the Kansas miners. You and our paper have done all we can to help them. There is a bond between us now. Frank Farrington will help."

I went, expecting nothing.

When I arrived in Springfield the following day my guardian angel had arranged to have the executive board of the Illinois miners in session. Had this not been the case, the delay would have meant the end of the *Leader* and, hence, the *Guardian*.

At my request, Farrington met me outside the room in which his board was meeting. "Well, Oscar, what do you want? Make it snappy. I have no time to waste," was his not too promising greeting.

"All right." I made it snappy. "Unless you let us have twenty-five thousand dollars right now, our plant in Oklahoma is busted."

"Snappy enough," replied Farrington. "Go in there, tell your tale of woe to the board, and they may let you have it."

"No," I said. "Before going to the board, I want to know where you, its president, stand."

"Get in there and tell your tale."

I went in. I told my tale of woe to the board, and told it not with tears in my eyes, but with all the humor I could muster. It was the very thing to do. If there is one thing miners love, it is a cheerful fighter. And so, amid laughter and back-slapping, President Frank Farrington said, "Come on, fellows. Make it snappy. We can't stay here all afternoon listening to this wise-cracker. Somebody move to let him have that twenty-five thousand, then tell the son of a bitch to get the hell out of here." The motion was made, and passed, fourteen to one.

On parting, I referred to the sentiment expressed by President Farrington, saying, "Well, I'd rather have you say, 'Give that son of a bitch his twenty-five thousand and tell him to get the hell out of here,' than 'Tell the gentleman we are sorry we can't do anything for him.'"

Why had I asked for twenty-five, when I had come for ten thousand? Search me. Was it the guardian angel's advice, or is it just good psychology always to ask for more and leave it to the cheerful giver to decide? Some months later, I was compelled to make a second pilgrimage to Springfield, Illinois. This time, my plea was for twenty thousand. It, too, was freely granted. The very salt of the earth, those miners, and so are their brave, scrapping wives and children. Nine years later we had repaid every cent of the forty-five thousand. Furthermore, we are still doing business with the bank, whose president, in the capacity of chairman of the open-shop committee of Oklahoma City's Chamber of Commerce, had scared the eternal daylights out of us.

Those loans totalling forty-five thousand dollars were only the good beginning. Soon after, a special convention of the Illinois miners voted for an official publication of their own, elected me as editor, and gave the job of printing the paper to our Oklahoma plant. The agreement entered into was that for the sum of $1520 per week I was to edit, print and mail an eight-page, eight-column paper, known as *The Illinois Miner,* whose policy was to be in harmony with the constitution, by-laws and convention resolutions of the organization. With $1520 every Thursday, on the dot, the Saturday payroll ceased to be the nightmare it had been. We started beating back to windward. In return, we gave to the Illinois miners, their wives and children, the best our hearts and minds had to offer. *The Illinois Miner* was more than a labor paper. It was a family paper, enjoyed by young and old. Of course, we printed labor news and labor editorials. But besides that we had at least one great classic poem in every issue. We conducted drawing, coloring, and essay contests which gave our children an opportunity to express themselves, and what talent there was, hidden and usually lost, among those children! We printed short stories—the best short stories of all lands and ages. We printed step-savers, cooking and household recipes carefully selected from those supplied by our own women. Tucked away in the files of *The Illinois Miner* is an international cookbook, not of landscape cooking, but healthful, stick-to-the-ribs cooking, for our women hailed from virtually every country of Europe, and they knew how to feed working families. For our serial we ran Wells's *Outline of History.* This was a frank experiment. How well it fared we soon learned. Coal diggers came to the Springfield office looking for back copies so that they could keep the whole fascinating story intact. H. G. Wells is out of favor now with our intellectuals, and indeed he has lost prestige everywhere by his latter-day advocacy of the rule of the "élite." The rule of the "élite" has gone the way of his earlier League of Nations pet. The far-ranging, fine-visioned Englishman might better have stuck to his first love: socialism—free socialism, that is, not the thing he saw and instinctively distrusted in Russia. He is, however, still the peerless popularizer in the best sense of that much-abused word. His outlines of history, economics, and science provide a far better understanding of the world we have unfortunately inherited and in which we eke out our precarious existence, than is contained in most university courses. They are ideal material for a general background to labor educational courses.

Today Wells writes in a mood of utter despair. Everything for which he has struggled—collective intelligence, planning, the great society—seems to him to have gone to pot. But the ideas and visions which he implanted in successive generations of alert-minded Americans have not gone to pot. That among these same Americans were our own Illinois miners may make a footnote for the future biographer of the leading encyclopedist of the twentieth century.

Of course *The Illinois Miner* crusaded for the new social order, but we did it without employing the stock phrases of Marxism. Such strange words as "proletariat," "bourgeoisie" and the rest of the old-line socialist patter never appeared in this American-language labor paper. At repeated conventions the miners had come out in favor of nationalization of the mines. They had gone so far as to appoint a committee, headed by John Brophy and aided in their research work by such wholehearted sympathizers as Robert Bruere and Heber Blankenhorn, to draw up a practical plan for running coal for the benefit of the three parties most concerned with the production of cheap and abundant fuel —the consumers, the miners, and the technicians. This committee was chosen over the opposition of the union's president, John L.

Lewis, then in his most reactionary phase. Lewis forbade all mention of nationalization in his court organ, the official paper of the United Mine Workers, which was, and is, probably the dullest labor publication in all Christendom.

We went into the nationalization proposal, however, with full pages devoted to the ins and outs of this man-sized problem. And we got results in the shape of endorsements from most of the mining camps, and the reprinting of our material in the progressive press as a whole. That there was never a greater need than now for some such educational campaign as we conducted back in the Nineteen-twenties is my firm conviction.

I was the columnist for the *Miner*. I took the pen name of "Adam Coaldigger" for my by-line. The pleasure on the face of a miner who had puzzled out "a damn' coaldigger," a familiar enough epithet among the upper crust, was wonderful to behold. I was soon being introduced on my swing around the camps as "Adam," and the name today is used as frequently as Oscar by the farmers and miners who still follow my Adam Coaldigger columns in *The American Guardian*.

The paper was edited, the news gathered in Springfield. It was made up and put to bed by Freda Hogan in Oklahoma City at our printing plant, one of the best equipped in the Southwest, by that time. In Springfield such competent workers as Len De Caux, the present editor of the *C.I.O. News*, who had been a steel worker; Carl Leathwood, who is a mainstay on the *Guardian* today; Richard Glover, a young miner fresh from the pits; Jesse Gelders, Karl Pretshold, now labor reporter on the St. Louis *Star-Times*, and Elizabeth Coleman were on my staff at one time or another. Needless to say, I let them very much alone. Regularly, at the deadline, they sent down human-interest copy of the sort that soon established the *Miner* as the "most readable labor paper in the United States," as our friendly critics put it. That there was not much competition from the standpoint of readability on the part of the rest of the labor papers does not detract from this estimate.

In view of the fact that mine was the comparatively simple job of getting out a weekly column and some editorials, I can say with all modesty that *The Illinois Miner* was one bang-up paper. The appeal of it lay in the fact that we wrote rank-and-file pieces for rank-and-file readers. I don't mean "writing down," either. No people in this country are quicker to understand when they are being patronized than the coal diggers. Interlarding miner stories with tough talk, the use of slang where slang was not called for, and the baby babble all too frequently resorted to by labor writers who never bother to keep in touch with the rank and file, was as "verboten" on our paper as the Marxian dialectic.

When I felt that any of our crowd were losing the rank-and-file touch I would tell them the story of Antaeus, brought somewhat up to date:

There is a feller you read about on the fringes of Greek mythology whose name was Antaeus. He was a giant. He lived in one of the African countries that the Greeks were trying to colonize. He was the leader of the rank and file of that country and he was one tough hombre. Whenever a Greek fighting man would land on that African coast with the announcement that the folks thereabouts were about to be liberated by the altruistic Greeks, Antaeus, with his admiring rank and file behind him, would come down to the dock and challenge the would-be liberator to a rassling match. Year after year, Antaeus would bump around the most doughty representatives of the wily Greeks, throw them onto their ships and bundle them back to where they came from.

Things looked pretty black for the Greeks' chances of colonizing Antaeus's country and bestowing upon it the blessings of Greek civilization, including of course, slavery, the most advanced forms of sex perversion, and the arts of what was then the last word in up-to-date warfare.

However, one day the usual rat turned up in the ranks of Antaeus's followers. This fellow got the good-natured giant drunk, and in the course of the ensuing bibulous conversation extracted from Antaeus the secret of the giant's power. A few nights later this pioneer industrial spy slipped aboard a boat bound for Greece which was taking home what was left of the last Greek to rassle with the big boy.

Arrived in Greece, the Pearl Bergoff of antiquity hustled off to see Hercules and tell him, for a price, the low-down on Antaeus. Hercules was delighted to get this information and promptly set sail for Africa, not forgetting to leave word behind among his followers to hang the rat when the latter came around for some more jack.

When he got to Antaeus's country, Hercules made the usual spiel about how the Greeks required *Lebensraum* in order to take care of their rapidly mounting birth rate and how they had picked out this African garden spot as the best place on earth in which to expand. He assured his listeners that the intentions of the Greeks were perfectly honorable, that they had come not to make war upon their neighbors but rather to offer them the right hand of fellowship. Then he added that they had better take that hand or else. . . . The Antaeans assembled on the beach had heard all this before and they gave Hercules the mythological equivalent of the raspberry. "Wait until the big boy comes," they told Hercules, "and he will proceed to take you to pieces and forget to put you back."

Finally Antaeus showed up, amid the cheers of his followers, and walking up to Hercules, he slapped the Greek liberator in the face, kicked him in the shins and dared him to rassle. Everyone laughed when Hercules accepted the challenge. "Now," said the rank and file, "old Charon is about to get another passenger for his ferryboat."

Then something happened. Instead of rushing in and getting slapped down for an easy fall, Hercules stalled around until he got a good grip around Antaeus's middle. Groaning and sweating in the age-long manner of rasslers, Hercules lifted the giant up from the ground with a mighty heave. Instantly Antaeus collapsed. All his enormous strength oozed out of him the moment that his two feet left the good earth, and he became a wet rag in Hercules' hands. With those same hands Hercules, still holding the giant up, neatly squeezed Antaeus to death, threw him into the water, and then went around asking the rank and file who was next. There were no takers, so the colonizers, whom Hercules had brought along on the boat, came ashore and proceeded to colonize those backward natives in a style and with a thoroughness which has been the admiration of every English schoolboy ever since.

You see, Antaeus was the son of the Earth goddess and his amazing strength came from his mother. As long as he was in touch with the earth, nothing could prevail against him, but the moment his big feet left the ground he was a dead cooky. That was the inside dope that the rat had slipped to Hercules.

When I see labor leaders and self-anointed guardians of the proletariat putting their feet up on desks in offices far removed from the grass roots and the people who work therein, I always feel like saying, "Buddy, remember Antaeus." But I never do, because when these leaders learned that I was talking about a Greek, all they would think of was some Greek restaurant down the block where they would presently line up at the pie counter.

At Christmas time we distributed prizes among our tens of thousands of contributors—books, ranging in price from twenty-five cents to four dollars, but the best books always. In order to render this service to our women and children readers the executive board permitted us to employ the advertising income of the paper for the purpose.

The more than nine years I served as editor and publisher of *The Illinois Miner* belong to the best of my life. No worry about payrolls, paper bills and bill collectors. No worry at all about what an advertiser would think of what I wrote. If he didn't like it, he could lump it. No worry, even, of what my boss, the executive board, might think of my writing. In all those more than nine years, I received but two letters from President Farrington in which he criticized something I had written—and those two letters were mainly addressed to his own constituents. I was never requested to turn *The Illinois Miner* into a court organ for the reigning family, which is the curse of the great bulk of official labor organs. I dare say I enjoyed a greater liberty of expression than the editor of any labor, socialist, or communist publication up to this very day. Above all, there was that glorious feeling of doing one's best for a good cause, and that other, perhaps still more glorious feeling, of being in contact with teeming, useful lives, and fully in tune with them.

45

IN "Egypt," the vast, wind-swept flat lands that run down
from Centralia to Cairo to make southern Illinois a little
world of its own, shut off from Chicago and the cities of
the north, I found another America.

My Illinois headquarters were at Springfield, in the business-
like, substantial building owned by the Illinois district of the
United Mine Workers of America. In a way, that building was
emblematic of the strength, the solidity, and the hell-for-leather
independence of the coal diggers of the state as they were organized under Frank Farrington, the president of the district. There
was none of the litter and confusion so usual in most union headquarters around those offices. In an anteroom, spick-and-span as
that of any big-shot executive, the diggers sat, awaiting their
turn to see the "big boy." Once inside they would state their
grievances, ranging from troubles with a hard-boiled straw boss
in some remote little mine to wholesale violations of the union
contract in one of the largest operations in the state. With a
world of patience, the big-muscled man with the blue eyes and
look of a born leader would hear them out and render judgment
on the separate cases—a judgment based on years of pick-and-
shovel work at the dangerous face of the coal beneath the corn
fields of Illinois, and based, further, on a knowledge of every
line of the union contract with the operators. The miners had a
saying that you could wake Farrington up in the middle of the

night and start to read the contract out loud at any section of it, and he would go on and recite it for you, word for word, backwards and forwards.

Frank Farrington was as unlike the layman's conception of that mythical being called a "labor leader" as anyone could possibly be. To be sure, he had a commanding presence. He wore good clothes over that big frame of his. When he went through hotel lobbies in New York at national conferences with the operators, or in Chicago when local issues were to be fought out, people turned around to look at him. I took an Eastern labor sympathizer once into a room where a group of Illinois miners were standing about "chewing the fat" after a convention meeting.

"Tell me," I asked, "who is the bull of that particular herd?" My companion pointed instantly to Farrington. The man stood out in any crowd as one set apart for leadership.

As a youth, Farrington had joined the Knights of Labor. He had seen or taken part in all the pioneering struggles of the United Mine Workers. His hero was John Mitchell, the lean, ascetic fighter for the under dog who had brought the anthracite miners of Pennsylvania up from serfdom in the pits to the stature of freemen, in the bitterly fought strike of 1902. Farrington had an understanding, not from books but from the lips of countless agitators, of the underlying principles of anarchism, communism, socialism. Coal-miners were and are instinctive radicals, genuine American proletarians, and at one time or another they have been first to hear the expression of every dissident opinion from that of Johann Most, the old anarchist leader, to the latest recruit in the cause of production for use. To none of these radical doctrines did Farrington subscribe. He followed the Gompers philosophy of no-philosophy. When he fought his way up to the presidency of the Illinois miners and built them into the strongest single unit in the American labor movement, his dominating thought always centered on the contract. He had seen too many agitators take command of a tense situation, bring the workers out onto the picket lines with fiery exhortations—and leave them there. Leave them because the rarest thing in the world is the combination of effective agitator and competent negotiator.

The noblest philosophy of brotherhood, solidarity, and militancy is just so much baloney if it does not finally put into the worker's hand a tightly drawn contract with his boss assuring him three square meals a day, decent working hours, and a pay envelope at the end of the week.

So Farrington early came to look on the contract with something of the reverence with which a confirmed Marxist looks upon the Communist Manifesto. Only, unlike the Marxist, Farrington was for constant revision of his Bible, a revision upward. Year by year, irrespective of what the national organization of the miners' union won or lost, he would go striding into negotiations with the hard-boiled operators of his state and come out with some raise in wages or reduction of hours for his rank and file. The Illinois district under Farrington's leadership was the pace setter for the miners of the nation and more often than not the rest of the fields lagged far behind. Naturally this created no love for Farrington among the union's national officials, who were hard put to it to explain to a restless rank and file why in Ohio, Pennsylvania, Iowa and the rest of what was then organized territory, they could not get such contracts as Illinois enjoyed. Rumors began to run round the pits outside Illinois that Farrington was starting a separatist movement, that he had Napoleonic aspirations, that he was building up an autonomous state within a state where there would be no concern for the welfare of the miners as a whole.

Trade-union politics are as incomprehensible and, incidentally, as boring to the layman as the politics of any other mass organization. I often marvel at how much time and energy is devoted to their interpretation by highbrow writers. Considering the fact that their articles are rarely read by the labor politicians whom they are supposed to affect, and that, more often than not, by the time they appear the entire situation has been radically changed, of what conceivable value to anybody is all this printer's ink spilled out in discussions of the maneuverings of John L. Lewis at the last convention of the C.I.O., or the attempt of the West Coast seamen to unhorse Harry Bridges? Then I realize that some persons have made themselves a lifelong reputation as "brilliant analysts of the labor scene," and that they are regarded by their fellow academicians (whose entire contact with the labor movement is through New York taxi drivers or Chicago house painters) as miraculous soothsayers who have their dope straight from Sidney Hillman or Dave Dubinsky or mayhap John Llewellyn Lewis himself. And after all, when you have been at it for several years you can always write for *The Saturday Evening Post*. Then the open-shoppers and union busters will reprint your stuff as the "considered judgment of a brilliant writer who has devoted his life to a sympathetic study of the labor problem." From then on you will lead the fat life of lecturing to women's clubs on "The inside story of the C.I.O.," or writing anonymous pamphlets for the National Association of Manufacturers on the glories of the back-to-work movement.

This is not to say that there is no need for interpreting the labor movement to the public. Labor reporters of integrity such as Louis Stark, Edward Levinson, Frederick Woltman, and the veteran Charles Ervin have done a magnificent job in giving the man in the subway some inkling of what is bothering the man in the mine or the factory. But the George Sokolskys and Benjamin Stolbergs have revived, with their irresponsible tittle-tattle, the old public suspicion of all highbrows which so obsessed Sam Gompers, William Green, Frank Farrington, and the other old-timers in the A. F. of L.

Farrington, when I first worked for him, had the traditional hostility of the worker for all the scribbling tribe. His first instinct was to "throw the son of a bitch out," irrespective of whether the inquiring reporter was friend or foe. He had naturally incurred the enmity of the local Springfield reporters and the wire-service men stationed at the state's capital. Consequently the average citizen of the little city where Lincoln spent most of his life, regarded the miners' organization, which was contributing so greatly to the wealth and welfare of the community, as an alien invasion. The ordinary Springfield citizen was confirmed in this by reading the Chicago *Tribune*, which never failed to take a dirty crack at Farrington. In times of crisis this hostility on the part of the local and state press could be effectively marshaled against the Illinois miners, as we were to find out to our sorrow.

Part of my job was to break down this inimical attitude toward the press on the part of the union officials. I found at the outset that it even extended toward those whom I intended to hire as writers and editors for the union's own paper. I was all right. Farrington had known me of old as a union organizer, and though he always kidded me about my socialism, he knew I could talk the language of the rank and file. But when I suggested bringing on trained newspapermen to help our regular staff cover the important stories that were breaking all around us, he growled:

"Sure. Bring 'em on. A lot of sob sisters, male and female, tearing their shirts about the poor, dear proletariat, getting up all sorts of cock-and-bull articles about the wicked operators and the emancipation of the working classes. What the hell? Can't you write this paper yourself?"

Patiently I explained that I was not qualified as a newshawk, that I couldn't even run a typewriter, and that the reporting of the activities of a highly active organization numbering some ninety thousand very active members was no part-time job. At length, and reluctantly, he consented to let me hire one or two professional newspapermen who I knew could be trusted not to run off the reservation. But it took a long time to overcome Farrington's distrust. In one instance it came startlingly to the surface when I introduced a radical writer from New York who came on with recommendations from trusted Eastern laborites. He apparently formed his idea of coal miners from reading *The Masses*, which Morris Hillquit once called the *Vanity Fair* of the labor movement. In *The Masses* all miners were six feet two inches tall, had the chests, arms, and legs of gorillas, and were forever breaking chains around their bulging biceps.

Anyway, my journalistic discovery arrived at the staid headquarters at Springfield wearing a dark shirt open at the neck, corduroy trousers, a huge black hat of the sort that Big Bill Haywood affected on his New York trips, and smoking an evil-smelling pipe. He talked tough out of the side of his mouth, and his talk was mostly a repetition of the expletive "goddam." When he came into Farrington's spotless office he kept his hat on, spat voluminously into the cuspidor, and puffing a cloud of smoke in the direction of Frank, wanted to know what he could do to "put the goddam operators out of business." The well-groomed Farrington, who was in the midst of the most delicate negotiations with the "goddam" operators, negotiations affecting the welfare of the entire industry in the state, looked on this intruder with intense disgust. Then he sent for me. (Of course I had no idea that my man had arrived. He had decided, as he told me later, to go straight to the top, as Farrington would presumably talk his language.)

"Oscar," Farrington roared, "take this proletarian faker of yours out of here, give him a bath, and put him on the next train east."

I followed instructions. To this day I have always been sorry for that journalist, a man of real ability who had simply accepted on faith the prevalent impression of his Eastern radical friends to the effect that coal diggers always wear pit lamps, on or off duty, never wash the coal dust off their faces, and rejoice in blowing up the mine operators who give them their living.

Later on, remembering this incident, I had another writer, who had won the confidence of Farrington, line up a bunch of rank-and-file delegates to a union convention and take their pictures. McAlister Coleman's story of the convention, together with the picture showing as upstanding and well dressed a group of American citizens as you would want to see, appeared in *Collier's*.

The caption of the picture read: "We don't always wear our pit clothes." It created a mild sensation and some disillusionment among the Greenwich Village radicals. But even today a large number of young and old radicals still hold to the belief that the way to win the friendship of the worker is to talk tough, dress like a bum, and damn the bosses.

There was, too, criticism of the way in which Farrington and Lewis lived, of their custom of riding in Pullmans, stopping at good hotels and eating good food. It rarely came from the rank and file. Union members take a vicarious pride in having their officials meet the operators on the latter's level. When, in those days, Farrington, and now Lewis, come back with a contract it doesn't bother a miner a bit that his leader wears clean linen, shines his shoes, or even puts on a little dog by quoting from Tennyson. It's only when he begins to give signs of being softened by his "upper-crust" contacts that there is grumbling among the rank and file over the official expense accounts.

Springfield, however, with its efficient, smooth-running headquarters in the heart of an historic American city, a city of considerable natural beauty marred chiefly by the presence of the state legislature, was only a part of the whole Illinois mine-field picture. There was another side in that "Egypt" to which I referred at the beginning of this chapter. Whenever I had to go down to the southern Illinois fields I felt as though I were definitely passing from one civilization to another older and darker one.

Historians have long debated how southern Illinois got the name of "Egypt." There is the suggestion of the Nile delta in the triangle of lowlands bordered by the Ohio and Mississippi rivers. Again, there is the story of how the good crops in the south saved the state from famine when the northern crops failed. At any rate, Egypt it is, and darkest Egypt as well. In Chicago and Springfield I heard the natives of Egypt contemptuously referred to as "swamp angels." I was warned against the ferocity of the natives, urged to arm myself when I took the train from St. Louis on the endless trip to Williamson County in the heart of the southern coal fields. "Bloody Williamson," they called it and bloody it certainly was, though there were reasons, historic and economic, for its reputation of which the Chicago and St. Louis sophisticates knew nothing and cared less.

As far back as the Civil War, when this countryside was only sparsely settled, it was a no-man's land fought over by wandering bands of guerillas from North and South. This was a debatable territory until the war was well under way. Then General John Logan put it definitely into the Northern column, and stamped it with a stiff-necked Republicanism which it bears to this day. When the fighting ended, mountaineers from Kentucky and Tennessee swarmed over the Ohio, bringing their family feuds with them. In the library of the county seat of Williamson, at Marion, a sweet-faced librarian answered my request for a history of the locality by handing me one of the most terrible books into which I have ever delved. It was called *Bloody Williamson*, and for page after hair-raising page it was a chronicle of assault and battery, arson, mayhem and manslaughter that might have been lifted straight from a Chicago police blotter. Beginning around 1870, when it was recorded how one member of a feuding family was worshipping in a Baptist church when an "intimate friend of his" walked in and blew the worshipper's head off with a shotgun, it went down a trail dripping gore from one end of the county to another.

Feuding and farming were the two chief occupations of the post-war settlers on this territory which, while generally regarded as part of a Northern state, is geographically farther south than Louisville, Kentucky. Then, in the early 'Nineties, coal was discovered beneath the corn fields, rich veins of it, some just below the surface, and all of it easier to mine than the coal farther north around Springfield.

One of the first to exploit the new fields was Joseph Leiter, the Harvard graduate and Chicago millionaire whose wife was reputed to be the Mrs. Malaprop of her day. (It was this lady who announced that she was going to a fancy-dress ball "in the garbage of a nun.") Leiter and the miners' union arrived in Egypt at about the same time. They met head on. Leiter attempted to import strike breakers from Chicago into an organized mine. Pickets and private detectives fought it out with guns. As is usual in these cases, the worst casualties were suffered by the strike breakers, ignorant Negroes who never did find out what the shooting was all about.

Finally Leiter bowed to the militancy of the union. There were other bloody battles before Egypt was fully organized, but for years before I went down there the union had become as integral a part of the lives of those working people as were the churches and lodge halls part of the lives of the small business and professional men who lived off the miners. In fact, unionism was all the miners knew in the way of recreation, education, and social life.

The pioneer unionists were the sons of the farmers who found in the coal beneath their feet unexpected sources of income beyond anything they could gather from the corn. Then the English and Welsh, the best of the world's miners, who still form the solid backbone of the union, came in, and after them the men from southern Europe, hot-tempered and quarrelsome as the southern Americans, but like them, faithful to their union trust.

In the coal "camps," as the little towns of Egypt were still called when I left the district in the early 'Twenties, except for the Elks' halls, where the crème de la crème curdled in sullen hostility toward the "red-neck" miners, by all odds the most imposing buildings were the labor temples. Each hall was supported by the local of the United Mine Workers, and here also the organized hotel clerks, baggage smashers, jitney drivers, store employees, carpenters, barbers—in short, the entire working population of the town—held their union meetings. There was great rivalry among the union bands of the various towns. On gala days they paraded in bright red uniforms round and round the courthouse squares. May Day, the date set apart by radicals for the celebration of the coming emancipation of the workers of the world, was observed with enormous barbecues and the voluminous speeches of visiting union heroes. (No speech of less than an hour is regarded by the American miner as anything worth listening to. The average is from an hour and a half to three hours, and I have heard convention orators speak from four to five hours without appreciably wearing down their audiences.)

Eugene Debs always received a great welcome when he went down to Egypt. Mother Jones is buried in a miners' cemetery near Egypt, next the graves of the victims of the Virden massacre, another bloody affair in the history of unionism. But though radicals were invariably accorded a respectful reception, the overwhelming majority of the southern Illinois miners stayed stubbornly inside the folds of the G.O.P. By voting Republican they were able to send their men to the Springfield legislature, there to put through laws forcing the absentee mine owners to grant measures of protection for the underground workers far in advance of the other coal states. Through their full-time lobbyists they kept a close watch on the Chicago legislators sent down to do the bidding of the operators.

We socialists had early recognized this situation and had concentrated on co-operative and educational rather than political activity. But what a shock it was for the young communists, coming out from New York to talk Marxian dialectics to these widely advertised coal-field proletarians, to discover that the latter were voting for Harding and Coolidge and turning out in numbers to hear Columbia's Nicholas Murray Butler on his frequent visits to Egypt on behalf of the G.O.P.!

46

SOON after I took on the job of editor of *The Illinois Miner*, the paper was put to as severe a test as any minority organ in this country has ever had to face. In June, 1922, a bloody massacre of the mine guards and strike breakers took place in and about the mining town of Herrin in Williamson County. It shocked the nation, set the entire press of the country howling for the destruction of the Illinois miners' union, and arrayed against our organization every powerful weapon the forces of capitalism could bring into play. Led by the Chicago *Tribune*, papers from coast to coast, including at first the so-called liberal press, released a barrage against the miners. The repercussions of that blast are heard to this day. And in truth it seemed that the events of that blood-stained June morning justified every adjective employed by the editorial writers in New York, Chicago, St. Louis, and San Francisco.

What happened at Herrin? Early in 1922 the country was swept by extensive strikes. The strike was labor's only effective answer to the open-shop drive which had smashed the steel strike of 1919 and now, aided by the effects of the post-War Red scare, was everywhere going great guns. Attorney-General Daugherty, with the blessing of Warren Harding, was issuing injunctions hand over fist. Coal and iron police in Pennsylvania and West Virginia, deputy sheriffs all over the lot, Pinkertons, gun thugs and gangsters generally were beating up strikers from the railroad shops in Jersey City to the Colorado coal pits. Despite those previous charges of "separatism," the Illinois miners had walked out in a body when a national strike of the bituminous diggers had been called early in the year. But there were no strike breakers, guards, or picket lines in Illinois at the commencement of the strike. In this one-hundred-per-cent unionized territory, what operator would be foolish enough to attempt to open his struck mine? Such a thing had not been tried in the memory of this generation of diggers. The men simply took their tools out in routine fashion and went home when the strike was called. They knew that no Illinois operator would risk his economic neck by trying to buck Farrington's close-knit organization.

There was, however, one operator who had his headquarters in Cleveland and who knew nothing of conditions in Illinois. His name was William J. Lester. He thought he saw a chance to invade Illinois and, of all places, Egypt, to make some big money quick and get away with it. He acquired title to a strip mine halfway between Herrin and Marion, in Williamson County. Then he bought machinery on credit to take off the overlay of the few feet of soil that covered a thick outcropping of rich coal. He negotiated with a small independent union of steam-shovel operators, who sent him some men to run a mammoth Bucyrus shovel of the type that had been used in digging the Panama Canal. He hired for his superintendent a professional union buster who boasted of the fact that he had smashed strikes in Howat's Kansas district.

The arrival of this ominous gentleman in the sleepy little town of Marion early in April created a lot of talk. The super himself, whose leg had been shattered by a bullet in a Kansas mine war, limped around town, ostentatiously wearing a large revolver, and boasting that he was going to split the union wide open. The local in Herrin with jurisdiction over the mine became interested. They opened negotiations with the Lester representatives in the course of which it was agreed that while the organized steam-shovel men might strip the overlay, no coal whatsoever was to be loaded for shipment until the conclusion of the strike.

Although this was apparently an arrangement satisfactory to both sides, union officials soon had cause to be uneasy about the goings-on at the strip mine. Strangers began getting off the trains from the north stopping at Marion. They were met by the super in a truck closed on all sides, and hurried off to the mine. Presently mysterious crates of the sort that could contain no known kind of mine machinery appeared at the little freight station. They, too, were carted off to the strip.

Alarmed miners were soon striding into the Herrin headquarters reporting that these strangers were sent down by the Thiel detective agency and from the strike-breakers' "hotel" run by the future Vice-President of the United States, Charlie "Hell 'n' Maria" Dawes, and that the crates in reality contained ammunition, high-powered rifles, tear-gas bombs, and at least one machine gun. These rumors were verified by the story of two young diggers who had been driving their Ford down a public road near the mine. The road had been torn up by a steam shovel, completely blocking off all access to the mine. As the two miners stared at the barricade, a man carrying a high-powered rifle stepped around it and ordered them to get out of their car. He then herded them up to the office of the super inside the mine. After a display of profane fireworks, the lame super took them to an adjoining building which, the miners said, contained a veritable arsenal. The super then told them that if any goddam union diggers were caught hanging around that strip it would mean their necks. On their way out they had seen the barracks where the guards and strike breakers were living, and the elaborate commissary nearby. Evidently the Lester men had made every preparation for a long-drawn-out siege.

With the sheriff, the heads of the miners' local drove out to the mine to talk to the super. They warned him not to attempt to load coal, and ordered him to open up the public road and leave their men alone. The super laughed at them and patted his gun at his hip. Then he took them over to the arsenal and showed them his munitions. He said that he could get Lester eighteen dollars a ton for coal in Chicago and that, union or no union, he was going to get it.

For the next ten days the mine guards had their way. They drove off at the points of their guns any passer-by suspected of being a union man. They were paid ten dollars a day and given all the "white mule" they could guzzle. Under the influence of this fiery stuff they would sally out through a rear entrance to the mine and ride around the countryside shooting at the stock on surrounding farms, shouting insults at the farm wives, and generally raising hell. In this fashion they forged a strong united front among the farmers and miners, normally as antagonistic as industrial and field workers are the world over.

On the tenth day, several young miners were gathered in front of a farmhouse some half-mile distant from the mine. The super crawled up on the bank around the strip and, taking deliberate aim, fired, killing one of the union men instantly. His fellow miners propped up the body of the murdered man in the back of a Ford and drove through the camps all that afternoon, calling on the diggers to look at their dead.

In the meantime the harassed union officials had found the situation getting out of their hands. Farrington was away from the state and out of telegraphic reach. They sent off a telegram to John L. Lewis, stressing, characteristically enough, the fact that the steam shovelers were union men, but adding that they were helping load coal in violation of the agreement. Lewis, who had no first-hand knowledge of the events in remote Williamson, wired back to treat the steam shovelers as they would any other strike breakers.

This telegram, sent off in the course of a busy day's routine handling of a national strike, has since been used by the enemies of Lewis and the C.I.O. as proof that Lewis sanctioned the Herrin massacres. Westbrook Pegler, the erratic and reactionary columnist, implacable foe of the C.I.O., has referred to the Herrin massacres repeatedly as an indication of what labor would do if it achieved power. After the appearance of one of Pegler's Herrin columns, a friend of mine, a correspondent for *The Illinois Miner*, who had investigated every phase of the Herrin massacre, wrote at length to Pegler, explaining the circumstances regarding the Lewis telegram. Pegler never acknowledged receipt of this letter and continues to this day to write of the fighting at Herrin as though it were led in person by John L. Lewis. For a former sports writer, Mr. Pegler shows a strange conception of sportsmanship. . . .

Word of the shooting of the miner sent automobiles loaded with armed men toward the strip from every camp in Egypt. The miners were joined by farmers armed with every sort of weapon from squirrel rifles to shotguns. At dusk of the tenth day men were crawling toward the strip through a corn field, firing at each head that bobbed up over the mine bank. On that bank, covered with a heavy camouflage of bushes, the guards had set up a machine gun that raked the field. The miners' army was led by World War veterans, many of whom wore their old trench helmets and all of whom were versed in the latest tactics of offensive warfare. Inside the mine the strike breakers were huddled under a shelter of railroad ties to escape improvised dynamite bombs thrown over the bank by the more daring of the diggers.

All that night the sound of battle rolled across the flat lands, terrifying the inhabitants of the little towns for miles around. At daybreak a cook's apron at the end of a long pole was swung up over the bank as a token of surrender. The exultant miners started surging toward the mine, holding their weapons over their heads. When the miners were within a short distance of the bank, the guards opened up again with their machine gun. By the time the firing from the mine was finally silenced, the attackers were in a mighty ugly mood. They swarmed up over the bank and headed toward the cars, back of which stood the trembling strike breakers and their sullen guards, one of whom had been killed by his own men while attempting to escape during the night. In the lifted scoop of the giant shovel high above the mine, a guard who had been sniping at the corn field peered anxiously down. The miners dynamited the deck of the shovel, letting the scoop fall with a resounding crash. The sniper rolled out half dead. Other miners dynamited the loaded cars on the tracks running out at the rear of the mine, leaving enough of them, however, to furnish proof that Lester had violated his agreement.

Then the worn victors rounded up their captives and started them on the long, hot march to Herrin. The original intention was to bundle strike breakers and gun thugs onto the train leaving Herrin for Chicago. A mile from the mine was a little wood-lot around which ran a barbed-wire fence. By the time the woods were reached, a great throng of men and women, who had taken no part in the night's battle, came down the road from Herrin. They took over the prisoners from the miners, most of whom drifted off to get some sleep or to celebrate their victory. A huge man, waving a revolver, climbed up on a hillock and made an incendiary speech. "The hell with letting these scabs go free," he shouted, "let's stop the breed right here." He hauled the limping super from the head of the line and dragged him down a little lane out of sight of the mob. There was the sound of shots and presently the speaker came back, alone.

Thereupon the mob lined the Lester men with their backs to the barbed-wire fence and the woods, and told them they would give them a chance to run, an American adaptation of the *ley de fuego*. In a moment three hundred men were pouring bullets into the panic-stricken crowd of strike breakers and guards. Many were killed outright then and there. Others who managed to crawl through the fence ran for their lives through the woods with bullets whipping around them. A few hid in the marshes by a little lake and eventually got back to Chicago. There was a brutal man hunt for some hours after that, with throat slitting and hanging all through the woods. Seven of the strike breakers were taken into Herrin, forced to crawl for a long distance on their hands and knees to the cemetery, and there shot down like animals, in the presence of cheering schoolchildren, who ran to get fresh cartridges for their men folk. In all, twenty-three guards and scabs were killed and many others wounded.

All this was bad enough, but the first story to come out of Herrin, sent by an Associated Press correspondent and written in the first person, as though the reporter had been an eye-witness to these horrors, made it appear that the killings were deliberately planned by the officials of the miners' union. The highlight of his story was a gruesome description of the cutting of the throat of a scab on the road to Herrin. The correspondent told how he had run to a farmhouse for water for the dying man and how a miner had kicked the glass out of the correspondent's hand, growling, "That son of a bitch ain't going to need no water where he's going to." On the strength of this macabre tale the reporter was rewarded with a job on the Chicago *Tribune*. Later, at the trials of the miners, where the reporter appeared as a star witness for the prosecution, the defense had no trouble in proving conclusively that the correspondent had arrived in Williamson hours after the last body had been taken to the temporary morgue in Herrin.

As a matter of fact, no newspaperman saw anything of the killings. But this did not prevent correspondents from indulging in the wildest yarns, all to the effect that innocent men had been done to death at the command of the leaders of the United Mine Workers of America. A notable exception was the coverage of Thoreau Cronin of the ultraconservative New York *Sun*. He not only gave his readers something of the background of the affair, but took pains to interview the Lester strike breakers who had escaped and who were bitter in their denunciation of the Cleveland operator for sending them into a union territory at the time of a national strike with assurances that there was "no labor trouble in Williamson." As for the guards who got away, they regarded it as all in the course of a day's work and made no bones of the fact that they had been sent in to terrorize the miners.

The Chicago *Tribune* was printing a map of Williamson County each day on its front page under the caption: "Wipe out this blot." Chambers of commerce all over the state raised special funds for the hiring of special prosecutors to go down to Williamson and hang the miners. On the heels of the indictments found against two hundred natives, the bulk of them members of the miners' union, a distinguished legal staff from Chicago, headed by Attorney-General Brundage and heeled with the funds of open-shoppers, arrived in Marion where the trials were to be held. After them came correspondents from six of the leading newspapers of the country and all the wire services.

The only newspaper at the beginning of the trials which attempted to give a picture of the situation as a whole was *The Illinois Miner*. We supplied a regular service to the handful of struggling sheets euphemistically called "the labor press." We prepared a pamphlet called *The Other Side of Herrin*, which we put on the desk of every important editor in the country. We showed the correspondents how the miners lived and how they worked in constant fear of sudden, crashing death. We told them something of the history of Egypt, and they came to see for themselves how those people, cut off from the main stream of American civilization, set out on these desolate flat lands with their monotonous repetition of corn field and coal tipple, had come to look upon their union as their mighty shield and buckler against a hostile world. We even took the scribes down into a mine, and took them up again with some speed in response to their earnest request to get back to the sunlight. Little by little this educational work showed its effects in the dispatches sent off from the courthouse. In fact, one reporter leaned so far to the side of the defense that he was reprimanded by his indignant editor, who reminded him by wire that he had not been sent there to exonerate the miners, but to execute them.

The trials of a dozen leading union men picked from the mass of those indicted dragged out through a rainy autumn and a hail-swept winter until well into the following spring. Under the able direction of Angus Kerr, chief counsel for the miners, the entire picture of the Williamson scene was painted not only for the jury but for the outside world as well. With all the array of the open-shop legal brain trust against him, Kerr and his assistant, Acquilla Lewis, succeeded in getting every miner off scot free. No juror in Williamson would believe for one moment the testimony of such miserable mercenaries as came down from the Chicago detective and fink agencies. Ultimately a Terre Haute paper remarked of the result of the trials: "One more acquittal in the Herrin cases and the rumors that there was any violence down that way will be permanently set to rest."

But the verdicts of the juries were understandable enough to anyone who knew the fierce provincialism of the Egyptians. To the traditional hostility of these despised "swamp angels" for city slickers, there was added the prejudice created by the activities of the chambers of commerce. And to cap it all was the campaign conducted by the Chicago *Tribune* against Williamson as a whole. If anything were needed to make certain verdicts of "not guilty," the fact that "The World's Greatest Newspaper" was backing the prosecution was a clincher. Among the working people of Illinois all that the *Tribune* has to do is to support some cause and every horny hand lines up dead against that cause.

Though the Illinois miners came through those crucial days without ever going outside the state organization with appeals for funds to defray the heavy expenses of the defense, it was evident enough that something more than driving scabs out of the mine fields was needed if the organization were to survive. Two enemies more dangerous than chambers of commerce, gun thugs and labor-baiting editorials were already at work tearing down the sturdy edifice which the pioneer unionists had built in Illinois. These were the failure to organize the fields south of the Ohio river, and the incredibly rapid advance of mine mechanization. Though today the Southern fields are organized, the

"Fordization" of the mines goes on apace, with that tragic toll of human wastage which is the inevitable result of what the high-brows call "technological unemployment." The cheery optimism with which some economists tell us that in the "long run" tech-nological improvements will work out for the benefit of the laborer becomes a ghastly farce to anyone who has seen, as I have, hordes of out-of-work miners wandering in dull despair across the abandoned coal fields. There is no "long run" for these men thrown out of employment by the introduction of power-driven undercutting machines, conveyors, and the rest of the labor-saving gadgets. Long before the end of their "long run" is in sight these workless miners, the "shock troops of the American labor movement," will be put underground for the last time beneath the shallow earth of paupers' cemeteries.

This spectre of increasing unemployment that haunts the coal mines of America is not going to be laid by any halfway meas-ures. It takes an unusual degree of courage and intelligence to tackle this key problem. In my opinion, and in the opinion of every serious student of the question, we will get nowhere until we recognize the fact that coal is the natural heritage of the whole people; that Nature or God, whichever you will, did not bury it away aeons ago for the benefit of any small group of profit-hungry men like those who today are laying waste our common birthright. When this truth is admitted, and only then, we shall be able to plan the operation of our mines from a civilized view-point. We must declare war upon the cruel waste of our coal and and human beings who mine it, but where shall we find volunteers for this war? Among the wise men of the East? Don't make me laugh. Among the miners and their union leaders? No. The leaders are up to their collective necks in union politics and in-ternecine warfare. They have abandoned even the pitifully inade-quate educational efforts that were begun some years ago to en-lighten the rank and file.

This coal question is just another headache which I bequeath to posterity, with the warning, however, that unless posterity does a lot better than its immediate ancestors, the black basis of our industrial civilization is on its way to catastrophic collapse.

Elsewhere I have said my say about factional rows inside the labor, liberal, and radical movement, and remarked that nothing is more boring to the general reader than the tortuous details of these rows. Therefore I cannot with consistency inflict upon such patient readers as have trailed thus far with me the details of the struggle for power between Lewis and Farrington and the schism in the United Mine Workers of America which followed.

It is sufficient to say here that, in ill health, and worn out with this internal bickering, Farrington, a few months before his announced resignation as president of the Illinois miners was to take effect in 1931, signed a contract with the Peabody Coal Company, the largest and most powerful operators in his state, whereby he would become the company's "labor adviser" at a salary of twenty-five thousand a year. Lewis was quick to take advantage of the publication of this damning contract and force Farrington out of the labor movement forever. In his place, Lewis set up a provisional government of his friends in Illinois. For a year the insurgent rank and file fought Lewis in the camps and the courts of the state. Much blood was spilled, a vast amount of money expended, many lawyers grew rich through appearing in the courts for one side or the other.

I was active in organizing the opposition to Lewis, who at that time seemed to me to give every indication of suffering from a rule-or-ruin complex. I am not ashamed of the part I played. However, Lewis is, again in my opinion, on the right track today. The industrial unionism for which the C.I.O. stands is the form of mass unionism for which old radicals had been fighting since the turn of the century. It is the only conceivably effective weapon with which to fight the tight organization of the bosses in heavy industry. It may be ironical that the same John L. Lewis, who was ruthlessly booting out from his union spokesmen for industrial unionism as late as 1931, should now, in 1940, be sending these same spokesmen out as his trusted lieutenants to organize mass unions. But the ironic touch has never been lacking in labor history.

Frank Farrington is dead. He died with the objurgations of many honestly indignant progressives ringing in his weary ears. So far as I am concerned, he was my friend, and the friend of the causes which I held most dear, in a time of dire need. I leave the stone-throwing to those in the liberal and labor movements who have never sinned.

Book Nine

NO THOROUGHFARE
TO UTOPIA

47

IN my first years as editor of *The Illinois Miner* it became clear to me that, no matter what was done, not more than perhaps fifty thousand out of the then ninety thousand union members would find permanent employment in the mines of Illinois. What an incurable optimist I was! Today not more than thirty thousand are employed, and these considerably less than full time. Why, I asked myself, let these men and their families decay in dying mining towns, waiting to hear mine whistles that were silenced forever? Outside of our English, Scotch, Welsh, and the small number of German miners, the overwhelming majority of the others were not born miners, but rather sons of the soil. So why not restore them to the soil?

There still was around a million dollars in the treasury of the union. We were paying the widows of demised miners a three-hundred-dollar death benefit. The widows never got it. The undertakers did. When that death benefit was a hundred dollars, funerals cost one hundred. When we raised it to two hundred funerals cost two hundred. When we raised it to three hundred, miners' funerals cost three hundred dollars. Well then, why not take some of the money in the union treasury and buy land for our unemployed never-again-to-be-employed brothers, then, that done, rob the undertaker of the dead miner by giving the three hundred dollars as grub stake to a live miner?

A truly brilliant idea and quite a few jumps ahead of the New

Deal. I talked my associates among the Illinois miners into the notion. I always could talk anybody into almost any notion, provided I had first firmly convinced myself that it was a good one. And so, as the only agriculture expert of the miners' union, I set forth in search of the right location on which to rear my subsistence-homestead Utopia.

After a search extending as far as old Mexico, I selected a fifty-five hundred acre cut-over tract in the Mississippi delta, near Lake Providence, Louisiana. Lake Providence is a beautiful lake full of fish, with clear water, bordered by cypress, pin oak and magnolia trees. However, don't think it was the beauty of that lake and my love of fishing that captured my heart. They were contributing factors, no doubt, but man does not live on beauty and fish alone. To subsist, even on a subsistence homestead, he must have good soil under his feet. Neither did I trust myself to be a soil expert. I had three soil experts with me—two from the Louisiana agricultural college, the other from the colonization department of the Missouri Pacific Railroad, which passes through that country.

In addition, I had it on the authority of one H. H. Bennett, of the soil department in the Department of Agriculture of the U. S. A. (now chief of soil conservation of the U. S. A.), that in all this wide world there was no other great body of land exceeding in productivity and fertility the soil of the Tensas Basin of the Mississippi bottoms.

Acting on the advice of my array of eminent experts I paid down the earnest money, solemnly contracted to pay the sum of five thousand dollars within a certain short period, and the balance in five annual installments of ten thousand each. To the credit of my experts I must say they did not misrepresent the land. It was all they recommended it to be. My troubles came from sources that had nothing to do with the quality of that soil. Moreover, once one of these troubles appeared, it wasn't long until all of its friends, relatives and neighbors followed.

Two Views of Oscar Ameringer's Resettlement Project in Louisiana

THE AUTHOR IN HIS DEN

(The pictures over the desk include many of Mr. Ameringer's closest friends. In the top row, at the left, is a photograph of a bust of Charles Ervin by Jo Davidson. Next to it hangs a portrait of the author's daughter, Susan, aged one, painted by the author at the age of sixty-two. Then come two photographs, one of Mark Twain, the other of Edward Bellamy. In the next row, from left to right, are Eugene V. Debs, Charney Vladeck, Victor Berger and Henry George. And the picture at the bottom, in the center of his desk, is of the author's son, Carl.)

The first trouble I ran into was that, when I returned to Springfield with my glad tidings, our legal department held that under our charter the union could not go into the real-estate business outside of the State of Illinois. Well, what of it? I had only five thousand dollars to raise for the present, and the next ten thousand not sooner than a year from now. A year is a long time. All kinds of things happen in a year. As the intelligent reader who has followed me thus far will already have surmised, I raised the five thousand. The land was ours, except for the fifty thousand still owing on it.

The next trouble did not originate in Illinois. It originated in the thirty-one states which, in the early spring of 1927, contributed their surplus rainfall to the Mississippi flood of that year. The union could not go into the colonization business under its fraternal charter. But it certainly could donate money out of the treasury to assist brothers who had put it there to gain a new foothold in life. But now we couldn't persuade the brothers to settle on the land designated for them. The big flood scared the very life out of them.

Shortly after the big flood the union got into a six-months' strike. By the time *that* was over, we were in the midst of the internal war with John L. Lewis. By the time that was over, the union treasury was as bare as Mother Hubbard's cupboard, our membership completely pauperized, my friends out of office, I no longer editor of *The Illinois Miner*, and forty thousand dollars still to pay on that land. Of the additional ten thousand we had managed to pay, I had raised five thousand and my guardian angel the other five through the sordid instrumentality of a plutocratic oil corporation which suspected a fortune under the surface of our tract. For the second, or was it the third? time in my life, I found myself "financially embarrassed," if that be the right term for dead broke, out of work, and forty thousand dollars in debt. I was getting up in the world. It takes a financial genius to accumulate forty thousand dollars' worth of liabilities.

How I got through those first four years of the temporary business depression that started in 1929 and is still going strong without losing that forty-thousand-dollar liability is still a mystery to me. However, help was near. The lynching bee of 1932, sometimes formally described as a presidential election, swept the New Deal into power. There was great talk about rural rehabilitation, subsistence homesteads, of jobless men and manless soil and so forth. All this was in my line. Was I not the father of subsistence homesteads for unemployed proletarians? Better still, the New Deal wave had washed a good number of my forward-looking friends into power—or at least, almost power. I packed my carpet bag and went to Washington.

One of the first New Dealers I called on was Harry Hopkins. Sure, my project was exactly what they were looking for. Of course Harry couldn't attend to all details. He referred me to a Colonel Westervelt who would take care of me. Colonel Westervelt was deeply impressed. I had made a fine start. My project was exactly what they were looking for. Of course, the colonel could not attend to all details. He referred me to a Mr. Nelson, in New Orleans, in charge of Louisiana projects. For good measure he dictated in my presence a letter to Mr. Nelson in which he strongly recommended both me and my project. While still in Colonel Westervelt's office I received a phone call from my old friend, Jacob Baker, then *alter ego* of Harry Hopkins. When I saw him, he added his recommendation of me and my project to that of Colonel Westervelt. At last I was in the hands of friends, and fortified by that assurance I repacked my carpet bag and went to New Orleans.

Mr. Nelson of New Orleans had the accumulated recommendations lying on his desk when I was ushered into his presence. Unfortunately, Mr. Nelson was in no position to act on my project. Projects, in that particular corner of Louisiana, were in the hands of the district office in Shreveport. So I went to Shreveport, where the presiding elder was all afire for my project but very sorry he couldn't do anything for me, as the matter was in the hands of their county manager, of East Carroll Parish, Louisiana, in which my project was located. I knew there was no use consulting that gentleman. I had consulted him before. There was but one thing that good man was empowered to do, and that was to refer the whole thing back to Washington, via Shreveport, Little Rock, and New Orleans.

But why worry? I had other friends in Washington. One of them was chief of the planning department of the Subsistence Homestead Corporation. I returned to Washington and saw him. He was a doctor of philosophy, of course; all chiefs in the Washington of that epoch were. I couldn't see how doctors of philosophy were better qualified to judge land, build houses and barns, than practical farmers, bricklayers and carpenters; however, my Ph.D. friend, Bill, had some redeeming qualities. He grew up on a farm, knew how to hitch up horses, hold plow handles, mow hay, husk corn, milk cows, and twist the tails of cream separators. In addition, he had built houses, had experience in co-operative farm enterprises, and was well acquainted with the soil and the people of the locality in which my project was located. Yes, he told me, I had a most excellent project.

"Sure," I replied. "Now, Bill, send somebody down there, look the tract over and then, if found suitable, title good and price right, you buy it and go ahead with the project."

Bill allowed that this undoubtedly would make good sense. But the government wouldn't do business that way. The first step toward a project was to get up a project book. When Bill showed me one of the four hundred and seventy project books already on hand, I almost fainted. "Why, Bill, it will take me months, and goodness knows how many hundred dollars, to get up a project book like that."

"Yes," admitted Bill. "It will require all that and perhaps more. But no project book, no project."

As a guide, time, and step saver, Bill handed me an outline of the project book demanded. It was composed by a Columbia Ph.D. specializing in higher agriculture. Why this influx into

Washington, D. C., of Ph.D.'s from Columbia University in the City of New York at Broadway and 116th Street? Why particularly this deluge of the doctorate into the Department of Agriculture? Before Columbia moved uptown to its present site (formerly occupied by the Bloomingdale Insane Asylum), the countryside thereabout consisted chiefly of rocks, truck gardens and far-ranging goats. It was never, so far as I understand, what might be called a natural granary. Columbia, once described as "a mausoleum completely surrounded by factories," was hardly a likely breeding ground for either farm products or farm experts. Under the leadership of Raymond Moley, however, the rush from Columbia's campus to Washington's public buildings overflowed into the Department of Agriculture so that in the honeymoon days of the New Deal the visitor to the Department everywhere tripped over the canes and spats of pedigreed Columbia farm experts, and the salutation, "Good morning, Doctor," was as common in the corridors as the greeting, "Good morning, colonel," is common in Louisville, Kentucky. When I had been roaming those vast and windy corridors long enough for my face to become familiar, even I was hailed as "doctor."

According to the outline, I had only to compile a comprehensive encyclopedia of the soil, climate, agriculture, history, geology, and meteorology of the Mississippi Basin, with special relation to East Carroll Parish, where my project was to be located. Included in the data demanded by the Government of the United States before it would even look at my project were the following:

> Chemical composition of soil
> Low temperature, high temperature, mean temperature by
> months, for the last ten years
> Annual rainfall per month (ten years)
> First day of frost (twelve years)
> Last day of frost (thirteen years)
> Local conditions

Educational facilities
Population movement
Church facilities
Kinds of crops
Where sold
Average price of crops (if any)
Death rates
Condition of roads and bridges
General transportation facilities
Analysis of drinking water certified by two reputable physi-
 cians
Status of farm and labor market
Birth rates and why
Distance from centers of population and how to get there

In short, there were so many questions in that outline that if
the rugged individualists who redeemed the North American
wilderness had been compelled to answer one per cent of them
before getting down to ground clearing, the site of Columbia's
campus would still resound with the war whoops of the local
Iroquois.

"But, Bill," I protested to my Ph.D. friend, "would it not be
more sensible to send a practical farmer down there to look the
country over? Then, if everything is found satisfactory, price ac-
ceptable and title good, you buy the land and get up your own
project book. After all," I continued, "if I wanted to sell you
people a lot for a skyscraper you wouldn't expect me to supply
blueprints, detailed drawings and estimates. You'd buy the lot
first, and then call in your own architects and contractors."

Bill admitted this was one way to do it. But the government
did not indulge in haphazard business like that. Besides, he did
not think he could locate a practical farmer among the legion of
Ph.D.'s who were directing the back-to-the-land movement of
the New Deal.

The first hard knot I was called upon to untie was to furnish correct data concerning the number and kind of families I intended to settle on the five thousand acres of land the government had not yet seen. And from where would I get them? I allowed there were some fifty thousand coal miners in Illinois alone who hadn't seen a pay day for years. Many of them could easily be induced to go back to Mother Earth and Father Eats. I also stated that I had it on the authority of another Ph.D. that there were ten thousand Oklahoma farm families whose farms had been blown from under their feet by dust storms, and that most of them were too poor to follow the farmsteads down the wind to Atlantic City and parts east. But all this was mere hearsay. The government demanded official data in black and white.

Eventually I discovered the official data sequestered in the atlas compiled by the Rural Rehabilitation Administration, on whose advice I had made the round trip from Washington, D. C., to New Orleans, Shreveport, Lake Providence and back. As usual, I had been in error regarding the number of Oklahoma families whose farms had migrated to the distant east. Instead of ten thousand families, it was thirty thousand.

"Fine," I said. "Now put those figures in writing on official stationery, and my troubles are ended." But alas, the custodian of the atlas could not do that. He was not allowed to give out information. It might lose him his job. Besides, there was a later survey showing that sixty thousand Oklahoma farm families had lost their real estate by way of meteorological disturbances. This was better still. But again, the custodian would not even let me make a copy of the official data contained in Atlas II. As it turned out, I never did succeed in getting that data. Wherever John Steinbeck may have secured the number of "Okies" described in his The Grapes of Wrath, I am sure he did not get it from one of the Ph.D.'s of the Rural Rehabilitation Administration in Washington.

I struck a still more serious snag when it came to preparing a budget, showing in detail what it would cost to settle a family on forty acres of the kind of land the government refused to look at. What made the budget almost as difficult to balance as the national budget was the fact that there are many kinds of farm edifices—barns, chicken coops, sheep pens and the homes of cows, mules, and pigs. Some of them cost more than others. Others are too cheap at any price. My own notion about a subsistence-homestead habitation was a modest four-room frame cottage, with a toilet in the backyard and water in the cow lot. I had built some similar residences myself. They cost six hundred dollars, and some of my neighbors down in luxurious Louisiana haven't spoken to me since, on the grounds that I was "spoiling po' whites," building better homes for them than most near-by planters sported.

In the opinion of the Ph.D. colonizers, my six-hundred-dollar palaces were not good enough for homeless dust-farmers, landless share croppers and jobless coal diggers. Nothing but four-room cottages, with screened porches, electric lights, bath, indoor toilet and hot-and-cold running water would do.* This naturally complicated matters a bit. Before I got through with the budget I had made an intensive study of low-cost housing in England, Germany, Sweden and Norway, and had collected a library of plans and estimates from an army of architects, building-material caterers, bathroom-fixture manufacturers and private and public utility corporations, supplemented by charts setting forth the wage differentials between Northern and Southern, union and non-union building-trade mechanics.

When the returns, and I, were all in, the cost of settling a family was four thousand dollars, or some three thousand, nine hundred more than the First Families of the land had on their persons when they landed at Plymouth Rock.

The next serious question I had to answer was how people who

---

* When I consulted some of my prospective resettlers, a considerable divergence of views developed. The women agreed it would be awfully nice to have running water in the kitchen. On the other hand, nearly all their husbands opined that running water in cow-lot and barn would be preferable, inasmuch as it is quite a chore pumping water for the stock. However, both sexes joined in the opinion that having the privy in the house wouldn't be sanitary.

had lost the land their fathers had got for nothing might somehow subsist, starting with a debt of four thousand dollars. Working out a scientific budget on farm income is not as easy a matter as some people think. There are droughts, floods, hailstorms, chinch bugs, Hessian flies, cattle ticks, hog cholera, germs, mites, boll weevils, army worms and other acts of God which are liable to throw the best farm budget out of kilter. Nor do farm prices stay put, as they ought. When crops are good the farmers get nothing for them, while when farm prices are good the farmer usually has nothing to sell.

The soil the government was not yet sure of buying was especially adapted to the raising of corn, alfalfa, oats, cotton, and many nutritious grasses. I always regarded cow, sow, and hen as the holy trinity of farming, and I knew from experience that everything that goes into the belly of man and beast grows luxuriantly on that alluvial soil in the Mississippi bottoms. In fact, in all my life I have never seen another farming region where soil and climate are kinder to man than is the delta of the Father of Waters.

However, there still remained the problem of earning two hundred dollars cash per annum to pay interest and amortization on four thousand dollars, to say nothing of shoes, clothing, schoolbooks, medical service, spiritual consolation and related luxuries. In order to supply these incidentals, my budget specified cotton as a cash crop. But at this point a whole swarm of new problems emerged.

First, in view of the fact that the government was paying cotton raisers to plow under cotton, and not raise it, how much of the snowy staple would my prospective subsistence homesteader be permitted to raise?

Second, how much would the Triple A pay them per pound of cotton sold, plowed under, or not raised?

Third, how many pounds of cotton can be grown on an unspecified number of acres of land?

Etc.

Fortunately, I never received a definite official answer to the first of these moot questions, which made answers to the others nonessential. Some of the Ph.D.'s I consulted allowed that my potential subsistence homesteaders might plant three acres of cotton. More liberal-minded Ph.D.'s opined they could plant as much as ten acres. One Ph.D. positively knew they could plant eight acres. But as he was not permitted to divulge that valuable information in writing, and I had promised him I would not divulge it orally, it didn't help me at all.

However, it's a long lane that has no turning, and so in the course of human events my project book was finished, pronounced satisfactory, and blessed with the recommendation of the Chief of the Planning Department of the Subsistence Homestead Corporation. Now forward with the project!

Not so fast. The project book would now go to the Interior Department, presided over by Mr. Ickes. Mr. Ickes is a most conscientious public servant. Unless he fully approved the most minute details of my project, or anybody else's project, it would be turned down cold. However, if he approved, it would then go to the Department of Justice for scrutiny of its legal aspect. Legal aspects found satisfactory, it would then go to Comptroller McCarl, who, finding the project worthy in every respect, would issue the check for my part of it.

While I was awaiting latest reports on the prospects of my project, I learned the mournful news that the funds of the Subsistence Homestead Corporation had evaporated in the process of collecting project books. Fortunately, Congress was in session. No doubt it would vote the four-billion-dollar appropriation requested by the President. Out of this, the Subsistence Homestead Corporation would receive a hundred and thirty-five million, out of which, if everything went right, and nothing worse showed up, I would get the check.

Well, everything comes to him who waits, and doesn't die waiting. Congress voted the four billion requested by the President. Money galore for no end of projects. The only fly in the ointment was that, in the meantime, the President had abolished the

Subsistence Homestead Corporation and turned the job of settling some three millions of poor but deserving jobless proletarians and landless peasants over to the newly created Resettlement Administration.

Well, it might have been worse. I had friends in court. And one of them was no other than Dr. T. I hastened to him. Sure, he would help. But at present, all was confusion. First job was a new set-up. When I heard that word "set-up," cold gooseflesh crept up my back. By that time I had learned all about it. The government would lease one more big building in which to set up the new set-up. Old partitions would be torn out—new partitions put in. Desks, swivel chairs, filing cases, clerks, stenographe. ', private secretaries, would be installed in the outer offices to conspire against folk who came to discuss business with the Ph.D.'s occupying the inner offices.

That done, the aggregated set-uppers would sit down to get up set-ups. When one set-upper had set up his particular set-up, he would pass it down the line for comments, corrections, and suggestions. Each set-upper would do likewise. When the set-up had made its destined pilgrimage and had returned to its particular author and there was nothing left of the original, each and all set-uppers would sit down to get up new set-ups.

But maybe it served me right. For thirty-five years I had advocated the common ownership and democratic management of all the means of production and here was the start of it. What right had I, an old Red, to scorn red tape?

All was not lost yet. I still had those friends in court. Dr. T. advised me to get my project book out of the demised Subsistence Homestead Corporation before Mr. Ickes got his clutches on it and used it to show how he had forestalled another raid on the treasury of the U. S. A. Also, none of the four hundred and seventy project books slumbering in the library of the Subsistence Homestead Corporation had as yet been transferred to the Resettlement Administration. "First come, first served, you know."

I knew.

Now the gentle reader may think it would be no trick at all

to take a project book from number so and so, New York Avenue, to K and Thirteenth Streets, especially as the distance is only a few miles and taxi fare no more than two bits, including a five-cent tip for the driver. But right there the gentle reader would be wrong. It wasn't easy at all. The death warrant had been read to the Subsistence Homestead Corporation, but execution had not yet taken place. Each condemned doctor was hanging like grim death to one of the four hundred and seventy project books. So long as one of them had a project book there was hope for him. Someone in authority might inquire what was in his particular project book, whereupon he could blossom forth with information and—perhaps—secure another job.

It took me two weeks to rescue my project book from the poor dragon guarding it, and it required a special messenger from the Resettlement Administration to get that far. However, my project was now safe in the hands of the new set-up and all I could do was sit down and wait. After waiting for two weeks, I grew a little impatient. After the third week I grew wrathful, went to my friends in court and secured a peremptory order from the chief of the new set-up that whosoever was in possession of my project book should immediately sit up and read it, or learn the reason why.

There was consternation in the halls of the new set-up. They had lost my precious book. But patience, heart. All things come to him who waits, or have I said that before? Anyhow, a week later, my project was found under some papers on the desk of the chief of the set-uppers. Now action followed upon action. When I next entered the new set-up territory, a conclave of Ph.D.'s was reading my book. I didn't want the doctors to hurry too much. Give the boys a chance to study my project thoroughly. On my return two days later I was gleefully informed by the assembled doctors that the project book was already on the way to Fayette-ville, Arkansas, where the regional office of the Resettlement Administration would take prompt action.

It's a long way from Washington, D. C., to Fayetteville, Arkansas, by way of Oklahoma City. I was bound not to let my project book out of sight again, but I had to return to Oklahoma City for my car. It was mighty lucky I went in my car to Fayetteville, because when I got there the regional office of the Resettlement Administration had moved to Little Rock, and train connections between Fayetteville and Little Rock, Arkansas, are none too good.

When I arrived at the new regional set-up at Little Rock they were still tearing out old and putting in new partitions. Yes, things were a little upsetting, vouchsafed the private secretary of the regional chief of the new regional set-up. But regarding my project book, everything was O.K. It was already on the way to the state office of the new set-up in New Orleans.

No, I did not go to New Orleans. I'd been there once before on the same mission. I knew that project book would sooner or later find its way back to Washington, and it did.

At long last, my project received thumbs down, on the part of one of the late Joe Robinson's political agronomists, on the ground that the soil of our tract would not raise vegetables. I had shown the agronomist vegetables growing on that soil. I had shown him no end of glass jars in which our women had canned vegetables they themselves had grown on that soil. I even offered to eat some of those vegetables—raw, canned, or cooked, to convince him they were not made of plaster of Paris, or papier-mâché. All in vain.

Instead of taking over my beloved project, the Resettlement Administration purchased a plantation adjoining our tract on the east and south. The Absom, Crump, and Wyn plantation the R.A. purchased was one of the best-managed in that territory. It was occupied by some three hundred and fifty Negro families, many of whom had lived and worked on it all their lives. These three hundred and fifty desettled Negro families were removed in favor of some hundred and twenty white families, who, I am sure, will have no trouble raising vegetables, since the Mr. Crump of the firm of Absom, Crump, and Wyn is none other than Democratic Boss Crump of Memphis, Tennessee. As I said, "Nothing like having friends in court."

But how about my own project? Well, it's still projecting. Around a hundred families are living on it, raising cotton, corn, cows, pigs, chickens—and vegetables. When I last saw them, they all looked fairly well dressed and well fed. There is a good school, which even boasts a small library. The neat, white-painted cottages are surrounded by flower and vegetable gardens. It really is a nice place, my garden home down in luxurious Louisiana. I am rather proud of it—especially of our children with their bright eyes, red cheeks and plump legs. Sunshine and plenty of milk and vegetables did it. It was, I admit, an almost heartbreaking job. I'm not through yet. It isn't all I had hoped it would be. But where twelve years ago there were eight square miles of jungle, populated by wild cats, hoot owls, and skunks, there are now laughing fields and smiling children. Especially am I proud of some twenty colored families, for whom I had reserved forty acres each. They have not yet won their war against the jungle and poverty, but they will.

On November 19, 1939, Freda, our daughter, Susan, and I went down there to celebrate emancipation day in terms of forty acres and a mule. We brought ice cream and watermelons. They brought us flowers and vegetables, and sang Negro spirituals. Their preacher preached a sermon on the blessing of work. Fred Holt, one time secretary-treasurer of the Oklahoma-Arkansas Miners, now a farmer and a county commissioner, made a speech, and I made a speech, and everybody was happy.

Besides, I still cherish that precious project book. It may not be as valuable as Morgan's Gutenberg Bible. But even a three-thousand-dollar book is nothing to sneeze at.

Book Ten

WHEN ALL IS SAID

48

THE somber shadows of the dying days of the Old Deal covered the land. Out of the murk and mist rose the specter of abundance accompanied by dire want. Wherever the eye fell, it beheld an incredible wealth of the things that make life livable, lovable, secure, and beautiful. Surrounded by this wealth were men struggling for the basic necessities of brute existence. The writers of Ecclesiastes were wrong. There *was* some new thing under the sun, something the world had never seen before: want in the midst of plenty. Even stranger still, want begot by plenty.

For aeons man had striven for the stuff whereof life, liberty, and happiness are shaped. For this he had fashioned weapons, and tools; had harnessed beast, wind, water, fire, and finally lightning. For this he had spanned mighty rivers, tunneled mountain ranges, crossed oceans. In quest of this he had spun philosophical systems, founded great religions, devised codes of law and government.

In 1932, standing on an elevation overlooking the Columbia river, I observed a pall of smoke hiding the panorama of snow-crested mountains. To my question, my companion explained that that was the smoke from forest fires. He added, "They've been burning all this summer and fall."

"But," I asked, "is there no way of putting them out?"

"Sure there is," my companion replied, "but what's the use? No sooner is one put out than they start another one."

"Who is 'they'?" I asked.

"Why, busted farmers and jobless lumberjacks. The government is paying fifty cents an hour for fighting forest fires, and this is the only way they can make their living."

The floor of the orchard was strewn with rose-red Oregon apples, stinking to high heaven, polluting the air for miles around. "Why are these tons of good Oregon apples left to rot, instead of being gathered, crated and shipped to market?" I asked my Virgil.

"Because it costs forty cents to pick, pack and ship a crate of Oregon apples, whereas the price in the market is less than thirty cents."

The Sunday-Daily Oregonian, staunch, stodgy, and Republican, prints a solemn editorial bemoaning the wholesale slaughter of mother sheep by their rightful owners. The reason for this wholesale slaughter of ewes, I learn, is threefold. It costs more to ship a mother sheep to market than it pays at the market. The sheepmen are too poor to buy the necessary feed to see their wards through the long Oregon winter. But it is against the laws of the State of Oregon to let sheep starve to death.

In the rear of a Seattle, Washington, market, I see pale, shabbily garbed mothers and children fighting for decayed vegetables thrown out by worried greens-merchants. Near Bakersfield, in California, ragged men mounted on caterpillar tractors are pulling out fruit trees to make room for the planting of five-cent cotton on land once sold for five hundred dollars an acre. In the alley below the window of my hotel in the City of Angels I see children quarreling over the spill of a garbage barrel.

Highway 66, crawling over the staked plains toward the land of promise, is already covered with hitch-hikers, forlorn jalopies, devastated trucks, and here and there remnants of a covered wagon, bearing the army of refugees from the marching desert.

Mounds of wheat, whitewashed by flocks of blackbirds, are rotting in Kansas fields.

In Wichita the law-and-order forces of Kansas are breaking up a bread riot.

Liquid gold from a new oil field is selling at ten cents a barrel, drinking water for twenty-five cents a barrel.

At a filling station in the Texas Panhandle, a well-dressed woman in an almost new Packard, with a crying child at her side and a deathly pale husband wrapped in a blanket on the rear seat, is pleading with the filling-station man to let her go. They are, she explains between sobs, not gasoline tramps, but respectable property owners of Miami, Florida. The crash wiped out their equity in real estate. Bank failure had wiped out their last cash. "For God's sake, man, let me go. We are down to sixty cents and still a thousand miles to go to my mother's ranch near Santa Barbara. She lost father's life insurance in a bank failure a few days after she received it. But there are fruit, vegetables, chickens, some cows and pigs on mother's ranch. If we can get there we can manage somehow." Then, stepping on the gas, she drives off with filled radiator, splash pan and tank.

"That's the third one today," says the filling-station man despairingly. "The next fine dame that comes along has got to show me the cash before she gets the goods, same as I make the Okies do."

"You're the very man I'm looking for," a cow man told me at an auto camp a few hundred miles further east. "Oh, you don't know me from Adam's off ox. But I know you. I used to hear you make Socialist speeches down in the Comanche pasture after the opening. I always took you for a damned fool preaching dividing up and social revolution. This country was good enough for me, and if that Dutchman don't like it, why in hell don't he go back where he came from? Anybody, I says to myself, *anybody* can get ahead in this country if he knows his business, works hard and saves his money. I came to the Territory with nothing but a saddle and a horse to my name. I barely could make out a check and read print. But I worked hard and saved my money. You didn't catch me hanging around saloons, pool halls and gambling joints, like most of the cow men, and that's how come I got a little bunch of cows of my own together, leased a good pasture, and finally bought a section of grass land. By the time the big war came I owned over a thousand white-faced steers, and as beef went up so did I. Toward the end of the War I bought two more sections.

"Of course I didn't pay all cash for it. But with beef around two bits the pound and going up, I could easily see my way through. Then the War stopped and things began to happen. Corn went down from a dollar and six bits to six bits, four bits, and finally two bits. And as the price of corn went down so did the price of beef, until I finally got less than four cents on the last bunch I took to Chicago. I always had to borrow money from the bank to finish off my steers with corn, and I always paid off the notes after I sold the stock. But now with beef at four cents and going lower, I couldn't meet the notes. So the bank took my breeding stock. Then a New York insurance company that held the mortgage on my land foreclosed. Now I'm cleaned out and by God I won't stand for it. I've played the game according to rule. I knew cows, I saved my money. I didn't booze, gamble or run around with whores, and still I'm cleaned out and by God, I won't stand for it."

"Well," I asked my enraged cattleman, "what are you proposing to do about it?"

"Do!" he almost shouted. "That's what I want to talk to you about. What we got to have is this here revolution you used to preach about."

"You mean divide up and start all over again?" I asked mildly.

"No, not divide up," he exclaimed angrily, "but own our land and cattle and things in common like the Indians used to do before the government robbed them of everything by giving them title deeds."

"That's better," I acknowledged, "provided we add railroads, banks, packing plants and a great many other things to those you mentioned. However, who's going to start this revolution?"

"That's what I want to talk over with you," my cow man came back. "You've been preaching revolution all over the country. You must know lots of people who believe revolution is the only way out. All I can do is my part."

"And what do you call your part?"

"My part is to capture Fort Sill."

"But how can you capture Fort Sill?"

"Easy as rolling off a log," my one-hundred-per-cent American tovarich snapped back. "I know Fort Sill like the palm of my hand. I almost saw it grow before my eyes. I've been in it hundreds of times. I know every one of the few guys who carry loaded arms, and where they are stationed. I can take twenty-five picked men and take that fort as easy as taking candy from a baby."

"And then?"

"And then," he continued, "we have enough arms and munitions to supply an army of twenty-five thousand men."

"And where will you get the army?"

"Army, hell! Give a general ring over the rural telephone lines and I'll have more army than you can shake a stick at. Everybody is busted, out of jobs and mad enough to fight catamounts bare handed. Don't you worry about the army, I'll get it."

"Then what?"

"We'll march till we come to the Mississippi, blow up the bridges, and stay there till those damned Eastern highbinders are starved to death."

"But will an army of twenty-five thousand be strong enough to hold the Mississippi line until the Easterners are starved to death?"

"Of course it won't. What I'm telling you has got to be done at all the military posts west of the Mississippi. And that's why I'm glad I met up with you again. There must be millions of people west of the river who feel exactly as I do and are sore enough to take chances. You know scads of them. Let's round 'em up and get going. You've talked about revolution long enough. Now we want action."

I patiently explained that the social revolution I preached was a matter of education and ballot, not starvation and bullets. That, moreover, revolutions are not made by a few bold spirits, but are in the nature of spontaneous combustion induced by the breakdown of economic and political systems no longer capable of maintaining accustomed standards of living. Revolutions come when the masses have reached the point of desperation to conclude that no matter what happens, things can't be made worse.

"Well," replied my cow man bitterly, "can you think of anything worse than the way they cleaned me out? I worked hard, saved my money, I know cows. Now all I've got to show for my life work is that sickly tin lizzie over there—and how the hell can I get a new start in the cow business with that?"

In the ditches of Highway 80, near Monroe, Louisiana, two groups of made-work workers were cutting weeds in water reaching to their knees. A month sooner or two months later the weeds could have been removed by a judicious investment of two matches. It was a cold, drizzly day. On the shoulders of the highway two sickly fires were smoking; at one the whites warmed themselves, at the other the Negroes. Whether cold and pneumonia germs respect the Jim Crow law I never learned. However, the lucky devils had work and the color line was religiously observed.

Night was coming on. I heard behind me the frantic tooting of a wheezy horn. I drove to the edge of the almost impossible buckshot road. A mud-encrusted Ford stopped by my side. "This here gang is lucky we caught up with you," was the greeting of the mud-encrusted driver who happened to be an acquaintance of mine. Then he added, "You won't mind giving them a lift. They're going your way."

The gang—six mud-covered, ragged, shivering share croppers —had walked seven miles that morning to a made-work project on the plantation of a Louisiana statesman. My acquaintance had mercifully picked them up on the seven-mile homeward trudge. I was glad to have the company of the six cold and hungry madework beneficiaries, for misery loves company. I was warm, well fed, and comfortably dressed, yet sick and weary in mind and heart at the sights I had seen and the tales I had heard on my return from the end of the Oregon Trail.

Along the right side of the road were miles of unpicked, long-staple cotton, drooping like dirty rags from long-opened bolls. That wealth of once snowy cotton was no longer worth harvesting at the cost of forty cents a hundred pounds. To the left, on what was once a lake—now partly drained for the planting of more cotton—on the branches of the remaining cypress trees hung bedraggled Spanish moss reminiscent of the faded mourning veils one sees on the mounds of month-old graves. At my side and behind me in my car were six "lazy louts." So lazy and shiftless that they had trudged seven miles that morning and would have trudged seven more that dreary evening over the near bottomless buckshot road had not two good Samaritans given them a lift—and all this for a dollar and a half, the price of a cotton jumper and overalls, a sack of corn meal, a few pounds of rancid sow belly and a can of molasses. So lazy and shiftless that every time my auto bogged down in the foot-deep mud of that God-forsaken road these cold, hungry, and almost barefoot men cheerfully lifted body, engine, and steaming radiator back on to semi-terra firma.

A few evenings later I was comfortably seated before the glowing fireplace of a plantation home. My host was the most progressive and successful cotton lord of the parish. My passengers of a few nights before were some of his tenants. "Yes, it's hell," he exclaimed, rising from his chair and pacing the room, "but what can I do, what can any of us do for the poor devils? They are freezing and starving because the price of cotton has fallen to where it is no longer worth the picking, while I worry my head off and lie sleepless at night wondering how to repay the money I borrowed to plant, cultivate and hoe the cotton you saw rotting in the fields. I am their captain, they my seamen, but we are all in the same boat and the boat is sinking. Something must be done. Communism, socialism, bolshevism—it's all the same to me. I'm sick and tired of this endless fluctuation of prices. When cotton goes over twenty cents a pound I strut around like a plutocrat. When it goes below seven cents I beg my banker, hat in hand, to extend my notes. I've long ago given up the notion of getting rich raising cotton. It's too much of a gamble, with all the cards stacked against me. What I want is security. I've got to get that security, a steady yearly income, no matter what."

I had learned another lesson. The war of planter and share cropper was a war between bankrupts and paupers, fighting over what money lenders, gamblers, stock jobbers and farm-implement corporations had left them out of last year's cotton crop. Which of the two victims of our glorious profit system suffers more depends on whether bodily want is preferable to spiritual agony, or vice versa.

Knoxville, Tennessee: There is a rumor about the reclamation of the Tennessee Valley, its eroded hillsides and poverty-stricken denizens, in a large way. It sounds too good to be true. Too much like national planning, the socialist violation of the good old tenets, every man for himself and may the devil take the hindmost.

Chattanooga: More closed banks and stores, cold factory stacks, bigger and better bread lines. On the road eastward more hitchhikers, tin lizzies, atavistic covered wagons, fear-stricken men, women, and children, whole families fleeing in every direction, as if pursued by unknown foes.

Washington, D. C.: Throngs of eager young men and women crowding the corridors and outer offices of the temple of commerce reared by hapless Herbert, and all of them dreaming dreams of a better life, working like beavers for its realization into the wee small hours of the night, while old men in the inner sanctuaries scheme how best to preserve the old order of things, not forgetting the nearly three hundred billion dollars of public, private and capitalized debt under which the nation is smothering to death.

Apple sellers on every street corner. Beggars shabby and beggars genteel, beggars in spats and limousines beseeching the new savior in the White House to save them, their banks, plants, and corporations, and for Christ's sake, do it now—right now, before the panicky rabble in streets and alleys bite their long-eared heads off.

The ruin on Pennsylvania Avenue from which the bonus army had been smoked was not yet cold. The forgotten heroes had been disbanded by Presidential ukase, sabers, night-sticks, and tear gas. Doctors, doctors everywhere, and not a one to suggest the reason for this want in the midst of plenty for all.

New York: The richest city of the richest country in the world. Still more apple sellers, mendicants in leaky shoes, taxis and shining Rolls-Royces. Executives toppling from twenty-story windows. Stocks hitting lower lows with every tick of the tickers. Gilt-edge securities collecting mold in deserted bank vaults; security for neither high nor low, bishop, banker or beggar man. Brokers, bank clerks, counter jumpers, A.B.'s, M.D.'s, Ph.D.'s, D.D.'s, shoveling snow in the lowly company of bricklayers, 'cellists, hod carriers, oboeists, garment workers, concert masters, stevedores, dramatists, and dock wallopers. A nightmare of want, woe and despair. You find it fittingly described in the great, forgotten drama *1931—*, by Paul and Claire Sifton: greater than Hauptmann's *Die Weber* which describes the toilers' life in the beginning of the machine age, whose fruits are exhibited in *1931—*.

Above all, a babble of tongues, confusion worse confounded. Learned clowns in caps and gowns uttering scholarly nonsense about the mysteries of the "business cycle," assuring a gasping world that what goes up must come down (but how about that which is down going up?), explaining the changed behavior of the stock market registering all down and no up. Economic morons in top hats and pince-nez uttering prophecies concerning the temporariness of the temporary business depression (ten years old by now) and predicting that Dame Prosperity was lurking just around the corner. Journalistic medicine men brewing good medicine to cheer the despondent, while social voodoo doctors cast the spell of seven-jointed words upon the evil spirits haunting the land of the free and the home of the brave.

The rattle, gabble, prattle of the upper floors echo throughout the whole rocking structure. Trotskyites, Gitlowites and Lovestoneites, Socialist Party members, Old Guards and Militants, are fighting over the soul of radical labor. Outworn shibboleths and shop-worn phrases coined under the smoke-hung atmosphere of Birmingham, Manchester and London of the Eighteen-sixties rend the air. Opinions, notions, nostrums and theories of uprooted revolutionists in Paris, Zurich and London are bandied about as the latest revelation from cloud-capped Sinai. The war between the sects of irate upheavers is far more savage than that between capital and labor. The strident cry from below: "Import the Russian revolution!" is answered by the piercing yell from on top: "Deport all revolutionists!" Just as though revolution were subject to importation, exportation or deportation—as feasible as transplanting the citrus industry of sunny California to Greenland's icy mountains!

Old labor unions reared in sacrifice, agony and blood are torn asunder for the sake of fine-spun and impossible theories. Such lifelong champions of the weary and heavy-laden as James Maurer, Charles Ervin, Charney Vladeck, Morris Hillquit and Norman Thomas, advocating social salvation by the slow but only sure road of understanding and political action, are being denounced as has-beens and "Social-Fascists." Labor leaders who, like my old friends Sidney Hillman and Benjamin Schlesinger, have been instrumental in raising hundreds of thousands of erstwhile sweatshop slaves out of poverty and degradation are smeared as "Mis-leaders of Labor" and "Counter-revolutionists."

Old friends and comrades assail one another's character and bloody one another's noses over policies and tactics the correctness of which only trial and error can prove or disprove. Wings over Union Square. Right wings, left wings and winglets of wings, and most of them attached to dead birds. For the problem that cries for solution is an exclusively American problem. Nowhere and at no earlier time in all the history of the race have men suffered widespread want because there is abundance for all.

This exclusive, new, and strictly American problem can neither be solved by theories spun in the Manchester or London of the long ago, nor by the new shibboleths and slogans emanating from the sick-beds of Europe. It can only be solved in America, in the American way of practical thinking, the ballot box, and a genuine love of country. We Americans must solve it.

I decided to flee New York, the nerve center of this distracted nation which is stricken by a deadly foe within itself.

Departing from my hotel on historic Gramercy Park one early, icy morning, I found the garbage cans still standing on the sidewalk. A shivering man was picking bread and meat scraps out of one of them. At a hash joint on Third Avenue I got the man's story. No, he was not a poor foreigner. He hailed from Vermont. Shades of Ethan Allen! A Green Mountain boy was picking meat scraps out of a garbage can in New York, while at the end of the Oregon Trail sheep ranchers murdered thousands of ewes because it was against the law to let sheep starve to death.

At Schenectady, after a lecture in which I expounded my ideas concerning the way out of want in the midst of plenty to a group of hopes-of-the-future, many of them technicians and engineers, I was berated for my moderation by one of them. The consensus was that a gallon of T.N.T. dropped into a manhole at the juncture of Forty-second Street and Broadway would get amazingly quick action.

An item in a Utica paper—by this time it is Christmas, 1932— tells of a letter found on the street by an old lady, which a little boy had addressed to Santa Claus:

"Please bring us three big slices of bread with lots of molasses on it. One for Mama, one for Sister, and one for me."

And wheat is rotting in Kansas by thousands of tons.

At the corner of Madison and State Streets, Chicago, harassed Christmas shoppers are milling by the tens of thousands, and not a happy face in all the milling mass. Under Wacker Drive that night, hundreds of homeless men wrapped in rags and newspapers are tossing in troubled sleep on icy-cold concrete floors.

Back home once more in Oklahoma City, reared on lakes of flowing gold, far richer than Athens in its glory, my sleep is disturbed by superfluous natural gas rushing out of oil wells, leaving the flowing gold at the mercy of declining rock pressure and invading salt water.

The morning paper tells of a little girl burned to death in one of the ramshackle shanties in Hooverville, down in the bottoms of the Canadian river. The poor thing had hugged the home-made stove in the dreadful shanty a bit too closely, and was burned to death a five-minutes' walk from where a million cubic feet of gas was going criminally to waste.

49

YULETIDE, 1939: I am busily pushing my worn pencil toward the end of the story of my many Americas, and in still another America—the intelligently planned suburban town of Radburn in northern New Jersey. Radburn is not just another suburban town for New York commuters to hang their hats in at the close of a routine Wall Street day. Not just another real-estate development conceived in lust for gain and perpetrated in jerry-built bungalows. Radburn was planned and charmingly carried out by my friend Clarence Stein and others as a haven of rest and peace from the human whirlpool of the near-by metropolis, with a special eye on the security of the young.

Rest—peace—security. They are no longer found even in this man-made oasis. For Mars is lowering again in a bigger and better war. The booming that heralded my birth, and modern Germany's first victory, on that August night of 1870 thunders again. There were no end of victories for the cannon to proclaim in the first years of my life in the Teutonic *Grosse Zeit*—the victory of Weissenburg and Wörth, of Strassburg, Mars-la-Tour, Metz and Sedan. More booming, bells ringing, waving of the new black-white-and-red banners announcing the crowning of William I in the glittering marble halls of Versailles. Establishing the might of United Germany for all time to come. Glorious victories one and all, and each victory sowing the seeds of new wars and new defeats.

My generation and my children's became the cannon fodder
of 1914-1918. I am thinking of my youngest son, a brilliant musician, who went overseas with the A.E.F. to return gassed, shell-
shocked, with seven shrapnel splinters in his body, received in
the bloody mire of the Argonne Forest. These children of Radburn, New Jersey, so carefully protected against speed maniacs
by underpassed streets and supervised playgrounds—for whom,
for what, and when shall they be the next cannon fodder?

In the seventy years of my life there have been three great
wars, each more bloody than its predecessor, each promising
eternal peace from the rattling rifles and thundering cannon. Take
all your wars and all their "victories" from the day when Samson
slew the Philistines with the jawbone of an ass, and they are not
worth a Schubert *Lied*, a Beethoven trio, a single movement
from any one of Papa Haydn's symphonies. Nor are they worth
a single discovery of a Jenner, Pasteur, Koch or Walter Reed,
slayers of pain, disease and death itself. If there is one lesson in
all the annals of history it is that war settles nothing. War is but
the sower of wars.

Today headlines and radio broadcasts bring the happy tidings
of more victories. A Nazi pocket battleship is blown up and
scuttled by its own crew. Its captain ended this war for himself
by blowing out his brains. One of Germany's luxury floating
hotels is most successfully sunk by its own "scuttle crew," picked
men assigned to the job of blowing up their own ships. But do
not gloat too much, my brave British and French propagandists!
Heroic Nazi airmen have brought down forty of your bombers
with the alleged loss of only two Messerschmitts, while U-boats
and magnetic mines have most heroically sunk your food ships.
What a heaven-crying, soul-killing, mind-staggering picture of
God's children shaping birds of prey and sharks of steel to feed
buzzards and sharks and worms with carcasses of their own kind.

Boom! boom! boom! from the frozen tundras of the Mur-
mansk coast to Uruguay, from off Cape May to Capetown and

Hong Kong. On the lower reaches of the Danube, oil and wheat barges are bringing the stuff of war to Hitler's armies. On the Danube's upper reaches, in the Swabia of my boyhood, peasant women are bemoaning the departure of their sons for the Siegfried line and praying that the day will give them their *Ersatzbrot*.

In Radburn, venders of festive spruce are crying their wares on the sidewalks before the town hall. Forests of lovely trees are sacrificed to print the latest news from the battle fields. And in all the welter of print, sound and fury not a word to tell us why we have war in a world that science, invention and discovery have welded into one. A world in which the tribes of men have been so inextricably interwoven by migration and the exchange of goods, science, arts and cultures that "an injury to one is the concern of all" is no longer a pious hope, but the fundamental law of man's well-being on earth.

Words! words! words! and the calling of names: Aggressors, non-aggressors, Communists, Fascists, imperialist and democratic nations and democratic imperialist nations! New demons called Stalin, Hitler and Mussolini. New angels named Chamberlain, Daladier and Churchill, in place of the evil spirits and beneficent spirits, personal gods and personal devils that governed the destinies of men in the childhood of the race. But not a word about the chain of events reaching back into antiquity, each link determining the character of the next.

The sagas of war make up the human tragedy called history. The dramatic growth of tools and weapons forced the human cells into clusters, clans, tribes, states, kingdoms, nations, empires and coalitions of empires by war, always by war and never by thought and understanding, not even on the part of the leading actors of the drama. The forces unleashed by the discovery of mechanical power, lifting man to ever greater heights of prosperity, cast him into an ever widening chasm of woe and despair, until at last the day has come when the twin forces of production and destruction are presenting man with the choice of rearing the kingdom of peace, plenty and security promised by both faith and science, or destroying himself in a welter of mechanized and scientific wars.

Yet I do not despair. Long has been the road, strewn with rocks and thorns, soaked with heart's blood, marked with tears, but an upward road always. Civilizations have risen and fallen. Great leaders of men have come and gone. Centuries of unbroken progress toward the better life have been followed by dark ages. But always, somewhere on this earth, was a people who preserved the inheritance of the race and carried it to greater heights. That you, my America, will be the carrier of the best of the ages and the herald of the better day is the prayer of my heart. Do not permit yourself to be sucked into the crimson whirlpool of the Old World. The blood of your sons cannot atone for the sins and errors of two hundred centuries. All the wealth of your fields, mines, and factories, all the energy of your falling waters, the riches of frozen sunshine and black gold beneath your fertile soil, can't buy liberty and democracy for the people of the woe-sick Old World. Give freely out of the fullness of your blessings and heal the wounds of war and its victims, forgetting ancient loves and hates, race, color, and clime, for all are as brothers. Above all, do not repeat the fatal error of bringing peace by war.

Before settling the troubles of distant lands, settle your own. If war there must be, make it war to the knife against poverty, disease, and ignorance at home. You have all that makes life livable, lovable and secure. You alone of all the countries of the earth have neared the land of promise. See that your gifts are neither hoarded by greed nor wasted in conquest and war, but are honestly earned and justly distributed for the good of all. Close your glorious arch of religious and political freedom with the keystone of industrial democracy, be the cost what it may. For economic autocracy and political democracy cannot dwell under the same roof. That much is certain if anything is certain in this ever changing world. Not to be the richest, the most powerful and most feared nation on earth, but the torchbearer of all that is good, true, and beautiful on earth—that is the mission of America. Hold fast to the words of the Carpenter: "It is more blessed to give than to receive." For life pays in kind, love for love, hate for hate, blow for blow, and song for song.

As for me, I have lived my little life and said my little piece. This world, with all its trials and tribulations, greed, cruelty, and stupidity, is still the best I ever got into. I have not succeeded in saving it from itself. . . . Perhaps it is well I failed, for what a dreary world it would be if there were nothing more to struggle for! My deepest regret is that the days are growing short and there is still so much to see, love, learn, enjoy and do. I would gladly spend my last dollar to deprive the heavenly orchestra of a good clarinet player capable of doubling in brass and strings!

Anyhow, it's a great life if you don't weaken. I have not weakened. And if there is a lesson in this tale, let it be told in the parting words of the dying Faust:

"This is wisdom's last conclusion:
Only he deserves liberty and life
Who earns them in the daily strife."

And so to sleep in the faith of a better tomorrow, always the eternal better tomorrow in spite of night and death.

INDEX